INDIA AND BAY OF BENGAL COMMUNITY

India and Bay of Bengal Community

The BIMSTEC Experiment

(Bangladesh-India-Myanmar-Sri Lanka-Thailand Economic Cooperation)

Editor

T. Nirmala Devi

GYAN

GYAN PUBLISHING HOUSE

NEW DELHI-110002

India and Bay of Bengal Community
The BIMSTEC Experiment
(Bangladesh-India-Myanmar-Sri Lanka-Thailand Economic Cooperation)

Rs. 740

ISBN: 81-212-0930-7

Published in 2007 in India by
Gyan Publishing House
5, Ansari Road, Darya Ganj,
New Delhi-110002
Phones : 23282060, 23261060
Fax : 011-23285914
E-mail : books@ gyanbooks.com
Website: www.gyanbooks.com

Lasser Type Setting by: Rudra Computer Graphics
Printed at : Salasar Imaging System, Delhi

Contents

Part-II: Cooperation in Trade and Investment in BIMSTEC

Part-III: Political Perspectives on BIMSTEC

Part-IV: Cooperation in Science and Technology in BIMSTEC

Part-V: Human Development and other Aspects of BIMSTEC

Foreword

Historically, the Bay of Bengal space has been an integral part of India's strategic, economic and civilization area of interest and consciousness. Its littoral and hinterland regions have profoundly impacted upon India's overall interests and well being and vice versa. Scholars like Prof. K M Panniker have extensively commented on the strategic significance of this region for India in their studies and books. In the more recent and contemporary context, the Bay of Bengal space has once again emerged as an integral and inseparable part of India's evolving Look East Policy; for example, the Andaman and Nicobar group of Islands and the North – East of our country bordering the Bay of Bengal region have been our traditional gateway to the hinterland of Southeast Asia and beyond. There are strong civilization, ethnic, cultural, linguistic, economic and political links with Southeast Asia, which have developed an imperative of interdependence through the ages. Arguably, the stability and prosperity of our Northeast is also closely linked to that of the Southeast Asian hinterland and, perhaps, beyond. Similarly, the security, strategic and economic interests of the Indian Ocean region, including the Andaman and Nicobar group of Islands, are also very closely linked to the Southeast Asian region surrounding it. It can, therefore, be said that the sub-region of the Bay of Bengal has its own unique history and imperative of interdependence and has been moulded and conditioned by the shared and enduring strategic, economic and civilization bonds.

BIMSTEC (now called the Bay of *Bengal Initiative for Multi Sectoral Techno – Economic Cooperation)* is a most recent manifestation of this imperative. All its seven Members – India, Sri Lanka, Bangladesh, Nepal, Bhutan, Thailand and Myanmar – are close Bay of Bengal neighbours of India with close links of history, geography and culture. India's now growing and considerable commerce with East and Southeast Asia passes through sea lanes in this sub-region; about two - thirds of India's exclusive economic zone (EEZ) and economic space is in this region; the combined size of the BIMSTEC economies is estimated to be in excess of US$ 900 billion – and growing – with a population of 1.6 billion, India alone accounting for the bulk of it both in GDP and population terms; India's maritime and strategic interests in this sub-region are of great importance for not only India but for the entire sub-region; the presence of foreign Navies in these waters make it necessary for the Indian Navy to maintain and monitor peace and stability in the region; being close to Indonesia and at the mouth of the strategically significant Malacca Straits, India has an important role in patrolling these waters and the sea lanes; China's now growing presence in and close to Myanmar has added a new and serious security dimension; the use by terrorists and other criminal elements of these waters for their nefarious activities is a new type of challenge for the Indian Navy. The Bay of Bengal sub-region accounts about ten percent of India's external economic relations; the sub- region is potentially resource and energy rich and increasingly vulnerable. India has to anchor the peace and prosperity of this sub-region for our common good and interdependent destiny.

BIMSTEC was established in December 1997, with India, Thailand, Sri Lanka, Bangladesh and Myanmar as the founding members. In fact, Bangladesh was not involved with the initial discussions having been admitted just before the Ministerial Meeting in Bangkok in December 1997. I had the honour and privilege of representing India at this Ministerial meeting and signing the Agreement for India. The membership of Bangladesh, and subsequently Nepal and Bhutan, changed somewhat the character of this grouping as all three of these countries, being least developed countries, brought a new dimension and a new set of issues to deal with; also, the membership of Bhutan and Nepal brought the hinterland of South Asia into BIMSTEC changing its original character. Some believe that Bangladesh's membership of the sub-regional grouping may have slowed down its progress towards integration and in developing a common approach on emerging challenges.

In the early 1990's while India had launched its Look East policy, largely motivated by the imperative of economics and post cold war strategic considerations, Southeast Asia was also ready to embark on a new Look West policy departing from its decades old policy of not looking westwards, beyond Myanmar. Southeast Asia too was propelled by the same considerations as India. In the post-cold war globalized world, India and Southeast Asia had begun to discover new and compelling convergences giving the relationship a substantive and meaningful momentum. While this growing strategic and economic convergence was rapidly evolving, India's disappointment with the progress of SAARC due to Pakistan's obduracy led her to think in terms of evolving alternate regional and sub-regional cooperation mechanisms. ASEAN too, anxious to forge new partnerships, had developed some experience with sub-regional cooperation arrangements such as growth triangles and quadrangles and was not averse to looking westwards for new opportunities, which would provide incrementality to its somewhat plateauing efforts with other ASEAN countries, compounded by recent economic hiccups such as the East and Southeast Asian financial crisis of 1998 and the new challenges of a globalized economic order. The BIMSTEC proposal was, in fact, first mooted by Thailand in 1992-93. India took a while to respond and to embark on this new sub-regional cooperation arrangement. For India, BIMSTEC with five of the original seven SAARC countries as members, was one way of promoting sub-regional cooperation bypassing an obdurate Pakistan. With existing Free Trade Arrangements with Sri Lanka, Nepal and Bhutan and proposed FTAs with Thailand, Singapore and Bangladesh – and the whole of ASEAN – it was not difficult to conceive of a genuine Bay of Bengal Economic Community with a common FTA for the free movement of goods and services, investments, tourism and eventually an integrated economic community. According to an estimate by a Delhi based Think Tank, the trade creation potential of the BIMSTEC FTA is between US$ 43 to 59 billion. This then was the reason d'etre of BIMSTEC and its relevance and importance in today's rapidly changing regional context.

BIMSTEC, admittedly, has been slow in taking off. Even after nearly ten years of existence, it still faces serious challenges such as coping with incompatibilities and the onerous demands of regionalism over nationalism; hastening the process of meaningful integration; deepening and expanding cooperation areas and arrangements; and launching quick and result-oriented short gestation cooperation projects, etc. India, as the largest country, has the responsibility to initiate more effective and proactive measures to hasten cooperation, including by developing enduring and mutually beneficial trade, infrastructure, investment and other linkages, which alone will create and sustain a vested interest in sub regional cooperation. This is necessary, if BIMSTEC is to avoid going the SAARC way. BIMSTEC, nevertheless, is a modest experiment in pragmatic politics and realistic economics in a fiercely competitive globalised and rapidly changing environment; it is an experiment aimed at achieving incrementality without having to redefine or reorder existing arrangements; it is an experiment to forge an arrangement to optimize, step by step, opportunities through cooperation in select identified areas and to make up for missed opportunities; it is an experiment in moving forward without waiting for all political or economic challenges to be overcome; it is, above all, a modest experiment in promoting sub-regional cooperation, optimizing synergies, complementarities and advantages of shared geography and history. No one seriously believes that BIMSTEC will dramatically alter or redefine the compulsions of the larger canvass. If, as a non-exclusive grouping, it helps provide additional and new opportunities and incrementality it would have served its short-term objective. India and Thailand, particularly, are among the rapidly growing economies of the Bay of Bengal region and could together pilot the sub-region towards greater prosperity through cooperation, interdependence and a sub-regional common approach on crucial issues. Ultimately, the Bay of Bengal community has to be seen as a small sub-regional building block of a larger Asian economic community and the emerging macro level integration process.

I would like to congratulate Prof. T. Nirmala Devi, Director, Centre for SAARC Studies, Andhra University, Visakhapatnam for taking this laudable and timely initiative to focus, through the Seminar organized by the Centre in November 2005, and this compilation of essays on the Bay of Bengal region. The papers presented at this Seminar and the themes covered provide a deep insight into issues ranging from the emerging political architecture of the region, trade and investment, science and technology to new areas of cooperation such as human resource development, role of the gender etc. BIMSTEC is an important option for our policy makers to consider and explore. This book, no doubt, will help them to focus on an area, which holds immense promise but which was ignored until recently by policy makers and academics alike.

New Delhi
May 30, 2006

A N Ram
Former Secretary,
Ministry of External Affairs
and
Chairman, CSCAP (India)

Preface

Regional economic integration among developing countries is advocated in the context of preferential and free trade arrangements, specialization, economies of scale and enlargement of markets, as most of these countries can not achieve them in isolation. Unlike the success of economic integration among the developed countries, regional groupings in the developing world are by and large not successful, barring the ASEAN which is frequently commended as a model of Third World regional cooperation. The SAARC, the other major regional grouping in Asia has not been very successful, owing mainly to political reasons. The BIMSTEC grouping, brainchild of Thailand, is a unique initiative in sub-regional economic cooperation. It has the distinction of combining five geographically contiguous countries of SAARC with two of ASEAN, thus creating a vast scope for regional development.

The emergence of SAARC as an economic bloc was impeded mainly due to mutual mistrust and as such India needs a better alternative like the BIMSTEC. India's keen desire to promote regional cooperation in the South Asian region has been fulfilled after obtaining membership in the regional grouping of the BIMSTEC. The need to diversify India's external economic relations manifested in phase-2 of its Look East policy, is to some extent a consequence of the non-functioning of SAARC in the economic arena in a desired manner. India's role is pivotal in the evolution and growth of this regional grouping. Along with another lead country, Thailand, India should play a proactive role in forging a meaningful cooperation in the region.

The formation of BIMSTEC in 1997 with the objective of promoting the economic development of the member nations through fair trade is a good augury, as liberalization of regional trade is quite essential to achieve the expected results. Signing of framework agreement to establish FTA in February 2004 and the Summit

Declaration in July 2004 are the major achievements of the BIMSTEC, which gave momentum to the member countries to gear up to face the global challenges in the new economy. The existing bilateral and multilateral agreements among the BIMSTEC nations under the earlier regional initiatives strengthen the economic rationale as well as mitigate the political tensions, if any. The present regional arrangement under the BIMSTEC framework helps provide additional and better opportunities for the overall betterment of its members. However, it is an admitted fact that the functioning mechanism of this grouping at present is slow, owing to some of the challenges such as the presence of national perspectives over regional outlook. The key members of the group, India and Thailand, the former in particular, need to encourage the pace of cooperation as well as execution at a faster pace. If the BIMSTEC has to be spared of the SAARC experience, greater positive thrust is expected from the leading members.

The present volume is designed to examine the current dynamics of regional cooperation under BIMSTEC and explore some of the issues of regional concern. It is a collection of papers presented at the National Seminar on "BIMSTEC: Towards a Bay of Bengal Economic Community", conducted by the Centre for SAARC Studies, Andhra University, Visakhapatnam during November 19-20, 2005. The major objective of the Seminar was to examine the trends and dynamics of cooperation in the BIMSTEC region and assess the strengths and limitations of mutual engagement in the chosen areas of cooperation.

The broad themes of the Seminar are: (i) India's role in the future growth of the BIMSTEC; (ii) cooperation in trade and investment in the BIMSTEC; (iii) political perspectives of the BIMSTEC; (iv) science and technological cooperation in the BIMSTEC; and (v) human development aspects in the BIMSTEC region. All these major issues relating to the functioning and progress of the BIMSTEC grouping have been comprehensively dealt with. The Seminar was participated by informed scholars across the country including the Directors of concerned UGC Area Study Centres, besides scholars from Andhra University specialized in the common concerns of the Bay of Bengal region also took active part. In all, twenty eight papers were presented at the Seminar, of which twenty three papers are revised and edited for the purpose of publication.

I am extremely beholden to Amb. A.N. Ram, Former Secretary (East), Ministry of External Affairs, Government of India and Chairman, CSCAP (India) for writing an excellent foreword to this volume at a very short notice. I express my deep sense of gratitude to Prof. K.C. Reddy, Chairman, A.P. State Council of Higher Education, Hyderabad and former Hon.Director, Centre for SAARC Studies, Andhra University, for his comprehensive keynote address and for being a constant source of encouragement. I am greatly indebted to Prof. L. Venugopal Reddy, Vice-Chancellor, Andhra University for kindly inaugurating the Seminar and for extending all the necessary support. I am highly grateful to Prof. P.V. Rao, Director, Centre for Indian Ocean Studies, Osmania University, Hyderabad for his valuable guidance and support in editing this volume. My gratitude is due to Prof. A. Lakshmana Chetty, Former Director, Centre for Southeast Asian and Pacific Studies, Sri Venkateswara University, Tirupati and Prof. I.N. Mukherji, Former Dean of School of South Asian Studies, Jawaharlal Nehru University, New Delhi for their expert advice, enthusiastic participation and valuable contribution to this volume. I place on record my sincere thanks to all the authors who have contributed to this volume.

July, 2006

T. Nirmala Devi

List of Contributors

1	K.C. Reddy	:	Chairman, A.P State Council of Higher Education, Hyderabad and Professor and Former Hon.Director Centre for SAARC Studies, Andhra University
2	Indra N. Mukherji and Nawal Kishore Paswan	:	Former Dean and Professor and Research Nawal Kishore Paswan Associate, South Asian Division, School of International Studies, Jawaharlal Nehru University, New Delhi.
3	P.V. Rao	:	Professor and Director, Centre for Indian Ocean Studies, Osmania University, Hyderabad
4	A. Lakshmana Chetty	:	Professor and Former Director Centre for Southeast Asian and Pacific Studies, Sri Venkateswara University, Tirupati
5	T. Nirmala Devi	:	Professor & Director, Centre for SAARC Studies Andhra University, Visakhapatnam
6	Tridib Chakraborti	:	Professor, Dept. of International Relations, Jadavpur University, Kolkata
7	E.V. Gangadharam	:	Professor and Director, Centre for Marine Archaeology, Andhra University, Visakhapatnam
8	B.C. Upreti	:	Professor, South Asia Studies Centre, University of Rajasthan, Jaipur

9	D. Panduranga Rao & K.V. Mohan Kumar	:	Professor and Research Scholar Dept. of Commerce & Management Studies, Andhra University, Visakhapatnam.
10	P. Rajendra Prasad	:	Professor and Director, Dr. Amrik Singh Centre for Bay of Bengal Andhra University, Visakhapatnam
11	G. Ramachandrudu, Ch. Appa Rao & A. Rajani	:	Professor; Assistant Professor and Research Scholar, Dept. of Economics, Andhra University, Visakhapatnam
12	A.Narayana Swamy & A. Sivaparvathi	:	Professor and Research Scholar, Dept. of Geo-physics, Andhra University, Visakhapatnam
13	P. Leela	:	Professor, Dept. of Applied Economics Andhra University, Visakhapatnam
14	K. Sreerama Murthy, K.Sailaja & R.Radha	:	Professor, Assistant Professor and Research Scholar, School of Economics, Andhra University, Visakhapatnam.
15	B. Meena Rao & S.Subba Rao	:	Professor, Dept. of Politics & Public Administration, Andhra University, Visakhapatnam & Asst. Professor, PG Centre, Vizianagaram.
16	P. Tara Kumari	:	Professor, Dept. of Economics, Andhra University, Visakhapatnam
17	B. Ratna Kumari	:	Associate Professor, Centre for Women's Studies, Andhra University Visakhapatnam.
18	M. Chandrasekhar & Ravi kumar Rao	:	Professor & Research Scholar, Integrated Institute of Advanced Management, Visakhapatnam
19	A.Vanajamani	:	Assistant Professor, Integrated Institute of Advanced Management, Visakhapatnam
20	C.Praseeda	:	Assistant Professor, Integrated Institute of Advanced Management, Visakhapatnam

21 G. Lakshmi and S. Vanaja Rani	:	Teaching Associates, Dept. of Politics and Dept. of Sociology, Andhra University, Visakhapatnam.
22 V. Srilatha	:	Research Scholar, Centre for Indian Ocean Studies, Osmania University, Hyderabad
23 Padmaja Murthy	:	Research Scholar, School of South Asian Studies, Jawaharlal Nehru University, New Delhi

Introduction

T. Nirmala Devi

A sub-regional grouping arrangement like the BIMSTEC serves as an instrument in promoting development and enhancing peace and stability in its area of coverage. Regional economic arrangements among the developing countries, with the exception of the ASEAN, are not a success story. The dismantling of cold war barriers, the slow rate of progress in the SAARC, India's interest in the ASEAN region and furthermore the interest of Thailand to enhance its economic relations with the South Asian countries are the contributing factors behind the formation of the BIMSTEC. Thus, the establishment of BIMSTEC grouping in the Asian subcontinent, covering the countries on the Bay of Bengal Rim, is a significant step ahead in combining the potential areas of regional development into a sub-regional forum. The asymmetry in the size of population, resource endowment and economic development is more or less the common characteristic of most of the regional groupings and thus it need not necessarily be a constraint on economic cooperation in the BIMSTEC region. Moreover, the existence of strong complementarities among the members will contribute to the facilitation of trade and industrial growth in the region. The realization of the potential and the exploitation of synergies, however, is subjected to several geo-political and economic factors. Yet, it is hoped that the member nations will overcome the challenges and strengthen the economic rationale by giving priority to the regional perspective.

The present volume is arranged into five parts: (i) India's role in the future growth of BIMSTEC; (ii) cooperation in the areas of trade and investment among the BIMSTEC nations; (iii) political perspectives of the BIMSTEC; (iv) science and technological cooperation in the BIMSTEC grouping; and (v) human development aspects in the BIMSTEC region. All these themes are extremely relevant to the successful working mechanism of the BIMSTEC and its further development prospects.

Part-I analyses the role of India in the future growth of BIMSTEC. Being the lead country in the grouping, India draws attention in the BIMSTEC framework and its functioning in the backdrop of the fast changing global economic environment. India is one of the fast emerging global power and is both a factor for peace and stability as well as a dynamic economic player in the region. India with its recent economic clout, capacity building measures and IT prowess, together with the gradual shift in the foreign policy outlook to suit to the rapid changes in global geo-political issues deserves a special status in the BIMSTEC region. Together with Thailand, India can change the economic profile of the region and provide the edge of regional perspective over national sovereignties. Four papers are presented in this section which project the importance of India in the political and politico-economic interface of the sub regional cooperation of the BIMSTEC. Whilemaking a strong case for the Bay of Bengal Community encompassing the rim countries, P.V. Rao explains the reasons for the slow progress of the BIMSTEC, among which the prominent were the financial crisis in 1997 which struck Thailand seriously and the lukewarm interest exhibited by India towards the BIMSTEC grouping . He opines that the non inclusion of two SAARC members in the BIMSTEC grouping, Pakistan and Maldives, which earlier opposed the South Asia Growth Quadrangle (SAGQ),could augur well for the growth of the BIMSTEC. Rao also points out that given the political mistrust in SAARC, the BIMSTEC grouping serves as an alternative to SAARC in which India could play a meaningful role. Lakshmana Chetty makes a survey of issues of cooperation connected with the BIMSTEC framework before and after the summit, while evaluating the role of India in the BIMSTEC. He underlines the importance of India's bilateral relations with Thailand, Sri Lanka and other LDCs for exploiting the synergies and thereby moving towards feasible cooperation. He opines that India's interest in the BIMSTEC can be viewed as an integral part of its Look East Policy and the smooth sailing of India in the BIMSTEC process depends upon the motives of Bangladesh and Nepal. Indranath Mukherji and Paswan undertake a broad survey of India's trade and investment opportunities under the BIMSTEC process. They highlighted the trade potential at the sectoral and product levels and suggest that these be brought under the fast track liberalization to improve the intra-regional trade. They estimate both the indices of trade complementarity as well as the intra-industry of India with the rest of the BIMSTEC nations in order to ensure trade complementarities in the region. While observing the absence of membership of both Pakistan and China in the grouping a likely contributing factor to a more politically cohesive regional grouping, the authors argue that a low share of intra-regional trade in the BIMSTEC owes to similarity of export products of the SAARC countries. However, the optimistic note is that the intra-trade is growing, resulting from the emerging trade potential of the members. Another positive phenomenon, the authors feel, is that the negotiating mechanism of the BIMSTEC FTA is based on negative list approach, unlike the positive list approach of the SAARC. Tridib Chakraborthy argues for contextualizing the BIMSTEC process through India's Look East policy and assesses the first summit of the grouping. He concludes that the Bay of Bengal Community could act as a complement rather than a substitute to SAARC, because the efforts to promote FTA offers a larger space for the SAARC nations to engage in trade and commerce with the markets of Southeast Asia, particularly Thailand. He also opines that India's outward orientation depends upon its trade with APEC in the backdrop of Asia emerging an important engine of growth.

Part-II examines prospects for cooperation in trade and investment under the BIMSTEC. Regional economic integration in the form of FTAs among the geographically contiguous countries is a good start. Facilitation of trade and investment are essentially required to complement the implementation of FTAs, besides strengthening of the economic and political links. The BIMSTEC provides an opportunity to strengthen external competitiveness for the member countries and the fruitful cooperation in the region also lies in technology management, capacity building as well as dealing with WTO commitments. The status of intra-regional trade in the BIMSTEC at present and the facilitation measures and implementation of relaxation of certain tax and customs duties required for its future expansion are dealt with in this section. Five papers have focused upon the opportunities and challenges for the BIMSTEC nations; economic cooperation in the BIMSTEC, trade and investment linkages in this direction; the regional economic arrangements; and exploration of the possibilities of the cooperation in the BIMSTEC grouping. K.C. Reddy, while analyzing the objective of the formation of the BIMSTEC grouping in his keynote presentation, observes that owing to the strong existence of complementarities in the regional context, the divergence in social and economic indicators of the member nations is unlikely to come in the way of enhancement of regional cooperation. Pointing to the reasons for the lack of success in the SAARC and their inclination towards industrial countries for trade, besides the other problems being faced by these developing countries at the WTO system, he highlighted the role of India in utilizing the untapped potential available in the BIMSTEC grouping for the future strengthening of complementarities and the necessity of physical connectivity with the other members. He stresses the need to exploit the synergies for mutual benefit through implementation of efficiency-seeking measures to restructure industry in the region. He concludes with an optimistic note that the BIMSTEC should not become another SAARC for which this new regional grouping should set up a time table to move towards a customs union, like the E.U. By comparing the socio-economic indicators of the BIMSTEC countries, Nirmala Devi surveys the global trade of the member countries and its structure and the intra-regional trade scenario for examining the possibilities of cooperation. She presents an account of India's engagement with the BIMSTEC nations through bilateral trade with a special focus on India-Thailand FTA and the key products traded between the two countries. To support this analysis, she estimates the index of trade reciprocity of individual BIMSTEC nations with the rest of regional members and also India's trade reciprocity with each BIMSTEC nation. While emphasizing the softening and liberalizing of complex trade formalities, she suggests the formation of a new formula on mutually beneficial basis in the case of FTAs by taking care of rules of origin and value addition etc. While discussing the functioning of various regional economic arrangements, different phases of old and new regionalism; and also the concept of sub regionalism, Padmaja Murthy examines the evolution of the BIMSTEC through different stages and suggests some specified measures for better performance. She concludes that this new grouping has the advantage of learning both from the mistakes and the successes of the other groupings and underscores the critical importance of a clear focused agenda and identifying mechanism. Another paper on the BIMSTEC economic community by Leela deals with the comparative trade analysis of the SAARC and the ASEAN and suggests the future dimensions for the successful functioning of the BIMSTEC region. The paper of Sreerama Murthy et.al., examines the performance of the BIMSTEC countries in terms of millennium development goals, in presenting the countries' output and trade. They emphasize the need to improve the quality of life and recommend the establishment of regional payments union for the BIMSTEC countries.

Part-III examines the political perspectives of the BIMSTEC nations in the rapidly changing global geo-political scenario. The fragmentation of the world into regional and sub-regional groupings is a consequence of various geo-political factors, besides the economic divisions. The need for integrating national economies is more felt today than in the past, because every country is eager to enhance its economic growth through integration with global market forces. The political and foreign policy options of individual countries and the two phases of Look East policy are reflected in this section. It contains five analytical papers, covering a wide gamut of regional issues of Asia and the significant application of Look East policy of India and the BIMSTEC interface. Upreti's paper examines the conceptualization of the sub-regional idea in the context of the BIMSTEC formation. Before emphasizing the adoption of specific target approach instead of populist approach, he rightly questions the BIMSTEC's ability to translate its goals as majority of its members belong to the SAARC, whose effectiveness has been very limited. The paper by Chandrasekhar and Ravi Kumar discuss the political perspectives of the BIMSTEC nations through the country-specific problems. They emphasize the redressal of the problems of the common folk, in order to attain some progress in these nations. A paper on maritime cooperation between India and Sri Lanka by Srilatha examines the role of LTTE, while discussing the pros and cons of the pre and post-Tsunami maritime cooperation. She undertakes the geo-political dimension of Seethusamudram ship canal project and argues for the protection of sea-lanes of communications and other network for uninterrupted services. Discussing the various ups and downs of India-Myanmar relations over time and the underlying factors, Meena Rao and Subba Rao observe that China threat and India's interest in deep engagement with the ASEAN countries are the major reasons for India's readiness to establish close ties with Myanmar. They emphasize this re-envisioning of the two countries' relations through India's efforts to restore peace talks with Myanmar. Vanajamani in her paper, explains the geography- based consolidation and India's political and economic relations with the other members of the region by analysing the major disputes and the improvement in the relations with the members. Apart from presenting trade and the other economic matters, she stresses the role of India for the fruitful cooperation in the region.

Part-IV is devoted to the scientific and technological cooperation among the BIMSTEC countries. The potential for cooperation in the areas of science and technology is another primary consideration under the BIMSTEC process. The huge quantity of resources in the Bay of Bengal Ocean points out to the sharing of information and understanding among the member nations under its coverage. Technology management and capacity building are the need of the hour, for which countries require interaction, collaboration in R & D projects, besides human resource development. The BIMSTEC nations need to go through a special understanding with reference to scientific and technological cooperation in order to ensure speedy growth. Mutual cooperation in the coastal oceanic resources of the Bay of Bengal with an emphasis on space, earth and atmospheric sciences are dealt with along with cooperation in marine archaeology in this section. Rajendra Prasad provides a broad survey of a number of coastal and oceanic resources and underlines the need for intimate collaboration among the BIMSTEC nations. He emphasizes the necessity of undertaking a concerted R&D and management strategies of the mangrove ecosystems unitedly. Further, he elaborates several fields of cooperation among the member countries, in view of the similarities in coastal, near shore and ocean environment and particularly of the enormous scope for cooperation. Narayana Swamy and Siva Parvathi explain the necessicity of collaboration in space, earth and atmospheric sciences. They emphasize the importance of environment-development linkage to the Bay of Bengal Community, through which the ocean plays an appropriate role in the area of global science. They plead for arresting the damage to the earth and atmospheric environment through proper measures. Gangadharam's paper projects a different dimension, i.e., cooperation in maritime archaeology among BIMSTEC countries. While explaining the importance of marine archaeology and well-known global marine archaeological case histories including that of India, he argues for preserving the common maritime heritage of the BIMSTEC and calls for common research in marine archaeology. He concludes that a consortium approach by maritime nations in the BIMSTEC results in promoting marine archaeology projects.

Part-V of the volume deals with the human development and the other related aspects of the BIMSTEC countries, viz., human poverty, transport cooperation, disaster management and gender's role. In this section, six papers make out an assessment of the evolution and development of the BIMSTEC grouping in the sphere of human development. The paper on Asian Drama by Ramachandrudu et.al., surveys human poverty in the regional groupings in Asia. While recalling the Asian Drama of Gunnar Myrdal in order to counter the imperialist policies of the U.S, the authors underline India's involvement in the cooperative policies to attain a win-win situation. Regional cooperation in transport sector, an important area of cooperation is discussed in the paper of Panduranga Rao and Mohan Kumar with an emphasis on road transport. While outlining the strategies for attaining regional cooperation, the paper identifies both the potential areas between bilateral countries as well as the problems existing in the inter-country routes. Praseeda examines the state of disaster management in India, a major player in the BIMSTEC grouping. She feels that since most of the landmass of the BIMSTEC countries touches the Bay of Bengal and the experience reveals the vulnerability of these countries to disasters, they need to incorporate comprehensive disaster management measures into their plans. The author suggests that in view of India's size, history of disasters and the disaster management exercises and initiatives, the BIMSTEC members can emulate the same. The issue of women in development of the BIMSTEC countries is discussed in three papers by Tara Kumari, Ratna Kumari and Lakshmi and Vanaja Rani, focusing on socio-economic development of women, gender mainstreaming in trade policies, and gender inequality in the region.

1

India and BIMST-EC: Experiment with Sub-Regional Cooperation

P.V. Rao

Even a cursory look at the growth of regional cooperation organizations in South Asia cannot miss the fact that almost all of them are under expansion. Once the era of globalization paralleled by the Indian market reforms dawned in nineties, regional cooperation has shifted away from the earlier pattern of restricting to region per se to trans-regional expansion. BIMST-EC, established in 1997 with five members – Bangladesh, India, Myanmar, Sri Lanka, Thailand – was expanded to seven by admitting the Himalayan states of Bhutan and Nepal. Its numerical strength thus, now is equivalent to that of SAARC. Of course, SAARC itself is under expansion following the Dacca summit's decision in November 2005 to admit Afghanistan as the eighth member, along with China and Japan as observes. Of course, the United States of America and South Korea too want to sit as observers and the admission of the former as observer at the 2008 SAARC summit appears to be imminent. ASEAN, basically a Southeast Asian organization had admitted India as a summit member in 2001 (ASEAN+1), and Pakistan as a member of its security forum, the ASEAN Regional Forum (ARF) in 2005. Thus, what we see is a new phenomenon of trans-regional expansion of the SAARC and ASEAN by admitting into their fold countries, which do not belong to their respective regions. Geopolitics and geo-economics are the prime movers in enlarging the membership of these regional organizations.

Such trans-regional cooperative engagement has had its impact on the sub-regional efforts too, the BIMSTEC in particular, which combines part of SAARC and part of ASEAN membership into its fold.

Sec. I. Introduction

BIMST-EC was created mainly due to the initiative taken by Thailand. Bangkok, goaded by it Look West policy convinced India to support its westward regional association. Sri Lanka and Bangladesh, the two smaller members of the SAARC which were always in search of extra-regional identity joined the BIMST-EC along with India. Hence, for the first time South Asia had moved in an eastward direction, linking it with the institutions of Southeast Asia. From an Indian point, the BIMST-EC initiative perfectly complements her Look East policy. The MEA Annual Report (2002-03) endorses similar view in stating that this "sub-regional economic cooperation grouping on the rim of the Bay of Bengal, constitutes an important component of India's Look East Policy," and concurs with the Group's view that it "will further strengthen relations between South and Southeast Asia." (Government of India 2003). The Indian Prime Minister Manmohan Singh reinforced the same point while addressing the BIMST-EC summit at Bangkok on July 31, 2004: "We consider our partnership in BIMST-EC as a key element in our 'Look East Policy' and long-standing approach of good neighbourliness towards all our neighbours – by land and sea." (http// :in.news.yahoo.com 2004a). Such frequent reference by Indian leadership to the relevance of BIMST-EC to New Delhi's Look East policy does not fail to carry the message that the sub-regional group's value and interest to India is just confined to its Asean relevance and hence does not enjoy a separate policy treatment. India surely, given its size, geopolitical location and strategic expansion, remains the leading member of the newly formed sub-regional group in the Bay of Bengal region. Perhaps South Asia's inability to form a sub-regional group of its own had boosted the prospects for BIMST-EC, and in both, the proposed South Asian Growth Quadrangle (SAGQ) as well as the BIMST-EC, India remains the prime sector (Rao P.V 2003).

Thailand's initiative on BIMST-EC indicates her objective to enhance relations in a multi-faceted manner with countries beyond the ASEAN. India, obviously, figures as the major partner in Bangkok's South Asia strategy. True to the declared objective, Thailand has been developing relations with India in various fields, primarily in trade, investment, maritime security, defence, tourism and infrastructure. The

Thai prime minister who visited India in June 2005 stated: "We are moving in a right track in deepening our friendship and cooperation ranging from trade an investment, land and air transportation linkages, security, science and technology, culture to education. Our efforts are not confined to relations at the government level, but we also put emphasis on people-to-people ties." (http//: in.news.yahoo.com 2004b).

BIMST-EC after its formation assigned to each of the member countries a lead role to coordinate activities in the designed sector in the following order: Bangladesh: trade and investment; India: technology; Thailand: transportation and communication; Myanmar: energy; Sri Lanka: tourism and fisheries. However, since such country roles alter every three years, country responsibility of each member was redesignated in 2002 in the given order; Bangladesh: trade and investment; Sri Lanka: technology; India: tourism, transportation and communication: Myanmar: energy; Thailand: fisheries, BIMST-EC expressly recognizes the importance of private sector participation in the implementation of the above sectoral cooperation.

Sec. II. Trade and Investment

A BIMST-EC Economic Forum thus was formed in 1999, consisting representatives from public and private sectors, with the objective of making policy recommendations to be debated at the grouping's annual ministerial meetings. As a sub regional group BIMST-EC made reasonable progress in enhancing its share in global trade. Public expression was given to the group's progress by the Indian prime minister on the summit occasion. To quote him:

Considerable progress has already been achieved in terms of a Framework Agreement on Free Trade and valuable expert-level studies under the six Listed areas of cooperation. For instance, we consider the trilateral India-Myanmar – Thailand Highway proposal and the proposed Optical Fibre Telecommunication Link alongside the Highway as projects, which would have considerable importance in the BIMST-EC context. (Assocham 2005)

It should be admitted that going by the less than one decade of its existence BIMST-EC's achievements are not really commendable. No doubt, considering the region's backwardness (nicknamed as the Himalayan Poverty Triangle), it did gain, in economic terms, in increasing its export-import ratios. According to Assocham, an Indian business representative group, BIMST-EC's exports have grown from $104.9 billion in 1999-2000 to $143.2 billion in 2003-04, while imports to this region have surged significantly from $103.4 billion in 1999-2000 to $152.4 billion in 2003-04. For the poor performance of the FDI sector, Assocham reasons basically three factors: first, the BIMST-EC countries are still within the framework of regulatory reforms: second, infrastructural and procedural bottlenecks continue to persist in this region, which restrict the investors for parking their surpluses in the region; and third, the socio-political conditions in the region are not liberally conducive to catch the attention of overseas investors. India alone accounted for 69.6 percent of total FDIs followed by Thailand, which accounted for 21.7 percent of the total FDI inflows in the region. Countries such as Sri Lanka, Myanmar and Bangladesh accounted for 4.9 percent, 2.6 percent and less than 0.10 percent of the total FDI inflows respectively during the period (www.eximbankindia.com)

In other words, most of the capital flows into the BIMST-EC are intra-regional, with India, the largest and growing economy of the region obviously registering the highest share, followed by Thailand. India's largest share in the BIMST-EC's foreign capital investment, and also the increase in the group's exports and imports as mentioned above could be due to the bilateral free/preferential trade pacts signed between India and other member countries. Only two countries, Myanmar and Thailand, are the non-SAARC countries in BIMST-EC, while the rest including the recent members, Bhutan and Pakistan, are part of the South Asian Regional Association, with two decades of cooperation in trade and investment, whatever be its progress.

Much of the intra-regional growth in trade and investment can be attributed to the bilateral agreements of cooperation between India and her SAARC partners. In fact, a Exim Bank study titled "BIMST-EC Initiative: A Study of India's Trade and Investment Potential with Select Asian Countries" indicates high potential for increasing bilateral trade and investment between India and the BIMST-EC countries (Research and Information Systems 2004a). Thus there is the India-Bangladesh PTA of 1997; India-Sri Lanka FTA signed in 1998; India-Nepal treaties of trade and transit periodically renewed; India-Bhutan treaty of 1949 provides for free trade and commerce between the two countries. As in the case of Nepal, India and Bhutan too periodically renew the 1949 Treaty, the latest renewal being in 1995 that is valid for a ten-year period. The tiny Himalayan Kingdom is heavily dependent on India for its trade and economic development. In addition to the formal trade, informal trade across the borders accounts for a vast unofficial economic engagement between the region's trading networks. It was after India's FTA/PTA arrangements with the above countries that a free trade area agreement was signed on February 8, 2004 between all the member countries including the latest members, Bhutan and Nepal. Bangladesh, which had certain reservations at the time of signing the FTA, joined later in June 2004.

The BIMST-EC Trade and Economic Ministers constituted an Inter-Government Group (IGG) in April 2000 to prepare a concept paper on Free Trade Area in the region. The IGG in its report, while recommending FTA, emphasized that its basic objective should be to encourage harmonious development of economic relations among the members through the expansion of trade and creation of fair conditions of intra-regional competition. In particular it felt that FTA's ultimate objective should be to 'create' trade in the region and should not lead to the 'diversion' of trade. The Group of Experts (GOE) has made steady progress for establishing a BIMSTEC FTA and since 2003,

BIMSTEC is contemplating on finding ways and means for augmenting investment flows among the BIMSTEC members as well as studying in-depth the possibilities of sectoral cooperation. The Group of Experts was of the view that through market enlargement and liberalization as well as measures for trade facilitation, the FTA in the BIMST-EC region will create an environment conducive to the improvement of efficiency and competitiveness of firms and industries in member countries. It will also help in establishing a conducive framework for intra-regional investment flows and attracting investments from outside the region (The Hindu 2005a).

Perhaps India's bilateral free trade agreements with the BIMST-EC countries paved the way for a multilateral sub-regional FTA. This, at least, is the inference drawn by a former senior official of India's Ministry of External Affairs (MEA) who headed the East Asia desk. According to him: "With India already having free trade area regimes with Sri Lanka, Nepal and Bhutan and close to finalizing an FTA with Thailand, a broad preparatory background was already in place. The BIMST-EC Group of Experts had prepared a draft Framework Agreement for the FTA." (Sudhir Devare 2006). The BIMST-EC FTA would cover all those original sectors such as trade, investment, energy, tourism and transportation, which are part of the group's original agenda of multilateral cooperation. In fact the first meeting of the group's Trade Negotiating Committee (TNC) was held in September 2004.

Sub-regional cooperation is surely dependent on the overall progress of the regional association, SAARC or BIMST-EC, and the interest of the prime actors in sharing, mobilizing and giving political thrust to the sub-regional idea. In fact, it is often argued that India's initial lack of interest in SAGQ and BIMST-EC contributed to their slow growth. Moreover, given the political dynamics in the SAARC region and the mutual suspicion between the member countries, India has demonstrated greater preference for bilateral economic cooperation.

India and Thailand signed a Free Trade Area (FTA) agreement in 2003. Initially under the bilateral FTA both agreed to cover eighty items for trade concessions. However, further progress on FTA ran into some problems as both the countries could not reach consensus on additional list of coverage, rules of origin, etc. In fact, the Thai prime minister visited New Delhi in 2005 with FTA as a major item on his negotiating agenda and held talks with the Indian businessmen to clear some of their misgivings about the bilateral FTA. He expressed his country's commitment to complete the FTA process with India by 2010. As part of her business promotion activities, Bangkok has been seriously promoting to encourage what it call the 'Thailand brand' products in India.

Series of Thailand Business Exhibitions are being held in important metropolitan cities of India including Delhi, Chennai, Bombay, Hyderabad and Bangalore. Among the business areas which Thailand wants to promote and which are also part of the bilateral FTA with India are: automobile spares, textiles, food items, computer software and accessories, chemicals, cosmetics, ceramics, garments, footwear, furniture, household goods and decoratives, plastics and construction. Though it is too early to assess the Indian consumer response to the Thai brands a preliminary survey conducted by this author on the local response to Thai goods at a Thailand Business Exhibition held in Hyderabad in 2004, might give an idea of future prospects for Thai goods in the Indian market. Flower decoratives, artificial jewellery, marker pens and plastic products received good response from Indian buyers. Thai shirts and rubber wood products had an average demand. In the automobile sector, Indian automobile manufacturers expressed some apprehensions about the Thai FTA impact on auto ancillary industry. It is felt that Thailand "has a definite manufacturing cost advantage vis-à-vis India" and that "imports from Thailand could start within 1-2 years of the FTA signing unless the Indian government makes systemic changes in policy and operating conditions for the Indian components industry." (The Hindu 2005b). The government too feels that the automobile sector's fears were unfounded.

As part of the FTA implementation, India and Thailand, signed an Early Harvest Scheme (EHS), to be operational beginning with September 2004. It facilitates fast track elimination of tariff barriers on export items of mutual interest. EHS plans tariff elimination over two years on eighty two items which include: gear boxes; refrigerators; pipes, textile spindles; ball bearings; pulleys; wrist watches and signaling equipment.

India and Sri Lanka have expanded their relations deeply into several sectors, which include energy, defence, trade and investment. The India-Sri Lanka Free Trade Area Agreement signed in 1998 is another bilaterally significant trade arrangement between the BIMST-EC partners. The FTA is generally recognized as a successful bilateral economic arrangement, which had given fillip to expansion of cooperation into other fields. Since the implementation of ISFTA there has been a phenomenal increase in the two-way trade between the partners. Exports of Sri Lanka more than doubled from US$ 71 million in 2001 to 168 million in 2002. India's export to Sri Lanka increased from $ 604 million in 2001 to $ 831 million to 2002 thus crossing the one billion dollar mark for the bilateral trade turnover. Furthermore, although investment is not covered by the FTA, it stimulated 37 investment projects with India emerging as the third largest foreign investor in Sri Lanka (Research and Information Systems 2004b). As noted earlier such bilateral agreement had a spillover effect on establishing regional multilateral trade and investment arrangement, the BIMST-EC in particular.

Sec. III. Infrastructure

The Bay of Bengal region is a historically well-linked area. Its physical topography, though a very difficult one to enable human passage was yet conquered by invaders traders, travelers, seamen and religious zealots. Modern advances in transport and communication technologies provide immense opportunities to connect the neighbouring countries more cohesively into a close and engaging regional system. Enough studies were conducted by ADB and ESCAP to develop roads, railways and rivers navigation linkages and integrate them into a regional transport mode. Asian Highway project thus is the most ambitious of such plans and in fact work, though in piecemeal, is underway on the trans-regional route designed to run from Hanoi to Tehran.

Thailand is known to be one of the Asian countries with developed infrastructure skills in road construction and airports. A great potential to promote cooperation between India and Thailand in this area is recognized. In fact, it is interesting to note that India, Myanmar and Thailand signed a trilateral agreement in 2003 to construct land repair 1360 km. Moreh-Bagan-Mae Sot Highway. The project is already under execution, which promises to serve as a key road link between South and Southeast Asian countries. The three countries also consider the possibility of constructing a road from Kanchanaburi in Thailand to Dawei in Myanmar and development of a seaport at Dawei.

Sec. IV. Tourism

Tourism is another promising area of cooperation in the region, which is identified by the BIMST-EC agreement. The ancient religious and ethnic ties which link the member countries of India, Sri Lanka, Myanmar, Thailand on the one hand and the more recent phenomenon of Indian film industry choosing shooting sites in Southeast Asian countries on the other are viewed as contributing factors to the growth of tourism between the BIMST-EC members. The draft paper on India-ASEAN *Vision 2020* which was later adopted at the 2004 India-ASEAN summit, Laos (officially known as the *India-ASEAN Partnership Agreement*) assesses the potential for tourism in the following language:

"The shared history and culture dating back to several centuries provides as base for a lot of tourism exchanges. A lot of tourists from Southeast Asia come to centres of Buddhist pilgrimage in India every year. With the rise of Indian middle class with higher purchasing power, India has emerged as a big market for ASEAN countries as a source of tourists." (Research and Information Systems 2003).

The documents further states that promotion of Buddhist tourism, eco-tourism, monumental tourism and joint tourist packages could be some of strategies of attracting tourists from the Southeast Asian countries like Thailand, Burma and Indonesia. Sri Lanka, Thailand and Myanmar have sizeable Buddhist population land the Indian Buddhist sites in Gaya, Rajgarh, Saranath, Sanchi and Amaravati are among the cherished destinations for Buddhist devotees from thee countries. Now that Nepal and Bhutan too have joined the BIMST-EC, their membership further supports the regional tourism-religion linkage. The ESCAP also recognizes the potential for promoting religious tourism between the member countries. However, a survey conducted by this author informs that the younger generation tourists from Thailand are attracted to India more by the latter's high-tech hubs and knowledge parks than religious centres. South Indian film industry has shown much interest in shooting outdoor films in Thailand. Thus, in 2004 alone about thirty-five Tamil and Telugu films were shooted in Thailand's scenic locations and the number is expected to increase in coming years.

Policy measures toward augmenting tourist flow in the Bay of Bengal region are already through. In the civil aviation sector, an 'open skies' agreement has been signed between India and Thailand following the policy announcement made by the Indian prime minister on the eve of the Bali ASEAN Summit. The policy initiative aims at increasing the air connectivity, frequency, seat sharing, joint collaboration and carrier services between the Indiana and Southeast Asian airlines. Initially, India planned under the 'open skies' policy to offer unlimited access to eighteen tourist destinations by the Southeast Asian airlines.

Apart from the 'open skies' policy enabling the prospects for tourist promotion by air service, the potential for promotion of holiday cruise services between the islands of Bay of Bengal littorals is also viewed seriously. For instance, a cruise service between the picturesque Thai island of Phuket and Port Blair in the Andamans is a much proposed tourist idea. In fact, in June 2005, the Port Blair Municipal Council and Phuket Province of Thailand signed an agreement at Phuket which while calling for cooperation in other areas such as health and education, identifies tourism also. The two local governments are taking many steps for reviving tourism industry and this agreement is very important component of that strategy. (Vijay Sakhuja 2005). The above policy initiatives on promoting tourism notwithstanding, India needs to undertake several long-term measures to lure tourists from Thailand and the other countries in the region. A familiar refrain, rather complaint made is that India's tourist infrastructure is poor and hence the reason for the poor inflow of tourists from the neighbouring countries. Long-term steps in improving local facilities, particularly accommodation and travel, could be gainful. At the same time India also has to campaign more seriously in Southeast Asian countries and her places of tourist interest. Despite much talk about luring Thai tourists to India, this author learnt from a Thai tourist representative that the Indian tourist information center set up following the former prime minister P.V.Narasimha Rao's visit to Bangkok was subsequently shifted out to a gulf country.

The open skies policy of Indian government has opened new vistas in the India-Sri Lanka tourism cooperation. More Indian cities are linked by air to Colombo both by public and private airlines offering budget packages. As a result Sri Lanka's potential as a tourist hub linking the Indian subcontinent with Southeast Asian countries is already evident. It may be recalled that the BIMST-EC identified tourism and civil aviation among it first priorities. A 'Buddhist circuit' linking India-Sri Lanka-Thailand-Myanmar is among the serious proposals, which by road, sea and air can provide easy connectivity between the Buddhist neighbours. Acknowledging the 'vast potential' for developing tourism in the region, the Indian prime minister declared at the BIMST-EC Summit in 2004 that India would host a Round Table and Workshop of tourism ministers of BIMST-EC "with the participation of tour operators, hotel representatives and others associated with the tourism industry with the objective of at least doubling tourism within BIMST-EC region in the next five years." (www.in.news.yahoo.com 2004c).

Sec. V. Energy

Energy cooperation is potentially an important aspect of BIMST-EC. There is tremendous unexplored quantity of hydropower, gas and oil resources in the Bay of Bengal region. India's northeast, Nepal and Bhutan are known for their hydropower resources, while Bangladesh and Burma have recognized deposits of natural gas and oil respectively. Negotiations between India, Bangladesh and Burma are already initiated for joint exploration and sharing of their energy resources. In January, energy ministers of three countries met and reached broad consensus on building a regional pipeline, which would carry offshore gas from Burma through Bangladesh to India. The Indian delegation presented several options of pumping gas from Burma which include: four overland pipelines running from Tripura and Bangladesh to West Bengal; two shallow sea routes of about 400km length through the EEZ of Bangladesh; and one 700km keep sea pipeline. Though Burma and India are very keen on finalizing trilateral energy supply deals, Bangladesh is not cooperative. Dacca demands a quid pro from India seeking greater transit facilities from Nepal and Bhutan for goods and electricity to Bangladesh, in return for transiting gas through its territory to India (The Hindu 2005).

India and Sri Lanka are actively involved in the exploration, storage and marketing of oil. The Indian Oil Corporation (IOC) is already marketing through more than one hundred retail outlets its products. New Delhi and Colombo also reached an agreement in May 2003 under which the island government has committed to lease its oil farm in the

China Bay of its eastern port of Trincomalee harbour is one of the world's best natural shallow harbours which served imperial Britain's strategic objectives in South East Asia during the Second World War. An oil storage facility comprising 99 tanks with a capacity of 12,250 each built to serve Britain's war requirements has been lying idle ever since.

Sec. VI. Assessment

Since its establishment in 1997, BIMST-EC had not been able to achieve much in terms of reaching it objectives. The very first year of its creation saw Southeast Asia melting under the financial breakdown. It jolted the ASEAN members, of which Thailand and Myanmar being partners, so severely that their multilateral approach to development suffered a set back, though briefly. Thailand, the leading member of ASEAN and BIMST-EC, herself was one of the seriously affected countries. India too, despite her enthusiasm to pursue the Look East policy, failed to come up with any rescue package to bail out the affected ASEAN countries from the financial breakdown. There was, therefore, an eerie mood in both the regions, which sullied the newly established BIMST-EC march.

India's approach to the BIMST-EC is one of the reasons for its progress. New Delhi does not see this sub-regional group as an independent regional initiative, the way ASEAN or SAARC is considered. In fact, in the early years of its formation there was dissatisfaction among the BIMST-EC members, Myanmar and Thailand in particular, that New Delhi was not taking sufficient interest to put teeth into the new group Rather, BIMST-EC is seen as a supplementary body to serve India's trans-regional interests in South and Southeast Asia. Burma's inclusion in the new group as well as her membership in ASEAN was to India's advantage, as it would have balanced the growing Chinese role in that country. Sri Lanka and Bangladesh, which at one time sought ASEAN membership, would help boost India's image as a responsible regional power with concern for the smaller neighbours.

Lately in 2004, Nepal and Bhutan too were admitted into the BIMST-EC which increased its membership from five to seven. By a numerical reckoning, BIMST-EC's strength equaled that of the SAARC. The absence of Pakistan and Maldives in it was made up by Thailand and Burma. Such an arrangement suited India's interest. It may be recalled that Pakistan and Maldives opposed the proposal for a sub-regional arrangement in South Asia, a South Asia Growth Quadrangle (SAGQ). Moreover, there always had been a strong case for a Bay of Bengal Community encompassing the rim countries of the Bay. BIMST-EC eminently fulfils such regional aspiration. Thus, in assessing the performance of the BIMST-EC and India's role in it, the SAARC inputs and India's dominant role in it are a major consideration. Therefore, onward movement of SAARC in the economic, tourism, technology etc, sectors has a positive impact on the BIMST-EC progress. Above all, BIMST-EC serves as an alternative SAARC for India. There was speculation that New Delhi in fact was toying with such idea – an alternative SAARC, minus Pakistan.

References

1. Assocham (2005), "FDI inflows in BIMST-EC decline" http://sify.com/finance/fullstory.php?id. October 4.
2. Government of India, Ministry of External Affairs (2003), *Annual Report, 2002-03*, New Delhi, p.104.
3. http://in.news.yahoo.com/040731/43/2f9em.html.July31, 2004a.
4. See Rao, P.V (2003), "India and Regional Cooperation: Multiple Strategies in an Elusive Region", in, P.V.Rao (ed.,), *India and Indian Ocean*, New Delhi: South Asian Publishers, p.144.
5. http://in.news.yahoo.com, 2004b, *Op.cit.*,
6. http://in.news.yahoo.com, 2004c, *Ibid.*,
7. http://www.eximbankindia.com/publi/main.html.
8. Research and Information System for the Developing Countries (2003), *ASEAN-India Vision 2020: Working Together for Shared Prosperity*, New Delhi.
9. RIS (2004a), *South Asia Development and Cooperation, Report*, p.51.
10. For detailed account of ISFTA and its achievements, See, RIS (2004b), *Ibid.*,
11. Sudhir Devare (2006), *India & Southeast Asia, Towards Security Convergence*, New Delhi: Capital Publishing Company, p.136.
12. *The Hindu* (2005), January 13
13. *The Hindu* (2005a), June 6
14. *The Hindu* (2005b), *Ibid.*
15. See, Vijay Sakhuja (2005), "Andamans-Phuket link", http://saharatime.com /fullstory. June 17.

2

India's Role in BIMST-EC: Prospects and Problems

A. Lakshmana Chetty

India's constant preoccupation with the inward-looking policy for long, tended to retard its success in fathoming the potentials of regionalism as a cooperative mechanism for advancing the cause of peace and prosperity in the region and the world at large. However, taking advantage of the broad direction of change that coloured India's foreign policy in early 1990s, manifest in the unveiling of the 'Look East' policy, New Delhi began associating itself willingly with the regional organizations to emerge as a beneficiary eventually. This became very much pronounced in the rapid growth of India-ASEAN partnership. It was against this backdrop that India joined the new sub-regional organization called BIMST-EC. Therefore, this paper seeks to trace BIMST-EC's "steady progress" and India's role therein. However, the basic thrust of the paper is in exploring the factors – both internal and foreign that hampered India's advances to take BIMST-EC to a higher plane of cooperation.

Sec. I. Birth of BIMSTEC

Bangladesh-India-Sri Lanka-Thailand Economic Cooperation (BISTEC), the brainchild of Thailand, was formally launched by the Foreign Ministers of the prospective member nations in Bangkok on June 6, 1997 (Kumar 1997). The entry of Myanmar in December 1997 (web: bimstec.a), and Nepal and Bhutan in 2003, demanded the reordering of the acronym BIST-EC so as to read as the 'Bay of Bengal

Initiative for Multi-Sectoral Technical and Economic Cooperation, (BIMSTEC). This rechristening prompted some to comment that this sub-regional grouping was renamed in such a way as "to keep Pak from gate-crashing." Dismissing such remarks as a merely wild conjecture, Prime Minister Manmohan Singh made the stand clear by avowing thus: "We are not trying to isolate any country. Pakistan is not linked geographically to Bay of Bengal and it is as simple as that." (web: times of India).

BIMSTEC offered India an opportunity to get its ties with its eastern neighbours reinforced, much in conformity with the core of India's Look East policy. Describing BIMSTEC's relevance to India, Prime Minister Manmohan Singh noted:

We consider our participation in BIMSTEC as a key element in our 'Look East Policy' and long standing approach of good neighbourliness towards all our neighbours – by land and sea. The challenge before us is to transform the richness of our human and natural resources into cooperative regional activities promoting development, enhancing prosperity and the well-being of our people, and ensuring our collective security in all its multifarious dimensions (web: meaindia 2004.a)

Against the backdrop of Pakistan's reluctance to trade with India, which impeded the emergence of the SAARC as an economic bloc, BIMSTEC cooperative framework appeared quite attractive and fruitful to India (The Hindu 2003), especially as it would quench the latter's thirst for the growth and development of South Asia which encompasses all the South Asian countries, sans Pakistan and Maldives, as members.

Interestingly enough, prior to the successful SAARC summit in Islamabad on June 4-6, 2004, New Delhi had prophetically maintained, that in case of the failure of the summit meeting, BIMSTEC (where there was no Pakistan), would turn out to be a major project for India (The Hindu 2004). This pragmatic approach was readily endorsed by the Indian general public. In a letter to the Editor of *Indian Express*, a reader wrote to say:

I think it is right time to bury saarc process as it has hardly achieved anything other than bringing futile hopes of increased south Asian cooperation which seems next to impossible with Pakistan's chronic obsession for Kashmir. India is very intelligently pursuing a better alternative of BIMSTEC ...(web: Express India) Besides meeting India's immediate need of countering China's growing influence in Myanmar (Far Eastern Economic Review 1997), BIMSTEC served various other purposes including the promotion of cooperation to ensure the security of waterways, the eradication of organized crime, piracy and drug trafficking and the sharing of expertise in the fields of information technology, space technology, infrastructure development and tourism. Thus, it has rightly been pointed out that BIMSTEC represented the reinforcement of India's relations with four of its South Asian neighbours and that of its link with ASEAN (Myanmar and Thailand) with all of which India has had deep and abiding cultural ties and with which India sought to strengthen its bilateral trade, investment and technology links. This agenda of India is quite in conformity with the main aim of BIMSTEC, namely, harnessing the existing potential of member countries for promoting economic cooperation in the spheres of investment, industry, technology, human resource development, agriculture and infrastructure so as to improve the "living standards" of the people and the cooperation with other international organizations (web: bimstec.b).

Sec.II. Multi-lateral Cooperation

Being a founder member and the largest member in terms of population as well as territory, India, despite being preoccupied with the idea of getting its partnership with ASEAN enhanced, made every effort to live up to the expectations of its colleagues in the BIMSTEC and "to carry forward the BIMSTEC vision of mutually beneficial regional cooperation" by wholeheartedly supporting and cooperating with its BIMSTEC partners so as "to translate ideals into meaningful cooperation on the ground." (web: meaindia.b). India, therefore, played its part in renewing multilateral cooperation and bilateral cooperation in the sub-region.

Designated as Lead Country of the 'Transport and Communication' as well as 'Tourism' – two of the six priority sectors of cooperation identified at the Economic Ministerial Retreat in Bangkok on August 7, 1998 – offered India an opportunity to demonstrate its firm political commitment to reinforce the mutually beneficial regional cooperation.

2.1. Transport and Communication

As a country, which was seeking to develop its infrastructure sector with an outlay of US $150 billion (The Hindu 2004), India became convinced that the prerequisite for the success of BIMSTEC's cooperation in all fields, tourism and trade and investment in particular, was the "availability of a sound infrastructure in transport and communications." (web: meaindia.c). In fact, the Regional Integration Arrangements (RIAs) throughout the world have perceived that the Transport and Communication constituted a lifeline for the development of cooperation in various spheres. The first major step in this direction was taken, when the BIMSTEC Expert Group on Transport and Communication Sector meeting for the first time in New Delhi on April 23-24, 2001 sharpened focus on key issues such as transport and cross-border facilitation, multimode transport and logistics, infrastructure development, maritime transport, human resource development, communication linkages and networking (web: meaindia.d).

At a trilateral meeting between the Foreign Ministers of India, Myanmar and Thailand in New Delhi on December 24, 2003, a decision was taken to take up Trilateral India-Myanmar-Thailand Highway Project (The Hindu 2003), which formed an integral part of the larger Trans-Asian Highway project – designed to link Istanbul with Tokyo (Sahgal 2004a). The Trilateral Highway of 1360 Km. would provide a land corridor connecting Moreh in Manipur to Mae Sot town in North Thailand through Bagan in Central Myanmar. Hailing this project, India's Ambassador in Bangkok Leela K. Ponappa told *The Indian Express:* "The Project symbolizes what economic cooperation among BIMSTEC countries actually means. Once fully constructed, there will be significant improvement in tourist and pilgrim traffic." (The Indian Express 2004). The Highway would turn out to be a boon to hundreds of plywood factories in the Northeast as the hardwood logs could be transported by land from Myanmar, Cambodia and Laos. Tourism industry would receive a tremendous fillip, as Meghalaya, Nagaland and Arunachal Pradesh are famous for their pristine natural beauty. The Highway would certainly lead to an upsurge in smuggling, particularly of opium, arms trafficking and insurgency. But, just as every cloud has a silver lining, the hope cherished is that the growth in economic opportunities which carries the prospects of the employment avenues, might serve as a disincentive to all those, who are lured to join the ranks of the militants (Sahgal 2004b). India was so immensely pleased with the full cooperation of Myanmar and Thailand that it volunteered to lay out the optic fibre lines along this highway, and ventured to meet the estimated expenditure of US $ 10 million dollar, so as to promote the quick movement of the telecommunication data (web: meaindia 2004.e). In addition to the Trilateral Highway project, BIMSTEC members have evinced a keen interest in yet another flagship project between Thailand-Myanmar and Bangladesh that would facilitate the land transport from the Bay of Bengal to the South China Sea. Recognizing the importance of air linkages, BIMSTEC members began advocating an open sky policy. Equally important is the sea transport because India relied on sea for 50 per cent of its trade with the BIMSTEC countries, especially, Myanmar, Sri Lanka and Thailand. In 2003, India, Myanmar and Thailand entered into an agreement to build a road linkage from Dawei (Tavoy) Deep Sea Port in Myanmar to Kanchanburi in Thailand for ocean-cum-overland intermodal transit from the Indian ports (The Hindu 2003). India offered to undertake a feasibility study on this road linkage. BIMSTEC also focused attention on the development of rail tracks, which need to be harmonized. India hosted the first Meeting of the Chief Executives of Railways of BIMSTEC countries in New Delhi on September 20-21, 2004. The Meeting stressed the need to create a genuinely regional cooperative effort aimed at human resource development by raising a corpus fund, to which the Asian Institute of Transport Development contributed US$ 2 million, as seed capital. The Meeting appreciated the offer of the Indian Railways to train the railway personnel from the member countries free of cost (web: meaindia.f). The successful completion of the programme of expansion of transportation links between South and Southeast Asia would not only facilitate the free flow of goods and passengers but would also bring in buoyancy to trade, investment services and tourism. Besides boosting India's economic interaction with Southeast Asia, the transport corridors would provide India with land access to the South China Sea. India's interest in developing transport linkage assumes importance in the context of New Delhi's determination to end the physical isolation of NER and transform its economy. In a statement, Prime Minister Manmohan Singh said on July 31, 2004:

The Northeastern region of India faces considerable handicaps because of the high cost of transport. The BIMSTEC initiative opens up the possibilities of making more effectively arrangements for transportation of goods and services to other countries of Southeast Asia through the land routes, making use of roads, railways and ports that would certainly help to promote the development of the North-Eastern region. (web: meaindia.g).

2.2. Tourism

Perceiving tourism as "an engine of growth," BIMSTEC accorded top priority to the promotion of tourism and accordingly paid due attention to the development of tourism at its official and Ministerial level meetings. Though, originally the responsibility for Tourism sector was delegated to Sri Lanka in 1998, India became the Lead Country of the Tourism Sector since 2002.

In addition to the Annual Ministerial Meetings where Tourism also figured prominently, Tourism Expert Group Meetings were held for seven times, till 2004. As a result of the discussions and decisions at these fora, certain concrete steps were taken to advance the cause of tourism, like the adoption of Action Plan for Cooperation in tourism, the designation of the year 2001 as the "Visit BIMSTEC Tourism Year" and the adoption of an action plan for the "Visit BIMSTEC Year 2004" which was subsequently extended to 2005, to mention the most important decisions. In accordance with the Action Plan whose chief objectives were attracting the foreign currencies and enhancing the regional employment, BIMSTEC undertook various projects including a joint marketing plan and information exchange, to attract intra-regional as well as foreign tourists, and to promote Buddhist tourism, ecotourism and sustainable regional tourism, excursions in the member countries for tourism entrepreneurs and media, a yacht cruising along Thailand-Myanmar-India and a training on tourism IT. The Tourism Authority of India shouldered the responsibility of developing the promotional website for the "Visit BIMSTEC Years 2004-2005". (Web: bimstec). A major step to promote tourism was taken at the instance of the Indian Prime Minister Manmohan Singh when the first ever BIMSTEC Tourism Ministers' Roundtable and Workshop took place in Kolkata on February 21-23, 2005. The Meeting adopted the 'Kolkata Declaration on Tourism Cooperation' with the Proposed Plan of Action as its annexure. The proposed Plan of Action envisaged the establishment of the BIMSTEC Tourism Information Centre in India and the exploration of the possibility of instituting a 'BIMSTEC Tourism Fund' bankrolled by the member countries.

India's record of development of its own tourism sector has not been encouraging. It is a sad comment that the funds of the Union Tourism Ministry offered to the state governments for the implementation of various tourism projects, remained unutilized (Deccan Chronicle 2005). It is hoped that BIMSTEC's initiatives in the tourism sector would stimulate Indian tourism industry. In an interview to Thai Newspapers on July 30, 2004, Premier Manmohan Singh said:

The regional tourism potential is ... immense and joint tourism projects can provide a joint marketing strategy interlinking and promoting Buddhist destinations in all BIMSTEC countries. Visit BIMSTEC year 2004-2005 is an effort in this direction. (web: meaindia.h).

For the least developed as well as developing countries of BIMSTEC sub-region, tourism is not just about the showcasing of their national heritage. It is a real job-spinner. The creation of more jobs and generation of more income meant alleviation of poverty and sustainable development.

India's role in BIMSTEC's multilateral cooperation has not been confined to tending the two priority sectors assigned to it – Transport and Communications and Tourism – but embraced on the other hand, various other areas of cooperation. Being a country which made rapid strides in the field of science and technology, India volunteered to host the first and second BIMSTEC Expert Group Meetings on Technology Sector in New Delhi in 2000 and 2002 respectively where discussion centered on agro-based technology and ICT. India organized the BIMSTEC workshop on "Monitoring and Warning of Tropical Cyclones and Monsoon" in March 2003 and the "BIMSTEC Workshop on Weather and Climate" in July 2005. India also organized a "Training Programme on Renewable Energy Policy Options" in December 2004. India served as 'Lead Country' also for the sub-sectors such as Coconut and Spices, Automotive Industry and Parts, Drugs/Pharmaceuticals, e-BIMSTEC, Intellectual Property Rights (IPR) and promotion of intra-BIMSTEC Investment. In 1999 India hosted a Forum on IPR among BIMSTEC countries designed to foster cooperation in the area of IPR.

2.3. BIMSTEC Free Trade Agreement

India had reached a milestone in its participation in the BIMSTEC process when it joined its BIMSTEC colleagues to sign the Framework Agreement for a BIMSTEC Free Trade Area (BIMSTEC FTA) in Phuket in February 2004. The BIMSTEC FTA would be implemented in two phases. In the first phase, also called the Fast Track, the three developing countries – Thailand, India and Sri Lanka – would give free access to a number of goods of the Least Developed countries (LCDs) – Bangladesh, Myanmar, Nepal and Bhutan – between July 1, 2006 and July 1, 2007. In the second phase, also termed the Normal Tack, the three developing nations would give free access to most of the LDC goods from July 1, 2010. For their part, the LDCs would provide free access to a number of products of the developing countries from July 1, 2011 under the Fast Track and from July 1, 2017 under the

Normal Track (web: meaindia.i). With the conclusion of the Framework Agreement for a BIMSTEC FTA which covered trade in goods, investments and services, the stage has been set for a sharp upswing in the economic integration of the grouping that encompasses 1.3 billion people and has a GDP of about US $ 50 billion.

2.4. BIMSTEC Summit

Yet another landmark in India's 7-year association with BIMSTEC was its participation in the much-awaited BIMSTEC Summit held in Bangkok in July 2004. In fact, this Summit, which was originally planned to be held in February 2004, was postponed by five months because of the political developments leading to the change of government in India. The level of interaction raised from deputy Foreign Minister to that of Foreign Minister in 2002, has now been further enhanced to Summit level so as "to give a push" to this organization by involving the leaders of the member countries. Delineating the significance of this first ever summit, Premier Manmohan said:

This was the first meeting of the leaders of these countries at the level of the Summit. This is one manifestation of our keen desire to promote regional cooperation in this area, to work with our neighbours, to strengthen our traditional bonds, to impart a new element of vigour, vitality and dynamism to and relations with our neighbouring countries. (web: meaindia.j).

The Summit meeting adopted a Declaration, in which leaders called for sharpening focus on the areas of cooperation in progress, including "timely completion" of the FTA negotiations, development of transportation infrastructure, inter-connection of energy grids, enhancement of tourism and business travel and people-to-people exchanges. The leaders expressed grave concern over the scourge of international terrorism and transnational crime, which marred the economic and social progress. During the Retreat, Leaders took "an important step" to set up a BIMSTEC Joint Working Group on Counter-Terrorism and International Crimes (JWG-CTIC) to coordinate the efforts of member countries (web: meaindia/BIMSTEC.pdf.a).

2.5. Post-Summit Development

India lost no time in fulfilling the commitments made at the Summit meeting. India thus hosted the First Meeting of the BIMSTEC JWG-CTIC in New Delhi in December 2004. Member nations perceived BIMSTEC JWG-CTIC as a "platform for cooperation among member States to enhance their operational and strategic capabilities in preventing and suppressing terrorism and transnational crime." India agreed to continue as Chairman and to host the second meeting of BIMSTEC JWG-CTIC (web: meaindia.k). The Department of Science and Technology set up the "BIMSTEC Centre on Weather and Climate" on August 19, 2004 (web: meaindia/BIMSTEC.pdf.b). India expressed its readiness to share remote sensing data for agriculture, environment and disaster management (web: meaindia/BIMSTEC.pdf.c).

India hosted the "First BIMSTEC Energy Ministers' Conference" in New Delhi on October 4, 2005 which produced a "Plan of Action for Energy Cooperation in BIMSTEC." (Web: bimstec). India offered 150 Indian Technical and Economic Cooperation (ITEC) scholarships over and 150 training scholarships it offered to BIMSTEC personnel at the BIMSTEC Ministerial Meeting in Phuket in February 2004. India also offered another 30 scholarships for studying the traditional systems of medicine in India (web: BIMSTEC.pdf.c).

A Workshop and Round Table of BIMSTEC Tourism Ministers with travel industry representatives held in Kolkata on February 21-23, 2005 came out with a declaration and an action plan to enhance intra-BIMSTEC Cooperation in the tourism sector (web: BIMSTEC.pdf.d).

Sec. III. Bilateral Relations

In its interaction with the individual countries of BIMSTEC, India has been treading carefully in the light of its experience in SAARC. In view of its size and strength, quite a few SAARC members perceived India as a major source of their insecurity. Even a section of the strategic analysts held the view that SAARC has "suffered from the preponderance of India vis-à-vis smaller partners." Holding India a 'hegemonic power' they argued that India's role was in sharp contrast to "an informal guiding role" played by Indonesia in ASEAN (Krishnamva 1999). The notion of India as a sub-imperial power was said to exist in the minds of the elites of the member nations of SAARC which was proved untrue and unfounded by India's benign moves such as the military help extended in support of the government in Maldives in 1988 (Yatanoor 2002) and the withdrawal of IPKF from Sri Lanka in 1990. New Delhi pursued a policy designed to promote the genuine spirit of trust and goodwill among the BIMSTEC member nations. Cognizant of the inherent weaknesses of some of the nations of BIMSTEC, in particular the LDCs, India displayed a political will to promote peace and harmony by way of fulfilling the expectations of the peoples for a prosperous future.

3.1. Bilateral Relations with Developing Countries

3.1.1. Thailand: Thanks to the convergence of their 'Look East' and 'Look West' policies, India and Thailand have been involved in forging a fruitful partnership in diverse areas. The intensity of warmth between the leaders of India and Thailand was such that on April 15, 2002 the Thai Premier Thaksin Shinawatra, despite his hospitalization, received in Bangkok the then Foreign Minister Jaswant Singh when the latter was on his way to Myanmar. Commenting on this episode, *The Hindu* observed: "Mr. Thaksin is once again signalling his extraordinary enthusiasm for building a new relationship with India." (The Hindu 2002). India duly reciprocated Thailand's sentiments and gestures. Prime Minister Manmohan Singh told Thai Newspapers, *Nation* and *Khao Sod* on July 30, 2004:

Our (India and Thailand) ties continue to expand, covering the full range of economic, technical, social and cultural fields that are important to our respective peoples. The shared will and desire at the highest levels in both countries, have given substantial content and new dimensions to our multi-faceted ties. Our exchanges in recent years have helped to lay strong foundation for building up a vibrant partnership for the mutual benefit of our two peoples and countries. (meaindia 2004.l).

The Framework Agreement on Free Trade Area signed in 2003, was hailed as a "landmark development" in India–Thailand relations. Growing security cooperation was reflected in the signing of an MoU by both on July 20, 2005 for joint maritime patrols to check piracy and arms smuggling (The Hindu 2002). Earlier, India and Thailand entered into an agreement to link the Andaman Sea and Gulf of Thailand with an oil/gas pipeline, and to twin Port Blair with Phuket in a tourist circuit (Verghese 2003). On February 2, 2002, both the sides signed an agreement to exchange technologies developed in either of the countries in the areas of pollution control and waste and environmental management. They also decided to launch joint research, development and design projects in different fields of science and technology (Hindu 2002). During Premier Thaksin's working visit to India on June 30, 2005, it was agreed to set a target of a bilateral trade volume of US $ 4 billion by 2007. The two countries (New Asia Monitor 2005) also signed a high profile Educational Exchange Programme (EEP).

3.1.2. Sri Lanka: India-Sri Lanka relations have been passing through an exciting phase manifested in very frequent high-level political exchanges and enhanced cooperation in diverse areas. India offered assistance to Sri Lanka at a time when the latter was in the thick of refurbishing its economy, in the wake of the dawn of peace (after decades of ethnic strife) in the aftermath of the ceasefire agreement between Colombo and the LTTE. Frequent bilateral political exchanges have facilitated close and routine consultation and cooperation. No year passed in the recent past, without a state visit to India by the Sri Lankan President. During her latest visit to India in June 2005, President Chandrika Kumaratunga along with Premier Manmohan Singh impliedly expressed concern over cease-fire violations and "the illegal acquisition of air capability" by the LTTE (The Hindu 2005a). Interestingly enough, both the chief contestants of the Sri Lankan Presidential election held on November 17, 2005, were positively disposed towards India and they even favoured the Indian model of federalism on the election platform. Colombo enjoys the distinction of being the first BIMSTEC country to conclude Free Trade Agreement (FTA) with India in December 1998, which became operational in December 2001. In May 2003, when Sri Lanka appealed to India for assistance, following the havoc, created by the heaviest rainfall recorded since 1870, India responded promptly and effectively. Indian Oil Corporation (IOC) and Ceylon Petroleum Corporation (CPC) joint venture in Trincomalee district and India's assistance to Trincomalee Technical College were hailed as symbolic and representative of the close and enduring ties that India has cultivated with northeastern Sri Lanka. On April 30, 2005, India gifted four ambulances for the benefit of the people of Sri Lanka's central plantation districts (Hindu 2005b). India has committed itself to setting up an India Cancer Centre in Sri Lanka. New Delhi has been offering Credit lines to Colombo from time to time of which the largest being the one amounting to US $ 100 million provided in June 2000. The other areas of cooperation include, travel, information and technology, space and telecommunication, agriculture sector, culture and education (web: meaindia.m).

3.2. Bilateral Relations with LDCs

3.2.1. Myanmar: India and Myanmar share a long border of 1640 Km. Of the seven northeastern states; four have been really fortunate to share this tranquil border. Indian Insurgent Groups (IIGs) taking shelter in countries like Bangladesh, Bhutan, and Nepal besides Myanmar, have been constantly disturbing the peace and security of the NER. Especially in Myanmar, the IIGs find safe haven because, some of their units have been able to establish sympathetically active links with their counterparts in Myanmar. This demanded cooperation for a concerted action against the IIGs by both the countries. It is gratifying to note that much to the delight of the Government of India, Myanmar has been coming out from time to time with statements of assurances in a forthright language to wipe out the menace of the insurgency. Addressing the CII in New Delhi on January 20, 2003, Myanmar Foreign Minister U Win Aung stated: "Myanmar is ready to share its border with India for the prosperity of the entire region." (The Hindu 2003). During his first ever visit to India in October 2004, the head of Myanmar's military government Gen. Than She not only stated that his government would forbid the use of its territory for insurgent activities against India, but also assured the Indian leadership that Yangon would undertake an operation against IIGs hiding in Myanmar similar to that by Bhutan the previous year (The Hindu 2004). Under an MOU for cooperation in the field of non-traditional security issues, signed on October 25, 2004, both countries agreed to cooperate in preventing the cross border crimes including terrorism (web: meaindia.n). During the Foreign Minister Natwar Singh's visit to Myanmar in March 2005, both the sides expressed "satisfaction that the evolution of bilateral defence cooperation is moving in the right direction." (The Hindu 2005).

The growing cordiality between the two countries has also been manifested in various transport corridors, jointly developed by them in Myanmar. Particular mention should be made of the 160 km. Tamu-Kalay road – connecting Manipur with Myanmar – which was built by India and inaugurated on February 13, 2001 by the then Indian Foreign Minister Jaswant Singh. Hailing it as a "highway of friendship," Myanmar Foreign Minister U Win Aung observed:

It is a symbol of close cooperation between two neighbouring countries. The new road will help promote economic development and cooperation based on our common desire to have good relations between our countries and to uplift the socio-economic standards of the national races living along the border.

Apart from this, India and Myanmar have been cooperating with each other, on a wide range of areas including remote sensing, gas exploration and hydel power generation in Myanmar. Of the high level visits exchanged by the two particular mention may be made of the visit of Gen. Maung Aye, the Myanmar Vice-Chairman of the ruling State Peace and Development Council (SPDC) in 2000, during which, he was accorded a red carpet-welcome, a gesture, normally extended to a Head of the State (News 2000) and of the state visit of the Chairman of SPDC Than Shwe in October 2004, during which he was accorded a high profile welcome. These two instances bespeak of the strategic importance accorded to Myanmar, in the context of the vigorous pursuit of 'Look East' policy.

3.2.2. Nepal: In view of their ancient historical, geographical, cultural and linguistic links, relations between India and Nepal have been 'consistently' good despite certain simmering differences on issues like the movement for democracy. Mutually beneficial bilateral relations and cooperation have been facilitated by the frequent exchange of high level visits between the two nations. As per the 2002 figures, India's exports to Nepal accounted for about 41 per cent of Nepal's global imports while Nepal's exports to India accounted for 48 per cent of Nepal's global exports. Indian investment in Nepal comes to about 36 per cent of the total FDIs in Nepal. India offers a generous aid package to Nepal with an average annual budget of Rs.60 to Rs.75 crores. Of the several Government of India assisted projects in Nepal, special mention must be made of two health projects – the B.P. Koirala Institute of Health Science at Dharan and the Maternity & Neo-natal Intensive Care Units at the Paropkar Hospital in Katmandu –, and the construction of two Bridges on Khalpur Mahakali Sector of East West Highway (web: meaindia.o). Even though Nepal's "economic geography is inextricably intertwined with that of India" Kathmandu has been seeking closer ties with Beijing much to the chagrin of New Delhi. King Gyanendra, like his farther King Mahendra, has been playing the China card in order to legitimise his "power grab" and to perpetuate monarchy at the cost of Parliamentary democracy. China's unceasing arms supplies to Nepal and the latter's vocal support to the farmer's entry into SAARC at a time when Beijing has been relentlessly exploiting every opportunity to undermine India's influence in the region, speak of bad state of relations between India and Nepal (Deccan Chronicle 2005). Unless India took effective steps to bring round King Gyanendra, external forces would entrench themselves in the affairs of the region seriously challenging India's primacy.

3.2.3. Bhutan: India and Bhutan share not only a border of about 700 kms. but also the threat from the Maoist groups which have been hand in glove with Indian leftwing extremists and the IIGs. "The open borders, Visa regime and duty-free trade across this border" are, as India's Foreign Secretary Shyam Saran has pointed out, a testimony to the "complete understanding between our two leaderships of our mutual security concerns." (web: meaindia.p). India remained the principal donor for the economic development of Bhutan. During the state visit of the King of Bhutan, His Majesty Jigme Singye Wangchuk, to India, took place in January 2005, New Delhi agreed to hike its assistance from Rs.430 crores to Rs.710 crores during the Ninth Plan period, (2002-2007). India has also offered the financial assistance for several hydroelectric projects in Bhutan including Chukha and Kurichi (projects which were successfully completed) and the mega 1020 MW Tala project (scheduled to be commissioned in 2006) and agreed to buy the surplus power (Chandrasekharan).

In December 2003- January 2004, Bhutan whose southeastern point adjoins Assam, demonstrated its spectacular security cooperation with India – which was in tune with Thimphu's policy of denying its territory to be used for anti-India activities – when it destroyed 31 and odd camps and killed many insurgents belonging to IIGs including the United Liberation Front of Assam (ULFA), the National Democratic Front of Bodoland (NDFB), and the Kamptapur Liberation Oganisation (KLO) (The Hindu 2005). The Bhutan Home Secretary Penden Wangchuck proclaimed at a press conference in Hyderabad on September 15, 2005, that there were no camps of IIGs or militants operating on Bhutanese soil (web: meaindia.q). The Government of India – which hailed these military operations as "a mile stone in our joint response to terrorist activities" (Deccan Chronicle 2003) – expressed its appreciation for Bhutan's successful operation when the King of Bhutan visited India in January 2005. There are few inter-state boundaries, which turned out to be "the gate ways to joint and mutually beneficial undertakings" as the one between India and Bhutan.

3.2.4. Bangladesh: It is really deplorable that, thirty years after Bangladesh had achieved liberation, rather deliverance from the shackles of Pakistan, largely through India's timely intercession and help, India is being denied certain facilities like the legitimate transit of goods and passengers to the NER, which India had enjoyed even in the erstwhile East Pakistan until 1971 (The Hindu 2005). As if to add injury to the indignity, Dhaka entered into an agreement with Beijing to get a road link between the two opened up through Myanmar to facilitate the flow of goods to China which on many an occasion had avowed repeatedly that "Indian Ocean is not India's Ocean," (web: meaindia.r) and thus had rubbed India on the wrong side. In fact, India piously began its interaction with Bangladesh by adopting a positive approach. India had offered help to Bangladesh in the IT sector as well as in cyclonic-tidal-surge-management, besides providing five computers to two schools in each of the 64 districts of Bangladesh. India volunteered to undertake the training of 250 schoolteachers, by Indian IT experts. But, far from returning these gestures, Bangladesh pursued policies and programmes, which wounded the Indian sentiments.

Bangladesh Prime Minister Khaleda Zia, whose term of office will be ending in less than one year, did not find it appropriate to visit India whereas she could find time to go to China in August 2005. Of the 4,095 Km. long porous borders, a small stretch of 6.5 km. remains undemarcated. That Dhaka remained utterly insensitive to India's security concerns on cross-border terrorism is very much in evidence in many instances. Following the razing of their camps in Bhutan and Myanmar, the IIGs have cleverly moved their bases and established them firmly along the Indo-Bangla border and thus, have been posing threat to the safety, security and stability of not only India but also of Bangladesh itself (The Hindu 2005). Curiously enough, Bangladesh authorities have been denying the knowledge of the very existence of such camps (web: meaindia.s). Yet another serious problem about which India has been gravely concerned, is the large scale illegal immigration of Bangla nationals as a result of the 'push of poverty' and the very high rate of 40 per cent unemployment, prevailing in Bangladesh. India proposed the fencing of the border but Dhaka was not forthcoming, the reason offered by Bangladesh Foreign Minister Morshed Khan, being what he told *The Hindu*: "Neither... should act unilaterally when there is a (1974) bilateral agreement that no defence barrier or structure be raised by either side within 150 yards from the zero line." (The Hindu 2005). In January 2005, India, Myanmar and Bangladesh did reach a formal agreement on the export of natural gas from Myanmar by pipeline through the territory of Bangladesh, but Dhaka made its cooperation conditional to India's acceptance of three of its demands: the transformation of hydro-electricity from Nepal and Bhutan to Bangladesh through Indian territory; the corridor for the movement of goods between Nepal and Bhutan and Bangladesh through Indian territory; and the reduction of trade imbalance (Deccan Chronicle 2005). An Indian scholar noted wryly that the Petroleum Minister "Mani Shankar's Aiyar's unrealistic Mynamar-Bagladesh-India gas-line cannot take off precisely because of the blind hatred for what, in Bangladesh, is called 'Hindu Bharat." [64] While several Southeast Asian countries sought India's cooperation in the field of nuclear energy, Dhaka turned to China for the same. It is obvious that Bangladesh has been trying to bully India into conceding its demands by playing China card.

When the former Prime Minister Vajpayee unveiled the "hands of friendship" policy towards India's neighbours, Pakistan was pragmatic enough to avail itself of the opportunity but Bangladesh remained obdurate. This did not bode well for a country like Bangladesh, which depended on India for 70 per cent of its imports (which either added to Bangladesh's export and manufacturing competitiveness or met the basic needs of the people of Bangladesh) worth over US $ 2 billion (The Hindu 2005).

Sec. IV. Conclusion

The inevitable disenchantment with the SAARC and the new found enthusiasm to associate itself with as many regional cooperative frameworks as possible and a crying need to diversify its external economic relations manifested in the launch of the 'Look East' policy, inspired India to become the founder member of BIST-EC which was eventually rechristened BIMSTEC. The BIMSTEC enjoys the distinction of bringing together the countries of South and Southeast Asia in a sub-regional grouping. To begin with, India could hardly find time and energy to address the strategic challenges as well as opportunities presented by BIMSTEC because of its preoccupation with the enhancement of its level of interaction with ASEAN. In due course, New Delhi got on to business to play its part in exploiting the synergies latent in the capabilities and resource endowments of the member nations for the prosperity and well being of all the peoples of the sub-region.

Though India's attitude towards the BIMSTEC has to be viewed as an integral part of its 'Look East' policy, one can discern from certain rapidly unfolding events, four main elements which constitute the core of India's policy towards BIMSTEC and of which the most important is the staunch support extended to the policies and programmes designed to turn the sub-region economically vibrant, socially cohesive and politically integrated. In the furtherance of this objective, the sub-regional grouping took certain measures such as the enhancement of the level of interaction among the member countries to that of the summit, an identification of six core areas of cooperation each of which was entrusted to a member of the grouping designated as a Lead Country, an initiation of the process of establishment of BIMSTEC FTA, to mention the most important ones. Second, to assist the individual members of BIMSTEC through bilateral cooperation in a wide range of areas including trade, investment, industry, science and technology, transport and communication, energy, tourism, agriculture, fisheries and human resource development. Glaring examples included, development of transport corridors including the road between Tamu and Kalemyo, trilateral high-way project and focus on mega projects in energy sector such as natural gas pipelines, to mention a few.

Third, forging of a common front against terrorism of all hues and transnational crimes including gunrunning and trafficking in narcotics, which have affected all the member countries without exception. Fourth, transforming NER into India's economic bridge to Southeast Asia. India's moves to improve the politico-socio-economic landscape of the NER, the assistance offered to develop transport networks in the neighbouring countries and the coordinated campaign against the insurgency, have all aimed at turning the NER into a land of peace and prosperity.

A cursory glance at India's bilateral relations with its BIMSTEC partners would reveal that Bangladesh and Nepal to some extent – which have been pursuing the policy of courting China and of alienating India – constitute the single encumbrance to take the BIMSTEC process to a higher plane. But, for India – a fast emerging global power, the accomplishment of image changeover from a country confined to South Asia (which has been long overdue), demands the heralding of a new era of positive collaboration with Bangladesh by burying the hatchet. Negative factors could be overcome through the personal interactions at the leaders and official's levels. India would do well by offering generous assistance, which would help Bangladesh to get out of the economic conundrum, which is the source of several bilateral problems chief of which being the large-scale illegal migration to India. It may be recalled that at the SAARC summit at Dhaka on November 13-14, 2005, Prime Minister Manmohan Singh maintained that India would benefit from the prospering Bangladesh by all means! (Deccan Chronicle 2005). These friendly gestures, while contributing to the weakening of the hands of the religious nationalists and militant fundamentalists, would prevent Bangladesh from entering into the shoes of Pakistan especially at a time when Pakistan has committed itself to effecting a gradual thaw in its relations with India. It is high time India gave up its lackadaisical approach to the Royal Nepal Government and played a benign role in resolving the spat between King Gyanendra and the forces fighting for Multi-Party system so as to take the wind out of the sails of external powers waiting in the wings to undermine India's legitimate interests in the region. India's smooth sail in the BIMSTEC process also demands that Bangladesh and Nepal, the two "new irritants" of India, were made to realize the need for living in peace and friendship with India despite the disparities in size and strength.

References

1. Amrish Sahgal (2004), "Highway to Prosperity," *Sahara Times* (Luknow), January 24
2. *Ibid.*, p.15
3. Chandrakant Yatanoor (2002), "ASEAN and SAARC: A Comparative Analysis in International Regional Cooperation," *Indian Ocean Digest*, July-December, p.89.
4. Chandrasekharan S, "Bhutan: Crack down on Indian insurgent camps-Implications: Update 36," http://www.saag.org/notes3/note206.html.
5. *Deccan Chronicle* (2005), October 26
6. *Ibid.*, (2003), October 9
7. *Ibid.*, (2005), November 14
8. *Far Eastern Economic Review* (1997), July 10, p.32
9. Krishnamva Nadhavathna (1999), "ASEAN and the New Millennium," *World Affairs*, July-September, pp.31-32.
10. *New Asia Monitor* (2005), July
11. *News* (2000), November 1
12. Sampath Kumar (1997), "South Asian Association for Regional Cooperation (SAARC): New Imperatives," *World Affairs*, July-September, p.39
13. Saradindu Mukherji (2005), "Bangla Policy is out of Kilter," *The New Indian Express*, November 15
14. *The Hindu* (2003), October 7
15. *Ibid.*, (2004), October 20
16. *Ibid.*, (2003), November 25
17. *Ibid.*, (2003), December 25
18. *Ibid.*, (2002), April 16
19. *Ibid.*, (2002), February 3
20. *Ibid.*, (2005), May 21
21. *Ibid.*, (2005), June 10
22. *Ibid.*, (2003), January 21
23. *Ibid.*, (2005), March 28

24. *Ibid.*, (2005), December 4
25. *Ibid.*, (2005), September 16
26. *Ibid.*,(2005), October 29
27. *Ibid.*, (2005), March 27
28. *Ibid.*, (2005), September 27
29. *The Indian Express* (2004), August 2
30. *The New Indian Express* (2005), Editorial, "The King and We," November 28
31. Verghese B.G (2003), "For an Ocean Outlook," *The Hindu*, November 25
32. Web: bimstec.a, for the text of "Declaration on the Admission of the Union of Myanmar and the Re-Naming of BIST-EC" see http://www.mfa.go.th/bimstec/bimstecweb/htm/ declardec97.html.
33. Web: bimstec.b, for the text of "Declaration on the Establishment of the Bangladesh-India-Sri Lanka-Thailand Economic Cooperation (BIST-EC), Bangkok, 6 June 1997" see http://www.mfa.go.th/bimstec/bimstecweb/html/declarjune97.html.
34. Web: bimstec. c, http://www.mfa.go.th/bimstec/bimstecweb/html/sectors.html.
35. Web: bimstec.d, *Ibid.*,
36. Web:http://www.expressindia.com messeges. hph? content _id = 24770.
37. For the text of BIMSTEC Summit Declaration see http://meaindia.nic.in/declarestatement/2004/07/31jd01.htm. Also see meaindia.nic.in/onmouse/BIMSTEC.pdf
38. Web: http://meaindia.nic.in/onmouse/BIMSTEC.pdf.b
39. Web: http://meaindia.nic.in/onmouse/BIMSTEC.pdf.c. *Ibid.*,
40. Web: http://meaindia.nic.in/onmouse/BIMSTEC.pdf.d. *Ibid.*,
41. *Ibid.*,
42. *Ibid.*,
43. *Ibid.*,
44. Web: meaindia.ahttp://meaindia.nic.in/speech/2004/07/31ss03.htm.
45. Web: meaindia;b, *Ibid.*,
46. Web: meaindia.c, http://meaindia.nic.in/pressrelease/2001/04/20010425.htm.
47. Web: meaindia.d, *Ibid.*,
48. Web: meaindia.e, http://meaindia.nic.in/mediainteraction/2004/07/31mi01.htm.
49. Web: meaindia.f, http://meaindia.nic.in/onmouse/BIMSTEC.pdf
50. Web: meaindia.g, http://meaindia.nic.in/mediainteraction/2004/07/31mi01.htm.

51. Web: meaindia.h, http://meaindia.nic.in/interview/2004/07/30in01.html.
52. Web: meaindia.i, http://www.bilaterals.org/article.php3?idarticle=2509.
53. Web: meaindia.j, http://meaindia.nic.in/meainteraction/2004/07/31mi01.html.
54. Web: meaindia.k, *Ibid.*,
55. Web: meaindia.l, http://meaindia.nic.in/interview/2004/07/30in01.htm.
56. Web: meaindia.m, *Ibid.*,
57. Web: meaindia.n, http://meaindia.nic.in/foreignrelations/srilanka.htm.
58. Web: meaindia.o, *Ibid.*,
59. Web: meaindia.p, *Ibid.*,
60. Web: meaindia.q, *Ibid.*,
61. Web: meaindia.r, *Ibid.*,
62. Web: meaindia.s, *Ibid.*,
63. http://timesofindia.indiatimes.com/articleshow/798292.cms#top & http://www.geo.tr/mainfiles/world.aspx?id=33651;
64. *World Affairs* (2001), April-June

3

India's Trade and Investment Opportunities in BIMSTEC

Indra Nath Mukherji

Nawal Kishore Paswan

Sec. I. Background

The regional grouping, Bangladesh-India-Sri Lanka Economic Cooperation (BIST-EC) was born when the Foreign Ministers of these countries met on June 6, 1997 at Bangkok. Myanmar joined as a full member at a Special Ministerial Meeting held in Bangkok on December 22, 1997 upon which the name of the grouping was changed to BIMST-EC. In 2003 full membership was granted to Nepal and Bhutan. During the First Summit in Bangkok on 31 July 2004 the grouping's name was changed to the Bay of Bengal Initiative for Multi- Sectoral Technical and Economic Cooperation or BIMSTEC (http://www.mfa.go.th/bimstec/background.html)

A Framework Agreement on the BIMSTEC Free Trade Area was signed on February 8, 2004 at the 6th Ministerial Meeting. This was in pursuance to the Agreed Conclusions of the BIMSTEC Economic Ministerial Retreat held in Bangkok on August 7, 1998 that suggested a Free Trade Arrangement.

The Agreement adopted a Negative List approach under which all products, except those in the Negative List would be subject to tariff reduction or elimination on two tracks. Under the Fast Track, the products listed by a Member States would be reduced /eliminated within the following time frame. It will be noted that in both the Fast and Normal Tracks, LDCs are given a longer phase out period for reduction/ elimination of tariffs.

Countries	*For Developing Country Parties*	*For LDC Parties*
India, Sri Lanka and Thailand	1 July 2006 to 30 June 2009	1 July 2006 to 30 June 2007
Bangladesh, Bhutan, Myanmar and Nepal	1 July 2006 to 30 June 2011	1 July 2006 to 30 June 2009

Under Normal Track the following time frame has been decided:

Countries	*For Developing Country Parties*	*For LDC Parties*
India, Sri Lanka and Thailand	1 July 2007 to 30 June 2012	1 July 2007 to 30 June 2010
Bangladesh, Bhutan, Myanmar and Nepal	1 July 2006 to 30 June 2011	1 July 2007 to 30 June 2015

Source: Protocol to *The Framework Agreement on BIMST-EC Free Trade Area.*

Article 8 of the Framework Agreement provides for promotion and protection of investments, and endeavours to strengthen cooperation in investment, by facilitating it and improving transparency of its rules and regulations. Besides, it provides for initiating negotiations in order to progressively liberalise the investment regime through a positive list approach.

The next section examines the share BIMSTEC Member States (BMS) in world trade and also the share of each Member State in Intra regional trade. Next the trade complementarities among BMS are examined with reference to India and other BMS. The products that contribute to complementarity, both at the sectoral and product levels are highlighted. Noting that considerable export similarity exists among BMS, the possible trade investment linkages that could contribute to more intra regional trade is examined next by analysing intra industry trade between India and other BMS. The objective of this study is to identify products that have high trade potential and as such could be liberalised under Fast Track to give momentum to expansion of intra regional trade.

Sec. II. Share in World Trade

The share of BMS in world trade is presented in table 1. As a grouping, BMS' intra regional exports in world trade have been varying from 2-5 percent over our reference period 1990-2003. The share of the region's exports in world trade increased from 2.42 percent in 1990 to 4.90 percent in 2003. The share of intra regional exports of all Member States (except Bangladesh and Thailand) in world exports shows a significant increase during this period. This region is relatively more important for exports of Nepal and Myanmar. In 2003, it accounted for over 44 percent of these two countries' world trade.

As in case of exports, the share of intra regional imports in BMS countries ' world imports more than doubled from 2.42 per cent in 1990 to 4.90 percent in 2003, as may be seen in table 2. Also to be noted is that excluding Thailand, the share of this region in all BMS' imports increased during our reference period. This region accounted for nearly 50 per cent of Nepal's world imports. In case of Bangladesh, Myanmar, and Sri Lanka this region accounted for 17-18 percent of their world imports.

The share of BMS in total regional exports has been presented in table.3. The data reveals that India holds a predominant position in intra-regional exports of this grouping. This share varied from 50-81 percent during the period 1990-2003. Thailand came next in importance, its share varying from 11-28 percent during the same period the share of Myanmar varied from 3-20 percent .The shares of Bangladesh, Nepal and Sri Lanka varied from 2-4 percent. The share of Myanmar varied from 2-6 percent while that of Bhutan was less than one percent.

Table.4 presents the share of BMS in total intra-regional imports of the grouping. Bangladesh was the largest importer from the region, its share varying from 24-38 percent during 1990-2003. During this period the import shares of Thailand, India and Sri Lanka varied from 14-29 percent. The import shares of Nepal and Myanmar were relatively lower (varying from 7-8 percent in 2003) while that of Bhutan was less than one percent in all the years excluding 2003.

Sec. III. Trade Complementarity (Cosine Measures)

The cosine index of trade complementarity (Technical Appendix.A) gives us an idea of how well the export structure of County A matches the import structure of Country B. Reversing the relationship, it also tells us how well the import structure of Country A matches export structure of country B. Good complementariy is demonstrated, if there is good matching both ways. Partial complementarity exists if the matching is only one way.

Table - 1

BIMSTEC Member Countries' Exports to the World and Percentage Share in World Exports

(Value in US $ Million)

	1990	*1995*	*2000*	*2001*	*2002*	*2003*
BD's World Exports	1670.5	3129.13	5589.58	5735.61	5443.26	6229.39
Share of BIMSTEC Members (%):	2.33	2.04	1.66	1.46	1.08	1.26
India's Exports to World :	17813	30537.2	42624.4	45335.7	50940.2	60792.7
Share of BIMSTEC Members (%):	3.60	6.37	5.09	5.43	5.37	7.04
Myanmar's Exports to World :	408.74	1197.86	1977.71	2634.69	2653.88	2750.41
Share of BIMSTEC Members (%):	25.99	15.66	21.08	35.46	39.53	44.15
Nepal's Exports to World :	211.31	323.54	676.29	613.67	542.87	570.73
Share of BIMSTEC Members (%):	7.42	9.10	32.68	39.73	48.84	44.71
Sri Lanka's Exports to World :	1895.28	3801	5458.79	4722.42	4679.89	5133.3
Share of BIMSTEC Members (%):	2.73	1.66	2.73	2.54	4.19	5.25
Thailand's Exports to World:	23071.6	57200.5	68961.5	65111.9	68850.6	80329.5
Share of BIMSTEC Members (%):	1.03	1.45	2.17	1.90	1.66	1.92
BIMSTEC's Exports to World :	45070.43	96189.23	125288.27	124153.99	133110.7	155806.03
Share of BIMSTEC Members (%):	2.42	3.24	3.63	4.09	4.09	4.90

Source: Estimated from IMF (2005), *Direction of Trade Statistics Yearbook*

Table-2

BIMSTEC Member Countries Imports from the and Percentage Share in World Imports

(Value in US $ Million)

	1990	*1995*	*2000*	*2001*	*2002*	*2003*
BD's Imports from World :	3656.09	6496.05	9000.78	9010.64	7847.78	9672.29
Share of BIMSTEC Members (%)	6.11	16.83	13.03	15.67	17.18	17.80
India's Imports from World :	23991.4	34483.6	50335.8	59519.6	67254	69826.5
Share of BIMSTEC Members (%):	0.85	1.36	1.78	1.95	1.80	2.15
Myanmar's Imports from BIMSTEC :	667.71	2341.63	3039.16	2660.92	2950.53	3218.49
Share of BIMSTEC Members (%):	3.32	1.09	20.03	16.91	14.25	18.03
Nepal's Imports from World:	586.63	767.35	1058.1	907.94	872.7	1399.65
Share of BIMSTEC Members (%):	19.83	35.30	18.14	23.02	24.94	47.46
Sri Lanka's Imports from World :	2636.41	4481	6687.99	5730.82	6022.76	6671.9
Share of BIMSTEC Members (%):	8.29	13.19	11.57	13.12	16.32	18.44
Thailand's Imports from World :	33407.5	73692	61923.5	62057.1	64720.8	75804.6
Share of BIMSTEC Members (%):	2.12	0.97	1.60	2.50	2.66	2.41
BIMSTEC's Imports from World :	64945.74	122261.63	132045.33	139887.02	149668.57	166593.43
Share of BIMSTEC Members (%):	2.30	2.59	3.51	3.95	3.94	4.52

Source: Estimated from IMF (2005)

Table-3

Percentage Share of BIMSTEC Member Countries in Intra-Regional Exports

(Value in US $ Million)

Year	*Intra-BIMSTEC Exports (Value)*	*Bangladesh*	*Bhutan*	*India*	*Myanmar*	*Nepal*	*Sri Lanka*	*Thailand*	*All 7 Members*
1990	1492.44	2.77	0.50	59.80	15.32	1.13	4.22	16.27	100.00
1991	1763.06	1.46	0.25	81.44	2.92	1.10	2.14	10.69	100.00
1992	1480.34	2.97	0.36	68.23	7.29	3.19	2.87	15.08	100.00
1993	1883.68	3.30	0.29	71.37	6.94	1.05	2.42	14.63	100.00
1994	2276.71	3.10	0.49	66.66	7.05	0.71	2.77	19.21	100.00
1995	3160.98	3.72	0.63	70.66	6.53	1.02	2.31	15.13	100.00
1996	3504.01	2.64	0.61	77.42	4.68	1.59	1.92	11.13	100.00
1997	3427.34	2.27	0.66	71.06	6.45	3.02	2.19	14.35	100.00
1998	3727.71	2.55	0.34	70.45	5.35	3.98	2.27	15.06	100.00
1999	3969.29	3.20	0.49	55.02	7.55	4.71	2.73	26.29	100.00
2000	4638.77	2.75	0.54	51.22	9.89	5.24	2.79	27.57	100.00
2001	5531.58	1.82	0.50	48.84	18.57	4.83	2.30	23.15	100.00
2002	5899.26	1.31	0.47	50.94	19.55	4.93	3.43	19.38	100.00
2003	7524.33	1.45	0.68	55.44	17.75	3.73	2.50	18.45	100.00

Source: Estimated from IMF (2005)

Table - 4

Percentage Share of BIMSTEC Member Countries in Intra-Regional Imports (Value in US $ Million)

Year	*Intra-BIMSTEC Imports (Value)*	*Bangladesh*	*Bhutan*	*India*	*Myanmar*	*Nepal*	*Sri Lanka*	*Thailand*	*All 7 Members*
1990	1090.34	33.08	0.01	15.04	3.98	5.19	17.64	25.07	100.00
1991	1130.44	32.58	0.13	14.41	0.70	9.23	23.36	19.59	100.00
1992	1354.93	30.51	0.17	14.51	0.48	7.24	26.89	20.19	100.00
1993	1628.45	31.64	0.29	14.11	1.67	8.97	21.50	21.81	100.00
1994	2183.62	28.43	0.31	16.63	1.41	9.09	24.03	20.10	100.00
1995	3116.19	37.59	0.38	16.98	0.74	7.90	19.68	16.73	100.00
1996	2790.00	34.40	0.37	18.21	1.71	6.70	21.84	16.77	100.00
1997	2905.96	32.91	0.54	21.88	1.67	6.58	22.14	14.27	100.00
1998	2996.63	36.98	0.36	23.08	1.20	5.77	19.71	12.90	100.00
1999	3545.3	26.05	0.25	22.29	12.14	4.70	17.72	16.86	100.00
2000	4542.65	24.52	0.08	23.20	12.18	3.84	17.24	18.93	100.00
2001	5080.13	26.57	0.09	20.35	8.06	3.75	13.60	27.59	100.00
2002	5444.25	24.01	0.09	19.80	7.02	3.65	16.74	28.69	100.00
2003	7638.54	24.19	1.01	20.24	6.91	7.91	18.18	21.57	100.00

Source: Estimated from IMF (2005).

Generally previous studies have done this exercise at 3 digit HS classification. Our study is done at a more disaggregated 6-digit HS level (The 3- digit HS classification)

3.1. Overall Product Complementarity

In this section, it is examined that India's trade complementarity with BMS with India as a supplier (exporter) and other BMS as a market (importer) and vice versa for the year 2003 taking all products at 6-digit classification under the harmonized system (HS) The results are summarized in table.5. The data reveals that India had good export-import complementarity with Bangladesh and Nepal and moderate with Sri Lanka.

Table - 5

Trade Complementarity Index between India and other BIMSTEC Member Country (2003)

	Bangladesh	*Myanmar*	*Nepal*	*Sri Lanka*	*Thailand*
A : India Exporting and other BIMSTEC Member Countries Importing (2003):	0.553	0.100	0.800	0.262	0.118
B. India Importing and other BIMSTEC Member Countries Importing (2003):	0.142	0.499	0.694	0.105	0.157

Source: Estimated from *PC -TAS Database* (2005).

Reversing the trade complementarity with India as market and other BMS as suppliers, it is noticed that there exists a good import-export complementarity with Myanmar and Nepal.

Generally products are offered concessions at the level of 6-digit HS classification. In this context, it will be useful to identify those products that have good complementarity at the product level. Product level analysis reveals the complementarity matching of a large number of products between India's exports and BIMSTEC Member countries' imports and vice versa. The number of such matched products is presented in table 6.

Table - 6

Number of Matched Products between India and Other BIMSTEC Members' Global Trade

Matched Products	*Bangladesh*	*Myanmar*	*Nepal*	*Sri Lanka*	*Thailand*
A. Number of Matched Products between India's Export to World and other BIMSTEC Member Countries' Imports from World	2389	448	1225	3308	4056
B. Number of Matched Products between India's Import from World and other BIMSTEC Member Countries' Exports to World	2351	2314	150	898	3282

Source: Estimated from *PC-TAS Database* (2005).*Note*: The details of such matched products may be obtained from the author on request.

An illustration of how products could be selected on Fast Track mode is presented below in terms of India - BMS world trade in matched products. The products sorted in terms of top ten matched world imports. India's world exports matched with BMS' world imports is presented in Annex table A 1. BMS' world exports matched with India's world imports is presented in Annex table A 2. It is clear from the table that India would be beneficiary, if the products (list of products in (Annex table A 1) are put on Fast Track liberalisation by BMS. Similarly BMS would be a beneficiary, if the list of products in Annex table A 2 could similarly be put under Fast Track liberalisation by India.

Sectoral (India's Export-Import Complementarity):

At the sectoral level, all 6-digit products under each Chapter (2-digit HS) are grouped and then work out their trade complementarity. This is to find out whether India's trading partners have good complementarity at the sectoral level independently of such complementarity at the product level. India's export-import complementarity ranked in terms of top ten values and defined in terms of Chapters with other BMS is presented in Box.1 below.

Box.1

India's Export-Import Complementarity with BMS

Bangladesh

27 - Mineral Fuels, Oils, Waxes & Bituminous Sub (0.990); 81 - Base Metals Nes, Cermets, Articles etc. (0.990); 01 - Live Animals (0.983); 05 - Products Of Animal Origin (0.983); 65 - Headgear & Other Parts (0.967); 74 - Copper & Articles Thereof (0.967); 40 - Rubbers & Articles Thereof (0.961); 10 - Cereals (0.959); 24 - Tobacco & Manuf. Tobacco Substitutes (0.949); and 76 - Aluminum & Articles Thereof (0.937).

Myanmar

53 - Veg. Textile Fibers, Yarns & Woven etc. (0.999); 68 - Articles Of Stone, Plaster, Cement, Asbestos, Mica (0.997); 03 - Fish & Crustaceans (0.993); 16 - Ed. Prep. of Meat, Fish, Crustaceans, Etc (0.993); 69 - Ceramic Products (0.991); 65 - Headgear & Other Parts (0.986); 05 - Products Of Animal Origin (0.979); 40 - Rubbers & Articles Thereof (0.976); 96 - Miscellaneous Manufactured Articles (0.969); and 11 - Milling Industry Products (0.960).

Nepal

23 - Residues From Food Industries, Animal Feed (0.998); 17 - Sugars & Sugar Confectionery (0.997); 53 - Veg. Textile Fibers Nesoi, Yarns & Woven Etc. (0.978); 93 - Arms & Ammunition, Parts & Accessories (0.975); 29 - Organic Chemicals (0.965); 25 - Salt, Sulphur, Earth & Stone, Lime & Cement (0.957); 65 - Headgear & Other Parts (0.948); 30 - Pharmaceutical Products (0.943); 24 - Tobacco & Manuf. Tobacco Substitutes (0.938) and 66 - Umbrellas, Sun Umbrellas, Walking -Sticks, Whips, (0.937)

Sri Lanka

14 - Vegetable Plaiting Materials (0.953); 30 - Pharmaceutical Products (0.934); 18 - Cocoa & Cocoa Preparations (0.913); 43 - Furskins & Artificial Fur, Manufactures (0.891); 23 - Residues From Food Industries, Animal Feed (0.859); 69 - Ceramic Products (0.845); 19 - Preps. Of Cereals, Flour, Starch Or Milk (0.805); 70 - Glass & Glassware (0.793); 22 - Beverages, Spirits & Vinegar (0.772) and 25 - Salt, Sulphur, Earth & Stone, Lime & Cement (0.772).

Thailand

88 - Aircraft, Spacecraft, & Parts Thereof (0.989); 30 - Pharmaceutical Products (0.984); 23 - Residues From Food Industries, Animal Feed (0.976); 79 - Zinc & Articles Thereof (0.944); 45 - Cork & Articles Of Cork (0.903); 74 - Copper & Articles Thereof (0.882); 22 - Beverages, Spirits & Vinegar (0.865); 86 - Railway Or Tramway Locomotives, Rolling Stock, Tra (0.842); 63 - Made -Up Textile Articles Nesoi, Needlecraft Sets, (0.825) and 97 - Works Of Art. Collectors' Pieces, Antiques (0.792).

Since India has good export-import complementarity with respect to the group of products contained under Chapters indicated above, it will be in India's interest to have these included under fast track liberalisation of its partner BMS (barring those that considered sensitive in nature by India's partners). Annex table A.3 presents Complementarity Index between India exporting and other BIMSTEC Member Countries Importing in respect of all the Chapters.(2003).

Sectoral (India's Import-Export Complemetarity):

In Box.2, India's import-export complementarity with BMS is presented

Box.2

India's Import-Export Complementarity with BMS

Bhutan

20 - Preps Of Vegs, Fruits, Nuts, Etc. (0.9990); 09 - Coffee, Tea, Mate & Spices (0.8321); 39 - Plastics & Articles Thereof (0.6386); 22 - Beverages, Spirits & Vinegar (0.2648); 07 - Edible Vegetables (0.1464); 08 - Ed. Fruits & Nuts, Peel Of Citrus/Melons (0.0987); 44 - Wood & Articles Of Wood, Wood Charcoal (0.0885) and 25 - Salt, Sulphur, Earth & Stone, Lime & Cement (0.0282).

Bangladesh

65 - Headgear & Other Parts (0.999); 79 - Zinc & Articles Thereof (0.990); 44 - Wood & Articles Of Wood, Wood Charcoal (0.988); 66 - Umbrellas, Sun Umbrellas, Walking -Sticks, Whips, R (0.985); 31 - Fertilizers (0.976); 75 - Nickel & Articles Thereof (0.973); 57 - Carpets

& Other Textile Floor Coverings (0.958); 52 - Cotton, Inc. Yarns & Woven Fabrics Thereof (0.946); 13 - Lac, Gums, Resins, Etc. (0.930) and 06 - Live Trees & Other Plants (0.922).

Myanmar

88 - Aircraft, Spacecraft, & Parts Thereof (0.997); 43 - Fur skins & Artificial Fur, Manufactures (0.988); 03 - Fish & Crustaceans (0.976); 27 - Mineral Fuels, Oils, Waxes & Bituminous Sub (0.965); 81 - Base Metals Nes, Cermets, Articles etc. (0.935); 21 - Misc. Edible Preparations (0.928); 89 - Ships, Boats, & Floating Structures (0.914) ; 42 - Articles Of Leather, Saddlery & Harness, Travel Go (0.909); 08 - Ed. Fruits & Nuts, Peel Of Citrus/Melons (0.906) and 35 - Albuminoidal Sub, Starches, Glues, Enzymes (0.903).

Nepal

30 - Pharmaceutical Products (0.961); 65 - Headgear & Other Parts (0.952); 44 - Wood & Articles Of Wood, Wood Charcoal (0.952); 33 - Oils & Resinoids, Perfumery, Cosmetic Or Toilet Pr (0.950); 37 - Photographic Or Cinematographic Goods (0.945); 12 - Oil Seeds/Misc. Grains/Med. Plants/Straw (0.908) and 34 - Soaps, Waxes, Scouring Products, Candles, Modelling (0.904). 47 - Pulp Of Wood, Waste & Scrap Of Paper (0.840) 62 - Articles Of Apparel & Clothing Accessories -Not Knit (0.828) 09 - Coffee, Tea, Mate & Spices (0.792)

Sri Lanka

88 - Aircraft, Spacecraft, & Parts Thereof (0.999); 05 - Products Of Animal Origin (0.998); 46 - Manu. Of Straw, Esparto, Or Other Plaiting Materials (0.991); 35 - Albuminoidal Sub, Starches, Glues, Enzymes (0.985); 68 - Articles Of Stone, Plaster, Cement, Asbestos, Mica (0.979); 16 - Ed. Prep. Of Meat, Fish, Crustaceans, Etc (0.943); 92 - Musical Instruments, Parts & Accessories (0.923); 18 - Cocoa & Cocoa Preparations (0.895); 06 - Live Trees & Other Plants (0.894) and 04 - Dairy, Eggs, Honey, & Ed. Products (0.844).

Thailand

93 - Arms & Ammunition, Parts & Accessories (0.997); 80 - Tin & Articles Thereof (0.994); 59 - Impregnated, Coated, Covered, Or Laminated

Textile (0.969); 65 - Headgear & Other Parts (0.945); 78 - Lead & Articles Thereof (0.926); 21 - Misc. Edible Preparations (0.908) ; 84 - Nuclear Reactors, Boilers, Machinery & Mechanical (0.846); 42 - Articles Of Leather, Saddlery & Harness, Travel Go (0.837); 74 - Copper & Articles Thereof (0.817) and 12 - Oil Seeds/Misc. Grains/Med. Plants/ Straw (0.808).

Since the products contained under indicated chapters above, have good import- export complementarity with other BMS, it would be desirable to have as many of them contained under Fast Track liberalization in India's list of concessions offered (barring those that are considered sensitive in nature by India). Annex table A.4 presents Complementarity Index between India importing and other BIMSTEC Member Countries exporting (2003).

Sec. II. Investment Linkages

It is now well known that the extent of intra regional trade is constrained by the limited export capabilities of less and least developed member countries. In this context importance need to be assigned to promote intra-regional investment flows from relatively more developed to less developed member States. In this context the flow of intra - industry trade (Technical Appendix B) between BMS could provide some direction for investment flows. This is because a Member State, instead of exporting and importing the same product from another Member State could choose to invest in the latter country to manufacture such a product for either for the domestic market, export to third countries or to further to buyback the same in the investing country. In the latter case this would also contribute to better balancing of bilateral trade between the two countries. Such a decision to invest in another partner country would, however, depend on the investment climate prevailing in that country. This section examine the nature and magnitude of India's intra- industry trade with other BMS. The choice of products has been based on the top intra industry trade value as also those having high intra industry trade index value.

The nature of India's intra industry trade (IIT) with Bangladesh points to the possibility of India setting up petroleum refinery in Bangladesh for manufacture of naphtha utilising the latter country's abundant natural gas as feedstock. In addition, there is considerable scope for India to set up integrated textile mills in Bangladesh to manufacture men's/ boy's shirts. The manufacture of electric accumulators or their parts could be other possibilities (table.7).

Table - 7

India's Intra-Industry with Bangladesh 2003

(Value in US Thousand Us Dollar)

HS Code	*Product Description*	*Exports*	*Imports*	*Total Trade*	*IIT Value*
271000	Petroleum oils & oils obtained from bituminous minerals,o/than crude etc	10649	5059	15708	64.413
620520	Mens/boys shirts, of cotton, not knitted	112	1949	2061	10.869
850710	Lead-acid electric accumulators of a kind usd f startg piston engines	269	283	552	97.464
030559	Fish nes, dried, whether or not salted but not smoked	365	79	444	35.586
370239	Photo film,nes in rolls,sensitisd,unexposd w/o sprocket holes,</=105mm	89	156	245	72.653
520210	Cotton yarn waste (including thread waste)	120	100	220	90.909
392310	Boxes, cases, crates & similar articles of plastic	119	91	210	86.667
850790	Parts of electric accumulators, including separators therefor	133	66	199	66.332

Source: Estimated from *PC-TAS Database* (2005).

The nature of India's intra industry trade with Bhutan, as presented in table.8 points to the possibility of setting up flour mills, food processing units and mineral water manufacturing units in Bhutan. The possibility of manufacturing office wooden furniture could further be explored.

India's intra industry trade with Nepal, as presented in table.9 points to the possibility of Indian companies setting up joint ventures in engineering industries manufacturing flat rolled products, herbicidal based pharmaceutical industries, manufacturing of plastic and textile products.

India's intra industry trade with Sri Lanka (table.10) shows the possibilities of Indian companies setting up manufacturing units in copper products, parts and accessories of automatic data processing machines, tyres and color television receivers.

The nature of India's intra industry trade with Thailand, as presented in table.11 points to the possibility of India setting up units in the latter country to manufacture parts and accessories of automatic data processing machines, motor vehicles parts, organic compounds, precious, semi precious stones, P-xylene, parts of spark-ignition engines nes., etc.

Sec. III. Concluding Observations

The origin of BIMSTEC is to be traced to the initiative of Thailand. Politically it marks a convergence between Thailand's 'Look West' policy with South Asia's 'Look East' policy. Its membership is similar to that of SAARC minus Pakistan and Maldives, but addition of Thailand and Myanmar. The absence of both Pakistan and China in the grouping is likely to contribute to a more politically cohesive regional grouping unlike in SAARC. Nevertheless some problems that are prevalent in SAARC are also visible in this grouping such as similarity of export products and consequent lack of complementarity. This has been one of the factors causing such low share of BMS in their intra regional trade. However, one positive feature to be noted (unlike SAARC), is the fairly rapid growth in the intra regional trade and their growing share in world trade, pointing to the emerging trade potential of the BMS. Besides unlike SAARC, the negotiating mechanism is based on Negative List approach to start with, unlike SAARC, which followed a Positive List approach initially which was slow and protracted. This paper highlights the trade potential at the sectoral and product levels and suggests that these be brought under Fast Track liberalization to add dynamism to the growth in intra regional trade. It further suggests some manufacturing units that India could set up in the BMS to provide added impetus to intra regional trade.

Table - 8
India's Intra-Industry with Bhutan 2003
(Value in US Thousand Us Dollar)

HS Code	*Product Description*	*Exports*	*Imports*	*Total Trade*	*IIT Value*
110100	Wheat or meslin flour	447	1593	2040	43.824
070990	Vegetables, fresh or chilled nes	1542	258	1800	28.667
230230	Wheat bran, sharps and other residues, pelleted or not	795	258	1053	49.003
252210	Quicklime	507	59	566	20.848
441222	Panels, outer ply non-conifer + ply tropical wood	152	413	565	53.805
220210	Waters incl mineral&aeratd,containg sugar o sweeteng matter o flavourd	93	428	521	35.701
701092	Glass containers, capacity 0.33-1.0 litre	364	143	507	56.410
080510	Oranges, fresh or dried	66	365	431	30.626
080290	Nuts edible, fresh or dried, whether or not shelled or peeled, nes	366	50	416	24.038
940330	Office furniture, wooden, nes	161	135	296	91.216

Source: Estimated from *PC-TAS Database* (2005).

Table – 9

India's Intra-Industry with Nepal 2003 (Value in US Thousand Us Dollar)

HS Code	*Product Description*	*Exports*	*Imports*	*Total Trade*	*IIT Value*
721230	Flat rolled prod, i/nas, <600mm wide, o/w plated or coated with zinc	21572	1464	23036	12.711
300490	Medicaments nes, in dosage	1374	19221	20595	13.343
330610	Dentifrices	10005	815	10820	15.065
071340	Lentils dried, shelled, whether or not skinned or split	6648	2060	8708	47.313
300390	Medicaments nes, formulated, in bulk	1321	3483	4804	54.996
392690	Articles of plastics or of other materials of Nos 39.01 to 39.14 nes	2609	1903	4512	84.353
721790	Wire of iron or non-alloy steel, nes	4022	329	4351	15.123
330590	Hair preparations, nes	2788	1370	4158	65.897
600210	Knittd or crochetd tex fab,w</=30 cm,>/=5% of elastomeric/rubber	221	3248	3469	12.741
391721	Tubes, pipes and hoses, rigid; of polyethylene	2699	767	3466	44.259

Source: Estimated from *PC-TAS Database* (2005).

Table - 10
India's Intra-Industry with Sri Lanka 2003
(Value in US Thousand Us Dollar)

HS Code	*Product Description*	*Exports*	*Imports*	*Total Trade*	*IIT Value*
740311	Copper cathodes and sections of cathodes unwrought	56239	3697	59936	12.336
740811	Wire of refind copper of which the max cross sectional dimension > 6mm	614	10444	11058	11.105
847330	Parts & accessories of automatic data processg machines&units thereof	4609	5918	10527	87.565
392690	Articles of plastics or of other materials of Nos 39.01 to 39.14 nes	4364	2690	7054	76.269
710239	Diamonds non-industrial nes excluding mounted or set diamonds	1623	3900	5523	58.772
401120	Pneumatic tires new of rubber for buses or lorries	937	4510	5447	34.404
852812	Colour television receivers	3330	1493	4823	61.912
090240	Black tea (fermented) & partly fermented tea in packages exceedg 3 kg	333	3534	3867	17.223
740710	Bars, rods and profiles of refined copper	2203	1436	3639	78.923

Source: Estimated from *PC-TAS Database* (2005).

Table - 11

India's Intra-Industry with Thailand 2003

(Value in US Thousand Us Dollar)

HS Code	*Product Description in brief*	*Exports*	*Imports*	*Total Trade*	*IIT Value*
847330	Parts & accessories of automatic data processing machines & units thereof	34891	26529	61420	86.39
870899	Motor vehicle parts nes	4758	16262	21020	45.27
294200	Organic compounds nes	16930	2314	19244	24.05
710399	Precious/semi-precious stones nes further workd than sawn/rough shapd	14635	1583	16218	19.52
710310	Prec/semi-prec stones (o/t diamonds) unworkd/simply sawn/rough shaped	1254	10396	11650	21.53
290243	P-xylene	5641	3398	9039	75.19
840991	Parts for spark-ignition type engines nes	878	6714	7592	23.13
540242	Yarn of polyester filaments, partially oriented,single,nes,not put up	1281	5264	6545	39.14
294190	Antibiotics nes, in bulk	3494	2966	6460	91.83
710391	Rubies, sapphires and emeralds further worked than sawn or rough shaped	4531	1928	6459	59.70

Source: Estimated from *PC-TAS Database* (2005).

Sec.V.Annex Tables:

Annex Table A.1: India's World Exports and BMS' World Imports (2003)
(Value in Thousand US Dollars)

Sl. No.	*HS-6 Code*	*Description in Brief*	*India's World Exports*	*Bangladesh's World Imports*
1	271000	Petroleum oils & oils obtained from bituminous miner	3443776	431228
2	520100	Cotton, not carded or combed	163143	384185
3	720839	Hot roll iron/steel nes, coil >600mm x <3mm	15214	203052
4	150710	Soya-bean oil crude, whether or not degummed	31	194465
5	100630	Rice, semi-milled or wholly milled, whether or not	889117	181804
6	151110	Palm oil, crude	786	159005
7	890800	Vessels and other floating structures for breaking	10991	155368
8	252310	Cement clinkers	99958	143660
9	100190	Wheat nes and meslin	387628	142533
10	170111	Raw sugar, cane	66677	97401

(Contd.)

(Contd. Table)

Sl. No.	*HS-6 Code*	*Description in Brief*	*India's World Exports*	*Myanmar's World Imports*
1	271121	Natural gas in gaseous state	2274	710078
2	440349	Logs, tropical hardwoods nes	1083	217047
3	440399	Logs, non-coniferous nes	1488	152118
4	071390	Leguminous vegetables dried,shelled,whether or not	29998	120245
5	030613	Shrimps and prawns, frozen, in shell or not, inclu	825958	115259
6	611030	Pullovers, cardigans and similar articles of man-m	14846	92933
7	611020	Pullovers, cardigans and similar articles of cotto	89984	84709
8	440729	Lumber, tropical hardwood nes, sawn lengthwise >6m	2063	84581
9	620193	Mens/boys anoraks and similar articles,of man-made	5195	64078
10	071331	Urd,mung,black/green gram beans drid shelld,whether	605	58991

(Contd.)

(Contd. Table)

Sl. No.	HS-6 Code	Description in Brief	India's World Exports	Nepal's World Imports
1	271000	Petroleum oils & oils obtained from bituminous miner	1898642	226153
2	580123	Woven weft pile fabrics of cotton, nes	502	47101
3	300490	Medicaments nes, in dosage	445504	43227
4	100630	Rice, semi-milled or wholly milled, whether or not	652294	41725
5	510710	Yarn of combed wool,>/=85% by wght of wool,not put	7451	37110
6	870390	Automobiles nes including gas turbine powered	12502	36584
7	847989	Machines & mechanical appliances nes having indivi	39259	35794
8	294200	Organic compounds nes	439558	30501
9	120500	Rape or colza seeds, whether or not broken	74	22618
10	151110	Palm oil, crude	78	21480

(Contd.)

(Contd. Table)

Sl. No.	HS-6 Code	Description in Brief	India's World Exports	Sri Lanka's World Imports
1	271000	Petroleum oils&oils obtained from bituminous miner	2505285	425038
2	270900	Petroleum oils and oils obtained from bituminous m	47	364633
3	710231	Diamonds non-industrial unworked or simply sawn, c	22646	155416
4	100190	Wheat nes and meslin	360977	129920
5	170199	Refined sugar, in solid form, nes	317476	119824
6	551219	Woven fabrics,containg>/=85% of polyester staple f	27124	105838
7	600299	Knitted or crocheted fabrics, of other materials,	205	81666
8	040221	Milk and cream powder unsweetened exceeding 1.5% f	4	77756
9	300490	Medicaments nes, in dosage	692957	76439
10	850213	Generatg sets,diesel/semi-diesel engines,of an out	9121	71778

(Contd.)

(Contd. Table)

Sl. No.	*HS-6 Code*	*Description in Brief*	*India's World Exports*	*Thailand's World Imports*
1	270900	Petroleum oils and oils obtained from bituminous m	23989	7195876
2	854290	Parts of electronic integrated circuits and microa	13597	2900708
3	847330	Parts&accessories of automatic data processg machi	214880	2475530
4	854230	Monolithic integrated circuits	3889	2383016
5	870899	Motor vehicle parts nes	345946	1756829
6	852520	Transmission apparatus,for radioteleph incorporatg	13485	1302726
7	854011	Cathode-ray television picture tubes,inc video mon	54186	823485
8	732690	Articles, iron or steel, nes	98944	815220
9	392690	Articles of plastics or of other materials of Nos	70577	795894
10	271000	Petroleum oils&oils obtained from bituminous miner	3443776	755002

Source: *PC-TAS* (2005)

Annex Table A.2: BMS' World Exports and India's world Imports (2003)

(Value in Thousand US Dollars)

Sl. No.	*HS-6 Code*	*Description in Brief*	*Bangladesh's World Exports*	*India's World Imports*
1	270900	Petroleum oils and oils obtained from bituminous miner	33878	18600672
2	852520	Transmission apparatus,for radioteleph incorporatg	79394	1842911
3	271000	Petroleum oils&oils obtained from bituminous miner	431228	1721776
4	151110	Palm oil, crude	159005	1234130
5	270119	Coal nes, whether or not pulverised but not agglom	55660	1075177
6	847330	Parts & accessories of automatic data processg machi	47583	807418
7	280920	Phosphoric acid and polyphosphoric acids	2434	643286
8	151190	Palm oil and its fractions refined but not chemica	4490	575889
9	150710	Soya-bean oil crude, whether or not degummed	194465	471961
10	880330	Aircraft parts nes	3320	387412

(Contd.)

(Contd. Table)

Sl. No.	*HS-6 Code*	*Description in Brief*	*Myanmar's World Exports*	*India's World Imports*
1	852520	Transmission apparatus,for radioteleph incorporatg	1071	1842911
2	271000	Petroleum oils&oils obtained from bituminous miner	261030	1721776
3	151110	Palm oil, crude	58	1234130
4	710239	Diamonds non-industrial nes excluding mounted or s	1464	1021095
5	847330	Parts&accessories of automatic data processg machi	7444	807418
6	151190	Palm oil and its fractions refined but not chemica	101625	575889
7	880330	Aircraft parts nes	4590	387412
8	294200	Organic compounds nes	416	352180
9	480100	Newsprint, in rolls or sheets	2416	346328
10	720449	Ferrous waste and scrap, iron or steel, nes	23	343678

(Contd.)

(Contd. Table)

Sl. No.	HS-6 Code	Description in Brief	Nepal's World Exports	India's World Imports
1	880330	Aircraft parts nes	412	77725
2	410429	Bovine and equine leather, tanned or retanned, nes	159	62758
3	300490	Medicaments nes, in dosage	5334	48558
4	330610	Dentifrices	31799	34476
5	071390	Leguminous vegetables dried,shelled,whether or not	14	33704
6	850490	Parts of electrical transformers, static converter	782	30121
7	370390	Photographic paper,paperboard and textiles,sensiti	971	29677
8	630510	Sacks&bags,for packg of goods,of jute or of other	7176	28588
9	230990	Animal feed preparations nes	2809	18047
10	340111	Toilet soap&prep,shaped;papers&nonwovens impreg wi	15202	14232

(Contd.)

(Contd. Table)

Sl. No.	HS-6 Code	Description in Brief	Sri Lanka's World Exports	India's World Imports
1	710231	Diamonds non-industrial unworked or simply sawn, c	37397	5429774
2	271000	Petroleum oils&oils obtained from bituminous miner	447	1571601
3	151110	Palm oil, crude	327	1064603
4	852520	Transmission apparatus,for radioteleph incorporatg	37	812623
5	847330	Parts&accessories of automatic data processg machi	7957	646422
6	710239	Diamonds non-industrial nes excluding mounted or s	176737	520421
7	880330	Aircraft parts nes	88941	330376
8	520100	Cotton, not carded or combed	4	253022
9	852990	Parts suitable f use solely/princ w the app of hea	2040	246041
10	852499	Recorded media for sound/image, nes	77	220535

(Contd.)

(Contd. Table)

Sl. No.	*HS-6 Code*	*Description in Brief*	*Thailand's World Exports*	*India's World Imports*
1	270900	Petroleum oils and oils obtained from bituminous miner	652619	18600672
2	710231	Diamonds non-industrial unworked or simply sawn, c	56317	5891068
3	710812	Gold in unwrought forms non-monetary	354139	4609346
4	852520	Transmission apparatus,for radioteleph incorporatg	156165	1842911
5	710813	Gold in oth semi-manufactd form n-monetary(inc gol	53239	1829286
6	271000	Petroleum oils&oils obtained from bituminous miner	1022157	1721776
7	151110	Palm oil, crude	28273	1234130
8	710239	Diamonds non-industrial nes excluding mounted or s	387954	1021095
9	847330	Parts&accessories of automatic data processg machi	3540575	807418
10	151190	Palm oil and its fractions refined but not chemica	32634	575889

(Source : PC-TAS 2005*)*

Annex Table A.3.1: Complementarity Index between India Exporting and other BIMSTEC Member Countries Importing 2003

HS-2	*Description*	*Bangladesh*	*Myanmar*	*Nepal*	*Sri Lanka*	*Thailand*
	All Commodities:	*0.553*	*0.100*	*0.800*	*0.262*	*0.118*
01	Live Animals	0.983	0.769	0.092	0.509	0.183
02	Meat & Edible Meat Offal	1.000	---	---	0.187	0.645
03	Fish & Crustaceans	0.597	0.993	---	0.008	0.408
04	Dairy, Eggs, Honey, & Ed. Products	0.269	0.673	0.065	0.179	0.273
05	Products Of Animal Origin	0.983	0.979	---	0.386	0.164
06	Live Trees & Other Plants	0.395	---	---	0.613	0.371
07	Edible Vegetables	0.297	0.173	0.590	0.767	0.412
08	Ed. Fruits & Nuts, Peel Of Citrus/Melons	0.254	0.018	0.301	0.043	0.043
09	Coffee, Tea, Mate & Spices	0.238	0.402	0.404	0.420	0.328
10	Cereals	0.959	0.658	1.000	0.412	0.410
11	Milling Industry Products	0.325	0.960	0.009	0.708	0.158
12	Oil Seeds/Misc. Grains/Med. Plants/Straw	0.054	0.867	0.003	0.447	0.326
13	Lac, Gums, Resins, Etc.	0.541	0.695	0.545	0.619	0.233
14	Vegetable Plaiting Materials	---	0.056	1.000	0.953	0.400
15	Animal Or Vegetable Fats, Oils &	0.007	1.000	0.025	0.023	0.690

(Contd.)

(Contd. Table)

HS-2	*Description*	*Bangladesh*	*Myanmar*	*Nepal*	*Sri Lanka*	*Thailand*
16	Ed. Prep. Of Meat, Fish, Crustaceans, Etc	1.000	0.993	0.634	0.015	0.242
17	Sugars & Sugar Confectionery	0.479	0.673	0.997	1.000	0.195
18	Cocoa & Cocoa Preparations	0.736	---	0.535	0.913	0.451
19	Preps. Of Cereals, Flour, Starch Or Milk	0.306	1.000	0.505	0.805	0.388
20	Preps Of Vegs, Fruits, Nuts, Etc.	0.487	1.000	0.639	0.351	0.132
21	Misc. Edible Preparations	0.415	1.000	0.311	0.758	0.470
22	Beverages, Spirits & Vinegar	0.875	0.649	0.634	0.772	0.865
23	Residues From Food Industries, Animal Feed	0.776	0.290	0.998	0.859	0.976
24	Tobacco & Manuf. Tobacco Substitutes	0.949	1.000	0.938	0.619	0.500
25	Salt, Sulphur, Earth & Stone, Lime & Cement	0.467	0.958	0.957	0.772	0.084
26	Ores Slag & Ash	0.061	0.722	---	0.262	0.390
27	Mineral Fuels, Oils, Waxes & Bituminous Sub	0.990	0.060	1.000	0.757	0.111

(Contd.)

(Contd. Table)

HS-2	Description	Bangladesh	Myanmar	Nepal	Sri Lanka	Thailand
27	Mineral Fuels, Oils, Waxes & Bituminous Sub	0.990	0.060	1.000	0.757	0.111
28	Inorganic Chem, Org/Inorg Compounds Of Precious Me	0.157	1.000	0.353	0.131	0.264
29	Organic Chemicals	0.233	1.000	0.965	0.121	0.110
30	Pharmaceutical Products	0.795	---	0.943	0.934	0.984
31	Fertilizers	0.176	---	1.000	0.182	0.661
32	Tanning Or Dyeing Extracts, Dyes, Pigments, Paints	0.746	1.000	0.276	0.515	0.424
33	Oils & Resinoids, Perfumery, Cosmetic Or Toilet Pr	0.344	0.406	0.437	0.359	0.498
34	Soaps, Waxes, Scouring Products, Candles, Modeling	0.392	---	0.929	0.474	0.401
35	Albuminoidal Sub, Starches, Glues, Enzymes	0.597	---	0.634	0.694	0.641
36	Explosives, Matches, Pyrotechnic Products	---	---	0.301	0.672	0.295
37	Photographic Or Cinematographic Goods	0.204	---	0.298	0.151	0.312
38	Miscellaneous Chemical Products	0.740	1.000	0.507	0.649	0.271
39	Plastics & Articles Thereof	0.781	0.462	0.344	0.644	0.342

(Contd.)

(Contd. Table)

HS-2	*Description*	*Bangladesh*	*Myanmar*	*Nepal*	*Sri Lanka*	*Thailand*
40	Rubbers & Articles Thereof	0.961	0.976	0.293	0.657	0.141
41	Raw Hides & Skins & Leather	0.819	0.079	---	0.316	0.633
42	Articles Of Leather, Saddlery & Harness, Travel Go	0.259	0.237	0.159	0.146	0.331
43	Furskins & Artificial Fur, Manufactures	---	---	---	0.891	0.581
44	Wood & Articles Of Wood, Wood Charcoal	0.225	0.233	0.840	0.371	0.197
45	Cork & Articles Of Cork	0.892	---	---	---	0.903
46	Manu. Of Straw, Esparto, Or Other Plaiting Materi	1.000	0.072	--	1.000	0.157
47	Pulp Of Wood, Waste & Scrap Of Paper	0.927	---	1.000	1.000	0.148
48	Paper & Paperboard, Articles Of Paper Pulp	0.417	0.284	0.836	0.331	0.384
49	Printed Books, Newspapers, Pictures, Manuscripts,	0.306	---	0.081	0.115	0.145
50	Silk, Inc. Yarns & Woven Fabrics Thereof	0.211	---	0.036	0.666	0.329
51	Wool & Fine Or Coarse Animal Hair, Inc. Yarns & Wo	0.193	---	0.356	0.278	0.502
52	Cotton, Inc. Yarns & Woven Fabrics Thereof	0.446	0.082	0.030	0.402	0.312

(Contd.)

(Contd. Table)

HS-2	Description	Bangladesh	Myanmar	Nepal	Sri Lanka	Thailand
53	Veg. Textile Fibers Nesoi, Yarns & Woven Etc.	0.214	0.999	0.978	0.038	0.028
54	Man-Made Filaments, Inc. Yarns & Woven Etc.	0.529	0.351	0.462	0.372	0.244
55	Man-Made Staple Fibers, Inc. Yarns Etc.	0.232	1.000	0.082	0.360	0.332
56	Wadding, Felt & Nonwovens, Special Yarns, Twine, C	0.408	---	1.000	0.304	0.176
57	Carpets & Other Textile Floor Coverings	0.420	1.000	0.078	0.084	0.510
58	Special Woven Fabrics, Tufted Textiles, Lace	0.187	---	0.155	0.126	0.259
59	Impregnated, Coated, Covered, Or Laminated Textile	0.863	---	0.238	0.278	0.523
60	Knitted Or Crocheted Fabrics	0.521	0.539	0.880	0.424	0.403
61	Articles Of Apparel & Clothing Accessories-Knitted	0.071	0.380	0.103	0.201	0.321
62	Articles Of Apparel & Clothing Accessories-Not Kni	0.025	0.387	0.098	0.155	0.304
63	Made-Up Textile Articles Nesoi, Needlecraft Sets,	0.478	0.037	0.097	0.183	0.825

(Contd.)

(Contd. Table)

HS-2	Description	Bangladesh	Myanmar	Nepal	Sri Lanka	Thailand
64	Footwear, Gaiters, & The Like	0.282	0.829	0.600	0.212	0.377
65	Headgear & Other Parts	0.967	0.986	0.948	0.466	0.657
66	Umbrellas, Sun Umbrellas, Walking-Sticks, Whips, R	0.504	---	0.937	0.416	0.486
67	Prepared Feathers, Human Hair & Articles Thereof,	1.000	1.000	---	0.166	0.785
68	Articles Of Stone, Plaster, Cement, Asbestos, Mica	0.153	0.997	1.000	0.299	0.020
69	Ceramic Products	0.729	0.991	0.564	0.845	0.397
70	Glass & Glassware	0.487	---	0.292	0.793	0.370
71	Pearls, Stones, Prec. Metals, Imitation Jewelry, C	1.000	0.038	0.007	0.148	0.680
72	Iron & Steel	0.100	0.021	0.378	0.334	0.155
73	Rticles Of Iron Or Steel	0.316	---	0.301	0.308	0.327
74	Copper & Articles Thereof	0.967	1.000	0.060	0.173	0.882
75	Nickel & Articles Thereof	0.171	---	---	1.000	0.154

(Contd. Table)

(Contd.Table)

HS-2	Description	Bangladesh	Myanmar	Nepal	Sri Lanka	Thailand
76	Aluminum & Articles Thereof	0.937	1.000	0.466	0.606	0.596
78	Lead & Articles Thereof	1.000	1.000	0.792	0.763	0.619
79	Zinc & Articles Thereof	0.670	1.000	0.109	0.400	0.944
80	Tin & Articles Thereof	1.000	---	0.313	0.054	0.129
81	Base Metals Nesoi, Cermets, Articles Etc.	0.990	---	---	0.725	0.176
82	Tools, Spoons & Forks Of Base Metal	0.566	---	0.605	0.536	0.253
83	Miscellaneous Articles Of Base Metal	0.145	---	0.073	0.096	0.260
84	Nuclear Reactors, Boilers, Machinery & Mechanical	0.483	0.093	0.270	0.559	0.748
85	Electrical Machinery & Equip. & Parts, Telecommuni	0.249	0.670	0.221	0.183	0.213
86	Railway Or Tramway Locomotives, Rolling Stock, Tra	0.338	---	---	0.670	0.842
87	Vehicles Other Than Railway Or Tramway Rolling Sto	0.582	1.000	0.150	0.394	0.712
88	Aircraft, Spacecraft, & Parts Thereof	0.816	1.000	1.000	1.000	0.989
89	Ships, Boats, & Floating Structures	0.248	0.256	---	0.057	0.178

(Contd)

(Contd. Table)

HS-2	*Description*	*Bangladesh*	*Myanmar*	*Nepal*	*Sri Lanka*	*Thailand*
90	Optical, Photographic, Cinematographic, Measuring,	0.456	0.224	0.312	0.430	0.221
91	Clocks & Watches & Parts Thereof	0.710	---	0.091	0.767	0.361
92	Musical Instruments, Parts & Accessories	1.000	1.000	1.000	0.370	0.506
93	Arms & Ammunition, Parts & Accessories	0.581	---	0.975	1.000	0.163
94	Furniture, Bedding, Cushions, Lamps & Lighting Fit	0.082	0.847	0.379	0.175	0.152
95	Toys, Games & Sports Equip, Parts & Acces.	0.628	---	0.545	0.330	0.203
96	Miscellaneous Manufactured Articles	0.102	0.969	0.445	0.105	0.378
97	Works Of Art. Collectors' Pieces, Antiques	1.000	0.303	---	---	0.792
99	Business Services, Health, Financial/Insur. Legal/	1.000	1.000	1.000	1.000	1.000

Note: Bhutan – not available; latest year data availability for Nepal is 2000 and Sri Lanka is 2002.

Source: Estimated from *PC-TAS Database* (2005).

Annex Table A.3.2: Complementarity Index between India Importing and other BIMSTEC Member Country Exporting 2003

HS-2	Description	Bhutan	Bangladesh	Myanmar	Nepal	Sri Lanka	Thialand
	All Commodities:	---	0.142	0.499	0.694	0.105	0.157
01	Live Animals	---	0.878	0.871	---		0.364
03	Fish & Crustaceans	---	0.715	0.976	---	0.704	0.555
04	Dairy, Eggs, Honey, & Ed. Products	---	0.641	0.435	0.028	0.844	0.130
05	Products Of Animal Origin	---	0.776	0.492	---	0.998	0.147
06	Live Trees & Other Plants	---	0.922	---	---	0.894	0.222
07	Edible Vegetables	0.146	0.611	0.057	0.260	0.014	0.136
08	Ed. Fruits & Nuts, Peel Of Citrus/Melons	0.099	0.313	0.906	---	0.018	0.005
09	Coffee, Tea, Mate & Spices	0.832	0.297	0.407	0.792	0.516	0.450
10	Cereals		0.195	0.110	---	1.000	0.128
11	Milling Industry Products	1.000	0.760	0.723	---	0.478	0.194
12	Oil Seeds/Misc. Grains/Med. Plants/Straw	---	0.245	0.330	0.908	0.081	0.808
13	Lac, Gums, Resins, Etc.	---	0.930	0.622	1.000	1.000	0.420
14	Vegetable Plaiting Materials	---	---	---	---	0.795	0.563
15	Animal Or Vegetable Fats, Oils & Waxes	---	0.800	0.421	---	0.127	0.706

(Contd)

(Contd. Table)

HS-2	Description	Bhutan	Bangladesh	Myanmar	Nepal	Sri Lanka	Thialand
16	Ed. Prep. Of Meat, Fish, Crustaceans, Etc	---	---	0.441	---	0.943	0.273
17	Sugars & Sugar Confectionery	---	0.879	0.414	1.000	0.362	0.562
18	Cocoa & Cocoa Preparations	---	0.671	0.085	---	0.895	0.399
19	Preps. Of Cereals, Flour, Starch Or Milk		0.206	0.243	0.311	0.190	0.354
20	Preps Of Vegs, Fruits, Nuts, Etc.	0.999	0.390	0.799	---	0.348	0.300
21	Misc. Edible Preparations		0.834	0.928	1.000	0.321	0.908
22	Beverages, Spirits & Vinegar	0.265	0.804	0.662	1.000	0.345	0.356
23	Residues From Food Industries, Animal Feed	1.000	0.393	0.613	0.711	0.045	0.207
24	Tobacco & Manuf. Tobacco Substitutes		0.294	0.786	---	0.075	0.329
25	Salt, Sulphur, Earth & Stone, Lime & Cement	0.028	0.026	0.041	0.764	0.818	0.013
26	Ores Slag & Ash	---	0.153	---	---	0.459	0.104
27	Mineral Fuels, Oils, Waxes & Bituminous Sub	1.000	0.176	0.965	---	0.085	0.602

(Contd)

(Contd. Table)

HS-2	*Description*	*Bhutan*	*Bangladesh*	*Myanmar*	*Nepal*	*Sri Lanka*	*Thialand*
28	Inorganic Chem, Org/Inorg Compounds Of Precious Me	1.000	0.162	0.324	---	0.748	0.796
29	Organic Chemicals	---	0.343	0.028	1.000	0.386	0.283
30	Pharmaceutical Products	---	0.914	0.831	0.961	0.719	0.795
31	Fertilizers	---	0.976	0.154		1.000	0.156
32	Tanning Or Dyeing Extracts, Dyes, Pigments, Paints	---	0.308	0.557	1.000	0.310	0.378
33	Oils & Resinoids, Perfumery, Cosmetic Or Toilet Pr	---	0.688	0.742	0.950	0.138	0.446
34	Soaps, Waxes, Scouring Products, Candles, Modeling	---	0.694	0.289	0.904	0.093	0.534
35	Albuminoidal Sub, Starches, Glues, Enzymes	---	0.869	0.903	---	0.985	0.308
36	Explosives, Matches, Pyrotechnic Products	---	---	0.830	---	---	0.086
37	Photographic Or Cinematographic Goods	---	0.643	0.682	0.945	---	0.211
38	Miscellaneous Chemical Products	---	0.618	0.744	1.000	0.064	0.689

(Contd)

(Contd. Table)

HS-2	*Description*	*Bhutan*	*Bangladesh*	*Myanmar*	*Nepal*	*Sri Lanka*	*Thialand*
39	Plastics & Articles Thereof	0.639	0.597	0.519	0.548	0.273	0.729
40	Rubbers & Articles Thereof	---	0.133	0.100	1.000	0.207	0.268
41	Raw Hides & Skins & Leather	---	0.738	0.288	0.139	0.784	0.651
42	Articles Of Leather, Saddlery & Harness, Travel Go	---	0.461	0.909	0.148	0.498	0.837
43	Furskins & Artificial Fur, Manufactures	---	1.000	0.988	---	---	0.472
44	Wood & Articles Of Wood, Wood Charcoal	0.089	0.988	0.394	0.952	0.430	0.020
45	Cork & Articles Of Cork	---	0.821	---	---	---	1.000
46	Manu. Of Straw, Esparto, Or Other Plaiting Materi	---	1.000	0.461		0.991	0.531
47	Pulp Of Wood, Waste & Scrap Of Paper	---	0.133	0.771	0.840	0.533	0.297
48	Paper & Paperboard, Articles Of Paper Pulp	---	0.503	0.314	0.301	0.610	0.171
49	Printed Books, Newspapers, Pictures, Manuscripts,	---	0.648	0.518	---	0.568	0.200
50	Silk, Inc. Yarns & Woven Fabrics Thereof	---	0.576	1.000	1.000	1.000	0.254

(Contd)

(Contd. Table)

HS-2	*Description*	*Bhutan*	*Bangladesh*	*Myanmar*	*Nepal*	*Sri Lanka*	*Thialand*
51	Wool & Fine Or Coarse Animal Hair, Inc. Yarns & Wo	---	0.176	0.320	1.000	0.510	0.437
52	Cotton, Inc. Yarns & Woven Fabrics Thereof	---	0.946	0.048		0.013	0.048
53	Veg. Textile Fibers Nesoi, Yarns & Woven Etc.	---	0.278	0.656	1.000	0.022	0.302
54	Man-Made Filaments, Inc. Yarns & Woven Etc.	---	0.446	0.306	1.000	0.312	0.632
55	Man-Made Staple Fibers, Inc. Yarns Etc.	---	0.290	0.405		0.273	0.490
56	Wadding, Felt & Nonwovens, Special Yarns, Twine, C	---	0.479	0.250	1.000	0.492	0.290
57	Carpets & Other Textile Floor Coverings	---	0.958	0.643	0.135	0.659	0.687
58	Special Woven Fabrics, Tufted Textiles, Lace	---	0.739	0.821	---	0.315	0.161
59	Impregnated, Coated, Covered, Or Laminated Textile	---	0.504	0.419	---	0.163	0.969
60	Knitted Or Crocheted Fabrics	---	0.371	0.441	---	0.338	0.645

(Contd)

(Contd. Table)

HS-2	Description	Bhutan	Bangladesh	Myanmar	Nepal	Sri Lanka	Thialand
61	Articles Of Apparel & Clothing Accessories-Knitted	1.000	0.200	0.566	0.174	0.729	0.559
62	Articles Of Apparel & Clothing Accessories-Not Kni	---	0.354	0.508	0.828	0.467	0.405
63	Made-Up Textile Articles Nesoi, Needlecraft Sets,	1.000	0.702	0.421	0.769	0.014	0.079
64	Footwear, Gaiters, & The Like	---	0.540	0.451	1.000	0.103	0.223
65	Headgear & Other Parts	---	0.999	0.608	0.952	0.364	0.945
66	Umbrellas, Sun Umbrellas, Walking-Sticks, Whips, R	---	0.985	0.777	---	---	0.172
67	Prepared Feathers, Human Hair & Articles Thereof,	---	1.000	---	---	1.000	0.490
68	Articles Of Stone, Plaster, Cement, Asbestos, Mica	---	0.530	0.189	---	0.979	0.308
69	Ceramic Products	---	0.483	0.536	---	0.152	0.289
70	Glass & Glassware	1.000	0.459	0.518	---	0.603	0.677
71	Pearls, Stones, Prec. Metals, Imitation Jewelry, C	---	1.000	1.000	1.000	0.280	0.325

(Contd)

(Contd. Table)

HS-2	Description	Bhutan	Bangladesh	Myanmar	Nepal	Sri Lanka	Thialand
72	Iron & Steel	---	0.047	0.140	---	0.180	0.176
73	Rticles Of Iron Or Steel	---	0.352	0.234	1.000	0.162	0.797
74	Copper & Articles Thereof	---	0.550	0.496	1.000	0.218	0.817
75	Nickel & Articles Thereof	---	0.973	1.000	---	---	0.016
76	Aluminum & Articles Thereof	---	0.652	0.285	---	0.240	0.143
78	Lead & Articles Thereof	---	0.902	0.555	---	0.386	0.926
79	Zinc & Articles Thereof	---	0.990	0.409	---	1.000	0.441
80	Tin & Articles Thereof	---	1.000	1.000	---	0.507	0.994
81	Base Metals Nesoi, Cermets, Articles Etc.	---	0.571	0.935	---	---	0.026
82	Tools, Spoons & Forks Of Base Metal	---	0.260	0.360	---	1.000	0.285
83	Miscellaneous Articles Of Base Metal	---	0.464	0.552	1.000	0.117	0.388
84	Nuclear Reactors, Boilers, Machinery & Mechanical	---	0.554	0.273	0.585	0.297	0.846
85	Electrical Machinery & Equip. & Parts, Telecommuni	---	0.902	0.153	1.000	0.140	0.208
86	Railway Or Tramway Locomotives, Rolling Stock, Tra	---	0.193	0.297	---	---	0.431

(Contd)

(Contd. Table)

HS-2	*Description*	*Bhutan*	*Bangladesh*	*Myanmar*	*Nepal*	*Sri Lanka*	*Thialand*
87	Vehicles Other Than Railway Or Tramway Rolling Sto	---	0.055	0.099	---	0.059	0.331
88	Aircraft, Spacecraft, & Parts Thereof	---	0.730	0.997	1.000	0.999	0.113
89	Ships, Boats, & Floating Structures	---	0.144	0.914	---	0.741	0.483
90	Optical, Photographic, Cinematographic, Measuring,	---	0.641	0.684	---	0.603	0.314
91	Clocks & Watches & Parts Thereof	---	0.905	0.823		1.000	0.428
92	Musical Instruments, Parts & Accessories	---	1.000	0.714	1.000	0.923	0.211
93	Arms & Ammunition, Parts & Accessories	---	0.373	---	---	---	0.997
94	Furniture, Bedding, Cushions, Lamps & Lighting Fit	---	0.224	0.562	1.000	0.567	0.452
95	Toys, Games & Sports Equip, Parts & Acces.	---	0.631	0.601	---	0.260	0.497
96	Miscellaneous Manufactured Articles	---	0.674	0.529	0.232	0.046	0.243
97	Works Of Art. Collectors' Pieces, Antiques	---	1.000	1.000	0.570	---	0.733
99	Business Services, Health, Financial/Insur. Legal/		1.000	1.000	1.000	1.000	1.000

Note: latest year data availability for Nepal is 2000 and Sri Lanka is 2002.

Source: Estimated from *PC-TAS Database* (2005).

Sec.IV. Technical Appendixes:

(A) Export – Import Complementarities

ΣXik*Mjk / (Xik2*Mjk2) and

Import –Export Complementaries :

ΣXjk*Mik / (Xjk2*Mik2)

Where X is Exports and M is Imports, superscripts *J*, *i*, and *k* are exporting country, importing country and commodity class respectively.

(B) Intra-Industry Trade Indices

Bilateral IIT in commodity ***k*** of country ***i*** with country ***j*** at disaggregate level:

IIT*ijk* = [(X*ijk*+M*ijk*)- |X*ijk*-M*ijk*| / (X*ijk*+M*ijk*)] *100

Where **IIT*iwk*** is the share of global IIT in the *i*th county in product ***k***; **IIT*ijk*** is the share of IIT in the *j*th country in product ***k*** ; **X*ijk*** and **M*ijk*** are respectively exports to and import from country ***j*** in industry ***k***. The measure should by definition, vary between 0 and 100 when expressed as an index. When exports exactly equal imports of an industry, IIT = 100; and where there are exports but no imports or vice-versa, ***IITiwk*** and **IITijk** = 0.

Note: For analytical purposes we may characterize good, moderate or poor complementarity when the cosine values are> 0.5, between 0.25- 0.50 and < 0.25 respectively. Further, we may characterize bilateral complementarity as mutual or partial depending on whether both or any one of the complementatities (export-import/ import/export) are favorable. The value tends to be biased upwards when number of matched products are fewer in number. In the limiting case of only one matched product the value becomes 1.

4

India's New Regionalism in Asia: Look East and BIMSTEC Interface

Tridib Chakraborti

Sec. I. Introduction

The years between 1989–91 should be regarded as a watershed period in the history of international relations. The reunification of Germany, the collapse of the Communist parties in Eastern Europe and the Soviet Union and the eventual disintegration of the latter and the impact of the Gulf War on the functioning of the United Nations Security Councils etc. indicated the redundancy of the concept of a multi–power world and the emergence of a new global political and economic scenario, characterized by positional shifts by and among all the actors. The withering away of the ideological struggle between capitalism and communism paved the way for globalization, and the world previously polarized by an ideological struggle rapidly fragmented into various regional and sub–regional trading blocs.

Sec. II. Contextualizing BIMSTEC: The Look East Initiative

India, in order to cope and adapt itself to this new international political and economic environment, on July 4, 1991, announced its New Economic Policy, under the leadership of Prime Minister P.V. Narasimha Rao, which was guided more by economic imperative and judiciousness and less by political rhetoric. In other words, this new policy was initiated to integrate the Indian economy into the global market economy and avail of the facilities being offered by the International Monetary Fund (IMF), as also by other international agencies and the industrialized countries. This paradigm shift in India's overall economic reforms and market liberalization policy led to a shift in New Delhi's overall foreign policy outlook. The structural similarities between the economies of the ASEAN countries and India, and partial withdrawal of the mixed economy system by New Delhi, naturally attracted many countries of Southeast Asia to develop better economic linkages with her. The concrete result of this was that the ASEAN countries since then considered India to be a favourable economic partner and took multifarious initiatives to promote trade link with New Delhi. The ASEAN countries, in the post–cold war globalized years, realized the growing importance of the role of economic diplomacy in relations between nations and were also drawn by the seriousness of New Delhi in her liberalization policy. This new economic dynamics and re–orientation of foreign policy prompted India to become a 'sectoral dialogue' partner of ASEAN in January 1992 on trade, investment, tourism and science and technology. At this Fifth ASEAN Summit in Bangkok in December 1995, the ASEAN leaders decided to elevate India's status from 'sectoral dialogue' to 'full dialogue' partner. In the following year at Jakarta, New Delhi took part in ASEAN's Annual Ministerial Meeting (AMM) and Post–Ministerial Conference (PMC) as a 'full dialogue' partner for the first time. In 1996, New Delhi also participated in the ASEAN Regional Forum (ARF) in Jakarta, and this helped to raise the profile of the security forum. Realizing its potential to contribute to regional economic development, New Delhi's status was further uplifted when India was made a Summit partner of ASEAN, called ASEAN + 1 in 2002. So far, India has participated four India–ASEAN Summit meetings, the first in 2002 at Phnom Penh, second in 2003 at Bali, third in 2004 at Vientiane and the fourth in 2005 at Kuala Lumpur.

However, the major achievement of India within the orbit of its 'Look East' policy has been its participation at the First East Asian Summit, held in December 2005, at Kuala Lumpur, Malaysia. This is no doubt, an unprecedented event in the history of Indian foreign policy, which in the words of Manmohan Singh, the Indian Prime Minister, was a 'historic meeting'. This Indian presence and participation in the First East Asian Summit was indeed a good beginning to its ultimate integration with the East Asian region and can be seen as a further stepping–stone in fulfilling its potential to play a major role in global affairs in the 21st Century. Thus, by uplifting India's position within the orbit of ASEAN and Farther East, the countries of Southeast Asian Nations recommenced and restored the ancient propinquity and re–

established a kinship that both civilizations had experienced in the past. Further, India in the context of new global order, tacitly preferred to strengthen its position in the Southeast Asian region and East Asia, initiated larger political partnerships, physical connectivity through road and rail links, free trade arrangements and other forms of cooperations with these countries. And for this, New Delhi has initiated several transnational and sub–regional fora between parts of India (including its Northeast) and Southeast Asian countries to promote cooperation between the economically dynamic regions. In 1997, India and Thailand proposed a new organization, known as BIST–EC (Bangladesh, India, Sri Lanka, Thailand – Economic Cooperation) – whose primary goal was to act as a vehicle for promoting trade and tourism in the Bay of Bengal region. The members of this trans–regional grouping have agreed to cooperate on trade and investment, technology, energy, transportation and communication, tourism and fisheries. In November 2000, India floated the Mekong–Ganga Cooperation (MGC) proposal with five of its eastern neighbours, namely – Cambodia, Laos, Vietnam, Myanmar and Thailand. Through this initiative, the six countries agreed to increase cooperation in tourism, culture and education, and further accelerated the development of bilateral relations between India and the less developed countries of Southeast Asia. The purpose of this paper is to analyse the evolution of the emergence of BIMSTEC as a sub–regional organization and trace its impact on India's Look East policy.

2.1. India's Look East Policy Unmasked

India's post–cold war New Regionalism doctrine, as part of its foreign policy agenda, towards the countries of Southeast Asia was officially proclaimed by Indian Prime Minister P.V. Narasimha Rao through his 'Singapore Lecture' in September 1994. Following this speech, the Government of India, for the first time officially endorsed the term 'Look East' as a major agenda of its overall foreign policy structure. The Ministry of External Affairs (MEA), for the first time, in its Annual Report of 1995–96, have used the term 'Look East' (Government of India 1996) red this policy as part of its major foreign policy agenda.

On September 4, 2003, Yashwant Sinha, the External Affairs Minister of India, in a speech delivered at the Plenary Session of the Second India–ASEAN Business Summit, at New Delhi said: "India's

'Look East' policy has now entered its Phase–II. Phase I was focused primarily on the ASEAN countries and on trade and investment linkages. Phase–II is characterised by an expanded definition of 'East' extending from Australia to China and East Asia with ASEAN as its core. Phase–II marks a shift in focus from exclusively economic issues to economic and security issues including joint efforts to protect sea-lanes, coordination on counter–terrorism etc. On the economic side, Phase II is also characterized by arrangements for FTAs and establishing of institutional economic linkages between the countries of the region and India."(www.meaindia.nic.in).

Besides this, one of the important reasons behind the announcement of New Delhi's 'Look East' Phase–II policy has been the physical connectivity and transportation links with Southeast Asian countries. In the context of rapidly changing global order, establishment of air and land links to East and Southeast Asia has emerged as an essential ingredient to Phase II of the policy. Hence, as part of its road diplomacy, New Delhi is at present building up its transport corridors with the region. These include the India–Myanmar–Thailand trilateral highway and the Delhi–Hanoi railway line, as part of the Ganga–Mekong project.

Furthermore, the 'Look East' Phase II policy of India has opened the window for the first time since 1997, to break out of the political confines of the South Asian subcontinent that have poorly limited India's grand strategic options. The 'Look East' diplomacy, for the first time, has allowed India to break the artificial political barriers between the South and Southeast Asia. The establishment of the Bay of Bengal Initiative for Multi–Sectoral Technical and Economic Cooperation (BIMSTEC) in its First Summit held in July 2004, at Thailand, included five nations of South Asia (i.e. Bangladesh, Sri Lanka, India, Nepal and Bhutan) together with two countries of Southeast Asia (i.e. Myanmar and Thailand), to strengthen regional cooperation among countries on the rim of or those seeking access to the Bay of Bengal. India's interests in fostering the establishing of BIMSTEC has opened up the possibilities of enhancing its trade linkages with Myanmar and Thailand as well as the opportunity to counter China's strategic designs within the region. This sub–regional organization might also act as a bridge of mutual understanding and cooperation between South and South Asia (The Hindu 2004), and could generate mobility in India's 'Look East' Phase II policy.

2.2. BIMSTEC: The Bridge Between South and Southeast Asia

The 'Look East' policy amounts to a paradigm shift in India's geo–strategic perceptions too. In terms of geo–politics, the contiguous sea spaces of the Bay of Bengal – South China Sea could be regarded as hubs of geo–economic and geo–strategic advantages and opportunities for India. It also aimed at political partnerships, physical connectivity through road and rail links, and free trade arrangements. Keeping this outlook in mind, in 1994, the idea of setting up a sub–regional cooperation bloc in the Bay of Bengal basin was first initiated in Bangkok, by India, Bangladesh, Sri Lanka and Thailand. After a number of deliberations of Inter–Ministerial consultation with the active support of Asian Development Bank (ADB) and ESCAP, on June 6, 1997, a regional economic forum was formed comprising of four countries namely, Bangladesh, India, Sri Lanka and Thailand. These four countries were selected because of their proximity and direct access to the Bay of Bengal. The main objective of this regional grouping, BIST-EC was to provide trade and technological cooperation among its members in the areas of trade and investment, tourism, transport and communication, technology, energy, fisheries, human resource development, agriculture and natural resources. This sub–regional grouping was formed with the intention of promoting sectoral cooperation in the above-mentioned areas and also to strengthen cooperation in trade and investment. It did not immediately form a Preferential Trading Agreement (PTA), but encouraged sectoral cooperation and an economic forum, which made it possible for business groups to interact with government officials and academics.

In 1998, Myanmar was included as a member and the name BISTEC was changed to BIMSTEC. Nepal was given observer status in 1999. The major intention to extend BIMSTEC to a PTA was announced in 2000. This initiative emerged from the three most developed members of the five countries. The two least developed members, Bangladesh and Myanmar, however expressed reservations and declared their wish to study the matter further. The First Ministerial Meeting was held in Thailand in 1997. By the time the Second Ministerial Meeting of BIMSTEC took place in Bangladesh in 1998, it was clear that Thailand had lost its initial momentum. However, the East Asian financial crisis in 1997, had taken a heavy toll on Thailand and this may perhaps explain the designation of her initial encouragement. Further, the projects that were allocated to some member countries had not made sufficient progress, since the private sector in all these countries were not enthusiastic about gains occurring from BIMSTEC. Besides this, the inclusion of Myanmar within ASEAN orbit in 1997, and the construction of Tamu–Kalemyo road, which was flagged off on October 29, 1997 for future establishment of transportation network, brought India more nearer towards its eastern neighbour, Myanmar. This resulted in that the then BIMSTEC members initiated 'Tourism' as a priority area and declared 2001 as the "Visit BIMSTEC Year". The probable construction of a trans–regional highway to facilitate tourism was also pondered about. In 2003, Nepal and Bhutan have been granted full membership of BIMSTEC. On July 31, 2004, the first BIMSTEC Summit took place in Thailand and the organization's name has been renamed as the Bay of Bengal Initiative for Multi–Sectoral Technical and Economic Cooperation (BIMSTEC) to generate greater further momentum in launching of the process of deeper integration in the region. BIMSTEC is conceived as a 'bridging link between two major regional groupings in the Asian region i.e. ASEAN and SAARC, and it has been an important element of India's 'Look East' strategy that has added a new dimension of New Delhi's economic cooperation with the Southeast Asian countries.

2.3. Evolution of BIMSTEC

The formation of BIMSTEC provides a matchless union of South Asia and Southeast Asia which might bring together more than 1.3 billion people i.e. nearly 21 percent of the world population, a combined GDP of US$ 750 billion, and a considerable amount of complementary, given geographical contiguity, differing levels of development and resource endowments (www/mofa/gov.bd/bimstec). Hence, its geographical contiguity could also facilitate the exploitation of potential of efficiency in seeking restructuring of industry, provided conditions for such restructuring are created. Although the intra–regional trade turnover is small, it is growing increasing faster than the overall trade of member countries. The full potential of intra–regional trade, however, although presently remains unrealized because of tariff and non–tariff barriers, weak communication links and lack of information regarding the supply capabilities and other important barriers (RIS 2004). One of the important agenda of the BIMSTEC sub–regional organization has been the regional cooperation through which its member countries might strengthen their external competitiveness. This cooperation might take the form of joint marketing and coordination in third country trading, regional cooperation for dealing with non-tariff barriers in developed world, coordination for WTO negotiations, technical assistance for compliance with WTO commitments and international standards (RIS 2004).

Besides this outlook, the aim and objectives of BIMSTEC, as pointed out by the 1997 Bangkok Declaration, are to create an enabling environment for rapid economic development through identification and implementation of specific cooperation projects in the sectors of trade, investment and industry, technology, human resource development, tourism, energy, and infrastructure and transportation. *Secondly,* to accelerate the economic growth and social progress in the sub–region through joint endeavors in a spirit of equality and partnership. *Thirdly,* to promote active collaboration and mutual assistance on matters of common interest in the economic, social, technical and scientific fields. *Fourthly* to provide assistance to each other in the form of training and research facilities in the educational, professional and technical spheres. *Fifthly*, to cooperate more effectively in joint efforts that are supportive of and complementary to national development plans of Member States which result in tangible benefits to the people in raising their living standards, including through generating employment and improving transportation and communication infrastructure. *Sixthly* to maintain close and beneficial cooperation with existing international and regional organization with similar aims and purposes. *Finally*, to cooperate in projects that can be dealt with most productively on a sub–regional basis among the BIST–EC countries and that make best use of available synergies (www.mofa.gov.bd/ bimstec).

Another objective of BIMSTEC was to create economic and social prosperity based on equality in order to enhance of mutual benefits in economic, social and technological aspects. It also involve intra–regional assistance in training, research and development as well as beneficial cooperation in industry, agriculture, expansion of trade and investment, improvement in communication and transport, improving living standards and cooperation with other international organizations.

BIMSTEC had a cooperative work program in six key sectors, namely trade and investment, technology, energy, tourism, transport and fisheries. Activities under each sector were to be coordinated and monitored by a BIMSTEC country nominated as lead country for the sector. Held in Bangkok on August 7, 1988, the first BIMSTEC economic and trade ministers' meeting termed as the 'Retreat', decided that

BIMST–EC would initially start cooperation process in six areas. It was agreed that each country would play a prominent role in planning and implementing programmes in each of the areas for a period of nearly three years. The sectors and prominent countries at the inception were:

Trade and Investment	–	Bangladesh
Technology	–	India
Transportation and Communication	–	Thailand
Energy	–	Myanmar
Tourism and Fisheries	–	Sri Lanka

Since some of the sectors are very large, for greater efficiency in achieving the aims and objectives of BIMST–EC, the six sectors have been further divided into sub–sectors with each sub–sector having a chair country responsible for co–coordinating activities of that sub–sector, reporting to the lead country. Further, recognizing that sub–regional cooperation can progress only through inter–governmental cooperation and co–ordination, and that the private sector is an engine of growth for enhancing interaction between government bodies and the private sector representatives of the five BIMST–EC countries, the BIMST–EC Economic Forum was conceptualized at a meeting in Dhaka in 1999. The BIMST–EC Economic Forum is a representative group of both the public and private sectors, formed to discuss way for achieving the objectives of BIMST–EC and making recommendations for the ministerial meetings each year. The Bangkok meeting of 1998, also imported a new dimension to economic cooperation between the member states. It was agreed that BIMST–EC should aim and strive to develop into a Free Trade Arrangement (FTA), and should focus on activities that facilitate trade, increase investment and promote technical cooperation among member countries. It was further reiterated that BIMST–EC activities should be designed to form a bridge between SAARC and ASEAN.

In its evolution from BIST–EC to BIMST–EC, this sub–regional organization have established various institutional mechanisms for its normal functioning and among them – Annual Ministerial Meeting, Senior Official Committee, Specialized Task Forces for necessary coordination, Senior Trade and Economic Officials Meeting, Trade Ministers Meeting, BIMST–EC Working Group, BIMST–EC Economic Forum and Business Forum etc. These various bodies have conducted important meetings from time to time and have taken important decisions as and when necessary in order to establish this sub–regional organization on a strong foothold. While established in June 1997, BIMST-EC is presently at the evolutionary stage to indicate spectacular results, but potentials for future cooperation are possible for the benefit of all its partners.

One of the important problems that the BIMST–EC sub–regional organization faced among its members are the uneven level of development among its members. The initial trade (pre–FTA) between member countries of BIMST–EC was very nominal. The intra–regional trade of BIMST–EC countries during 1999 was nearly 3 percent of their global imports and 2.9 percent of their total exports. The imports of Bangladesh and Sri Lanka were sole dependent on other BIMST–EC members to the extent of more than 13 percent in 1999. The corresponding import share of other countries of BIMST–EC (e.g. India, Myanmar and Thailand) is low in the range of 1.16 to 2.67 per cent.

Table - 1
Country–wise Shares in Intra–BIMSTEC Trade
(percentage of GDP)

(Value in US $ million)

Year	Exports		Imports		Total Trade	
Countries	1995	2001	1995	2001	1995	2001
Bangladesh	2.05	1.54	34.62	23.48	36.67	25.02
Myanmar	6.03	19.14	0.79	7.77	6.82	26.91
Nepal	0.96	3.67	8.58	10.36	9.54	14.03
India	62.39	50.71	14.78	20.11	77.17	70.82
Sri Lanka	2.02	2.20	18.70	12.49	20.72	14.69
Thailand	26.54	22.74	22.58	25.79	49.07	48.53

Source: IMF (2002), *Direction of Trade Statistics Yearbook.*

The export basket of Myanmar was totally dependent on other BIMST–EC countries to the extent of around 18 per cent in 1999, while that for Nepal was 21 percent. Similarly, India's export basket was dependent on other BIMST–EC countries to the extent of around 5 per cent of its total exports. Other members (i.e. Sri Lanka, Thailand and Bangladesh) export share to BIMST–EC was meagre to the extent of around 2.8, 1.7 and 1.2 per cent respectively. So far as total intra–regional export of India is concerned, she remains the major exporter within this sub–regional organization. Out of total amount of US $ 3.24 billion of intra–BIMST–EC trade, India exported US $ 2.02 billion in 1999. At the same time, intra–regional import was not concentrated to one country (Strategic Digest 2004).

Further more, among the BIMST–EC members during the period from 1995 to 2001, India and Thailand remained at the top so far as the shares of Intra–BIMST–EC trade are concerned (Table -1). Presently, this figure is changing very rapidly, and to increase this ratio, the BIMST–EC members have taken a number of important initiatives and, among them, improved transport network and the groundwork for a FTA are most important.

2.4. The First BIMSTEC Summit

India has actively supported the creation of bilateral and sub–regional groupings. These bilateral and sub–regional cooperation frameworks might complement its larger goal of enhancing ASEAN–India ties. On July 31, 2004, the first BIMSTEC Summit was held at Thailand. In this meeting, BIMSTEC has acquired its new incarnation – a Bay of Bengal Community. BIMSTEC earlier was known as SAARC minus Pakistan and Maldives plus Thailand and Myanmar. In its new incarnation, it is known as the Bay of Bengal Initiative for Multi–Sectoral Technical and Economic Cooperation. The Summit Declaration at Bangkok placed special emphasis on sectors such as trade and investment, transport and communications, tourism, energy, human resources development, agriculture, fisheries, science and technology and people to people contact. It was also agreed to expand the cooperation into areas of public health, education, rural community development, small and medium scale enterprises, construction, environment, information and communications technology, biotechnology, weather and climate research, and natural disaster mitigation and management. This Summit also laid importance on the development of transport and communication infrastructure, hydropower and hydrocarbon projects including intra–BIMSTEC inter connectivity of electricity and natural gas grids. Further joint development of BIMSTEC tourism package, introduction of BIMSTEC Travel Card / Visa, coordination of efforts of the member countries in combating the menace of international terrorism and transnational crime, promotion of exchanges of parliamentarians, media persons, students and faculty, sports persons etc. were also agreed in this Summit.

The Indian Prime Minister, Manmohan Singh at the inaugural BIMSTEC meeting at Bangkok, described the BIMSTEC "as a collective and effective forum for giving full expression to the widely rediscover the coherence of the region based on the commonality of many linkages around the Bay of Bengal." He further said in his speech: "Regional integrator is not antithetical to globalization, but can be useful building block. Our collective endeavours can be more than the sum of our individual efforts. BIMSTEC offers us the hope and the opportunity to fulfill this imperative of our times. We consider our participation in BIMSTEC as a key element of our 'Look East Policy' and long standing approach of good neighbours towards all other neighbours – by land and sea." (meaindia.nic.in/sshome.htm)

Besides this, the First Summit of BIMSTEC have accepted certain proposals made by India and they are: (i) India will organize a Round Table and Workshop of Tourism Ministers and Trade and Tourism Industry representatives in 2005. (ii)India will host a Ministerial meeting on Energy Cooperation in 2005. (iii) India will set up a BIMSTEC Center on Weather and Climate in New Delhi. (iv) New Delhi offered 150 additional ITEC scholarship and 30 scholarships for studying traditional systems of medicine in India, etc.

This meeting also endorsed a plant to start free trade negotiations in September 2004. The aim was to achieve regional free trade by 2017. Trade among seven member countries having a combined population of 1.3 billion was at that time more than $ 7 billion a year. The BIMSTEC free trade area, if implemented, would relax tariffs and give less developed countries a grace period during which they could protect their most vital industries (The Tribune, 2004). Thus, the Bangkok Summit of BIMSTEC was a watershed event in the history of pan–Asian regional and economic cooperation; paving the way for a free trade agreement eventually, was not very ambitious, but not insignificant either, and which in the words of Manmohan Singh "a bridge between the ASEAN and SAARC countries." (news.indiamart.com/news–analysis/bimst–ec–summit–a– mi–7074).

Another important achievement of the BIMSTEC was the Agreement on Free Trade Area signed in February 2004. Under this FTA different sectors were identified for economic cooperation. Joint projects in different areas were also identified with concrete steps to implement those projects. The Framework Agreement towards creating a FTA in the BIMSTEC region, signed in February 2004, was not endorsed by Bangladesh because it was not convinced about how it was going to get compensated for the loss of revenue due to the reduction of its custom duties on goods. Later on, Bangladesh expressed its interest in signing the Agreement and has acceded by signing a Protocol to this effect in June 2004. The Framework Agreement to establish BIMSTEC FTA includes provisions, for negotiations on FTA in goods, services and investment. The major highlights of the Framework Agreement are as follows: (i) Trade in goods will be liberalized through progressive elimination of tariffs and non-tariffs barriers. This will be done in two phases. Products will be identified for (a) Fast Track and (b) Normal Track. (ii) For the Fast Track products the non-Least Developed Countries (LDCs) will eliminate tariffs for LDC parties by 30 June 2007; but among themselves by 30 June 2009. The LDC parties will do so for non-LDCs by 30 June 2011; but among themselves by 30 June 2009. iii) For the normal track products the non-LDC will eliminate tariffs for LDCs by 30 June 2010; but among themselves by 30 June 2012. The LDCs will eliminate tariffs for non-LDCs by 2017; but among themselves by 30 June 2015. iv) in case of Trade in goods negotiations on specific issues namely Rules of Origin, Sensitive List and Dispute Settlement mechanism are to be concluded by December 2005. The negotiations on Trade in Services and Investment are to commence in December 2005 and to be concluded by the end of December 2007. The trade liberalization programme in goods is set to commence from July 1, 2006. Agreements for Trade in Services and Investment will begin to enter into effect from January 1, 2008 (www.mofa.gov.bd/bimstec). This agreement also kept social and differential treatment for LDC States Parties in BIMSTEC FTA. Thus, the objective of FTA among the member states has been to increase investments and tourism across their borders and to promote technical cooperation, since most of these countries in the past always looked to the West for trade. However, implementation of FTA among BIMSTEC member is not an easy task. It would take a long time to implement all its modalities, since uneven economic structure clearly exists among its members. One interesting point to be mentioned here in this connection is that recently (in 2006) a study, based on the latest available trade figures collected from the Ministry of Commerce and Industry, found that with the signing FTAs with Sri Lanka (1998) and Thailand (2004), India's imports from these two countries have increased over 300 percent and 125 percent respectively, between 2002-03 and 2004-05. India's exports to Sri

Lanka have gone up by 47 percent and that of Thailand by 19 percent during the same period. The study however pointed out that countries like China, Malaysia, Indonesia, Taiwan and the Philippines used Sri Lanka and Thailand as 'convenient destinations' to dump their products in India under the grab of FTAs. Due to this, Sri Lankan exports to India increased from $ 90.83 million in 2002–03 to $ 364.39 million towards the end of 2004–05. Finally, the study suggests that India should take precautionary measures before signing FTA with countries like Bangladesh, Bhutan and Myanmar so as to maintain surplus trade balance with these countries and its hegemony in the BIMSTEC region (www.bilaterals.org/article.=3732). Thus, inspite of these differences amongst countries in the BIMSTEC sub–region, opportunities for economic cooperation and exchange exist at multiferious levels. Such cooperation can build on the existing strengths of the various economies as well as alleviate many of the constraints and internal problems. Economic cooperation can and needs to be driven by the private sector and facilitated by supportive policy initiatives of the Governments of the sub–region. Long-term measures to establish the foundations for greater economic cooperation are to be match with practical short-term measures to remove bottlenecks and administrative barriers (UN Economic and Social Commission for Asia and Pacific 1997). Furthermore, the dismantling of cold war barriers has allowed BIMSTEC to respond positively to the aspirations of some of the smaller countries of South and Southeast Asia, and gave them larger economic and political space in a world of rapid global integration.

Sec. III. Conclusion

Having analyzed the evolution of BIMSTEC and its economic performance as a sub–regional organization in the context of new global order, certain questions still exist over the utility of this sub–regional organization. Is BIMSTEC an alternative model of SAARC? What is the utility of BIMSTEC in the context of India's Look East Policy? The answers of these questions could well be positive. It is true that regional integration is a building block, not a substitute, to greater integration with the global community. Regional integration agreements are required to be inclusive. An exclusive arrangement could pose a hindrance rather than a boon to global integration. BIMSTEC never offered an alternative model of SAARC. Since SAARC has always been bogged down by intra–regional differences, particularly due to Indo–Pak rivalries, it progress has been too slow to be tangible. It is in the economic field, first through preferential (SAPTA), followed by Free Trade Agreement (SAFTA), that SAARC has demonstrated some degree of tangible collective purpose, through much less in performance. Barring India and Pakistan, the other five member states had been consistent disciples of regional integration, as their destiny and identity remain deeply tied to the success of this regional organization. Amongst the momentous decisions adopted by the SAARC members so far, a large number of initiatives have come largely from the smaller states of South Asia (Rao, P.V 2005). The need to make the regional association a better platform has become far more essential with the advent of globalization. Given this situation, it is imperative for the SAARC members to think regionally rather than locally, in the context of a market driven global economy. Thus, in the context of regional economic integration in the new global order, the emergence of BIMSTEC does not stand in opposition to SAARC. In fact, the Bay of Bengal Community could act as a complement rather than a substitute to SAARC's prosperity and its efforts to promote a free trade area in South Asia by offering a larger space for the SAARC states to engage in trade, commerce and marketing with Southeast and East Asia. The BIMSTEC could also act as a spur to SAARC on economic cooperation (The Hindu 2004).

It is clear that India has taken a holistic view about the emergence of BIMSTEC in the context of new global order, particularly given its new Look East thrust. India, since the fall of former Soviet Union, has pioneered a number of multilateral initiatives for promotion of greater political and economic cooperation mainly with the Southeast and East Asian countries. India views the BIMSTEC as an extension or second phase of its 'Look East' policy. Atal Bihari Vajpayee's deepened the scope and substance of India's 'Look East' policy to cover much of Asia, including the ASEAN, China, Japan, Australia and New Zealand. If the first phase of the 'Look East' policy focused on developing commercial relations and institutional links with Asia, in its second phase India has aimed at fostering political partnerships, working out physical connectivity through road and railway links, and negotiating free trade arrangements. By linking SAARC with the ASEAN region, BIMSTEC has logistically put India closer to Southeast through the Myanmar–Thailand link. In other words, India has gained a natural gateway to the east through the territories of Myanmar and Thailand to reach the heart of the Southeast and East Asia. Thailand, as an important ASEAN component, can help to speed up the pace of trade liberalization and regional economic cooperation within BIMSTEC. It has played an important role before in bringing the Bay of Bengal littorals, India in particular, into common sub–regional fold. Thailand also visualizes the linkage between India– Thailand–Myanmar as part of the broader strategy of cooperation between India and Southeast Asia as a whole, and for that BIMSTEC has appeared as a major vehicle of connectivity between South and Southeast Asia through its initiatives. This would most certainly help India in the integration process with the countries of ASEAN.

Furthermore, it is now amply clear that eastern Asia will remain an important engine of growth in the 21st century and that its varying dynamic of growth will alter the overall balance of power, both within the region and globally. If the next phase of India's outward orientation has to proceed successfully and expeditiously, it is important that India's trade with the APEC economies increases and for that India needs to become a member of this body. To enable this, India must strengthen its 'Look East' policy and here the BIMSTEC could act as a bridge between South and Southeast Asia.

References

1. Government of India, Ministry of External Affairs (1996), *Annual Report: 1995-96*, New Delhi, p.17.
2. For details, see www.meaindia.nic.in/
3. See http://www/mofa/gov.bd/bimstec
4. IDSA (2004), *Strategic Digest,* New Delhi, Vol.34, No.5, May, p.675.
5. Raja Mohan. C (2004), "A Foreign Policy for the East", *The Hindu*, July 24.
6. Rao P.V (2005), "Sub-regional Strategies of Cooperation in ASEAN: The Indian Approach", in K. Raja Reddy (ed), *India and ASEAN: Foreign Policy Dimensions for the 21st Century*, New Delhi: New Century Publications, p.158.
7. Research and Information Systems (2004), *Future Directions of BIMSTEC: Towards A Bay of Bengal Economic Community*, RIS Policy Brief, No.12, February, p.1.
8. *Ibid.*, p.2.
9. For Bangkok Declaration of BIST-EC of 1997, see http://www.mofa.gov.bd/ bimstec
10. See http://meaindia.nic.in/sshome.htm.
11. *The Hindu* (2004), July 30.

12. *The Tribune* (2004), August 1.
13. See http://news.indiamart.com/news-analysis/bimst-ec-summit-a- mi-7074.
14. For details see http://www.mofa.gov.bd/bimstec.
15. See www.bilaterals.org/article.php3?id_article=3732
16. UN Economic and Social Commission for Asia and Pacific (1997), *The BIST-EC Development Programme: Overview and Sectoral Cooperation*, News York: United Nations, p.1.

5

Challenges and Opportunities for BIMSTEC

K.C. Reddy

Sec. I. Introduction

The conflict between regionalism and globalization is now considered irrelevant, as regionalism in gaining not only strong ground but also more importantly emerging as an important vehicle for international trade. Today, every country with significant share of international trade is a member of one regional grouping or the other. Also, the regional groupings themselves are looking for inter-group arrangements to accelerate and sustain trade through cooperation. BIMSTEC has to be contextualized in this changing international scenario. The emerging trend towards regionalism holds tremendous promise for the geographically proximate countries, given the size of the untapped potential and strong complementarities. Also, the inability of SAARC to grow into a significant regional grouping is another additional aspect that makes one to argue a strong case for the Bay of Bengal initiative for regional cooperation.

The Bay of Bengal Initiative for Multi-Sectoral Technical and Economic Cooperation (BIMSTEC), formerly the Bangladesh – India – Myanmar – Sri Lanka – Thailand – Economic Cooperation is a sub regional grouping, combining the geographically contiguous countries of Bangladesh, Bhutan, India, Nepal and Sri Lanka from the SAARC; and Myanmar and Thailand from ASEAN regions. BIMSTEC came into existence in 1997 to exploit the synergies of their capabilities and resource endowments for their development. Subsequently, BIMSTEC established a Free Trade Area in the region, with the objective of promoting harmonious development of economic relations among the members through fair conditions of trade. The emergence of BIMSTEC is especially striking, in the light of the moderate progress of SAPTA/ SAFTA and India's Look East policy as well as its interest in the likely formation of an 'Asian Economic Community'.

The BIMSTEC Group has identified six sectors for cooperation, viz., trade and investment, technology, transport and communication, energy, tourism and fisheries. The formation of BIMSTEC region and its subsequent moves viz., signing of Free Trade Agreement on BIMSTEC in February 2004, expansion of membership to Nepal and Bhutan and its first Summit in July 2004 have given a new impetus to cooperation in the region.

Sec. II. Structure of BIMSTEC

The combined size of BIMSTEC in terms of population in 2004 is 1.378 billion showing an average growth of 1.61 percent during 2000-04, as against a growth rate of 2.1 percent during 1980-90. The combined economic size of the region, (GDP) barring Bhutan and Myanmar is US $938.97 billions in 2004 with an average annual growth rate of 4.6 percent (World Bank 2006). The disparity in per capita incomes is glaring in the region, with Thailand having the highest and Nepal the least. The incidence of poverty is high in the region, with the exception of Thailand and Sri Lanka. Poverty, as measured in terms of $ 1 a day is well above one-third in Nepal, Bangladesh and India during 1990-2003. In terms of the national poverty line, the incidence of poverty is nearly one-half in Bangladesh; well above two-fifths in Nepal and 29 percent in India during the period. However, the positive sign is the steady decline. (UNDP 2005).

The economic indicators of the BIMSTEC region revealed rapid transformation of these economies. The shift from agriculture to services as contributors to GDP is viewed as an emerging strength in terms of productivity and contribution to employment. A heavy dependence on services is visible in the region. However, the exceptions are Thailand and Nepal in which the major contribution to GDP is from the industry and agriculture respectively.

The existence of strong complementarities, a basic rationale for the formation of a regional grouping appears to be quite apparent in the BIMSTEC context. There is enough evidence to show that the members are at different levels of industrial and economic development with different natural resource endowments. Therefore, it is presumed that they possess substantial complementarities. The geographical contiguity, as already indicated, is expected to facilitate the exploitation of potential of efficiency seeking restructuring of industry, provided conditions for such restructuring are created. The scope for enhancing economic cooperation in trade and investment in the region is clearly visible, despite the differences in the social and economic indicators of development among the member countries. The investment priorities in social sectors also differed in these countries, owing to the shift towards their policy regimes. The relevance of the region in enhancing the trade and investment patterns is also basing on the existing socio-economic performance of the individual members.

Sec. III. Regional Trade

Liberal trade policy regimes, together with procedural simplification are excepted to enhance the opportunities for trade and investment in an economic area. Economic reforms in the SAARC region, particularly in India facilitated the trade and investment pattern both in size and quality. The reduction in procedural complexities, though in a lesser degree in India relative to its neighbours improved the country's trade performance. In the past, the efforts of these countries to exploit their potential were not successful due to inadequate demand for the manufactured exports from the industrial markets. The protection and the demand recession in the industrial countries aggravated their problems on the external front. In recent years, these problems, though not mitigated, have lost their intensity due to the improvement in export competitiveness of these economies. In this context, viable economic integration measures are required in these countries to enlarge the size of the markets as well as to meet the complex conditions at the international markets. In the past, a number of initiatives towards intra-regional trade liberalization between individual member countries of BIMSTEC region under bilateral and multilateral trade agreements have been signed and implemented. They include India-Sri Lanka FTA, India-Thailand FTA, ASEAN Free Trade Agreement in the case of Thailand and Myanmar, SAPTA/SAFTA and Bangkok Agreement (in the case of India, Sri Lanka and Bangladesh). India's Framework Agreement on Comprehensive Economic Cooperation with ASEAN in October 2003, and the Mekong-Ganga Cooperation in which India, Thailand and Myanmar are cooperating are all indicators of closer trade interactions in the region

(RIS 2004). The formation of FTA in BIMSTEC is desirable and economically viable, in the light of the moderate progress made in trade liberalization under the above agreements. A fast track trade liberalization in the coming years under the umbrella of BIMSTEC is envisioned by the experts.

An RIS study finds the trade creating potential of BIMSTEC-FTA to be between US $ 43 to $ 59 billion a year. The potential of intra-regional trade remains untapped because of tariff and non-tariff barriers, poor communication and transport links, lack of information about the supply capabilities, among other barriers. Similarly, the intra-regional investment is negligible, despite tremendous potential that exists for market seeking as well as efficiency-seeking investments within the region. Regional economic integration may help in exploiting this hidden potential of intra-regional cooperation for mutual benefit.

The direction of exports of BIMSTEC nations showed a higher orientation towards industrial countries and this has been reduced in some countries like India recently. Despite the inclination of BIMSTEC countries towards the United States and the European Union in general, nearly 50 percent of the export market of India and Thailand in the recent years was directed to the Third World (Asian Development Bank 2003). The Intra-regional trade is rising in the region, despite the variation in the size of the trade among the member nations; the smaller countries recorded the highest and the bigger the lowest. The recent shift in the composition of trade, particularly in exports of the members towards manufactures and the sizeable share of high technology exports in Thailand revealed a marked diversification over the years. Notwithstanding, the advancement in software services, India could not attain a significant share in hi-tech exports. However, the trend appears to be improving in recent years. The current account imbalance in the balance of payments of the BIMSTEC region registered a gradual decline in recent years.

Sec. IV. India's Role

Mutual cooperation in a number of areas in the BIMSTEC region are more or less covered by India's bilateral economic relations with the individual members and this would further foster the rate of economic growth by tapping the regional synergies. The developments in the neighboring country's relations; India's bilateral trade agreements with Nepal and Bhutan; and its FTA with Sri Lanka; a transit traffic agreement between the governments of India, Nepal and Bangladesh;

a closer economic relation with Myanmar, as is seen from the India-Myanmar official meetings on border management; and the recent signing of FTA between India and Thailand are examples of India's positive neighbourhood policy.

Sec. V. Conclusion

The asymmetry both in size and level and patterns of economic development in the BIMSTEC region is unlikely to come in the way of enhancement of regional economic cooperation, as the improved performance of the smaller countries particularly in the recent years provides a favorable macro environment. Further, each member-country exhibits a typical success story in their development experience from which others are expected to emulate. The region's untapped potential, particularly in energy provides vast scope for further cooperation through a careful and economically viable utilization. The existing bilateral and multilateral agreements among BIMSTEC members under the SAARC umbrella are expected to strengthen the economic rationale and reduce the political differences, if any.

Trade liberalization, in particular liberalizing the regional trade is critical to move towards the Millennium Goals. The new found evidence in support of trade working positively as an instrument to reduce inequalities and alleviating poverty provides enough support for Free Trade particularly for the Third World. Otherwise, the existing high tariff barriers among these countries work against their basic development objectives. At the same time, softening and liberalizing of complex and extensive trade formalities need to be done away on an urgent basis, as they deter the progress of exports. The signing of FTA in the BIMSTEC region would assure the benefits to the member countries. Likewise, regional agreement on investment is also imperative to facilitate the trade flows, particularly trade in services. This kind of steps deepens the trade and investment engagements in the region to optimize the benefits.

In summary, it could be said that the BIMSTEC region has a rich potential for economic cooperation, arising from substantial complementarities existing between the economic structures and resource endowments of the member countries. These synergies could be exploited for mutual benefit through regional economic integration. BIMSTEC has made a good beginning with establishing a free Trade Area. However, to realize the potential and exploit the synergies totally, the implementation of FTA needs to be expedited apart from initiating steps to implement efficiency seeking measures to restructure industry. They need to be complemented with trade and investment facilitation measures. Development of transport and communication links is considered critical to exploit trade potential. Further BIMSTEC should set up a timetable to move towards a customs union drawing inspiration from the successful experience of the European Common Market. In other words, BIMSTEC should go beyond an FTA with a well-defined time frame. The hope is that the BIMSTEC story is a different one from that of SAARC and its trading arrangements, SAPTA and SAFTA.

References

1. Asian Development Bank (2003), *Asian Development Outlook*, New York: Oxford University Press, Table. A.12, p.292
2. RIS (2004), *Future Directions of BIMSTEC: Towards a Bay of Bengal Economic Community*, New Delhi, p.9
3. UNDP (2005), *Human Development Report*, New York: Oxford University Press, Table.3, pp.227-8
4. World Bank (2006), *World Development Report*, New York: Oxford University Press, Table.1, pp.292-3

6

Economic Cooperation in BIMSTEC: Emerging Trends and Prospects

T. Nirmala Devi

Regional economic integration under the framework of Bay of Bengal Initiative for Multi-Sectoral Technical and Economic Cooperation (BIMSTEC), formerly the Bangladesh – India – Myanmar – Sri Lanka – Thailand – Economic Cooperation does not collide with the similar initiatives of South Asian Association for Regional Cooperation (SAARC) and the Association of South East Asian Nations (ASEAN). It is a sub regional grouping, combining the geographically contiguous countries of Bangladesh, Bhutan, India, Nepal, Sri Lanka, Myanmar and Thailand and thus, serves as a bridge between the SAARC and the ASEAN regions. The goal of initiating South Asian Preferential Trading Arrangement (SAPTA) and its transition to South Asian Free Trade Area (SAFTA) have not yielded the expected results, considering the modest increase in the size of intra-regional trade. In the SAARC region, trade between neighbours is facilitated mostly by bilateral agreements, particularly in the case of India. Now India has extended its ties to the ASEAN region, especially to Thailand in the form of FTA. Besides its engagement with Myanmar on border management, the promotion of trade; travel; and transport linkages etc. with the Southeast Asian countries are steps in this direction. In the wake of these recent developments and India's consistent Look East policy, the formation of BIMSTEC in 1997 with the objective of promoting economic development among the members through fair trade is welcoming.

The likely formation of Asian Economic Community, encompassing India, ASEAN, China, Korea and Japan is envisioned by the experts in the coming future for enhancing overall growth in the Asian region. The unification process in Asia has now taken shape with the East Asia Summit in November 2005 and India's participation in this has elevated the country's position in global picture, which is a good augury. Evidence also suggests that a closer interaction among the geographically contiguous countries would surely be economically viable. Viewed against this backdrop, the paper attempts to examine the feasibility of deep economic relations among the member nations of BIMSTEC, in consideration of their recent engagement in the form of FTA to be functional from July 1, 2006. The paper also highlights the role of India in augmenting the trade within the region. It aims to explore the chances of trade promotion among the BIMSTEC members by estimating the trade reciprocity index. The paper is arranged into five sections. While the first section being the introduction, the second section discusses the macro economic performance of the individual member countries of the region and the third examines India's role in promoting trade and investment flows in the grouping in general and with Thailand in particular. The fourth section presents the trade reciprocity index by estimating each individual member country's trade with the rest of BIMSTEC nations. With a view to emphasize the future engagement of India in the economic matters of BIMSTEC, the estimation of India's trade reciprocity with each member country in the region is also dealt with in this section. The fifth section provides the conclusion.

Sec. I. Introduction

The rationale behind the formation of any regional grouping is the existence of strong complementarities, which is mostly visible in the BIMSTEC region. This provides a strong base for economic cooperation in trade and investment in the region. A study by RIS (2004) found that each individual member of the region exhibits different capabilities - Sri Lanka's success in social sector development; Thailand's strong industrial base in selected industries and its high economic growth; India's achievement in building up a highly competent scientific manpower and broad industrial base; Bangladesh's model of population management and its untapped resources like natural gas; and Myanmar's huge development potential in agriculture as well as in industry – which could be a source of inspiration to other countries.

There is a significant change in the trade orientation of BIMSTEC countries from the 1990s and most of them exhibited a higher outward orientation. Thailand in the ASEAN grouping has been experiencing tremendous growth prospects in its external trade, despite the financial crisis in 1997. The relevance of the regional bloc in enhancing the trading and investment patterns is to be judged by analyzing the existing socio-economic performance of the individual members. India's 1.08 billion population constitutes a huge share in the region's 1.378 billion population in 2004, which registered an average growth rate of population of 1.61 percent during the period 2000-04, relative to the growth rate of 2.1 percent during the period 1980-90 (World Bank 2006). The declining growth rate of population from the period 1980-90 to 2000-04 in Thailand and Bangladesh, as seen from table.1, is a positive move and the size of less than one percent in the former country is impressive in the context of reducing overhead costs on the existing population. The rise in the population growth rate of Bhutan may be attributed to its move to increase its indigenous population. The life expectancy at birth was not appreciable in general in the region with the exception of Sri Lanka and Thailand and the progress from 1990 to 2003 was significant in Bhutan, Bangladesh and Nepal, while Myanmar recorded a marginal decline. The adult literacy rate was significant in Thailand and Sri Lanka along with Myanmar in the latter period. The primary completion rate was above cent only in Sri Lanka, owing to its consistent priority to education at primary and secondary levels. In the latter period, Thailand and India followed Sri Lanka in this indicator. The progress in this ratio is conspicuous in the two Least Developed Countries (LDCs), Bangladesh and Nepal. As per the human development index estimated by the UNDP, Thailand and Sri Lanka registered a medium human development from 1990 onwards, while the rest of BIMSTEC countries were under the category of low human development. With improved performance on the dimension of social development, particularly in life expectancy at birth; adult literacy rate; combined gross enrolment ratio at the three levels of education together with the GDP per capita in PPP terms, the rest of members also joined the former group, despite the wide disparity in HDI values. The noteworthy feature in the HDI values is that the smaller countries like Nepal and Bhutan showed greater dynamism and progress over the years than the socially advanced countries in the region, Thailand and Sri Lanka, which had a marked performance even from the early 1990. The incidence of poverty is sizeable in the

Table – 1

BIMSTEC: Select Social Indicators

Country	*Total Population (millions)*		*Annual population growth rate (%)*		Life expectancy at birth (years)		*Adult literacy rate % ages 15 and older*	*Primary completion rate (%)*			*Human development index values*
	1990	*2004*	*1980-90*	*2000-04*	*1990*	*2003*	*1990*	*1998-2004*	*1988/89 - 1993/94*	*2000/0 - 2003/04*	*2003*
Bangladesh	106.7	140.5	2.4	1.7	52	63	38	41	46	73	0.520
Bhutan	--	0.9	2.1	2.7	49	63	--	--	--	--	0.536
India	849.5	1079.7	2.1	1.9	59	63	52	61	78	81	0.602
Myanmar	41.6	49.9	2.1	1.2	61	60	--	90	--	--	0.578
Nepal	18.9	25.2	2.6	2.2	52	62	28	49	55	78	0.526
Sri Lanka	17.0	19.4	1.4	1.3	71	74	90	90	103	113	0.751
Thailand	55.8	62.4	1.7	0.7	66	70	94	93	--	86	0.778

Source: World Bank (1992 & 2006), *World Development Report*, New York: Oxford University Press. UNDP (2005), *Human Development Report*, New York: Oxford University Press.

BIMSTEC region, with the exception of Thailand and Sri Lanka. However, it registered a slow decline in most of the countries. In terms of $ 1 a day, the poverty incidence was a well above one-third in Nepal, Bangladesh and India during the period 1990-03, in contrast to <2 and <8 percent of poverty in Thailand and Sri Lanka respectively. If measured on the basis of the national poverty line, the incidence of poverty was nearly one-half in Bangladesh; a well above two-fifths in Nepal; 29 percent in India; a quarter in Sri Lanka; and 13 percent in Thailand during the period 1990-2002 (UNDP 2005).

Sec. II. Regional Trade and Investment

Subsequent to the initiation of economic reforms in the SAARC region, particularly in India, liberalization of trade regimes and the simplification of procedures facilitated the trade and investment pattern, though not to the expected extent. The attempts of these countries to export their products at the international markets were not successful in the past owing to the protectionist policies of the advanced countries coupled with the lack of demand for their manufacturing exports. However, after the shift in the economic regimes, majority of the South Asian countries were able to improve their export competitiveness to some extent. As SAPTA and SAFTA in the SAARC regional grouping failed to deliver the goods, these countries together with Thailand and Myanmar signed the FTA under the BIMSTEC umbrella with a view to expand the size of their market. As five out of seven SAARC countries have now embraced BIMSTEC grouping, they are aiming to reap maximum benefits from the new regional economic cooperation, while meeting the complex conditions at international markets. The formation of BIMSTEC region and its moves viz., signing of FTA in February 2004, expansion of membership to Nepal and Bhutan and its first Summit in July 2004, have given a new impetus to the regional cooperation. The region has identified six sectors for cooperation, viz., trade and investment, technology, transport and communication, energy, tourism and fisheries. Intra-regional trade liberalization among individual member countries of the BIMSTEC have been undertaken in the past under bilateral and multilateral trade agreements. However, the moderate progress in the trade liberalization under most of the above agreements supports the formation of FTA for all the members of the BIMSTEC which is desirable and economically feasible. The success of trade liberalization under the framework of the BIMSTEC depends on the geo-political and economic linkages of the member countries in the coming years.

2.1. Trade – Trends and Potential

In 2004, the total GDP of the BIMSTEC region, barring Bhutan and Myanmar, was at US $ 938.97 billion with an average annual growth rate of 4.6 percent (World Bank 2006). The disparity in per capita incomes is glaring in the region, with Thailand was at the top and Nepal at the bottom in both the measures. In absolute terms, the progress in per capita income from 1995 to 2004 was more pronounced in Bhutan and Sri Lanka followed by India, while the decline in Thailand during this period as well as its moderate progress in PPP terms may be attributed to the impact of financial crisis in 1997. In PPP terms of per capita, India recorded a very significant progress in the region, followed by Sri Lanka and Bangladesh. The improvement in GDP per capita growth rate from the period 1985-95 to 2003-04 was appreciable in India and Sri Lanka with a rise of 2.2 percentage points each, in contrast to the notable decline in Thailand and Bhutan to a major extent and in Nepal to a lesser extent. The economic indicators of the BIMSTEC region, as shown in table.2. revealed the rapid transformation of their economies from agriculture to services. Some structural variations among the economies have been appearing in the region. The shift from the share of agriculture in GDP to that of services is viewed from the strength of the sector's productivity and contribution to employment. With the exception of Nepal, a heavy dependence on services was visible in the region in the recent years and its growth was significant in India. The share of services was declined in favour of industry in Thailand, in contrast to the above countries.

Growth dynamism of a country or a region can be judged from the size of its international trade, owing to its contribution to industrialization and foreign exchange earnings. As shown in table.3, the proportion of trade to GDP, which indicates an outward orientation of the economy has a moderate role in the BIMSTEC countries, however, displayed a better picture from the late 1990s. Thailand and Sri Lanka registered an impressive contribution of trade to the GDP. Leaving aside Myanmar, India's trade share in GDP was small in the BIMSTEC region, owing to the huge size of the population and the resultant high consumption. However, it registered a significant improvement from 1995 onwards. Thailand experienced a tremendous growth in its trade share in GDP, followed by Sri Lanka. Even Nepal's trade share ranged between one-half and three-fifths. The contribution of exports exceeded that of its imports in GDP of Thailand only, and registered a favourable balance from the year 1998 onwards, reflecting a sea change in its export orientation.

Table –2

BIMSTEC: Trends in Key Economic Indicators

Country	*Gross national income per capita (US $)*		*PPP Gross national income per capita (US $)*		*Gross domestic product (GDP) per capita % growth*		*Distribution of GDP (%)*					
	1995	*2004*	*1995*	*2004*	*1985-95*	*2003-04*	*Agriculture value added*		*Industry value added*		*Services value added*	
							1995	*2004*	*1995*	*2004*	*1995*	*2004*
Bangladesh	240	440	1380	1980	2.1	3.7	31	21	18	27	52	53
Bhutan	420	760	1260	--	4.9	2.3	--	--	--	--	--	--
India	340	620	1400	3100	3.2	5.4	29	22	29	26	41	52
Nepal	200	260	1170	1470	2.4	1.6	42	40	22	23	36	37
Sri Lanka	700	1010	3250	4000	2.6	4.8	23	17	25	25	52	58
Thailand	2740	2540	7590	8020	8.4	5.4	11	10	40	44	49	46

Source: As in table-1

Table – 3

Trade Dependency in BIMSTEC Region (% share of trade in GDP)

Year	*Bangladesh*			*India*			*Myanmar*		
	Export	*Import*	*Trade*	*Export*	*Import*	*Trade*	*Export*	*Import*	*Trade*
1990	9.7	18.6	28.3	7.5	9.7	17.2	1.3	2.5	3.8
1995	11.7	20.0	31.7	10.4	13.2	23.6	1.2	1.9	3.1
1996	11.6	18.7	30.3	10.6	14.2	24.8	1.0	1.6	2.6
1997	13.4	19.0	32.4	10.7	13.9	24.6	0.8	1.4	2.2
1998	13.7	18.6	32.3	10.8	14.1	24.9	0.7	1.1	1.8
1999	13.9	20.0	33.9	11.4	14.0	25.4	0.5	0.7	1.2
2000	15.9	21.3	37.2	13.9	16.5	30.4	–	–	–
2001	15.0	21.3	36.3	13.7	15.4	29.1	–	–	–
2002	14.7	19.5	34.2	15.3	16.5	31.8	–	–	–

Table – 3 (contd..)

Trade Dependency in BIMSTEC Region (% share of trade in GDP)

Year	*Nepal*			*Sri Lanka*			*Thailand*		
	Export	*Import*	*Trade*	*Export*	*Import*	*Trade*	*Export*	*Import*	*Trade*
1990	12.0	23.7	35.7	28.5	36.9	65.4	34.2	42.0	76.2
1995	24.4	38.5	62.9	35.4	45.9	81.3	41.8	48.9	90.7
1996	26.1	39.6	65.7	35.0	43.9	78.9	39.3	45.9	85.2
1997	26.5	39.6	66.1	36.5	43.6	80.1	48.0	48.0	96.0
1998	23.0	31.5	54.5	36.2	42.3	78.5	58.9	43.4	102.3
1999	25.3	34.0	59.3	35.5	43.3	78.8	58.2	45.9	104.1
2000	24.0	33.5	57.5	39.1	49.6	88.7	66.7	58.5	125.2
2001	20.7	31.1	51.8	39.2	45.4	84.6	66.0	60.0	126.0
2002	--	--	--	36.1	42.9	79.0	64.4	58.3	122.7

Source: IMF (2002 & 2004), *International Financial Statistics Yearbook*, Washington D.C

Table – 4

BIMSTEC: Growth Rate of Merchandise Exports (% per year)

Country	*1990*	*1995*	*1996*	*1997*	*1998*	*1999*	*2000*	*2001*	*2002*
Bangladesh	28.2	37.1	11.8	14.0	16.8	2.9	8.2	11.4	-7.6
Bhutan	-11.9	10.3	39.6	1.7	12.1	-5.9	9.1	-12.9	-1.8
India	9.0	20.3	4.2	4.5	-3.9	9.5	19.6	0.1	11.4
Myanmar	-0.1	1.9	-0.4	8.7	4.3	36.0	36.8	30.0	–
Nepal	35.2	-9.7	1.9	10.2	11.9	18.23	37.5	4.6	-18.0
Sri Lanka	23.1	18.6	7.6	13.3	3.4	-3.9	19.8	-12.8	-2.4
Thailand	4.7	24.8	-1.9	3.8	-6.8	7.4	19.5	-6.9	5.8

Source: Asian Development Bank (various years), *Asian Development Outlook*, New York: Oxford University Press

The growth rate of exports of BIMSTEC countries recorded an inconsistent trend over the years, as seen from table.4. Majority of these countries experienced a negative rate in the later 1990s and the early years of the new millennium. About one-third of growth rate in Myanmar from 1999 onwards and a considerable growth rate in the year 2000 in Sri Lanka and Nepal were exceptions to the above trend. India recorded a continuous deceleration in its growth rate after 1995, however, regained to this figure more or less in 2000, and ended up with a growth rate of above one-tenth in its exports in 2002. Owing to the visible reason of Asian crisis, the export growth rate in Thailand declined from nearly one-fourth in 1995 to nearly one-fifth in 2000, which dropped further in the subsequent years.

2.2. Intra-regional Trade

In intra-BIMSTEC trade, (table.5) major countries, Thailand and India registered a lower share, indicating a high concentration of exports towards extra-region, particularly with the U.S, the E.U and other developing countries. In contrast, the smaller countries, Nepal and Myanmar revealed a better orientation towards intra-bloc with a well below one-half and one-third shares in their total trade respectively in the year 2003. In this year, Sri Lanka and Bangladesh recorded a well above one-tenth shares each. The common thread in all these countries, by and large, is the rising trend over the years, barring Bangladesh and Nepal in 2000 and Myanmar in 1995. The table also indicated that a lion's share of the region has been directed towards the extra-bloc, particularly in the cases of Thailand and India.

The exports of BIMSTEC nations revealed extra-regional tendency as they are directed towards industrial countries in general, however, this has been declining in some countries like India in the latter year. Japan, which was one of the major export destinations of BIMSTEC nations in the 1980s and early 1990s, has lost its prominence in the 1990s, due to the inclination of BIMSTEC countries towards the U.S and the E.U. The rise in the export share of these countries to the U.S was significant during 1990 to 2001 - a growth of 15 to 21 percent in India; 23 to 35 percent in Nepal; 26 to 41 percent in Sri Lanka; and 2 to 17 percent in Myanmar - barring a marginal fall from 31 to 30 percent in Bangladesh and the modest fall from 23 to 20 percent in Thailand, while the share of exports to the E.U has registered an increase from 32 to 41 percent in Bangladesh and from 7 to 15 percent in Myanmar. Notwithstanding the higher orientation towards industrial countries, nearly 50 percent of the export market of India and Thailand during the above years was directed to the developing world (Asian Development Bank 2003).

Table - 5

Intra-BIMSTEC Trade (in percent)

Country	*Intra-region*				*Extra-region*			
	1990	*1995*	*2000*	*2003*	*1990*	*1995*	*2000*	*2003*
Bangladesh	10.97	12.02	8.62	11.32	89.03	87.98	91.38	88.68
India	2.02	3.71	3.30	3.28	97.98	96.29	96.70	96.72
Myanmar	11.93	6.02	20.45	30.07	88.07	93.98	79.55	69.93
Nepal	16.54	27.59	23.81	46.66	83.46	72.41	76.19	53.34
Sri Lanka	5.96	7.90	7.59	12.70	94.04	92.10	92.41	87.30
Thailand	1.67	1.18	1.90	2.16	98.33	98.82	98.10	97.84

Source: Basic data obtained from IMF (various years), *Direction of Trade Statistics Yearbook*, Washington, D C.

Table – 6

BIMSTEC: Trends in Structure of Trade

Country	*External balance of goods & services (% of GDP)*	*Imports of goods and services (% of GDP)*		*Exports of goods and services (% of GDP)*		*Primary Exports (% of merchandise exports)*		*Manufactured Exports (% of merchandise exports)*		*High Technology Exports (% of manufactured exports*	
	2004	*1990*	*2003*	*1990*	*2003*	*1990*	*2003*	*1990*	*2003*	*1990*	*2003*
Bangladesh	-7	14	20	6	14	--	10	77	89	(.)	(.)
Bhutan	--	32	43*	28	22*	--	--	--	--	--	--
India	-1	9	16	7	14	28	22	71	77	2	5
Myanmar	--	5	--	3	--	--	--	--	--	--	--
Nepal	-12	22	29	11	17	--	--	83	--	--	--
Sri Lanka	-9	38	42	29	36	42	25*	54	74*	1	1*
Thailand	5	42	59	34	66	36	22	63	75	21	30

Source: UNDP (2005), *Human Development Report*, New York: Oxford University Press.

Note: (.) = Less than half the unit shown

* = Data refer to 2002

2.3. Composition of Trade

It is seen from the structure of trade of BIMSTEC countries (table.6.), that the share of primary products in the export composition was more than two-fifths in Sri Lanka, a well above one-third in Thailand and about one-fourth in Bangladesh and India each (though the share in the earlier year was not shown in the case of Bangladesh) in the BIMSTEC region in the former year. However, it declined notably in Sri Lanka, Bangladesh and Thailand in the latter year. The share of manufactured exports had climbed up from 1980s to 1990s in all the countries and the growth was conspicuous from 1990 to 2003 in Sri Lanka, followed by Bangladesh and Thailand. The share of high technology exports in the total of manufactured exports in the latter year was a well below one-third in Thailand, whereas it was at the lowest of 5 and 1 percent in India and Sri Lanka respectively.

The BIMSTEC region registered a current account imbalance in their balance of payments in GDP terms, as expected. However, the unfavourable balance had gradually declined in most of the members from the 1990s, particularly in Thailand from 1998 onwards, while India and Bangladesh were able to erase the negative balance in the early years of new millennium (IMF 2004). The Official Development Assistance (ODA) received as net disbursements from the industrial countries and its share in GDP in general had declined from 1990 to 2003, barring Bhutan and Nepal in the latter year. The proportion of total debt service in GDP during the above period reduced modestly in the region with the exception of Thailand and India, which experienced a significant and moderate increases respectively. On the other hand, the debt as a share of exports registered a sizeable decline in Bangladesh followed by Myanmar and India (UNDP 2005)

2.4. Foreign Direct Investment (FDI) Flows

FDI in general and in export-oriented services in particular, offers several economic benefits for the host countries in the fields of export earnings, job creation, higher wages and upgrading skills (UNCTAD 2004). In India, the FDI inflows which reached the highest in 1997 declined significantly in the subsequent three years, however, picked up from 2001 onwards, as seen from table.7.a. Thailand recorded a higher volume in the earlier period i.e., upto 1997 only and its consistent drop afterwards was an indication of the strong bearing of the financial crisis on the economy. In the rest of countries, Sri Lanka experienced

Table – 7.a

BIMSTEC: Foreign Direct Investment inflows

Country	*1990*	*1995*	*1996*	*1997*	*1998*	*1999*	*2000*	*2001*	*2002*	*2003*
Bangladesh	3	2	14	141	190	180	280	79	52	-121
India	162	2144	2426	3600	2633	2168	2319	3403	3449	4269
Myanmar	5	277	310	419	684[a]	304[a]	208[a]	192[a]	191[a]	128[a]
Nepal	6	8	19	23	12	4	--	21[b]	2[b]	30
Sri Lanka	43	65	133	435	150	201	175	82	197	229
Thailand	2444	2000	2405	3600	1700	1484	1289	1300	1200	1450

Source: UNCTAD (various years), *World Investment Report*, Geneva.

Note: a = annual average from 1996 to 97

b = annual average from 1993 to 97

Table – 7.b

BIMSTEC: Share of Services in total inward Foreign Direct Investment (in percent)

Country	*Flows*					*Stock*				
	Average 1990-94	*Average 1995-99*	*Average 2000-02*	*2001*	*2002*	*1990*	*1995*	*2000*	*2001*	*2002*
Bangladesh	--	28.5	45.7	58.0	68.5	--	5.3	27.7	28.9	--
India	10.5	28.3	--	--	--	--	--	--	--	--
Myanmar	--	8.7	28.3	24.8	31.1	23.0[a]	31.9[a]	35.1[a]	35.1[a]	34.7[a]
Nepal	52.7	68.3	--	--	--	44.2	48.2	--	--	--
Sri Lanka	--	75.4[a]	48.1[a]	42.6[a]	50.9[a]	--	43.2[a]	63.7	63.2	59.0[a]
Thailand	61.8	68.6	30.3	25.7	15.7	47.6	57.9	62.2	58.0	56.8

Source: As in table-7.a

Note: a = approval data

Table – 7.c

BIMSTEC: Inward and outward FDI stocks as a percentage of gross domestic product

Country	*1980*	*1985*	*1990*	*1995*	*2000*	*2002*	*2003*
Bangladesh							
Inward	1.7	1.5	1.1	0.9	5.2	5.2	5.0
Outward	--	--	--	--	0.1	0.1	0.1
Bhutan							
Inward	--	--	0.6	0.8	0.7	0.7	0.7
Outward	--	--	--	--	--	--	--
India:							
Inward	0.2	0.3	0.5	1.6	3.8	5.2	5.4
Outward	--	--	--	0.1	0.4	0.8	0.9
Nepal:							
Inward	0.1	0.1	0.3	0.9	1.8	2.0	2.5
Outward	--	--	--	--	--	--	--
Sri Lanka:							
Inward	5.7	8.6	8.5	10.0	14.4	16.1	15.6
Outward	--	--	0.1	0.3	0.5	0.6	0.6
Thailand:							
Inward	3.0	5.1	9.7	10.5	24.5	27.7	25.8
Outward	--	--	0.5	1.4	2.1	2.2	2.3

Source: As in table-7.a

stability in FDI inflows, except for the year 2001. The share of services in the total inward FDI inflows had increased substantially from the average of the period 1995-99 to that of 2000-02 in Bangladesh, in contrast to Thailand, which witnessed a drastic decline in the latter period due to the abovesaid reason. (table.7.b). The considerable rise in India, followed by Nepal from the average of 1990-94 to that of 1995-99 and in Myanmar in the later 1990s and the early years of new millennium and the decline of Sri Lanka from the average of the period 1995-99 to 2000-02 revealed the fast global shift as well as the individual country's political and economic stability. The visible share of services in the FDI stock in Thailand and Sri Lanka indicated a favourable move towards economic development. The shift towards services was not prominent in the early years in India; although the country has earned a good reputation in software industry in the subsequent years. Table.7.c shows that the FDI inward stock as a share of GDP was significant from the year 2000 onwards in Thailand (about one-fourth) followed by Sri Lanka (a well below one-sixth) while the outward stock was above 2 percent and slightly above 0.5 percent in the former and latter countries respectively. A mere share of 5 percent of FDI inward stock was contributed to the GDP by India and Bangladesh in 2002 and 2003 and the former country recorded a miniscule share in the outward stock in the above years. Generally, foreign capital supplements the domestic savings to achieve a higher rate of domestic investment. In most of these countries, the contribution of FDI to gross fixed capital formation has been limited due to their incapability to attract FDI, except in the case of Thailand and Sri Lanka (UNCTAD 2004)

Sec.III. India's Engagement with the BIMSTEC Region:

India's bilateral economic relations with the regional members contribute to the enhancement of complementarities and thus, to mutual cooperation in a number of areas. Though the BIMSTEC members differ in their intensity of economic relationship with India, the recent dynamism exhibited by India in forging economic ties with the neighbours would pave the way in fostering the rate of economic growth.

India is gradually emerging as an economic powerhouse in the developing countries and is ranked next to China and major - ASEAN in Asia. Consequently, it is a natural hub for most of its neighbours. All the BIMSTEC members share the long sea borders with India, with the exception of Nepal and Bhutan, the land-locked countries. The developments in the neighbouring countries' relations - India's bilateral trade agreements with Nepal and Bhutan and its recent signing of agreement with Nepal to set up the first ever rail link between the two; a transit traffic agreement between the governments of India, Nepal and Bangladesh in 1997, which allowed the movement of traffic by road from Nepal to Bangladesh through India; sharing of the broad gauge railways of India with Bangladesh along with Pakistan and a bilateral rail interchange agreements; the India and Bangladesh protocol on Inland Transit and Trade facilitates for the movement of cargo to the north-eastern states and several other similar arrangements – have intensified the cooperative measures in the region. India's FTA with Sri Lanka under which the duty concessions are being exchanged on bilateral basis are some of India's active economic interactions with the region. The country has entered into a close economic relationship with Myanmar, as revealed by the India-Myanmar official meetings on border management, promotion of trade and travel through road and building a highway, connecting India-Myanmar border.

Likewise, the meeting of foreign ministers of India, Myanmar and Thailand on transport linkage of three nations is also an example of India's neighbourhood policy (Parikh & Radhakrishna 2004-05).

3.1. India's Bilateral Trade with the BIMSTEC Nations

In its bilateral trade with each of BIMSTEC members from 1990 to 2003, India enjoyed a trade surplus with Bangladesh, Sri Lanka and Thailand, particularly with the former two countries which also showed more or less an increasing trend, as seen from table.8. On the other hand, India had a consistent trade deficit, reflecting the excess of its imports over exports with Myanmar, especially in the latest year under consideration. The bilateral trade balance of India was also mostly unfavourable with Bhutan and Nepal, which reversed in the year 2003.

The Energy Minister's Conference held in New Delhi in 2005 aimed at setting up of a BIMSTEC Centre of Energy to pool the strengths of members for capacity building in all areas of energy sectors, is a positive step in further strengthening the regional cooperation. This underscores the need for specific projects of cooperation such as building transmission lines or gas pipelines. India's overall interests and of its energy economics, in particular is reflected in the schemes of evaluating hydro power from Nepal in the north, to Bangladesh, Thailand and Myanmar in the south-east, and to build gas pipelines to Thailand and Sri Lanka (The Hindu 2005).

Table – 8

India's Bilateral Trade Balance with BIMSTEC Countries (US $ million)

Year	*Bangladesh*	*Bhutan*	*Myanmar*	*Nepal*	*Sri Lanka*	*Thailand*
1990	281.85	--	-88.71	24.44	79.47	138.83
1991	318.83	0.70	-47.38	58.09	163.02	150.19
1992	343.70	0.86	-99.87	49.93	217.78	175.41
1993	416.69	1.70	-102.65	56.07	229.66	259.41
1994	486.73	3.76	-96.47	70.63	302.61	228.54
1995	880.8	-4.71	-139.22	79.67	344.48	314.95
1996	774.49	-6.47	-102.48	108.26	423.50	258.24
1997	753.48	-3.02	-164.02	81.50	452.30	145.50
1998	883.83	2.60	-151.45	1.82	414.30	63.60
1999	651.88	-6.93	-139.05	-33.68	441.17	103.32
2000	780.47	-17.60	-139.13	-87.08	560.10	174.60
2001	1019.93	-19.35	-144.03	-104.01	467.62	81.64
2002	998.40	-21.00	-156.33	-112.88	568.80	250.53
2003	1461.39	27.50	-305.30	296.83	1051.95	246.85

Source : As in Table-5

Table – 9

Share of Top Five Imports and Exports of Thailand in India's Trade

(in per cent)

Imports				*Exports*			
Commodity	*1995-96*	*2000-01*	*2004-05*	*Commodity*	*1995-96*	*2000-01*	*2004-05*
Electronic goods	10.64	31.48	18.78	Gems & Jewellery	48.47	36.09	34.27
Non-electrical machinery	5.96	9.12	10.67	Non-ferrous metals	0.09	0.33	11.73
Artfcl. Resins, plastic matrls. etc.	10.54	7.14	8.51	Prim. &Semi-fin.iron & steel	4.50	4.20	5.80
Transport equipment	0.76	0.39	7.29	Oil meals	13.59	6.58	5.58
Electrical machinery	2.14	3.64	4.98	Drugs, pharm. & fine chemicals	2.88	6.21	5.53

Source: CMIE (2002 & 2005), *Foreign Trade & Balance of Payments*, Mumbai.

3.2. India-Thailand FTA

The economic interaction between the two fast growing and better performing countries in BIMSTEC, India and Thailand needs to be discussed. The recent signing of FTA between India and Thailand is a landmark in the history of BIMSTEC region and hopes to provide more opportunities for both the countries involved.

In the India-Thailand bilateral trade (table.9.), the trend in the top five import items of India sourced from Thailand increased from 30 percent in 1995-96 to nearly 52 percent in 2000-01, which registered a decline of nearly 2 percentage points in the latter year. In the year 1995-96, the items of electronic goods and artificial resins, plastic materials etc., constituted the main imports and the former import item outnumbered the others in the year 2000-01. It, however, registered a decline in the latter year in favour of transport equipment to a major extent. The five items of India's exports, which accounted for about 69 percent of its total to Thailand in the former year witnessed a decline of 16 percentage points in 2000-01 and recovered again to nearly 10 percentage points in the latter year. The substantial size of the export of gems and jewellery in the select three years indicated the consistent demand in Thailand. The significant rise in non-ferrous metals in 2004-05, in contrast to the sizeable decline in oil meals indicated the shift in the priority.

Under the frame work of FTA between India and Thailand, 82 items are to be enjoyed concessional tariffs now onwards under the 'Early Harvest Scheme' which include electronic components, grapes, apples, precious stone and articles of jewellery. The total trade between two countries stood at $1.7 billion in 2004-05 but Thailand's share in India's total exports and imports is just one and 0.8 percent respectively. This FTA was initially criticized, as it was against India's interests. However, the fears were dispelled after a closer observation of realities and the reassurance of Thailand towards the mutual benefits. A new formula needs to be evolved for the betterment of both countries, particularly in the sphere of investment and from the Indian point of view of trade in services (Business Line 2005).

Sec IV. Index of Trade Reciprocity

In order to measure the reciprocity in the overall balance of trade of any two partner countries (or group of countries not including all trade partners at the global level), the following Trade Reciprocity Index (Ø) has been devised.

$$\theta = 1 - \frac{\sum_{j=1}^{n}\left[\frac{a_{ij} - a_{ji}}{a_{ij} + a_{ji}} \sum_{i=1}^{n} a_{ij}\right]}{(n-1)\left[\sum_{i=1} \sum_{j=1} a_{ij}\right]}$$

Where

a_{ij} = exports of country i to partner j

a_{ji} = exports of country j to partner i

n = total number of countries involved in the context of bilateral or regional grouping being considered.

The index will always lie between zero and one. When every pair of countries in a group tends to have a balanced bilateral trade (case of perfectly balanced two-way trade), the value of Ø reaches its maximum (i.e., unity). On the other hand, when there exist only one way flow of trade between the pair of trading partners (say, complete dependence of country A on country B for its imports or exports), the value of Ø is at its minimum (i.e., Zero). This index, thus measures the degree of trade reciprocity. It can be measured at bilateral as well as multilateral level for a group of countries. It is extremely useful in the context of the schemes of regional trade cooperation among partners who are facing (or apprehending) balance of trade difficulties. Like most of the indices, this index too suffers from some limitations, i.e., trade reciprocity can be measured at a given level, but cannot clearly distinguish between the degrees of trade reciprocity at varying levels of trade (Wadhva 1987).

4.1. Construction of Trade Reciprocity Index

The trade reciprocity index is estimated for the six countries of BIMSTEC, viz., Bangladesh, India, Myanmar Nepal, Sri Lanka and Thailand for the select years 1990, 1995 and 2000 and 2003. In the estimation of the index, Bhutan has not been taken into consideration, owing to the paucity of data. In measuring the trade reciprocity index for the individual BIMSTEC countries with the rest of the region, 'n', i.e., the number of countries involved in trade has differed, particularly in the cases of Myanmar and Nepal. In Myanmar's trade with the region, Nepal was absent although the select years. The other non-participant countries are Sri Lanka in 1990; and Sri Lanka together with Thailand in 1995. In Nepal's trade too, Myanmar was not engaged in the years under consideration. Sri Lanka is the other exception in Nepal's trade

with the region in the years 1995 and 2003. The above two countries – Myanmar and Nepal – did not engage in some selected years in Sri Lanka's trade, hence Sri Lanka's trade reciprocity index was estimated with the absence of Myanmar in 1990; Myanmar and Nepal in 1995; and Nepal in 2003. Myanmar was also not a trade partner in Thailand's trade in 1995. Thus, exceptions are common in individual country's trade with the region, barring India and Bangladesh.

4.2. Analysis of the Results

The trade reciprocity index of individual BIMSTEC member countries with the region is presented in table 10.a. The values of the index are either unity or nearing unity in all the countries in the four selected years. Bangladesh registered a slight fall in its value from 1990, however, recovered again in 2003. Myanmar picked up its trade from 1995 to 2000, despite the marginal fall in 2003, as indicated by its value. Despite the notably high value in 1990, Nepal experienced a fall in the subsequent two selected years and became steady again in 2003. There was a visible increase in Sri Lanka's trade reciprocity with the region from 1990 to 1995, which declined modestly in the latter years. The initially high value of trade reciprocity in Thailand went down moderately in 1995 and picked up again gradually in the latter two years under consideration. Only India showed a consistent increase, despite a slightly lower value of trade reciprocity than the other regional members.

·Table 10.b provides India's trade reciprocity index with each BIMSTEC nation individually. As visualized in the previous table, the values of trade reciprocity index of India with Bangladesh, Myanmar, Nepal, Sri Lanka and Thailand have been consistently rising since 1990. These values showed a slightly higher trade with Thailand and a marginally lower trade with Bangladesh.

Sec.V. Conclusion

The members of BIMSTEC grouping are divergent in socio-economic characteristics viz., population size, per capita income, level of economic growth, yet these differences will not become a hurdle for their increased economic cooperation due to the favourable picture posted by the improved performance of the smaller countries. Each

Table – 10.a
Trade Reciprocity Index of Individual BIMSTEC Nations with Region

Year	*Bangladesh with BIMSTEC bloc*	*India with BIMSTEC bloc*	*Myanmar with BIMSTEC Bloc*	*Nepal with BIMSTEC bloc*	*Sri Lanka with BIMSTEC Bloc*	*Thailand with BIMSTEC bloc*
1990	1.004148	0.999815	0.998682	1.00903	1.002227	1.00006
1995	1.00282	0.999941	0.997919	1.008908	1.002583	0.999945
2000	1.001847	0.999968	1.000084	0.999867	1.000914	0.999964
2003	1.002423	0.999978	0.999919	1.000398	1.000626	1.000004

Source: Estimated from the basic data obtained from IMF (various years), *Direction of Trade Statistics Yearbook*, Washington D C.

Table – 10.b
India's Trade Reciprocity Index with BIMSTEC Nations

Year	*India with Bangladesh*	*India with Myanmar*	*India with Nepal*	*India with Sri Lanka*	*India with Thailand*
1990	0.9997018	0.999728	0.999702	0.999707	0.999744
1995	0.9999	0.999911	0.999899	0.9999	0.999924
2000	0.999912	0.999921	0.999924	0.999913	0.999946
2003	0.999954	0.99996	0.999958	0.999958	0.999965

Source: Same as the above table

member country exhibits some kind of success story or development experience from which the other member can emulate the same. Moreover, there are no serious political differences among the member nations. If meticulous study is undertaken, the region's untapped potential provides a vast scope for further cooperation. The existing complementarities, as evinced from the RIS study can be multiplied, if planned carefully.

The existing bilateral and multilateral agreements among BIMSTEC members under the regional initiatives not only strengthen the economic rationale but also mitigate the political tensions, if any. The new initiative of Bay of Bengal Economic Community would definitely support and enhance the economic interaction among the members. It is evident that a regular exchange of information and networking on trade and investment matters can be done with a political will, which plays a facilitating role in economic interactions.

Liberalization of regional trade is quite essential to achieve the desired targets. The existing high tariff barriers among these countries have deterred the trade flows to a major extent. In this context, the softening and liberalizing of complex and extensive trade formalities are to be done on an urgent basis, otherwise they slow down the progress of exports, increase the size of illegal trade on the borders and thus affect the economic relations with the neighbouring countries. India's FTAs with ASEAN nations, particularly with Thailand have faced criticism under the apprehension of inclusion of more areas of the economy. A new formula on mutually beneficial basis needs to be evolved in the case of FTAs, by taking extra-care on rules of origin, value-addition and other important issues. Liberalization of trade regimes should also be followed by regional arrangements on investment in course of time.

India's possibility of emerging as a regional energy hub in South Asia depends on its likely setting up of bilateral grids in the coming years – bilateral interconnections with Myanmar for exchange of power; a power station in Bangladesh and a similar initiative with Sri Lanka - besides strengthening of the existing grids with Nepal and Bhutan. These kinds of steps deepen the trade and investment engagements to optimize the benefits of individual nations under the BIMSTEC framework. The member countries should be wise enough in giving priority to the regional perspective by keeping aside their fears on geo-political and economic issues, otherwise the operating mechanism of the BIMSTEC region will be delayed further.

References

1. Asian Development Bank (2003), *Asian Development Outlook*, New York: Oxford University Press, Table. A.12, p.292
2. *Business Line* (2005), September 20
3. *Ibid.*,(2005), September 26
4. IMF (2004), *International Financial Statistics Yearbook*, Washington, D C.
5. Kirit S. Parikh & R. Radhakrishna (2004-05), *India Development Report*, New Delhi: Oxford University Press, p.164.
6. RIS (2004), *Future Directions of BIMSTEC: Towards a Bay of Bengal Economic Community*, New Delhi. pp.25-26
7. *The Hindu* (2005), October 7
8. UNCTAD (2004), *World Investment Report*, Geneva, pp.169-70
9. *Ibid.*, Annex table B.5.
10. UNDP (2005), *Human Development Report*, New York: Oxford University Press, Table.3, pp.227-8
11. *Ibid.*, Table.19, pp.280-2
12. World Bank (2006), *World Development Report*, New York: Oxford University Press, Table.1, pp.292-3
13. *Ibid.*,Table.3, pp.292-3

7

Regional Economic Arrangements: Understanding the Growth of BIMSTEC

Padmaja Murthy

Sec. I. Introduction

An important feature of present day international economic scenario is the proliferation of regional economic arrangements. They denote a process or a state of affairs involving the combination of separate economies into larger economic regions. At present, it is difficult to find a single region, which is free of any sort of trading arrangement or economic co-operation. However regional economic arrangements are not a new phenomenon. During the 1960s, there was a proliferation of such groupings primarily among the developing countries. These attempts did not meet with much success. Since mid-1980s, once again such groupings are being concluded not only by the developing countries but most significantly by the developed countries too. The former is termed as old regionalism and the later as new regionalism. The factors, which have influenced new regionalism, have also resulted in the formation of less formal arrangements, sometimes referred to as growth triangles or quadrangles or more generally as sub-regionalism.

The formation and evolution of BIMSTEC should be seen in the context of these global trends of regional economic arrangements. The process of BIMSTEC began with the establishment of the sub-regional grouping - Bangladesh –India – Sri Lanka- Thailand Economic

Co-operation (BIST-EC). In December 1997, Myanmar was admitted and the grouping was renamed as BIMST-EC (Bangladesh –India – Myanmar -Sri Lanka- Thailand- Economic Co-operation). In February 2004, Bhutan and Nepal joined the grouping. In July 2004, the grouping had its first summit level meeting and was rechristened as Bay of Bengal Initiative for Multi-Sectoral Technical and Economic Co-operation (BIMSTEC). The change of terminology captures in it both the expansion in the number of participating countries and the deepening of purpose of the grouping. It also indicates to the sub-regional grouping moving towards more formal structures. All this apparent movement does not mean that the going has been smooth for BIMSTEC. The observation by one of the member countries that the high potential projects agreed upon in various expert group meetings have not been implemented and that BIMSTEC risks becoming irrelevant, despite its high potential signals to the challenges the grouping faces as it moves towards completing a decade. Problems are however not unique to the BIMSTEC alone and are characteristic to other groupings too.

The aim of the paper is three fold. Section one briefly states the concepts related to regional economic integration. Section two identifies the main features of old regionalism and new regionalism and how they differ. The characteristics of sub regionalism are also brought out. Following this background of discussion on regionalism in the first two sections, Section three understands the growth and evolution of the BIMSTEC.

Sec. II. Regional Economic Integration - Concepts

A regional economic arrangement aims at integrating independent national economies into a larger economic region. It, therefore, involves the removal of trade impediments and establishment of coordination and cooperation among the countries concerned. (Curzon 1974). Depending on the level of integration, the regional economic arrangements take a variety of forms. The principle ones are the preferential trading arrangements, free trade area, customs union, common market and economic union. As of May 2003, 184 regional trade agreements (RTA) were in force. Almost every WTO (World Trade Organisation) member now formed at least one RTA and some have entered more. (Burfisher et.al 2003).

2.1. Preferential Trade Area

A preferential trade area is one where the member countries partially bring down tariffs towards each other's good. It is important to remember that tariffs still existing in trade among them. What they have done is to give preference to the goods of the member countries in comparison to the rest of the world.

2.2. Free Trade Area

A free trade area is an arrangement whereby the member countries do not have any barriers and restrictions with respect to trade among themselves. However, each of the member countries is at a liberty to determine the tariff structure with respect to the imports originating from non-member countries.

2.3. Customs Union

A customs union facilitates free flow of trade among the member countries, like that in a free trade area. However, unlike a free trade area, the member countries have an understanding for a common external tariff towards non-members.

2.4. Common Market

A common market has all the features of a customs union. In addition it is accompanied by free movement of factors of production. Thus, it is assumed that there is no constraint whatsoever among the member countries, whether it is transfer of goods, capital or services.

2.5. Economic Union

An economic union exists, if a common market is characterized also by union-wide economic policies. Going by this taxonomy, it may be deduced that the various economic arrangements are like steps towards different degrees of economic integration. However, in practice, the steps need not follow sequentially and these categories are indicative rather than clear-cut.

A glance at the above types of economic arrangements might lead one to conclude that the reasons for forming such arrangements are purely economic. However, there have been schemes that were proposed for definite political reasons. Many a times, the dominance of the political agenda over the economic agenda negatively effects the working and forward movement of the grouping. It might be safe to conclude that it is the combination of the political as well as the economic rationale, which goes into the making of an economic arrangement. (Agraa 1982). The formation of the European Economic Community (EEC) was a politically motivated move towards forming a

West European Union. Even the erstwhile COMECON (also known as CMEA i.e. Council for Mutual Economic Assistance founded in 1949) included the strengthening of political ties as one of its fundamental goals. These countries were bound together by the ideology of Communism. They basically catered to their needs of exports and imports by trading among themselves. (Shah 1968). In some cases, economic arrangements may even act as a low cost method of achieving political goals of foreign policy. In such situations, the trade policy becomes the foreign policy. The EU's pyramid of preferences with the African, Caribbean and Pacific (ACP) countries is such an example. Through such arrangements, the EU was able to extend its sphere of political influence, even in the post-colonial period. Commission of the European Communities, 1993) Even the NAFTA (North American Free Trade Area) is a vital tool in the hands of the USA to influence the regional actors politically.

Sec. III. The Evolution of Regional Economic Groupings - Old Regionalism and New Regionalism

During the 1930s, as countries carving out their own colonies proliferated, the areas open to trade on equal terms greatly reduced. As a consequence, towards the end of the World War II period, free trade had become the biggest casualty with the emergence of restrictive trade practices. The post-World War II economic order, therefore, sought to put an end to such attempts at regionalisation through the establishment of an International Trade Organization (ITO) to oversee the conduct of free and fair trade based on non-discriminatory practices.

Though the attempts at establishing an ITO failed, GATT came into existence in 1948. Its core principle is non-discrimination, as specified in Article 1 of GATT.

"...Any advantage, favour, privilege or immunity granted by any contracting party to any product originating in or destined for any other country shall be accorded immediately and unconditionally to the like product originating or destined for the territory of all other contracting parties"

In sum, the cornerstone of GATT is the extension of unconditional most favoured nation treatment to all fellow signatories. However, there is one exception to this Article, which is contained in Article 24. It states the conditions under which GATT signatories may form customs union and free trade areas, provided they fulfill some specific conditions, which would be economically sound for the overall goal of free trade.

(Chisti 1991). However, there were clear political motives behind this Article, one of which was to facilitate the British to retain their sphere of influence by keeping their system of imperial preferences intact. Further, the USA realized that European stability in the post-World War II scenario could be achieved only through cooperation among these countries. This political stability would have to be aided by economic integration and, therefore, Article 24 was supported by the USA. Many regional economic arrangements thus, arose but without complying to the letter and spirit of the provision of Article 24, clearly indicating the political goals which such arrangements sought to achieve. (Bhagwati 1991)

Attempts towards forming economic arrangements in the post-World War II period can be studied broadly under two phases. Each phase is characterized by a different set of factors and regional actors. While the first phase, beginning from the 1950s and undergoing intensification over the next two decades, saw a proliferation of regional arrangements primarily among developing countries, the second phase began from the mid-1980s and has been characterized by regional economic arrangements being concluded by the developed countries together with the developing countries. The former is termed as Old regionalism and the later as New regionalism.

3.1. First Phase - Old Regionalism

The first phase that witnessed groupings primarily among developing countries were a result of various factors. However, the timing coincided with the successful launching of the EEC in 1957, which set a positive tone for other economic groupings. The attempts were impressive enough to prompt a writer in 1964 to describe the period as the "age of integration". Some of the major regional groupings during this period were: 1957 – European Economic Community (EEC); 1960 – European Free Trade Area (EFTA); 1960 – Latin American Free Trade Area (LAFTA); 1960 – Central American Common Market (CACM); 1964 – Maghreb Permanent Consultative Committee; 1964 – Regional Cooperation and Development (RCD) among Iran, Pakistan and Turkey. (Agraa 1982)

Chronologically, LAFTA, set up in 1960, was the first important integration scheme agreed to by the fewer developing countries. The understanding of some of the factors that led to the setting up of LAFTA would help us in attributing reasons to the formation of regional groupings by several other developing countries. (Tussie 1987)

First, LAFTA arose out of the "demonstrative effect" of the establishment of EEC and EFTA. The second important factor lay in the interest of Argentina, Brazil, Chile and Uruguay to preserve their shrinking trade covered by bilateral agreements. The region was witnessing a rise in imports from the rest of the world and a decline in intra-regional trade. The countries desired to stop this trend. Since a customs union would have required closer coordination of foreign and economic policies, which they were not prepared to accept, they embarked instead on the idea of a free trade area. Clearly the groupings in this period were inward looking.

The third crucial factor that influenced LAFTA were the views of the United Nations Economic Commission for Latin America (ECLA). Import substitution and regional integration were among ECLA's central tenets in the area of international trade from the very outset. In fact, the dominant development strategy of the 1950s among developing counties was import-substituting industrialization. In ECLA's thinking, regional integration was crucial to obtain the economies of large-scale production offered by technology development of modern industry. It was of the opinion that without access to external markets, it would not be possible to sustain the growth of import substitution industries. But since Latin American goods were in competitive in world markets, regional economic integration was the way out. Thus, integration extended the policy of import substitution from a national to a continental scale.

This economic integration was thus, designed to work via the economies of scale. Countries could complement each other's markets and hence import substitution could become more efficient through the enlargement of the sheltered market. Latin America was believed to be producing much less than it could, owing to a fragmentation of what could and should have been a single market. This had to change, if production was to be efficient and low cost. In the absence of any cooperation among themselves, the Latin American countries did not have big markets to tap their production on a large scale. By cooperating amongst themselves they could transform small national markets into a large single market. As a result, they would be less dependent on traditional markets of the developed countries. Further, through their combined import potential, the developing countries could secure better terms of trade. These were the economic factors motivating them to forming the grouping.

Unfortunately, many of the regional economic arrangements of the developing countries failed to take off smoothly because, instead of using trade liberalization, and hence, prices to guide industry allocation, they sought to allocate industries by bureaucratic negotiations. Consequently, economic rationale did not dominate and had to remain subservient to the political demands of regional economic arrangements. This clearly indicates the political factors, which need to be understood while assessing the Performance of the grouping.

The advantages accruing from such arrangements were sought to be shared by negotiations between the countries. The smaller countries in the group feared that larger parties would benefit most. Many of these nations had acquired freedom from the colonial yoke and were jealous of sharing their policy-making autonomy. Added to this were also the political differences and problems that these countries had inherited from their colonial masters. These hampered genuine cooperation and progress. There was thus, absence of political will. (Bhagwati 1991). In the later years, in the face of regional debt crisis, among other factors, these arrangements disintegrated. Due to these reasons, such arrangements could not make any impact at a global level and their importance, if any is limited to the region concerned. Presently though, in the second phase, these are being revived.

3.2. Second Phase - New Regionalism

The second phase is dominated by regional economic arrangements having both the developed and the developing countries as its members. None other than the USA, which till then had, vociferously championed the cause of multilateralism, is leading it. These countries are the ones that have a major share in world trade. For example, the EU and NAFTA together accounted for nearly three-fifth of the world trade in 1993. (Halan 1993)

Three factors are primarily responsible for the proliferation of regional economic arrangements in the second phase.

(a) *Disenchantment with the GATT process. (Schott ed., 1989)*: Concern about the efficiency of the GATT process (prior to the World Trade Organization – WTO) had led some countries to focus more on regional economic arrangements than on their participation in the multilateral negotiations. The Tokyo Round lasted from 1973 to 1979 and the Uruguay Round, which started in 1986, was concluded after a full seven years in December 1993. With regard to the Uruguay Round, there were 15 negotiating groups and the implicit understanding of consensus during such negotiations meant that blocking the negotiations

was easy. Such problems normally do not rise in negotiations among a small group of countries and more importantly the pace of negotiations tends to be faster and results can be achieved more quickly. Further, while GATT had been successful in bringing down tariffs to a great extent, traded goods remained vulnerable to a broad range of non-tariff restrictions. Attempts to extend multilateral negotiations to such practices had not met with success.

(b) *The effects of US leadership and the impact of efforts to form the EMU (European Monetary Union)*: The multilateral trading system had the USA as its champion, having initiated each of the GATT rounds of talks. When the USA moved away to managing its trade deficit through unilateral, bilateral and regional measures, including conclusion of trade agreements with Canada and Israel, other countries followed suit. Similarly, the measures adopted to implement the Single European Market, led to a fear psychosis that a Fortress Europe was emerging which could be countered only by forming similar regional arrangements.

(c) *Lastly, and more significantly regional economic arrangements are being aided by globalism*: Generally, growth in Gross Domestic Product (GDP) worldwide has been related to growth in the use of basic materials as energy, steel, copper, cement, etc. However, since the late 1970s, the GDP growth has been accounted for by growth in new technology areas like electronics, computers, medical technologies, etc. These new areas are knowledge intensive and economic growth has since been driven by their application. Efficient manufacturing methods are resulting in improvement in the quality of products being sold at competitive prices. New product development has also become multi-disciplinary in character, requiring a large number of different technologies. (Miller 1992)

Companies are, therefore, engaging in a worldwide search for new technologies. The cost of R&D and the cost of establishing advanced manufacturing production lines are very high. In order to meet these costs, companies need to be assured of easy access to large markets and command over immense resources. The companies, therefore, find favorable conditions in regional arrangements. Modern regionalism in this sense becomes an inescapable development.

In the second phase, the groupings have been a mixture of developed and developing countries (e.g. Mexico in NAFTA, and in Asia Pacific Cooperation – APEC – too). It is not just South-South cooperation but linking the developed and developing and thus north –South co-operation too. Member countries themselves are carrying out unilateral liberalisation of their economies (as seen in SAPTA); these arrangements have a clear outward looking orientation (unlike LAFTA in the first phase, as observed above) and are not following policy of import substitution but of export orientated industrialization.; the countries are looking for faster growth in international trade and increase in Foreign Direct Investment(FDI); the members of the regional groupings do not owe their allegiance to one grouping only in a watertight arrangement, rather, they are part of more than one grouping at a time, as seen in the case of the USA which has formed a free trade area with Israel, is part of NAFTA along with Canada and Mexico, and a member of APEC as well. Integration under old regionalism was shallow in the sense that only reduction in tariffs were focused, but new regionalism aims at much deeper integration breaking down all barriers within the region and look upon it as a tool of integration into world economy. (Eden 2003)

3.3. Sub Regionalism

Another important outcome of the phase of new regionalism has been sub-regionalism. They are considered as less formal arrangements. The Greater Mekong Sub-region (GMS) program falls under this category. It is a case of market, as opposed to institutional integration. In this the member countries rely on non-official institutions that provide public and quasi-public goods that reduce transaction costs associated with international movement of goods, services and other production factors. On the other hand, institutional integration is characterized by legal arrangements that promote preferential trade among members. Thus, the GMS program devised economic corridors where in a network of roads were built to connect the region and reduce costs of transporting goods and people. Further these corridors also focused on interconnections for power transmission and telecommunication links. Thus, the belief that the role that transport and communication infrastructure play for economic integration should not be under-estimated. While these referred to as hard issues, GMS program later also looked into simplifying customs procedures, transparency in customs clearance, promoting tourism, single visa system etc. All these referred to as soft issues. Studies show that this process helped in regionalism as a whole. (Menno)

Sec. IV. Evolution of BIMSTEC

The discussion in the first two sections have clearly brought out that regional groupings are not a new phenomenon. The factors, which influenced their formation, differed in the first and second phases. The formation of a regional grouping is just the beginning and their success and failure depend upon many political and economic factors. More groupings have failed than succeeded. Many have found success overtime after going through a long period of stagnation. BIMSTEC should be understood and evaluated in this background. As a late starter, it has the benefit of learning from the experiences of the other groupings.

BIMSTEC was formed in June 1997. It was then known as the Bangladesh-India-Sri Lanka –Thailand Economic Cooperation (BIST-EC). (Refer Appendix 1 for the Declaration) The declaration clearly spells out the need to establish a firm foundation for common action to promote 'sub –regional cooperation' in the areas of trade, investment, technological exchange. It calls for specific co-operation projects at the sub-regional level. In 1997 Myanmar was admitted and the grouping renamed as Bangladesh-India-Myanmar-Sri Lanka Thailand Economic Cooperation (BIMSTEC). In February 2004 Nepal and Bhutan joined the grouping. In July 2004, the first summit meeting took place and the grouping was renamed as the Bay of Bengal Initiative for Multi-sectoral Technical and Economic co-operation (BIMSTEC).

The formation of BIMSTEC should be seen in the background of the factors characterizing new regionalism. The countries are desirous of expanding their international trade, focusing on export oriented liberalisation, attracting FDI, are liberalizing their own economies, looking at new technologies – all leading to economic development. Forming regional groups and being part of such groups is an important economic policy they are adopting. On the political factors, countries like Nepal, Bangladesh and Sri Lanka have always looked for extra regional linkages in order to reduce their dependence on India economically and reduce India's influence on them. In the South Asian Association for Regional Cooperation (SAARC) where all of them are members, the overwhelming presence of India is felt. Through groupings like the BIMSTEC they hope to dilute the Indian presence to some extent. Further, the BIMSTEC provides means to establish and deepen links with ASEAN. For India, the BIMSTEC provides another opportunity to deepen its Look East Policy. As for Myanmar and Thailand, through the BIMSTEC they hoped to tap the unsaturated markets of South Asia in general and India especially. A mix of political and economic factors motivated the member countries to join the grouping. In this there are five of the seven SAARC members. (except Pakistan and Maldives) and the other two i.e., Thailand and Myanmar are members of ASEAN (Association of South East Asian Nations).

A brief study of the functioning of the BIMSTEC and its various activities brings out two phases in its evolution. While initially the focus was on primarily economic areas, in the second phase this agenda has expanded to include the social issues too. The second phase also coincides with upgrading the interaction among the member countries to the summit level with the holding of the first summit in July 2004. It needs to be mentioned that the economic and the social are not two watertight areas and both influence each other and are meaningless without the other for development. However, groups and organizations identify certain issues and areas to focus on and co-operate and move ahead step by step.

4.1. First Phase - Focus on Economic Issues

The organization was established in 1997 and the member countries decided to co-operate in six areas with each of the member countries playing a lead role in planning and implementing programs in their specific areas. The six areas are: Trade and Investment, Technology, Transportation & Communication, Energy, Tourism, Fisheries. These six sectors have been further divided into sub sectors with each sub sector having a chair country responsible for co-ordinating activities of that sub sector reporting to the lead country. (Refer Appendix II for the Joint Statement of the BIMST-EC Ministerial Meeting December 1997). The members also indicated to discuss issues relating to promote intra regional cooperation on elimination of non-tariff barriers, market access issues, services and preferential trading arrangements among them. The grouping committed itself to the principle of open regionalism and enhanced south-south co-operation. With this as the sub structure for the programme of co-operation, the BIMSTEC attempted to build on them, deepen and expand the areas of co-operation and implement the decisions arrived at.

In 1998, the BIMST-EC Business Forum was formed. The aim was to enhance private sector co-operation among member countries in the identified sectors and sub-sectors. In 1999, the BIMST-EC Economic Forum was established with representative groups of both the public and private sectors to discuss matters pertaining to achieving the objectives of the group and make recommendations to be taken up at the ministerial meetings each year. In November 2003, the BIMSTEC- CCI (Chamber of Commerce and Industry) was launched to sustain regular interaction between the business communities. Thus, thereby institutionalizing the private and public synergy process.

The member countries also offered training scholarships in technical areas to emphasize on human resource development. As early as 2001, the member countries decided that year to be 'Visit Tourism Year' for the region, but it got implemented after being postponed time and again on 2004 only.

The various meetings in the six core areas and their sub-sectors in the first phase have taken place at the ministerial level and senior officials only. The visibility had not risen above that till 2004, when the first summit was held. These meetings have brought out reports spelling out projects, which could be undertaken leading to greater development of the region. However progress has been very slow. Areas have been identified and studies either carried out or commissioned, but on the ground no progress has been made.

4.2. Second Phase - Expansion to Social Issues

While economic issues continue to occupy prime space, the agenda has expanded to include issues of social concern too, thereby providing a holistic approach to development. This is a necessity because any country cannot isolate these very important social issues from economic growth. For example tourism, one of the six core areas gets affected with terrorism. In that sense, it is a positive step, but then the economic agenda should not be diluted with the broadening of the areas of concern. The grouping has entered the second phase and the first summit held in 2004 clearly signals this. Thus, there has been a clear upgradation of relations to the highest level to provide the necessary momentum. It was at this summit that the grouping was rechristened as Bay of Bengal Initiative for Multisectoral Technical and Economic Co-operation. It also marks a period, where serious critical rethinking is being done regarding the performance of the grouping.

People to people contact has thus, taken a priority so that a sense of one identity emerges thereby giving momentum to the grouping from below. (Refer appendix III for the BIMSTEC Summit Declaration, Bangkok July 31, 2004). It has been proposed that this should take the form of exchange programme of student and faculty, parliamentarians, media persons, sports persons and artists in performing arts. They also called for broadcasting the BIMSTEC member country television programmes, holding film festivals, art exhibitions and other mass media productions. The July Summit committed itself to expand into the areas of culture, education, public health, protection of biodiversity and traditional knowledge, rural community development, small and medium scale enterprises, construction, environment, information and communications technology, biotechnology, weather &and climate research, natural disaster mitigation and management. Co-operation was emphasized in the areas of public health for combating threats like malaria, tuberculoses and polio and also HIV/AIDS. More significantly, the member countries talked of the grave concern at the continuing threat of international terrorism and transnational crime that has affected the economic and social progress of the people of the region. The second phase of BIMSTEC also is marked by member countries calling for customs expert group for facilitation of intra–regional trade, need for more institutionalized banking arrangements and taking measures relating to trade facilitation. They have also concluded the Framework Agreement for BIMSTEC Free Trade Area and a detailed schedule has also been prepared on this count including the submission of negative lists by the agreed parties. The BIMSTEC FTA is set to be implemented by July1, 2006. However, some issues like the rules of origin criteria need to be agreed upon while that on mechanism for settlement of disputes has been agreed upon.

4.3. Assessment

4.3.1. Identity - Subregionalsim and Regionalism BIMSTEC began as a sub-regional grouping both in terms of the agenda, as observed in GMS and the member countries belonging to two sub-regions that is South Asia and Southeast Asia. Like the GMS, hardware issues were identified to begin with The six sub-sectors clearly point out to this and the aim was also to implement co-operative projects in the fields of investment and infrastructure. Slowly moved to softer issues without any progress on the hardware issues and expanded the agenda. Thus, the identity of sub regional grouping in terms of agenda no longer there, though that of a sub regional grouping in terms of member countries continues. Its agenda is now that of or similar to any other regional grouping. The structures are not informal or market oriented but legal and institutional. The problems and challenges too would be similar to that of any other regional grouping.

4.3.2. Absence of a Secretariat and Financing Mechanism Though BIMSTEC began with a limited specific agenda of six areas, it is seen that no progress has not been made. This is reflected in the observation of the member country, Thailand that high potential projects agreed upon mere not implemented. Thus, apprehensions were expressed that the organization risks becoming irrelevant, despite high potential as well as high expectations from outsiders. The absence of a secretariat was spelt as one of the reasons. There has been a view within the group that the grouping should first become mature and then have a secretariat. The other view questions as to how the grouping can become mature without a secretariat. The issue seems to have been resolved for the time being in the observation in the summit declaration that once a clear focused programme of co-operation is in place, appropriate formal institutional mechanisms would be established jointly and within each country for effective co-ordination and implementation. It needs to be noted that SAARC has a secretariat in Kathmandu, Nepal, but that has not helped matters in a major way. Member countries have also referred to the lack of funding mechanism to implement the various projects for otherwise even the best of the ideas are meaningless. Focus on funding the infrastructure projects would really give life to the grouping. The origins GMS program can be traced to the late 1950s but it was only in the early 1990s that it was revived with details of funding mechanism.

4.3.3.Need for a Proper Agenda and its Implementation The successes that were spelt out after seven years into co-operation at the summit meet in 2004 are regarding the launch of BIMSTEC tourism year 2004-05; the launch of BIMSTEC chambers of commerce; holding of the first BIMSTEC youth football tournament; establishment of BIMSTEC centre in Bangladesh and establishment of biomass gasifier plant in Myanmar. This is not much to speak off by any measure. There has to be clarity regarding the direction the group aims to take. The six sectors were identified, but nothing much happened and then the focus has shifted to the FTA. Experiences of other groupings have shown that without a proper infrastructure of roads, power and telecommunication integration is not effective. Further if bureaucrats and politicians see their narrow national interests and not the good of the region, then like some other groupings it too will make slow progress.

4.3.4. Political Commitment: Heart of a Regional Grouping: Just like the heart is important for a person to be alive, similarly political commitment is very essential without which nothing will work and can work. The grouping has to learn from the mistakes of the other groupings. No doubt BIMSTEC's relevance will continue to be there because it is a link between two regions - South and South East Asia and both want to improve links with the other. BIMSTEC should not be looked upon as just a link but an independent grouping having its own identity. However, if the grouping fails to move ahead as a group and the countries individually improve and stress on their bilateral relations and find success in it then forward movement will be difficult. Also important to stress that the member countries from South Asia together constitute the five out the seven members of SAARC. The other two being Pakistan and Myanmar. They bring with them the baggage of differences faced in SAARC and more specifically the negative feelings towards India. Unless this is overcome in co-operative projects involving one or more of them it will be difficult to move ahead. Political commitment is a serious issue of concern, which needs to be translated from words to deed. It needs to be noted that even within groupings in which there are no major differences it is not easy to balance national interests and the regions interests.

4.3.5. Non-Tariff Barriers: The non-tariff barriers have been a problem area even among the success groups like the European Union. The programme of the Single European Market was to remove the 300 odd fiscal, physical and technical barriers, which had divided the grouping into smaller markets rather than it being a single market. Free trade agreements need to specifically take care of them. It also needs to be observed that negative lists seem to include important goods, which are traded thus, reducing the FTA's effectiveness. This should be specifically avoided.

Sec. V. Conclusion

BIMSTEC has in it shades of both sub regionalism and regionalism. It has the advantages of learning from both the mistakes and success of the other groupings. Most significantly its member countries are themselves members of two significant groupings and bring with them rich experience of working in these groups. They know too well both the recipe of success and the route to failure. However, unless rationality prevails over other divisive issues and political commitment dominates, the grouping will become irrelevant. BIMSTEC should immediately focus on infrastructural projects – roads, power, and communication - which will facilitate the effective working of the FTA too. In addition, a clear focused agenda and identifying mechanisms to fund the projects are critical for BIMSTEC's working and success.

References

1. Ali M.El Agraa (1982), *International Trade*, London: MacMillan Ltd., pp. 160-161.
2. Diana Tussie (1991), *The Less Developing Countries and the World TradingSystem-A Challenge to the Gatt,* London: Francis Pinter, p.5. Also refer Richard Pompret (1991), *Unequal Trade: The Economics of Discriminatory Trade Policies,* Oxford: Basil Blackwell, p.178.
3. Commission of the European Communities (1993), *Europe in a Changing World: The External Relations of the European Community,* (Luxembourg), p.11.
4. Eden & Herman (2003), *The New Regionalsim in the Americas*, May 31, Texas A&M University
5. Jayant Menon (2000), "Building Blocks or Stumbling Blocks? Regional Cooperation Arrangements in Southeast Asia", ADB Discussion Paper No.41
6. Jagdish Bhagwati (1991), *The World Trading System At Risk*, Great Britain: Harvester Wheatshef, pp.72-75.
7. J. Schott, (ed., 1989), *Free Trade Areas and US Trade Policy*, Washington: Institute of International Economics
8. Mary E.Burfisher, (Economic Research Service, USDA), Sherman Robinson (IFPRI), Karen Thierfelder (US Naval Academy) (2003), The International Agricultural Trade Research Consortium (IATRC) Conference, Capri, Italy, June 23-26
9. Monika Halan (1993), "The World's Major Trade Blocs and Trading Nations" *Business Today,* January22, pp.26-27.
10. Manubhai Shah (1968), *Developing Countries and UNCTAD*, Bombay: Vora & Co. Publishers, p.48.
11. Padmaja Murthy (2000), *Managing Suspicions –Understanding India's Relations with Bangladesh, Bhutan, Nepal, Sri Lanka* (Knowledge World in association with IDSA, November, pp. 96-138.
12. Percy S.Mistry, *Regional Integration and Development: Panacea or Pitfalls?* RIS Occasional paper No.47, p.7.

13. Rajesh Mehta (1992), " Trading Blocs and the Developing Economies," *RIS Digest*, vol.9, n.3, September, p.87.
14. For details on exceptions to Article 1 of GATT, refer Sumitra Chisti (1991), *Restructuring of International Economic Relations*, New Delhi: Concept Publishers
15. Victoria Curzon (1974), *The Essentials of Economic Integration: Lessons of the EFTA Experience,* Great Britain: Macmillan, p.19.
16. William Miller. F (1992), "Regionalism and Globalism" Foreign *Trade Review*, Vol.24, n.4, January-March.
17. For details on the various activities of BIMSTEC, the various meetings held and the joint statements refer website: www.bimstec.org

8

Evolution of BIMSTEC: Towards A Bay of Bengal Economic Community

P. Leela

Sec. I. Introduction

The post-Second World War period witnessed a growing desire among the Nation States for cooperation and integration at different levels, due to the realisation of increased importance of regional cooperation (Rahman 1988). Several studies indicated from time to time the advantages associated with regional cooperation. Regional economic cooperation can help in the optimum utilisation of capabilities available in the member countries and can open up avenues of industrialisation by deploying the technical know-how of one member State in another. Regional economic integration can help in generating growth impulses from within (Kumar 2005). Regional preferential arrangements between countries geographically close to one another can constitute the building blocks of a global free trade regime (Waqif 1997). Regional cooperation has immense potential of success, if implemented in the economic field for the commercial exploitation of indigenous productive resources and turning them into internationally tradable commodities (Jain 1973). Similarities in the stages of development, endowments and commonness of concerns are the important factors, which make cooperation advantageous beyond the sub-regional level. However, in the areas of cooperation and the strategies required to implement the cooperation, schemes will have to be different for inter-regional cooperation from those relevant for intra-regional cooperation (Panchamukhi 1988).

Against this background, the object of the present paper is to analyse the evolution and progress of economic cooperation in the three regional groupings of SAARC, ASEAN and BIMSTEC and to examine the prospects and potential of trade generation in the context of a Bay of Bengal Economic Community.

Sec. II. Comparative Trade Analysis of SAARC and ASEAN :

The formation of South Asian Association for Regional Cooperation (SAARC) two decades ago in 1985 reflects an increasing awareness in the Member States of SAARC that a coordinated strategy of development can indeed help in realising the potential complementarities for the benefit of all. The formation of ASEAN earlier in 1967 gave a fillip to the hastening of the formation of SAARC. Intra-regional trade expansion has in fact gained importance since the establishment of E.E.C in 1957, which provided a model for regional economic cooperation both among the developed and the developing countries of the World (Wadhva 1988).

The seven SAARC member countries are Bangladesh, Bhutan, India, Maldives, Nepal, Pakistan and Sri Lanka. The SAARC Charter mentions that among the objectives of the Association shall be acceleration of economic growth, promotion of active collaboration in the economic, social, cultural, technical and scientific fields and cooperation in international forums on matters of common interest (SAARC 1991). The countries of the SAARC region belong to a low per capita income group and are primarily agricultural in nature.

Foreign trade gained in importance in the cooperation of the SAARC region, with the SAARC moving from its initial Integrated Programmed of Action (IPA) to the formation of South Asian Preferential Trading Agreement (SAPTA) and further to SAFTA, which came into effect from January 1, 2006. India being the largest member country in terms of size of population and geographical area in the SAARC region, much is expected from India's trade with other member countries of the SAARC region.

Trends in India's exports to the SAARC region in the second decade after the formation of SAARC, shown in Table 1, indicate that India's exports to the SAARC region increased from $ 1722.7 million in 1995-96 to $ 4309.1 million in 2004-05, while India's imports from the SAARC region increased from $ 256.8 million to $ 907.1 million. India has a trade surplus with the SAARC region.

Table - 1

Trends in India's Trade with Regional Groupings

(U.S $ Million)

	SAARC		*ASEAN*	
	Exports	*Imports*	*Exports*	*Imports*
1995-1996	1722.7	256.8	2710.0	2688.1
1996-1997	1703.1	241.8	2857.7	2912.2
1997-1998	1612.9	234.6	2421.8	3382.3
1998-1999	1678.8	465.5	1629.5	4318.8
1999-2000	1396.1	398.1	2235.0	5090.9
2000-2001	1858.1	435.1	2888.0	4064.9
2001-2002	2032.9	573.5	3468.8	4402.2
2002-2003	2731.2	513.3	4630.5	5163.5
2003-2004	4159.1	670.6	5837.2	7452.8
2004-2005	4309.1	907.1	8009.4	8824.2

Source: CMIE (2002 & 2005), *Foreign Trade and Balance of Payments*, Mumbai.

Trends in India's trade with ASEAN, as shown in table 1, indicate that India's exports to ASEAN increased from $ 2710 million in 1995-96 to $ 8009.4 million in 2004-05, while India's imports from ASEAN increased from $ 2688 million to $ 8824.2 million. India has a trade deficit with ASEAN.

Thus, it is found that India's total trade with SAARC at $ 5216.12 million is about one-third of India's total trade with ASEAN at $ 16,833.6 million in 2005. India imports more from ASEAN than from SAARC. Trade with SAARC accounts for about three per cent of India's total trade, while ASEAN accounts for about nine per cent of the total trade of India (GOI 2003-04). Growth of India's trade with ASEAN is greater than that with SAARC.

The intra-regional trade of SAARC, as shown in table 2 increased from $ 601 million in 1985 to $ 2024 million in 1995 and further to $ 4773 million in 2003. During this period, intra-regional trade of ASEAN increased from $ 14,343 million to $ 104,872 million. Thus, the intra-regional trade of ASEAN is a little over 20 times greater than the intra-regional trade of SAARC. The relative share of SAARC in world exports increased from 0.7 per cent in 1985 to only 1.1 per cent in 2003, while the relative share of ASEAN in world exports increased from 3.9 per cent to 6.1 per cent during the same period.

The slow growth of SAARC has led to the recognition of the scope and potential of a sub-regional grouping among the countries of the SAARC and the ASEAN leading to the concept of BIMSTEC, as a bridge between SAARC and ASEAN.

Sec. III. Progress of BIMSTEC

BIMSTEC, as a sub-regional grouping, was originally formed in 1997 covering geographically contiguous countries on the rim of Bay of Bengal. These included: Bangladesh, India, Myanmar, Sri Lanka and Thailand. BIMSTEC received a major impetus in the year 2004 from three important developments namely, (i) the signing of a Framework Agreement for a BIMSTEC Free Trade Area (FTA) in February 2004; (ii) the expansion of the Group with the entry of Bhutan and Nepal as member countries; and (iii) the first BIMSTEC Summit meeting held in July 2004 in Phuket, Bangkok at which BIMSTEC has been renamed as Bay of Bengal Initiative for Multi-Sectoral Technical and Economic Cooperation.

There are six priority areas of cooperation identified for BIMSTEC. These include:

- Trade and investment (led by Bangladesh)
- Technology (led by Sri Lanka)
- Energy (led by Myanmar)
- Transport and Communication (led by India)
- Tourism (led by India)
- Agriculture and fisheries (led by Thailand)

The lead country status for each country is for a period of three years.

The member countries of BIMSTEC, namely, Bangladesh, Bhutan, India, Myanmar, Nepal, Sri Lanka and Thailand are characterized by different levels of development and diverse natural endowments, giving rise to substantial scope for complementarities among these countries. The combined size of BIMSTEC economies is $ 750 billion with a population of 1.3 billion (Kumar 2004).

Table - 2

Trends in Intra-Regional Trade – Merchandise Exports

Year	*SAARC ($ Million)*	*Percentage of Total Bloc Exports*	*Percentage of World Exports*	*ASEAN ($ Million)*	*Percentage of Total Bloc Exports*	*Percentage of World Exports*
1985	601	4.5	0.7	14343	19.8	3.9
1990	863	3.2	0.8	28648	19.8	4.3
1995	2024	4.4	0.9	81911	25.4	6.4
1996	2147	4.3	0.9	86923	25.4	6.5
1997	2007	4.0	0.9	88770	25.0	6.5
1998	2466	4.8	0.9	72352	21.9	6.1
1999	2180	4.0	1.0	80415	22.4	6.3
2000	2593	4.1	1.0	101848	23.9	6.7
2001	2827	4.3	1.1	89478	23.2	6.3
2002	2998	4.2	1.1	95864	23.7	6.3
2003	4773	5.6	1.1	104872	23.0	6.1

Source: World Bank (2001), *World Economic Indicators*, Washington, D.C
World Bank (2005), *World Development Indicators*, Washington, D.C

Note: Exports within bloc are the sum of exports by members of a trade bloc to other members of the bloc. They are shown both in million $ as in col (2) and col (5) and as % of total exports by the bloc as in col (3) and col (6). Col (4) and col (7) show the share of the bloc's total exports in World exports.

"Trade blocs are groups of countries that have established special preferential arrangements governing trade between members" (World Bank 2001). The objective of BIMSTEC FTAAgreement is to strengthen and enhance economic, trade and investment cooperation (GOI, 2003-04). It proposes a fast track of liberalization between 2006 and 2011 and a normal track of liberalization between 2007 and 2017, depending on the level of development (Kumar 2004).

BIMSTEC /FTA /Agreement is a comprehensive Agreement, covering trade in goods as well as services and investments and provides a framework for liberalisation of trade in all these areas. The Bangkok Summit Declaration of 2004 emphasised on the steps to be taken for the timely completion of BIMSTEC FTA Agreement so that the full potential benefits of BIMSTEC trade and investment coordination programmes can be realized at the earliest.

Sec. IV. Future Directions

The signing of the BIMSTEC FTA Agreement has laid the foundation for the future road map of BIMSTEC as a sub-regional grouping involving deeper economic integration and the speedy expedition of economic reforms. This has led to a shift in focus towards the formation of a Bay of Bengal Economic Community by the year 2020 (RIS 2004). Moving from BIMSTEC towards a Bay of Bengal Economic Community has the long run advantage of fully exploiting the potential of economic integration in the Bay of Bengal region. However, poor communication and transport facilities, lack of information regarding capabilities and resources across the countries are important stumbling blocks, along with tariff and non-tariff barriers to the evolution of a Bay of Bengal Economic Community.

Hence, the successful promotion of mutually beneficial cooperation in the Bay of Bengal Region requires speedy development of transport and communication linkages, exchange of information relating to the supply capabilities, progress in science and technology and enhanced technical cooperation, simplification and coordination of customs procedures and formalities and above all the establishment of institutional support for hastening the utilization of enhanced opportunities for multilateral regional cooperation.

References

1. Government of India, (2003-04), *Economic Survey.*
2. Jain, O.P., (1973), *Regional Cooperation for Trade in Asia*, New Delhi: Commercial Publications Bureau.

3. Kumar, Nagesh (2004),"Towards a Bay of Bengal Community", *Financial Express*, February 11.
4. Kumar, Nagesh (2005), "A Broader Asian Community and a Possible Road Map", *Economic and Political Weekly*, September 3-9, Vol XL, No. 36.
5. Panchamukhi, V.R (1988), "Economic Cooperation between SAARC and ASEAN: Prospects and Problems", in Bhabani Sen Gupta (ed), *SAARC-ASEAN Prospects and Problems of Inter-Regional Cooperation*, South Asian Publishers, New Delhi.
6. Rahman, A (1988), "Political Economy of Inter-Regional Cooperation: The SAARC and ASEAN Experience" in Bhabani Sen Gupta (ed). *Ibid.*
7. Research and Information System for the Developing Countries (2004), *Future Directions of BIMSTEC: Towards a Bay of Bengal Economic Community*, New Delhi.
8. SAARC Secretariat (1991), *SAARC Study on Trade, Manufactures and Services*, Kathmandu.
9. Wadhva, Charan D (1988), "Possibilities of Trade Generating Joint Ventures among Countries of SAARC and ASEAN", in Bhabani Sen Gupta (ed),*Op.cit*.
10. Waqif, Arif A (1997), *Cooperative Development of Transport and Communications Sectors in South Asia*, Delhi: Macmillan India Ltd.

9

Possibilities of Cooperation in BIMSTEC Countries

K. Sreerama Murty, K. Sailaja and R. Radha

Sec. I. Introduction

Economic cooperation between developing countries, though gained widespread acceptance as an idea, has not been translated into action for a long period. The Brandt Commission has observed that regional and sub-regional economic integration is an important means for economic cooperation between developing countries (ECDC). However, the turbulent seventies, the uncertain Eighties and the dynamic nineties have affected the world nations - big and small, rich and poor - by throwing up challenges and creating opportunities.

The developing countries being largely dependent upon the developed countries as markets for their exports are faced with uncertain growth prospects (in their export earnings). Further, in the context of structural rigidities in the international division of labour and inadequate support from the developed countries, the developing countries have to initiate, measures of cooperation among themselves. In this context, regional schemes such as Andean Group, The Association of South East Asian Nations (ASEAN) and the South Asian Association for Regional Cooperation (SAARC) were launched for the economic cooperation of developing countries. BIMSTEC is the latest initiative for large-scale regional cooperation among the nations of Bay of Bengal region. It is argued that this sub-regional integration would lead to free trade and establishment of preferential trading arrangements contribute to specialization and economies of scale, which in turn result in rapid economic development. This form of cooperation is particularly useful for countries with small domestic markets, which cannot in isolation sustain efficient industrialization over a wide spectrum of activities. Thus, sub-regional cooperation has a vast scope for development. However, in order to achieve concrete results, it is important to identify the areas where such co-operation is feasible and mutually beneficial to the member countries. Hence an attempt is made in this paper to examine the structure of output, merchandise trade and the performance of BIMSTEC nations in terms of poverty eradication and better quality of life.

Sec. II. BIMSTEC - Structure of Output

Data relating to the structure of output in BIMSTEC countries are presented in table 1. The available data shows that all the BIMSTEC countries except Nepal are experiencing a decent average annual growth in GDP. Among the group, India accounts for the highest GDP of 691.9 billion dollars in 2004 with an annual growth rate of 6.2 percent followed by Thailand and to some extent by Bangladesh. In terms of average annual growth rate also, the same trend is observed. However, the dis-aggregate analysis of the structure of output shows variations in the contributions of agriculture, industry and services to the GDP. In all the countries with the exception of Nepal, service's sector contribution to GDP is found to be highest among all the sectors. Sri Lanka recorded the highest contribution of services value added to the GDP followed by Bangladesh and India. With regard to the contribution of industry to the countries' GDP, Thailand has highest proportion of value added followed by Bangladesh and India. However in terms of the contribution of agriculture sector to gross domestic product, Nepal with 40 percent of its GDP coming from agriculture heads the list. India and Bangladesh recorded above one-fifth in this sector. Thus, the analysis of the structure of output in BIMSTEC countries shows that services sector is predominant in Sri Lanka, Bangladesh and India.

The manufacturing sector is playing a significant role in Thailand. This is the case with Bangladesh and India to some extent. It is pertinent to note that agriculture is the main stay for Nepal followed by India and Bangladesh.

Table – 1

Structure of Output in BIMSTEC Nations

Country	*Gross Domestic Product (in millions of $) 2004*	*Value added as % of GDP 2004*			*Average annual growth rate (%) 2000-2004*
		Agriculture	Industry	Services	
Bangladesh	56,844	21	27	53	5.1
Bhutan	-	-	-	-	-
India	691,876	22	26	52	6.2
Myanmar	-	-	-	-	-
Nepal	6,707	40	23	37	2.6
Srilanka	20,055	17	25	58	3.8
Thailand	163,491	10	44	46	5.3

Source: World Bank (2006), *World Development Report*, New York: Oxford University Press.

Sec. III. The Merchandise Trade in BIMSTEC Countries

In order to identify the items of potential export and potential import, it would be useful to know the export-import component of the manufactured good in the BIMSTEC countries. The data relating to the merchandise trade are presented in table 2. From the data, it may be observed that among the BIMSTEC group excluding Bhutan and Myanmar for which data is not available, Thailand has the highest amount of merchandise exports as well as imports, followed by India, while Nepal registered the low volume in both. Bangladesh recorded a moderate size of exports and imports, however the proportion of manufacturing exports in the total merchandise exports is found to be significantly high in this country. This share is above three-fourths in India and nearly to that size in Thailand and Sri Lanka. From this, it is clear that both Thailand and India can give lead in merchandise trade among the BIMSTEC countries. Both Srilanka and Bangladesh are also emerging as important exporters of manufactured goods in the BIMSTEC region.

Table – 2

Merchandise Trade in BIMSTEC Countries
(in millions $)

Country	*Exports 2004*	*Imports 2004*	*Manufactured exports (%)of total merchandise exports 2003*
Bangladesh	8,150	12,100	89
Bhutan	-	-	-
India	72,530	95,156	77
Myanmar	-	-	-
Nepal	756	1,877	-
Srilanka	5,800	7,950	74
Thailand	97,701	95,384	75

Source: As in table-1.

3.1. Performance of BIMSTEC Countries in terms of Millennium Development Goals

In the development process of any country, human resources play a very crucial role. As such as understanding of the performance of BIMSTEC countries with respect to millennium development goals would help us to evolve a strategy involving human resources in the economic co-operation of these nations. Hence, an attempt is made to analyze the performance of the BIMSTEC countries in terms of eradicating poverty and improving the quality of life of the people in these countries. Data relating to these aspects are presented in table 3. From the table, it may be observed that the percentage of people with less than a $ a day are found to be highest in Nepal followed by Bangladesh and India, while it is the lowest in Sri Lanka and Thailand. With regard to the universal primary education, it may be observed that the percentage of children with primary education completion rate in 2003-04 is abnormal in Sri Lanka with more than a cent followed by Thailand and India. The data shows that child mortality rate per thousand is found to be highest in India and Nepal in the year 2003. In maternal mortality rate to Nepal and India have the highest rates. Thailand and Sri Lanka showed a better picture in the above two rates. With regard to the prevalence of HIV/AIDS, it is observed that Thailand has the highest percentage of population in the age group of 15 to 49 followed by India. From the above analysis, it may be concluded that poverty, child mortality and maternal mortality are significantly high in Nepal, Bangladesh and India. On the other hand, Thailand and Srilanka are better placed in terms of poverty eradication and better quality of life.

Sec. IV. Conclusion

In order to achieve high level of economic cooperation among the BIMSTEC countries, it is very important to understand and appreciate the structures of individual economies and identify the potential areas of trade and economic cooperation. In view of the vide prevalence of poverty and high mortality rates, efforts are to be made to improve the quality of life in the BIMSTEC countries. This enables the region to achieve rapid economic progress and cooperation. Further, the regional economic co-operation can be speeded up with the establishment of regional payments union for the BIMSTEC countries.

Selected Bibliography

1. Dominic Salvatore, *International Economics*.
2. Jacob Viner, *International trade and Economic Development*.
3. Jha.L.K.(1982); 'South Asian Regional Cooperation: A proposal for a Payment-Union' in K. Satya Murthy (ed.), *South Asian Regional Co-operation*, Institute of Asian Studies, Hyderabad.
4. World Bank (2001), *Global Economic Prospects*.
5. World Bank (2006), *World Development Report*.

10

Development of BIMST-EC: Nature, Direction,Challenges and Issues

B.C. Upreti

The post-Cold War World Order characterized by globalization and liberalization opened new opportunities for regional and sub-regional cooperation in different parts of the world. Regionalism as an instrument to build synergies had started taking roots nearly two decades ago and globalization, liberalization and expansion of multi-national corporation have unsealed avenues for regional and sub-regional economic integration. It is widely accepted that geo-economics has taken precedence over geo-political issues. The Third World countries have been in search of economic dynamism that would provide sustenance, stability and growth to their economies in the context of the changing world scenario. In this process, the need for integrating national economies has been acknowledged everywhere. Hence, sub-regional approach is getting prominence. This paper endeavors to examine the nature and growth of BIMST-EC as a sub-regional grouping.

Sec. I. Sub-Regional Cooperation - Some Conceptual References

Sub-regionalism is a new and innovative phenomenon, gaining prominence particularly in the past few decades. Just like regionalism and inter-regional cooperation, sub-regionalism is also considered to be a strategy for development in a particular geographical area. There are three pre-requisites for sub-regional cooperation: geographical proximity; economic commonalities in terms of natural resources, problems of development, etc.; and a sense of unanimity, willingness and urgency in promoting development and prosperity. Since the very idea of sub-regional grouping involves a common concern of the countries of a sub-region on certain economic issues affecting them, it ensures congenial bilateral relations between them. Hence, a sub-regional approach is not only an instrument to promote development, but it may also promote peace and stability in the region. And in this context, it may also be helpful in conflict resolution and confidence building.

The sub-regional cooperation seeks to build a cooperative framework, which aims at transforming efforts and benefits of economic development from nation states to a larger entity, namely a sub-region (Hansen 1967). Sub-regionalism is an approach towards interdependent development that seeks to replace national developmental efforts into inter-regional or sub-regional cooperation leading to collective benefits. It may be defined as a "controlled regional development strategy, a response to borderless economy as it is a means of enhancing competitiveness of the participating growth areas and promoting their exports in the global market place" (Kalam 2000).

It may also be treated as a localized version of regionalism, which tends to develop smaller growth oriented zones within a broader region. In a more simplistic way, it can be said that forming a regional grouping of the concerned countries can adequately attain where objectives of an action plan cannot be sufficiently achieved by the countries of a region by acting individually, these objectives. But there has to be sufficient scope and willingness to form such a group (Bhargava 1995). A sub-region can also be understood in terms of a production bloc within which free flow of goods, services and technology is possible. A similar idea is Growth Triangle that calls for trade and investment within a compact region.

There are three issues related to sub-regional approach at theoretical level:

(1) In certain academic circles, the concept of sub-region has not been welcomed on the ground that it conveys the impression of sub-nationalism thereby pointing towards a narrow outlook (ICSAC 1998). But such an objection is misperceived and based on certain preconceived notions. If sub-regionalism sounds a narrow approach the same can also be applied to regionalism. Actually sub-regional cooperation is a matter of convenience, needs and willingness. In a way it shows the widening of the concept of nation-state because a country has to agree to open its national economy to outsiders.

(2) Whether formation of sub-regional groups within a regional organization is possible or not is another important concern. When the question of the formation of a sub-regional group in the Eastern Himalayan block came up at the SAARC forum, (Upreti 1998) it was strongly opposed by Pakistan and Sri Lanka on the plea that such attempts could be detrimental to the idea of regional cooperation (Saxena 1997). But it may be made clear here that sub-regional approach does not clash with the existing regional or global organizations (Grover 1995). If these sub-groups are formed within the framework of regional organizations, they may provide strength to them. It may also be noted here that article XXIV of GATT that was incorporated in the charter of WTO permits formation of such groups. There are many examples of sub-regional groups within regional organization; for example, ASEAN has three sub-regional groups such as the *Mekong Delta Belt* and EU has Benelux.

(3) An equally important concern is whether a sub-regional organization should be confined to the regional framework or it can take roots beyond that? In this regard, it may be stated that there cannot be any definite criteria. It may be a part of a regional organization or acquire the form of an inter-regional cooperation. In this context, it may provide a linkage between different regions. Sub-regionalism cannot be a stumbling block to multilateral approach.

It can be said that sub-regionalism is a means of economic cooperation and coordination among physically proximate countries. It is being widely accepted as a strategy of development. The sub-regional approach can be effective in exploiting regional economic complementarities. Such an approach may also be helpful in enhancing regional peace and stability. It can also be helpful in restraining extra-regional influences and interventions to a certain extent (Murthy 1995).

Sec. II. Formation and Growth of BIMST-EC

BIMST-EC is a relatively young organization among the various regional and sub-regional groupings. The willingness of the countries of two regions of Asia to follow a sub-regional approach for the mutually beneficial development underline the vast prospects of beneficial multilateral cooperation in the Bay of Bengal (Rao 2001).

The idea of forming a sub-regional grouping of the member countries of the Bay of Bengal community was mooted by Thailand. Thailand, a developed economy of the ASEAN region was looking for expanding its economic relations with the South Asian countries. Hence it mooted the idea of a Bay of Bengal Economic Cooperation Organization. The Deputy foreign minister of Thailand paid a visit to India in 1996 and discussed this idea with the Indian leaders. India agreed to enter into such a venture. It seems that there were two important considerations behind India's acceptance of the proposal. The South Asian Association for Regional Cooperation (SAARC) had not been able to register any significant achievement towards regional cooperation in the region. It was proving to be a slow organization and it was also becoming a victim of the political animosities among the member countries. Secondly, India had larger economic interest in the ASEAN region. India was already forging a policy of closer relations with the ASEAN countries since 1992 under the banner of its Look East policy (Das 1997). India had succeeded in entering to ASEAN Regional Forum (ARF). Its ultimate goal was to entire to ASEAN with member (Mohan 1998). So it was encouraged to join a sub-regional groups consisting of a powerful ASEAN country.

The deputy foreign minister of Thailand also visited other countries and pursued the proposal. On June 6, 1997 in a meeting in Bangkok it was decided to form an organization called BIST-EC of Bangladesh, India, Sri Lanka and Thailand. On December 22, 1997 first meeting of BIST-EC was held in which Myanmar, was also given membership. The organization was accordingly renamed as BIMST-EC. In the Bangkok conference, charter of the BIMST-EC was adopted which prescribed the objectives and areas of cooperation of BIMST-EC.

In the Dhaka ministerial conference held in December 1998 Nepal was also given the observer's status in BIMST-EC. In 2004 Nepal and Bhutan were accorded full membership of BIMST-EC. Thus, it has now seven members.

All of these countries have developing yet fast upcoming economies. Bangladesh is an agricultural country and 75 percent of the people are dependent on it. It is the foremost raw jute exporting country. Other important products are rice, sugarcane, tobacco, etc. India too is largely dependent on agriculture, but it has a broader industrial base in comparison to the other neighbors. It has vast opportunities to trade with the neighboring countries. Myanmar is a rich rice growing country. Two-third of its cultivated land grows rice. It is also rich in forest resources. Burma teak has been in high demand all over the world. Myanmar's trade is fully nationalized. Agriculture is the most important sector of Sri Lankan economy. Rubber, tea coffee, are its main products. It does not grow sufficient food grains for its domestic needs. Thailand too is an agricultural country (85 percent). Rice is its staple crop and is grown quite in surplus. It is indeed third largest producer of rice. It is also third largest rubber producing country. Thailand provides market for consumer goods, machinery and raw material of various types. Nepal and Bhutan have agriculture economies and they are yet to register any significant economic growth. However, these countries are rich in river water resources that have tremendous scope for hydropower generation.

It gives an idea that the economies of these countries have similar characteristics, hence can learn from each other's experiences; they have economic complementarities and provide sufficient scope and opportunities for intra-regional trade. As a regional formation, the BIMST-EC can serve the following purposes:

(1) The BIMST-EC provides a linkage between two regional organizations of the Indian Ocean, SAARC and ASEAN. It indeed opens new avenues of regional and sub-regional economic cooperation. As a Bangladesh daily commented, "What seems to be of positive consequence is that the BIMST policy making body has a plan to design its activities to form a bridge linking the SAARC and ASEAN".

(2) It helps in the joint exploitation of maritime resources, and in the development of regional transport system like the Asian Highway and railway networks.

(3) Cooperation at the sub-regional level will reduce extra-regional economic dependence and thus, serve the goal of South-South Cooperation.

It may also be noted here that the members of the BIMSTEC are situated along an important and convenient sea trade route. Hence, inter-regional trade is possible at a high rate. These countries have rich and broad-based natural resource base.

Sec. III. Structure of BIMSTEC

3.1. Objectives and Orientation

BIMST-EC has come into existence with a primary objective to promote a closer cooperation among its member countries in social and economic sectors. It aims at creating an environment for rapid economic development in the region. It has focused upon certain specific projects that have been core to the development of the region (The Hindu 1998). The BIMST-EC has emphasized the need to create conditions for peace, stability and prosperity in the region and it recognizes the need for a rapid and sustained economic development, in order to realize these motives.

The formation of BIMST-EC recognizes the imperative need that in an age of globalization and liberalization, there is a need to build strong regional economic ties, in order to enhance capabilities to face the onslaughts of globalization in a collective manner and also at the same time, to utilize and avail of the opportunities provided by the process of globalization and liberalization.

More specifically, the BIMST-EC has the following major objectives: (i) to accelerate pace of development in the region with a view to attain the twin objectives of economic growth and human development through multilateral efforts based on the principles of equality and partnership; (ii) to develop the available pool of resources in the region for mutual benefits and development; (iii) to exchange the scientific and technological knowledge with an objective to enhance the capabilities of the member countries; (iv) forging better linkages between the countries of the region that would facilitate mutual cooperation in diverse fields; (v) enhance trade and investment in the region and build appropriate infra-structural facilities for that purpose; and (vi) promote mutually beneficial linkages and correlation with the other similar organizations and institutions.

It is clear from the objectives of the BIMST-EC that this organization is basically economic in nature. As such, it has confined its self to issues related to economic growth and social development. It may also be pointed here that the orientation of the BIMSTEC is project-specific. The areas of cooperation are already specified and it seeks to forge cooperation among the member countries in those areas on a priority basis. There are sub-areas as well.

Yet another important aspect is that the BIMEST-EC as a sub-regional organization is State-specific. It means that a State as a whole is the member of this organization, not its parts. Actually a sub-region generally gives the impression that the regional cooperation may take place between some identical parts of the adjoining States which have some common issues or problems to be dealt with. But it is not the case with the BIMST-EC. Actually the third world countries are highly State centered and the various regions of a State normally do not enjoy freedom to act independently in external affairs of what ever nature they might be.

In the context of the emerging challenges of terrorism, peace and security, the BIMST-EC has also expressed its concern to contain terrorism and promote peace and stability in the region. These issues have come up in the BIMST-EC forums in the last few years.

3.1.1. Areas and Dimensions of Cooperation: The BIMST-EC initially identified 5 areas of cooperation within its framework with a member country being the convener of the project. There are as following:

Transport and communication	-	India
Trade and Investment	-	Bangladesh
Technology	-	India
Tourism	-	Sri Lanka
Energy	-	Myanmar
Fisheries	-	Thailand

It has been accepted that the inadequate infrastructure is a major obstacle to the development of vital sectors of the economy. In this regard, development of a transport network has been considered a primary requirement. The ASEAN highway project is an important aspect of the development of inter-State road linkages in the BIMST-EC region.

The BIMST-EC has given importance to intra-regional trade. It has been accepted that taking trade facilitation measures can enhance the regional trade. There is a need for adequate infrastructure and adequate trade policies. It may be noted that the BIMST-EC region holds nearly one-fifth of the total world population but its share in international trade is only 1.4 per cent.

Technology cooperation is an important dimension. These countries can learn from each other's experiences and share the available pool of technology particularly information technology, biotechnology, pharmaceutical and bio-informatics. There is vast scope of cooperation for the utilization of commercial and non-commercial energy resources in the BIMST-EC region. The BIMST-EC has emphasized upon both the development of energy infrastructure and the development of renewable energy resources. Similarly, fisheries have also been identified as a potential area of cooperation. The fisheries development can provide nutrition, employment and income. Nearly 10 per cent of world's total fish production takes place in the BIMST-EC region.

It is also possible to develop tourism as a vital industry in the BIMST-EC region. Tourism may contribute significantly to the socio-economic development of the countries of the region. It may be noted that top ten tourist destinations are located in the BIMST-EC region. Thailand ranks 20 among 140 countries, in terms of tourism attraction. There is also scope for intra-regional tourism.

Apart from these core areas BIMST-EC has also accorded importance to cooperation in other areas. Education, health, agriculture, disaster management, peace, security, etc are other such areas.

The following sub-sections of the BIMST-EC cooperation have been agreed upon:

Automotive industry and parts	-	Thailand
Banking arrangements	-	Thailand
Coconut and Spices	-	India
Drugs and Pharmaceuticals	-	India
Gems and Jewellery	-	Sri Lanka
Horticulture and Floricultural products	-	Thailand
Processed food	-	Sri Lanka
Rubber, Tea and Coffee	-	Thailand
Textile and Clothing	-	Bangladesh

It is thus, clear that the BIMST-EC has tried to expand the scope of its activities.

3.2. Institutional Mechanism and Dynamics

The institutional mechanism of the BIMST-EC has been operative through various meetings, and institutions. The functioning of the BIMST-EC has surrounded the following major activities: (web: bimstec.a).

1. Meetings of the Ministers - Foreign, Economic and Commerce and Trade
2. Senior Officials Meetings (SOM)
3. Meetings of Economic / Technical Officials
4. Meetings of the Group Experts
5. Business Forum Meetings
6. Summit Meeting

The first ministerial meeting of the BIMST-EC foreign ministers was held in Bangkok in June 1997 and a special meeting on December 22, 1997, which adopted the charter of this organization and laid down its procedural details.

The second ministerial meeting was held in Dhaka on December 19, 1998. It emphasized the development of a comprehensive transport network. It was also agreed to forge BIMST-EC relations with financial and developmental institutions like World Bank, ADB, UNDP, and ESCAP etc. Nepal was accorded the status of an observer in the BIMST-EC ministerial meetings. The meeting emphasized Asian solidarity and South-. South cooperation in order to meet the challenges of globalization and liberalization.

The third ministerial meeting took place in New Delhi on July 6, 2000. It stressed upon strengthening the institutional mechanism of BIMST-EC. It was also decided to facilitate trade and investment opportunities in the region and also to expedite cooperation in the areas of agriculture development and disaster management.

The fourth ministerial meeting was held in Yangoon on December 21, 2001. The issues of terrorism, territorial integrity and security also figured in the meeting apart from dwelling upon the core issues. The fifth ministerial meeting was held in Colombo in December 2002 and sixth in Phuket (Thailand) on February 8, 2004. Nepal and Bhutan were offered full membership of BIMST-EC. The forum reiterated its commitment to socio-economic development of the region. It also laid emphasis on the development of hydrocarbon and hydropower potential.

Apart from this, five rounds of meetings of the economic and trade ministers had taken place till February 2004. These meetings emphasized on taking up variety of issues such as transport and communication, trade, simplification of rules relating to entry visa procedures, issuing business, travel card, development of inland waterways etc.

The issues relating to socio-economic cooperation in the BIMST-EC regions have also been discussed in the seven round meetings of Senior Official Meetings (SOM), meetings of the expert groups, etc.

3.3. BIMST-EC Economic Forum

In the Dhaka meeting of SOM held on December 19-20, 1997, it was recommended to constitute an economic forum of BIMST-EC countries, which would provide a platform for a closer interaction between the public and private sector representatives of the BIMST-EC countries (web: bimsetc.b). The main objective of this forum has been to exchange views regarding effective implementation of various schemes of mutual cooperation. The economic forum provides representation to both public and private sectors. It was decided that each member country would send two to six members in the forum representing both the public and private sectors. Three meetings of the economic forum have taken place till now. In the third meeting on January 13, 2004 at Bangkok, it emphasized the need to review the existing sectors and sub-sectors of cooperation accepted within the BIMST-EC framework.

3.4. BIMST-EC Chamber of Commerce and Industry

The BIMST-EC countries have also formed its chamber of commerce and industry (web: bimstec.c). The collective self-reliance has been the primary motive of the chamber. In its meeting on November 30, 2003 encouragements to trade, industry, agriculture, industry, intra-regional tourism, etc. was emphasized. It was also agreed to organize trade fairs, joint display centers, exhibitions, publicity, joint research programmes, etc.

3.5. BIMST-EC Free Trade Area

The BIMST-EC countries have also agreed for Free Trade Area. In this regard a Framework Agreement on FTA was concluded on January 15, 2004. The objectives of FTA were laid down as to strengthen trade and investment and facilitate effective economic integration. The FTA emphasized upon (i) liberalization of trade; (ii) removal of discrimination in trade services; (iii) promotion and protection of investments; (iv) liberalization of investment regimes; (v) cooperation in identified sectors; (vi) capacity building programmes; and (vii)reduction of tariff and non-tariff barriers.

3.6. BIMST-EC Summit Conference:

The first summit meeting of the BIMST-EC was held on July 31, 2004 at Bangkok. Nepal and Bhutan attended the summit as its full flagged members. It was agreed that the BMIST-EC should be known as the Bay of Bengal initiative for Multi-Sectoral Technical and Economic Cooperation (web: bimstec.d). The summit endorsed formation of BIMST-EC chamber of Commerce and framework agreement for FTA. It was also agreed to establish a BIMST-EC centre in Bangkok. The issues that were discussed and agreed upon were human resource development; establishment of biomass gasifier plant at Myanmar; explore cooperation in education, health, protection of bio-diversity and traditional knowledge; and coordinate efforts to combat the menace of terrorism.

Sec. IV. Challenges and Issues

Any regional or sub-regional organization is a welcome development, as the very idea rests upon coordinate approach to development. It not only fosters development, but also opens up the avenues for building a congenial regional atmosphere. In this perspective, formation of BIMST-EC is a welcome development. What is more important is that BIMST-EC also provides a linkage between two regions of Asia, South Asia and South East Asia. Such an organization can also offer benefit to the countries of South Asia to learn and seek benefits from the ASEAN.

It is a fact that the BIMSTEC countries offer vast scope for cooperation in the field of trade, investment, hydropower generation, natural gas, etc. BIMSTEC has expanded in terms of size as well as activities and of which BIMST-EC Chamber of Commerce and Industry and framework agreement on FTA are significant developments. The BIMST-EC has also reached to summit level conference. But then it is also a fact that BIMST-EC has not been able to record any substantial progress in any sector of its activities, except for organizing meetings and expert group meetings.

The working of BIMST-EC so far shows that it is also a regional grouping not a growth axis model. The organization has been expanding its areas of activities instead of concentrating on few selected areas. The BIMST-EC began with six core areas that were well identified. But instead of concentrating upon these areas, it also fell in the same trap of meetings, conferences and then including more and more areas of cooperation within its framework.

The member countries of BIMST-EC vary much in terms of size, population, resources, socio-cultural milieu, political regimes, economic development and scientific and technology attainments. These asymmetries at times play an adverse role in forging a meaningful cooperation. The political tangles between the member countries further compounded the adverse implications.

Majority of the member countries of BIMST-EC belong to South Asian region, which have not been able to provide any significant breakthrough to their own organization- SAARC. What would prompt them to be more effective in the case of BIMST-EC is an important issue.

It is also significant to note that the BIMST-EC countries are at different levels of trade liberalization. ASEAN has achieved the target of free trade but SAARC is yet to implement SAFTA. In such a situation is it possible to gain any substantial progress towards intra-regional trade is also a significant issue.

To sum up, it can be said that the BIMST-EC is a significant development. But it has to be noted that it is a sub-regional grouping not a routine regional organization. Hence, it can attain its objectives only if specific target based approach is followed instead of adopting a populist approach.

References

1. Abul Kalam (2000), "Sub-regional Cooperation in South Asia in Comparative Perspective" in B.C. Upreti (ed.), *SAARC Dynamics of Regional Cooperation in South Asia*, Delhi: Kalinga Publishers, pp.109-132.
2. Bhargava, K.K. (1995), "Possibilities of Interaction with SAARC", *World Focus*, (Special Issues of Indian Ocean), vol. 16, No. 7, July 14.
3. Grover, V.K (1995), "Recharging Economic Cooperation," *World Focus*, Vol. 16, No. 7, July.
4. Gautam Murthy (1995), "Regional Cooperation for Peace in the Indian Ocean: An Assessment of ASEAN and SAARC" in Rama S. Melkote (ed.), *Indian Ocean: Issues for Peace*, New Delhi: Manohar Publishers, 183.
5. Parimal Kumar Das (1997), "India's Move Towards ASEAN," *World Focus*, vol. 18, June 6, 1997: 10-12 and B.C. Upreti (2003), "India's Relations with the ASEAN Countries: Building a New Partnership," in B.C. Upreti et. al. (eds.), *India's Foreign Policy*, Vol. II, Delhi: Kalinga Publishers, pp.321-330.
6. Raja Mohan, C. (1998), "India Gains from the ARF Meet", *The Hindu*, 29 July.
7. Rao, P.V (ed., 2001), *Regional Cooperation in Indian Ocean: Trends and Perspectives*, South Asian Publishers, New Delhi.
8. Roger D. Hansen (1967), "Regional Integration: Reflection on a Decade of Theoretical Efforts," World Politics, vol. no. 2, January, pp.242-247.
9. Shobhan Saxena (1997), "Block Within a Block" *The Times of India*, February 9, and P.S. Suryanarayan (1997), "India Moots SAARC as Economic Block," *The Hindu*, May 9.
10. *The Hindu* (1998), 8 July.
11. Upreti, B.C (1998), "Sub-regional Cooperation in South Asia: Perceptions, Potentials and Problems of Cooperation among the Countries of the Eastern Himalayan Region," paper presented at a

seminar on *India's Role in Regional Cooperation in South Asia*, ICSAC & IIC, December 11-12; also see B.C. Upreti (2001), *Uneasy Friends*, Delhi: Kalinga Publishers, pp.155-174.

12. For details web: www.bimstec.org/e_meetings.htm.
13. www.bimstec.org/docs/meetings/eco-forum/001.htm.
14. www.bimstec.org/docs/september/bimstec_chamber_of_ commerc/0.1 htm.
15. www.bimstec.org/docs/meetings/working group/ 006. htm.

11

Political and Foreign Policy Perspectives of BIMSTEC

M.Chandrasekha

G. Ravi Kumar Rao

Sec. I. Introduction

In general, the volatile political environment and the nuances of foreign policy of the member States of the BIMSTEC have become an impediment to the progress of the region. The overall welfare of the population of the region is very much dependent on the improvement of the political environment in the respective member states.

The Maoist problem in Nepal is closely related to the restoration of democracy in the Himalayan State and as such there is a mounting pressure on the King to restore democracy. As such, if the Maoists are brought into the mainstream of political decision-making, the extremism is expected to be minimized and hence the efforts of the nation can be directed towards nation building. Similarly in Sri Lanka, the political leadership should deal effectively with the Tamil militants and work towards regional autonomy for the Tamils so that the extremist violence by Tamil Tigers is significantly reduced. This calls for an approach to reconciliation with the Tamil Tigers in the larger interests of the Simhala people. For instance, the stand off between the King of Nepal and the Maoists has hampered the progress of Nepal. Similarly the ethnic problem in Sri Lanka has posed several challenges to the political administration in Sri Lanka that is threatening the very unity of the Republic.

Likewise, the border skirmishes between India and Myanmar and the problem of ethnic minority problems existing between Myanmar and Thailand are creating a lot of distrust between the neighboring nations, which has affected the long term progress of the nation. The problem between Myanmar and India could be viewed as one of lack of communication and by resolving to maintain greater interaction between the two sides; the problem of insurgency across the border can be greatly reduced. This calls for a great political will on both sides and a spirit of compromise on the part of both countries. Similarly, the ethnic problem across the Thai-Myanmar border could be resolved on the basis of a spirit of mutual cooperation and respect.

Therefore, it is necessary for the littoral states bordering the Bay of Bengal to bring certain radical changes in their foreign policy perspectives so as to improve the standard of living of their masses in their respective countries.

Today, with the advancement in technologies and changes in the peoples aspirations in different countries, democracy becomes the inevitable political choice. Hence, the countries bordering the Bay of Bengal have to yield to the aspirations of the citizens of their respective nations so that speedy development can be achieved through democratic means.

Accordingly, the foreign policy of all the concerned countries have to be modified in line with the peoples aspirations and thereby bring about the overall progress in the standard of living of the people in the region on democratic lines. The foreign policy of the different nations have to be fine tuned in such a way that compromise gives way to confrontation and accordingly the countries energies are directed toward betterment of their respective. In conclusion, it may be stated that if the littoral nations bordering the Bay of Bengal utilize their energies towards co-operation as opposed to confrontation, the region's progress would be phenomenal and the entire region could achieve miracles in progress. How exactly this could be done would be analysed in the bilateral and multilateral aspects of the foreign policy of the respective nations.

Sec. II. Perspectives of BIMSTEC Nations

It is the avowed duty of the leadership of most countries to work for the upliftment of their citizens. No doubt, there are certain areas of difference of opinion with the neighboring states that is causing hardships in achieving the aspirations of the masses. This calls for an environment of compromise and reconciliation with the neighborhood so that the overall interests of the citizens of the respective nations is served effectively.

It is true that there are certain irreconcilable factors between neighbouring countries that have become the bones of contention between the nations and thereby the overall objective of the achievement of national welfare is affected. However, keeping in view of the welfare of the citizens, the respective countries should work towards a formula of compromise so that the broader objective of citizen's welfare could be achieved.

How exactly this could be achieved is discussed in this paper. The point is that there should be a political will on both sides to resolve issues so that the standard living of the people as well as their quality of life is improved. In order to achieve the political aspirations of the people, most nations have preferred democratic means of governance as opposed to others forms of governance to meet the people's aspirations.

2.1. Thailand

The Thai – Myanmar border has always been a contentious issue between the two nations and has been a major source of ill will between the two nations. The present Government of Thailand is been on settling the border dispute so that their efforts could be focused on development.

2.2. Myanmar

Myanmar is a country, which is ruled by the Military Junta and as such is not considered a representative of the people's aspirations. It is to be noted that most nations that have progressed significantly on the economic front have been following the Democratic model of governance. However, it is quite possible for a military regime to satisfy its people's aspirations by looking at the problems objectively and take steps to resolve the outstanding issues in the spirit of co-operation and compromise.

It is true that Myanmar is facing a tribal influx from across the border from Thailand and this is causing a grave threat to the Myanmar administration. But then, the point is that both Thailand and Myanmar have to re-formulate their respective foreign policy objectives, so as to achieve a lasting peace across their borders, so that the efforts of both countries could be directed towards human welfare.

Regarding drugs trafficking, it may be stated that the problem is one of economic necessity and unless steps are taken by both the nations to improve the economic well being of both the nations, it is difficult to implement the laws against illicit drug trafficking.

The problem of cross border infiltration with India could be resolved through a meaningful dialogue with the Indian Government so that the Nagas could be brought into the mainstream of the Indian political system and thereby the resources that Myanmar spends on sponsoring Naga separatists in India could be canalized for the economic upliftment of the Myanmar people, so that the overall objective of improving the standards of living of the Myanmar people could be improved.

2.3. Bangladesh

Bangladesh, a littoral state of Bay of Bengal has several differences with India regarding the distribution of water during the drought period but it has also problems with India regarding the diversion of water during the period when there are floods in river Ganges.

These issues have to be resolved by means of mutual discussions and as such the method of resolution through the interlinking of the rivers is the main issue between the two nations. The Farakka Barrage problem is the main issue that needs resolution through peaceful means. The problem of refugee inflows from Bangladesh has been a major irritant in ensuring smooth relations between the two nations. It is to be sorted out through mutual discussions and accordingly the relations between the littoral country's neighbours have to be solved through meaningful negations and through goodwill between the two neighbors

Unfortunately, it is observed that the two neighbours are having difference between them due to the intervention of China in the bilateral relations between India and Bangladesh. Therefore, it is necessary that the bilateral problems between India and Bangladesh have to be solved through bilateral discussion and not by the means advocated by China, a third force. Therefore, unless the littoral countries of the Bay of Bengal do not develop a common platform to address their bilateral issues, it is difficult for them to achieve the overall objective of the emancipation of their masses and accordingly the national objectives of the respective countries.

2.4. Sri Lanka

The case of Sri Lanka involves the resolution of the dispute between the Tamil Rebels headed by V. Prabhakaran and the Sri Lanka government. It is a fact that the LTTE have been harping on a separate a Tamil State in Sri Lanka, independent of the Sri Lanka government, which has been proved a non-stator. The Sri Lankan governments have to work with India and other neighbours to arrive at a formula so that lasting peace with LTTE rebels would be achieved. It is quite a different matter that Sri Lanka has achieved a considerable progress on the economic front through its liberalization policies during the last couple of decades, as evidenced by their economic performance. However, economic progress without internal peace is not a very healthy phenomenon considering the fact that the recent gunning down of the Foreign Minister of Sri Lanka has put the peace process on the back burner. Hence, the Government of Sri Lanka has to take certain pro-active measures to ensure that peace returns to the embattled island sooner or later. To this end, the Government of Sri Lanka has to work towards a means of national reconciliation with the LTTE, so that the objective of overall Sri Lankan welfare is achieved.

2.5. Indo-Nepal Affairs

The Indo-Nepal affairs have received a sever blow, following the sacking of the democratically elected government in Nepal as the King proclaimed himself as the leader of the Republic, and further the Maoist activists have threatened the democratic fabric of the country. Nepal, which has been a rather peaceful constitutional monarchy with Prime Minister as the head of government has recently witnessed a situation whereby the democracy has been usurped by the monarchy. This has led the Maoists to spring into action for the restoration of Democracy in the Kingdom of Nepal. However, as their Monarchy is quite powerful, it is felt that the restoration of democracy is a rather distant reality and the Maoist insurgency in the Republic is likely to cause a greater problem in the restoration of democracy. The government has put the country in jeopardy. Therefore, it is imperative for the nation to come to terms with the democratic aspirations of is people and work towards national reconciliation.

Sec. III. The Economic Implications

Most of the countries in the world have realized that a speedy growth of their economies can be achieved only through integrating their respective economies with the global economy. In order to achieve this, the governments of different countries have to focus their energies on liberalization and economic reforms (as opposed to minor political issues), which is very vital for improving their citizens' standard of living. Most of these countries have adopted an outward looking economic polices during the 1990s that has resulted in faster economic growth and prosperity for its people.

In conclusion, it may be stated that unless the problems of the masses are addressed, lasting peace cannot be attained and hence the littoral states of the Bay of Bengal have to bear in mind this fact, so that the welfare of the people is achieved.

Selected Bibliography

Newsweek
Time
Economic and Political Weekly
India Today
Internet – Websites of the various countries

12.

Indo-Sri Lanka Maritime Co-operation: Implications on the Bay of Bengal

V. Srilatha

Sec. I. Introduction

The Bay of Bengal occupies an area of 2,172,000 sq. kms. washing the shores of Indonesia, Myanmar, Bangladesh, India and Sri Lanka. Bay of Bengal as a maritime region enjoys several geopolitical advantages as a compact water body enclosed from three sides. Major sea-lanes traverse through it either via Malacca Strait to Southeast Asia and the Far East or to Australia. Closely connected via the Andaman Sea to the strategically important Malacca Strait, the area also covers most of the Bay of Bengal, which is under maritime sovereignty or/and jurisdiction of various littoral states. Only a small area in the middle remains as the high seas as defined under Article 86 of the UNCLOS-III (Singh 2001a). The Bay of Bengal is of utmost importance to almost half of Asia for its security and the Arabian Sea for its importance of oil supplies to enhance global prosperity. India's security concerns in the Indian Ocean will be increasing in the coming years as India's dependence on the sea has increased in terms of trade, energy resources, shipping, sustainable exploitation of marine resources and ocean research and exploration. Unless there is constant vigilance to deter incursions, its transportation routes will be increasingly vulnerable to disruption and a range of criminal and clandestine activities. The continuing militarization of the Indian Ocean and the dynamic role of technology on naval warfare will have an impact on India's strategic interests and security interests.

At the same time, Sri Lanka faces two distinct but interrelated problems i.e. acts of piracy against foreign merchant vessels; and the question of maritime insurgency as represented by the activities of the Sea Tigers; the naval wing of the LTTE. These acts of piracy are also linked to the overall insurgency activities in the region (Singh 2000b) As there is bound to be spill over effect in India and effect Indian Security, this could facilitate maritime cooperation between the two countries. India Maritime Doctrine 2004 has clearly implied upon some of the important policy outlook as maritime interest of India deals with extended neighbourhood and the possible assertive role to be played by Indian Navy in the process. In the context of India's growing economic development and its dependence on the energy, it becomes imperative to safeguard its sea-lanes from external aggression the naval doctrine advocating induction of nuclear submarine into the Indian Navy, envisages a sea-based deterrent to inflict unacceptable damage and raise the cost of intervention on the adversary. It also calls for exercising sea control in designated areas of the Arabian Sea and the Bay of Bengal to safeguard the country's mercantile, marine, sea borne trade and also to protect its coastline, island territories and offshore assets (India's Maritime Doctrine 2004).

Sec. II. The Liberation Tigers of Tamil Elam (LTTE)

The emergence of Sea Tigers, a naval wing of LTTE formed in 1984 as a credible fighting force in India's maritime neighborhood, can be a maritime threat. It has to be understood from the changing maritime environment in the neighborhood, Sea Tigers' objectives and maritime terrorism in the Pak Bay. Sri Lankan and foreign intelligence agencies estimate the strength of the Sea Tigers at 2,000 to 3,000 cadres (Suryanarayan 2004). LTTE has been using the present shallow Palk Strait for its illegal activities and depends on it greatly for its logistics sustenance by the sea. Both India and Sri Lanka are interested in tackling the presence of a third "rogue" navy in the area, which is not in their security interests. As early as in 1997, the Maritime Intelligence and Counter Piracy Operations Center had described Sri Lankan waters as an "extremely dangerous area for maritime traffic" and as the fifth most afflicted in terms of piracy (The Hindu 2005). During the several of the LTTE offensive campaigns, the Sea Tigers have landed troops to outflank Sri Lankan Army (SLA) units. The first Black Sea Tiger attack was off Valvettiturai on July 10, 1990, the guerrillas badly damaged the Sri Lankan naval ship Edithara. On May 4, 1991, they sank the Sri Lankan command ship Abitha. The largest operation was the capture of Mullaitivu in 1996, the SLA lost over a thousand soldiers with all their equipment. During the battle for Elephant Pass in 2000, the Sea Tigers conducted a massive amphibious operation, landing 1,500 guerrillas undetected in the Jaffna coast with their weapons and the subsequent surrender of the Elephant Pass complex to the Tamil.

The Sea Tigers also use a number of large merchant vessels to smuggle equipment from the neighboring countries. Attack divers were used to sink at least one freighter at the Sri Lanka Naval (SLN) base at Kankesanturai - KKS, at the northern point of the Jaffna peninsula. Since 2003 the Tigers under the leadership of Prabhakaran has begun to articulate their 'rights' in the seas and demanding control over marine resources and the right of access and exploitation over them in the proposals for interim government. As part of offence the latest is the LTTE attack on the Karuna faction in the east in 2004. Currently the LTTE controls the northern part of Sri Lanka, except the Jaffna peninsula. As far as the Palk Bay is concerned, the Sea Tigers dominate the entire coastline except the Jaffna region. The Sea Tigers fast patrol boats and smaller suicide boats have engaged and sunk around 30 SLN fast patrolboats, attacked the main SLN naval base at Trincomalee and sunk one of two SLN catamarans used for troop transports. The offensive weapons are light fiberglass boats. The Sea Tiger's attack vessels are used on the sea during operations and training; and when idle they are loaded on large trailers and hidden in the dense jungle southwest of Mullaitivu, thus avoiding from being trapped.

The Sea Tigers bases are strategically located for attacks on these shipments, and forces the SLN to keep a significant force of fast attack patrol boats on alert. Sea Tigers have also been a hindrance as they seized the cargo of Sri Lankan freighters. The LTTE has hijacked several vessels and some of the reported cases relate to the hijacking of Irish Mona (August 1995), Princess Wave (August 1996), Athena (May 1997), Misen (July 1997), and the attack on m.v.Moranbong in July 1997 (Sakhuja 2005a). Attacks on naval vessels and crew intensified after 1997. In September 1997, the Cosco-owned 35,110 dwt m.v. cordiality was captured near Trincomalee and five of the Chinese crew was killed. The Sri Lankan Navy, in its offensive, allegedly killed 25 'rebels' in small craft. 28, and the cargo ship was also lost (Sakhuja 2005b). The next major attack was on m.v. Princess Kash, which was a Belize-flagged vessel and had an Indian crew. It was also hijacked and when taken towards the LTTE stronghold in Mullaitivu, the ship was bombed by the Sri Lankan Air Force to prevent its cargo from falling into the hands of the LTTE. The status of 22 crew members is still unknown. Another ship, m.v. Yu Via, from China, was intercepted by the LTTE, while it was enroute from Sri Lanka to Chennai. When the Sri Lankan Navy intervened, the vessel was towed to Trincomalee. The crew were reportedly safe (The Hindu 1999). In November 2002, a mystery ship reportedly controlled by the LTTE was spotted 100 nautical miles north east of Mullaitivu. It off loaded weapons into small boats before the crew noticed that they were being watched by Indian forces and began dumping items overboard. Sri Lankan naval forces intercepted a dingy with six-armed LTTE cadres and communications equipment (Verghese 2003).

In February 2003, three Tamil Tiger rebels blew themselves up after monitors boarded their heavily armed boat off the northern coast of Jaffna as they tried to smuggle arms to the island. The possible damage to life and property increased in the region, as the distinction between piracy and terrorism seems to be fast eroding. According to the US think tank, Center for Strategic and International Studies, the Sea Tigers have destroyed 30 to 50 per cent of the coastal craft of the Sri Lankan Navy (Venkatesh 2005a). According to 2003 proposal for an Interim Self Governing Authority (ISGA) in the Tamil-speaking north east there was a demand for complete control of the coast and access to it from the sea, though sea and fishing come under Central authority. LTTE's interest is gaining control over the Sri Lankan north eastern coastline and the sea-lanes off. Prof. Suryanarayan also points out that the LTTE has been keen on controlling the coastline of the "Tamil Homeland" in Sri Lanka, which means two thirds of the Sri Lankan coastline is under its control. This poses a great threat to Sri Lanka and India. According to the writer "India can ignore this dangerous development only at its own peril" (Venkatesh 2005b).

Sec. III. Indo -Sri Lanka Maritime Co-operartion

India-Sri Lanka co-operation to combat LTTE was codified in the much debated Indo-Sri Lanka Accord of July 29, 1987. It needs to be underlined that it is still a valid document since neither India nor Sri Lanka has formally repudiated it.

Articles 2.16(a) and (b) are of particular significance.

Article 2.16 (a) says, "India will take all necessary steps to ensure that Indian territory (which also includes territorial waters) is not used for activities prejudicial to the unity, integrity and security of Sri Lanka".

Article 2.16 (b) is still more specific. "The Indian Navy/Coast Guard will cooperate with the Sri Lankan Navy in preventing Tamil militant activities from affecting Sri Lanka." It is also interesting to note that both these articles impose a unilateral obligation on the part of India without any reciprocal obligation on the part of Sri Lanka.

Article 12.1(c) makes it even more specific. "In the event that Government of Sri Lanka requests the Government of India to afford military assistance to implement these proposals the Government of India will cooperate by giving to the Government of Sri Lanka such military assistance as and when required" (Singh 2001c).

Letters dated July 29, 1987 between Rajiv Gandhi and J.R. Jayawardene; both States reaffirmed the decision not to allow their respective territories to be used for activities. As the Palk Strait was considered as one of the major sources of logistic and civilian supply of the LTTE, Sri Lanka tried to control and deny its use to the LTTE through various means .In 1986, Sri Lanka declared up to five miles of northern territorial sea waters as a prohibited zone, which also included the sea from Mullaitivu to Trincomalee. In 1993, after the Sea Tiger's attack in August in the Jaffna lagoon, Sri Lanka through a notification on September 3, banned all vessels, except its Navy operating from the northern territorial waters extending from the north of Manar in the west to Trincomalee in the east. Since the territory south of the Jaffna Peninsula was under LTTE's effective control, the sea route via these northern waters was the most viable supply route for Sri Lankan forces stationed in the north. While these tactical moves tied down Sri Lankan Navy to its inshore waters only, distant coastal waters and the high seas beyond were left largely unattended. LTTE continued to receive the bulk of its supplies via the high seas. It also mastered the maritime logistics by thoroughly exploiting the drugs and arms nexus and the loopholes in international shipping.

On January 15, 1993 m.v. Ahat, a small 400-ton ship registered in San Lorenzo was intercepted as Indian Coast Guard vessel Vivek noticed it in Indian EEZ. On January 16, m.v. Ahat was intercepted when it reportedly entered Indian "waters" and was suspected of carrying men and material for the LTTE. The members on board the ship were offered the choice of surrender. Some crewmembers did jump into the sea but many died when the ship was set on fire. Reportedly, Kittu, an important LTTE leader, was also killed. The episode raised several issues of international law as well as of domestic law prejudicial to each other's unity, territorial integrity and security (Singh 2001d). In 1995 when Sri Lankan President Chandrika Kumaratunga launched " War for Peace "against the LTTE, India stayed neutral & supported her indirectly. India reportedly set a naval blockade across the Palk Strait, a strip of sea dividing Srilanka from India, in a bid to prevent LTTE boats from smuggling arms & fuel from the coastal state of Tamil.Nadu India also agreed in principle to Colombo's request for the surveillance of the north eastern seas to monitor possible move of vessels smuggling arms for the militants (Gunaratna 1993). Following a strict watch by the Sri Lanka Navy, Indian Navy and the Coast Guard, the LTTE began to depend heavily on South-East Asia for its supplies (Singh 2003a). Thailand is one of the links (points) of supply where material is loaded and then transferred to smaller boats of LTTE about 60-70 n. miles off the Sri Lankan coast, particularly the LTTE base of Mullaitivu (Singh 2003b). Sea Tigers escort these small boats to the shore. Till 1995, LTTE had a base at Twante, an island off the coast of Myanmar. When a Tiger base in Myanmar was closed in 1996 after protests from Colombo, Thailand's Andaman Sea ports became more important as Thai ports are strategic for transhipment. Munitions are switched from ocean-going vessels to smaller craft that make the risky 1,900-km run to Sri Lanka's northeastern coast (Davis 2000a).

Figure-1

Source: http://flonnet.com/fl2101/stories/20040116001704200.htm

Munitions have moved not only through Phuket, but also Ranong and Krabi on the Andaman coast, as well as Sattahip on the Gulf of Thailand. In January, Thai police seized a trawler near Ranong, carrying Carl Gustav rocket launchers. Later Phuket in Thailand became the main backup base. It came to light when the Thai authorities arrested Christly Reginald Laurence, a Sri Lanka-born Tamil with Norway's passport, for his links with LTTE. The suspected submersible/ submarine constructing by LTTE was located in a shipyard connected to Laurence, on the island of Sirae near Phuket in the Andaman Sea coast. Hull was completed, but other systems were not yet installed. Laurance was deported from Thailand, as building a submersible/ submarine is not an offence according to the law in Thailand (Davis 200b). Thailand realized the importance in co-operating with these countries as it was also plagued by piracy as a link-up among the Tigers, anti-Yangon Karen guerrillas and the Arakan Liberation Party, another Myanmar insurgent group known to have contracted out its shipping services etc. The Tigers critically needed hardware (artillery and mortar rounds, surface-to-air missiles, big-caliber machine-gun ammunition) were bought in Bulgaria, the Czech Republic and North Korea (Davies & Web)

LTTE also used suicide attacks as a part of its naval tactics 'Suicide' attacks against ships of Sri Lanka Navy have been reported. On September 9, 1994, Sea Tigers rammed two explosive-laden boats into the OPV Sagarwardene in the Gulf of Manar (Sakhuja 2005a). In March 1996, Sea Tigers rammed a boat loaded with explosives into a Dovra-class fast attack craft which resulted in its sinking. Several more such attacks followed. According to Rohana Gunaratne, Sea Tigers have launched over 30 such 'suicide' attacks. According to Ashok K. Mehta, such operations normally involve 8-10 speedboats and fishing trawlers (powered by four 250-hp engines). A quarry is selected. While other boats act as decoy, the explosive – packed suicide craft rams into the target (Sakhuja 2005b). As suicide 'terrorists' against their targets are employing attacks. The Government of India expressed its concern over LTTE airbase at Wani, which could be used as to launch unconventional attacks using micro light aircraft against shipping and land targets across the Palk Straits. Though LTTE assured that the airbase was not intended to pose any threat to India, it acts rather than reacts to a possible situation. To meet the threat Indian Coast Guard was placed since July 1987 under the Navy for operational requirements (Sakhuja 2005c). Regular International Boundary Line

[IBL] meetings between the Sri Lankan Navy, the Indian Navy and the Indian Coast Guard on a regular basis are held where various issues including fishing violations, refugee repatriation, drug peddling, smuggling, communications and other issues are discussed and the meetings are invariably held close to the IBL on either an Indian Vessel or a Sri Lankan vessel.

The Naval Detachments along the TN Coast numbering seven in number, the two Coast Guard Stations one each in Gulf of Mannar (Tuticorin) and Palk Bay (Mandapam), the Naval Air Station (Ramnad) are engaged in the Operation code named "Tasha". In addition, there are regular patrols by the Coast Guard Dorniers operating from Chennai and staging through Ramnad as required. There have also been proposals for joint patrolling along the IBL to prevent the fishermen from crossing over to each other's side (Vasan & Web). The increasing activities of the Tamil groups, especially of the LTTE, led to tighten maritime security in the Palk Strait and the Gulf of Manar under Operation Tasha since June 1990. In August 1993, it was further buttressed with Operation Nakabandi. Both these operations continue even after 2002 AD. The Coast Guard, since its inception had till 2001 apprehended nearly 708 foreign fishing vessels and 7,404 crew.20 Indian naval exercises with Thailand and Indonesia are aimed in part at ensuring security for a new sea route linking the Indian and Pacific oceans.

Sec. IV. Sethusamudram Ship Canal Project

Sethusamudram Ship Canal project called as "Suez Canal of India "has a very important geo-political dimension as it diverts sea traffic through India's own maritime waters and gives India a firm grip on one of the world's most strategic and busiest sea-lanes. It is estimated nearly 3000 ships are likely to cross the canal directly every year The canal not only reduces the distance between Cape Comarin and Chennai but also time by 36 hours .If converted into monetary benefits it is of great advantage. Further the 200 nautical miles of exclusive (Daily Mirror 2004). Economic Zones rich in fishery, undersea metallic and fossil fuel can be better patrolled to prevent poaching and foreign intervention. Apart from the commercial aspect, the proposed channel will improve tremendously the power projection capabilities of the Indian armed forces in the Arabian Sea and the Bay of Bengal deep into the Indian Ocean as far as the Antarctic ice fields. It makes possible the quick transfer of warships and personnel between the

Figure-2

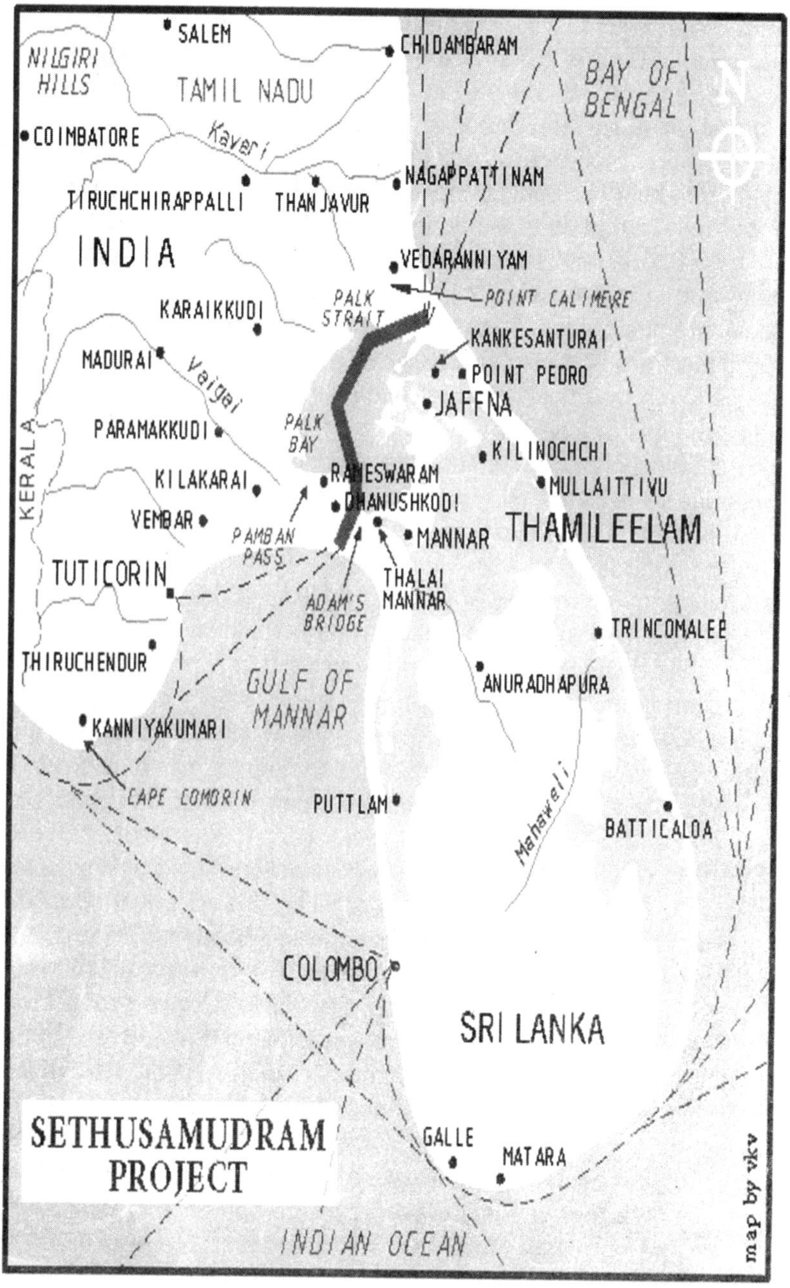

Source: http://www.tamilnet.com/art.html? catid=13&artid=15202

Southern Naval Command at Cochin and the Eastern Naval Command at Vishakhapatnam as well as the Coastguard installations on both Indian seaboards.

Bay of Bengal is also going to be a very exciting area as India's dependence on oil and its advanced technology in oil and gas exploration plays key factor in entering the energy sector in the neighborhood. Reliance in 2002 discovered both onshore and offshore gas reserves in Krishna Godhavari Basin, which is the single largest discovery of the year. In the northern arc of Bay of Bengal, ONGC rig block NEC26 is jointly exploited by Gasprom of Russia and GAIL of India. And in the south in the sea of Andamans two major offshore blocks are discovered. Further the ONGC has found gas reserves at Rameshwaram and also on Srilankan side of Palk Strait (The Week 2005). Thus making it a hub of energy interest .Sri Lanka can also reap benefits from the canal project as Sri Lanka has recently opened up marketing and storage facilities to India, signifying an important milestone in regional oil diplomacy .The $30 million project is the strategic prospect of the island's eastern port which could, once the oil farmland is modernized & start functioning can emerge as a commercial and the energy hub in the Bay of Bengal (Rao 2005).

Indo-Sri Lanka maritime cooperation should diversify, as energy security becomes a strategic security with the growing importance of protection of sea-lanes of communication, safety of oil tankers, technology availability, marine infrastructure and transportation facility, control of oil spillage, coastal pollution and illegal arms diffusion etc in the region. India should ensure that the maritime security apparatus functions at 24x7, 365 as India's security concerns would certainly shift from a defensive nature to preventive action in the coming years.

Indo-Sri Lanka maritime cooperation should enhance in the context of making Sri Lanka's use its Exclusive Economic Zone (EEZ), which is eight times its land area. Sri Lanka imports approx Rs 5 billion worth of fish per annum, while others poach in its own ocean area. The operational speed of Sri Lankan patrol aircraft available is in the range of 200 kts that can reach the outer limit of 200nm EEZ within one hour whereas Sri Lanka dependence, on a surface vessel capable of carrying out EEZ patrols with a speed of 15 kts which reach this limits only in 14 hrs. Thus, in the wake of Sethusamudram canal project, India and Sri Lanka should have maritime co-operation in exploitation of living and non-living maritime resources; development of maritime communications; shipbuilding and ship repair; weather forecasting; prevention of pollution and combating maritime terrorism

Figure.3

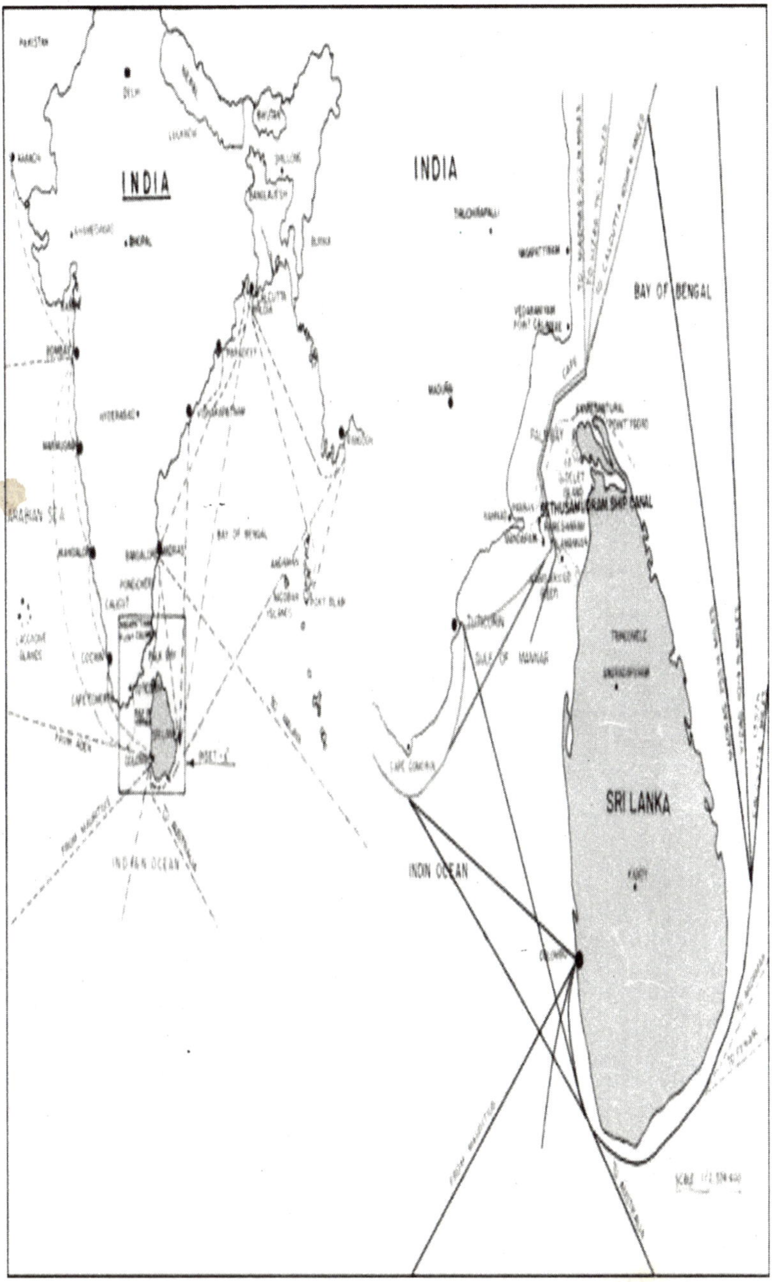

Source: http://www.climate.lk/sethu

Figure.4

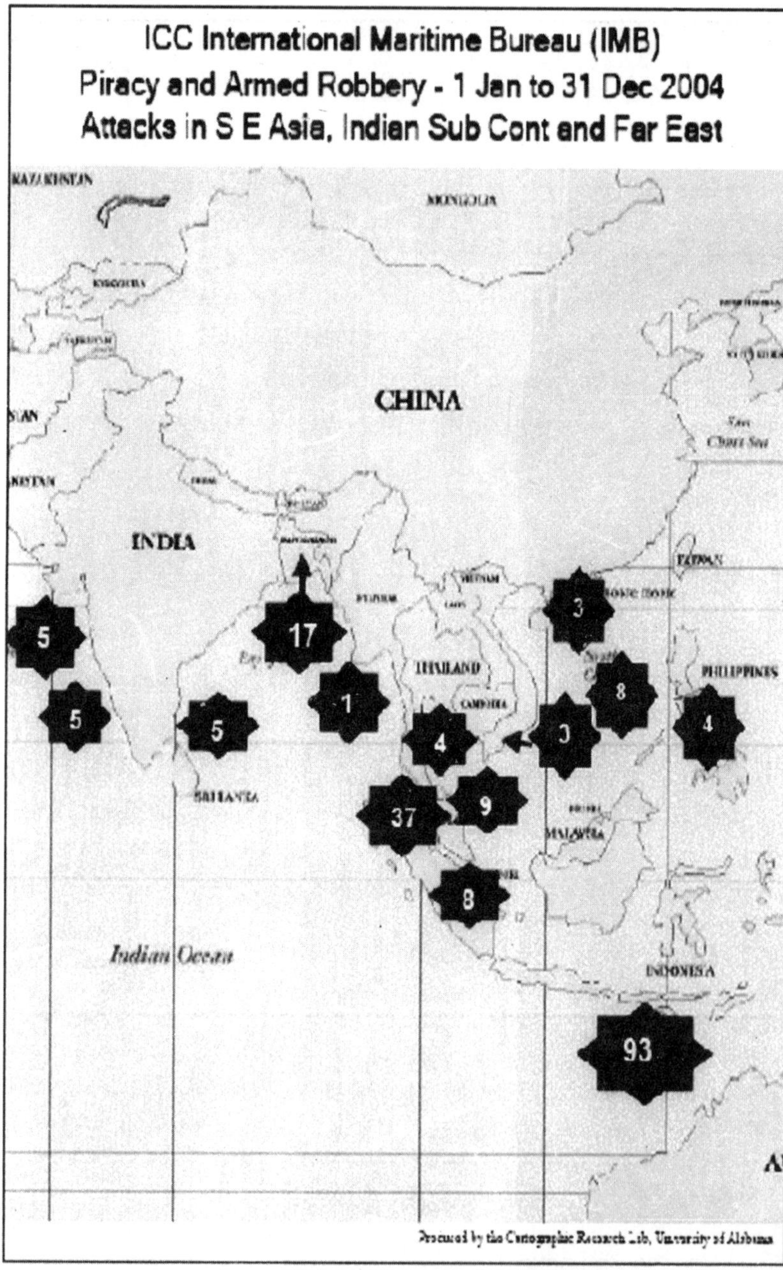

Source: http://www.icc-ccs.org/prc/piracy_maps_2004.php

Sec.V. Post-Tsunami Maritime Cooperation

India has deployed 14 ships, nearly 1,000 military personnel and several dozen helicopters and airplanes to Srilanka to cater to its needs during the devastation caused by tsunami on December 26, 2004. Indian Naval Ships were used to carry medical stores and relief material to Sri Lanka. India's Six MI-17 helicopters were used for search and rescue and relief missions. Naval vessels - INS Sandhayak - converted into a hospital ship and other ferried supplies, cleared the harbours and helped helicopter operations (Balachandran & Web.a). So far the harbors in Galle, Trincomalee and Colombo had been surveyed and the maps handed over to the Sri Lankan authorities, Tangalle, Hambantota, and Kankesanthuraiare were also taken up. While Galle harbor, had to be cleared of debris. Trincomalee survey showed that it was clear and intact for Kankesanthurai, and Jaffna's major port, will be taken up next, the official said. In fact, all the harbours in the affected coastline, except those, which are in the LTTE-controlled areas, will be surveyed and cleared (Balachandran & Web.b). In addition, India has pledged $23 million for reconstruction in Sri Lanka. Marine archeology is also viewed as a security concern in the region as various groups from international community are operating (officially and unofficially) in the maritime boundary areas of the SAARC region .It has come to notice that the archeological activities are conducted mainly by pirates for the international market. Some of the mapped particulars of coastal areas and lagoons coincidentally have become the strongest LTTE naval bases or hit and run covers in their escape routes. This area becomes an important issue to be dealt by the countries in the Bay of Bengal region (Front Line 2005).

India has MoUs with Singapore, Sri Lanka and Thailand on a variety of security subjects linked with cooperation, bilateral exercises and maritime security. With the recent resumption of defense ties between the US and India, the US has sought an arrangement for greater access to Trincomalee. This desire has led to the afore mentioned training programmes, a keen interest in Sri Lankan affairs and a continual improvement in Indo-US defence relations Sri Lanka, and the US security cooperation programme for armed forces helps to improve their preparedness, dealing with the Liberation Tigers of Tamil Eelam (LTTE). American frigate 'Courageous' renamed as B621 was sent as a gift to Sri Lanka. This frigate has a refurbished warship with a deck where helicopters can land while the ship is in motion. This ship helps the Sri Lankan Navy to patrol in the sea within Sri Lankan's Exclusive Economic Zone on the western, northern and eastern coasts (Web. Elam.Nation 2005).

Indo-Sri Lanka maritime cooperation could diversify with the growing importance of protection of sea-lanes of communication, safety of oil tankers, technology availability, marine infrastructure & transportation facility, control of oil spillage, coastal pollution and illegal arms diffusion etc. Maritime low intensity conflicts like exploitation of national resources by unauthorized persons, the attempt to intentionally pollute the sea thereby leading to ecological damage, the threat to life and property on board ship (or platform or structure in the continental shelf or near the shore), threat to national peace and security. Environment of maritime cooperation will also help to promote parallel moves for cooperation in civilian-developmental spheres like fishing, regional trade, disaster management etc. Surveillance, monitoring and enforcement demonstrate the nation's resolve and capability to exercise control over its area of jurisdiction.

References

1. Anthony Davis (2000a), "Tracking Tigers in Phuket A secret Tamil guerrilla base embarrasses Bangkok" *Asia Week*, June 16, vol.29, no.23
2. *Ibid.*, (2000b)
3. Balachandran P.K., *Indian Navy renders Lankan harbours Usable* http;//www.hindustantimes .com/news 181_1194771,00050002.htm.
4. *Ibid.*,
5. *Daily Mirror* (2004), 6 October. Also see *Indian Express* 15, and July 20
6. *Frontline* (2005), April 22, pp.36-37
7. *India's Maritime Doctrine*, (2004)
8. Mani Shankar Aiyar, "Take Risks for Energy Interest" (Interview), *The Week*, November13
9. Rao P.V (2005), "Regional Energy cooperation: The Indo-Srilanka Experience" *Indian Ocean Digest*, Jan-June, and vol.no1 p.55.
10. "Refurbished US frigate handed over to Sri Lanka" (2005), www Elam.Nation.com .March 29
11. Rohan Gunaratna (1993), *Indian Intervention in Srilanka: The Role Of India's Intelligence Agencies*, Colombo: Gunaritine office, p.36.
12. Roger Davies, "Sea Tigers, stealth technology and the North Korea n connections"http://www.janes.com/regional_news/asia_pacific/news/jir/jir010307_2_n.shtml.

13. *Ibid.*, See also Vijay Sakhuja (2005) *Sea Piracy in South Asia.* South Asia Analysis Group 18 Feb, p.no. 1259
14. *Ibid.*,
15. *Ibid.*,
16. Singh K.R (2001a), "Regional Cooperation in the Bay of Bengal: Non-Conventional Threats-Maritime Dimension" *Strategic Analysis*: March, Vol.24 no.12
17. *Ibid.* (2001b),
18. *Ibid.*, (2001c)
19. *Ibid.*, (2001d)
20. *Ibid.*, (2003a), "Maritime Violence and Non-state Actors: with special reference to the Andaman Sea and its Environment", *Dialogue*, April-June, Vol. 4, no 4.
21. *Ibid.*, (2003b)
22. Suryanarayan V (2004), "Sea Tigers — Threat To Indian Security" *The Hindu*, 28, July
23. *The Hindu* (1999), September 28, Also see Krishna Dev (2000), *Journal of Indian Ocean Studies*, March, p. 131 and Sakhuja Vijay (2000), *Strategic Analysis*, August, pp. 925-26.
24. *Ibid.*,(2005), 27 Sep.
25. *The Week*, (2005)
26. Vasan R.S, in "Palk Bay Issues and Security Concerns ", http://www.saag.org/%5Cpapers14%5Cpaper1355.htm,Paper No.13
27. Venkatesh (2005), "Sethusamudram: Strategic Asset", *Syndicate Features*, 26 May
28. See also Verghese B.G (2003), "For an Ocean Outlook", *The Hindu*, Nov25
29. *Ibid.*,
30. Vijay Sakhuja, (2005a), "Sea Piracies in South Asia", *South Asia AnalysisGroup* 18.Feb.p. 1259
31. *Ibid.*, (2005b)

13

Re-Envisioning India-Myanmar Relations

B. Meena Rao

S. Subba Rao

Sec. I. Introduction

Foreign policy is born out of a country's principles, interests and objectives. It is the interplay of forces like history, geography and domestic and international environment and history that it cannot change; geography which is normally durable; its domestic circumstances which evolve continuously; and its international environment, which is always in flux and largely out of the country's control. History and geography give continuity to foreign policy while domestic and international circumstances produce changes.

In order to understand foreign policy challenges, mere analysis of their external relations is not enough. It is also necessary to look inside nations, at their domestic developments. 'Domestic' and 'external' factors are tied closely together and each significantly affects the other. Gladstone, the British Prime Minister had once said, "the first condition of a good foreign policy is a good domestic policy" (Dutt 1984). India's foreign policy towards Myanmar is a case in point.

The Indian sub-continent stands distinct from the rest of Asia. It is the most natural geographic unit that has developed a very distinct culture. The countries of the Indian sub-continent are a part of one of the most ancient living civilizations, where all religions, faiths, ideologies of the world live together. Though geographical borders and boundaries divide the population of the sub-continent into separate political communities, it is difficult to separate the people from their moorings. India's foreign policy reflects the ethos of the sub-continent. Jawaharlal Nehru, in 1957 stated, "for India her external affairs will follow internal affairs." This was the guiding factor, why India adopted the principle of Panch Sheel in conducting her foreign policy. In India's perspective, Panch Sheel expresses the spiritual essence of both India's domestic and foreign policy (Dixit 1998).

The socio-cultural factors in the study of India's foreign policy making are gaining importance. I.K. Gujral, observed, "Indian foreign policy is not foreign. It is totally Indian and is rooted in India's realities." At one point of time, these factors were taken to be aspects, which influence the making of the domestic policies of a nation. But with the advent of globalisation such factors have crossed the boundaries of nations. Such links can sometimes facilitate, at other times impede in the making of India's foreign policy. There exists a two-way relationship between India's foreign policy and the domestic policy. Such connection may facilitate some kind of integration, but with the interference of a 'third nation' the same factors are manipulated to serve only selfish interest of the 'third nation.' This is especially true in the case of India, which shares contiguous and porous borders with her neighbours. India borders with Pakistan on the Northwest, Tibet, autonomous region of China and Nepal in the North, Bhutan in the Northeast, Bangladesh and Myanmar in the East and Sri Lanka and Maldives in the South. On the one hand, if it can facilitate trade and commerce it can also facilitate the crossing over of illegal migrants. Such fissiparous factors make the safeguarding of the national integration very demanding and challenging. For India, the maintenance of national interest depends on the kind of foreign policy she ensues with her neighbours. For example Myanmar, in the east serves as a hiding resort and training ground for insurgent elements operating in India's Northeast. For India, to counter these insurgents a lot will depend on the Sino-Indo relations (Ollapally 2005).

Since independence, India's foreign policy has been one of building bridges of friendship and cooperation with all countries regardless of the economic and political systems. No matter what contours international politics took, India pursued this basic code. Regrettably India's territorial integrity remains under threat from her neighbours. Internal centrifugal forces continue to affect India's geopolitical unity. Fanned by outside support there are demands for secession from segments of the population in Jammu and Kashmir and the Northeastern provinces. Adversarial relations with Pakistan and China have resulted in India having to divert its scarce financial, material and trained manpower resources for defence purposes, thereby reducing its capacities to formulate and implement social and economic policies for national consolidation and reconstruction.

Barring Bhutan and Maldives, India's relations with its others neighbours, namely, Nepal, Sri Lanka, Myanmar, Bangladesh, and Pakistan have remained problematic for one reason or the other. The quest for a new approach to the neighbours has been at the center of India's foreign policy debate throughout the 1990s. India's relation with her neighbours was governed in pursuit of safeguarding Indian security and the maximization of India's economic interest in a globalised world. This was most explicitly articulated in the form of Gujral Doctrine. India has undertaken negotiations with each one of its neighbours since the middle of 1991 to remove any misunderstandings and to stabilize economic and political relations, and implement confidence-building measures (Dutt).

The shifting trends of India's foreign policy after the end of cold war was in part about laying the foundation for a recovery of India's role in what increasingly came to be called as India's 'extended neighbourhood'. This period saw the re-establishment of expanded political dialogue and economic ties between India and its neighbours especially in the east. India never consciously articulated its approach in terms of theory that demanded activism in the regions to enhance its own security. However, its regional initiatives were now presented in terms of mutual economic benefit and the restoration of historic links. India's activism in East Asia, South-East Asia, Afghanistan, Central Asia, the Persian Gulf and parts of Africa became an important feature of India's altered foreign policy (Raja Mohan 2003).

In 1991, the then Prime Minister P.V. Narasimha Rao instituted a Look East policy that continued to pursue India's interests in the security of East and Southeast Asia. India started to reduce resistance to regional cooperation and committed itself to a new, more open economic policy. As India launched itself on the track of the Look East doctrine the eastern neighbours began to loom large in its national economic and political strategy. India's Look East went through two distinct phases. The first focused on renewing political and commercial contact. The second phase in India's Look East policy had a new dimension – the development of India's remote Northeast. India's search for a new economic relationship with the region was driven by considerations of globalisation and the domestic imperative of developing the Northeast by increasing its connectivity to the outside world. Instead of consciously trying to isolate the region from external influences as it had done in the past, India began to recognize the importance of opening it up for commercial linkages with its eastern neighbours. The post-Cold War atmosphere proposes an opportunity for this region to pursue the hitherto untested trend of creating new institutions to address both economic and political/security issues. Despite the fact that multilateral institutions, both for political and economic purposes, were created during the Cold War, the phenomenon of institutionalism as understood in the present context is both new and qualitatively different (Ravni Thakur 2004).

India is making several efforts towards sub-regional, cross-regional and bilateral regional trading arrangements. While bilateral initiatives largely involve ASEAN economies, some of the notable sub-regional economic cooperation efforts are the Bay of Bengal Initiative among Member States for Multi-Sectoral Technical and Economic Cooperation (BIMSTEC) comprising Bangladesh, India, Myanmar, Nepal, Bhutan, Sri Lanka and Thailand. Another regional organization of which both India and Myanmar are members of is the Mekong-Ganga Cooperation Group, the other members being Cambodia, Laos Vietnam and Thailand. India has sought to improve the road connections between the Northeast and by investing in the transport infrastructure of the neighbour. India and Thailand have planned a trilateral project with Myanmar to link the three nations through a road corridor. By taking advantage of Myanmar as a bridge to South-east Asia, India hopes to transform the Northeast from a security burden into a land of economic opportunity (Ravni Thakur).

In tune with these policies at the global level, India is responding to the process of globalisation at the regional level. In fact, India's policy towards its South Asian neighbours has a two-fold relevance. First, any worthwhile project of promoting regional cooperation is inconceivable without India's active participation, because South Asia is predominantly an Indo-centric region. Second as a corollary, it is only by consolidating cooperative ties with its eastern neighbours that India can contain secessionist movements, cross-border terrorism and diverse range of intra-state conflicts with its neighbours.

Sec. II. India-Myanmar Relations

Amongst India's eastern neighbours, Myanmar occupies an important place. As early as 1944 Sardar KM Panikar had focused attention on the strategic significance of Myanmar and remarked, " the defence of Myanmar is the defence of India and it is India's primary concern no less than India's to see that its frontiers remain inviolable" (Kuppuswamy). Consequently, neither of these two states can remain unaffected and unconcerned with the political and security situation in the other. Myanmar shares with four Indian Northeastern States of Arunachal Pradesh, Nagaland, Manipur and Mizoram a 1643 km-long border, and with a coastline of 1930 km wide open on the Andaman Sea and the Bay of Bengal facing the Indian territories of the Andaman Islands. As a result, Myanmar poses a strategic challenge to India's Eastern frontier.

Geo-strategically, Myanmar's importance for India arises because: First, Myanmar is the second largest of India's neighbour on the eastern flank. Secondly, Myanmar provides the eastern littoral of the Bay of Bengal. An unfriendly Myanmar hosting foreign naval presence would be a grave threat to India's security. Thirdly, Myanmar has a big border with China in the North, contiguous with the Sino-Indian disputed border, which makes possible various strategic complications, in case India maintains distance from Myanmar. Fourthly, Myanmar bridges South Asia and India with Southeast Asia. It also acts as a buffer between India's Northeastern States and the Southern provinces of China. Also, geo-economically, Myanmar is rich in natural resources and has appreciable production of crude oil, and natural gas. It has sizeable deposits of copper, lead, tin, tungsten, steel and gold. Some of these, especially crude oil and natural gas could be an attraction for India, being the next door. Accordingly, Myanmar holds a place of strategic significance to India's eastern frontier

Myanmar was one of the largest and one of the richest provinces of British India. The British integrated the whole Myanmar territory to their empire in India and ruled the province directly from India. Thus, Myanmar was given the new role of strategic frontier, of British India, and become a buffer territory between India and the French Indo-china and the decadent Chinese empire further north. Till 1937, Myanmar was a part of India. As a part of India during the British rule, the Myanmar administration was part of the overall Indian administrative structure, yet the Indian National Congress supported the Myanmar struggle for independence and separation from India. On April 1, 1937, Myanmar was separated from India and was made a separate State. With the first Myanmar Prime Minister, U Nu, along with other Asian leaders, especially Jawaharlal Nehru who was very close to him, Myanmar became one of the leading countries of the Non-Aligned Movement in the 1950s. What's more, in enunciating the Principles of Panch Sheel in 1954, along with Nehru and U Nu was also present. The important factor during this period was the support given by the Indian nationalist leaders to the Myanmar Nationalist Movement. India and Myanmar's attitude towards the political and economic issues that faced the world in 1950s were similar or identical and both worked to strengthen bilateral relations (Prakash Chander & Prem Arora 1990).

All this changed after the military coup in 1962 with the advent of military rule under General Ne Win, Myanmar opted for a self-isolation for almost three decades. Gen. Ne Win regime (under pressure from China) started distancing itself from India. Myanmar got out of the Non-Aligned Movement in 1979. The Myanmar regime cut links with all its neighbours, including India. Fearing no credible threat from the East, India was apparently satisfied with this "non-relations' followed by the Military regime. Moreover obsessed by the security on its western front against Pakistan, India had for long ignored its eastern neighbour. Pakistan and China forged close military ties with the new regime in their overall strategy of weakening India. China turned Myanmar practically into a client State through its political diplomacy and economic and military assistance. The Myanmar-Pak-China nexus has perhaps made the Indian policy planners to rethink on their approach towards the military regime and drop its neglected attitude towards Myanmar.

It may be recalled the turning point in the deterioration of India-Myanmar relations came with the mass resurgence for democracy in 1988. When Myanmar began to be shaken by a strong popular movement after twenty-six years of military rule, India clearly adopted a sympathetic stance towards the Pro-democracy uprising. After the demission of General Ne Win on July 23, 1988, demonstrations of students, monks and democracy activists followed one another till the general strike of August the 8, 1988. Tens of thousands indeed millions came out on the streets in support of the movement for the restoration of democracy led by Aung San Suu Kyi, daughter of the late Aung San (Dutt 1984). Several hundreds of demonstrators were slaughtered as thousands were thrown into jails. P M S Malik, the then Indian Ambassador, strongly stood against the new junta that seized power. India strongly denounced the bloody repression and the Indian Embassy was turned into a makeshift hospital and several students climbed over the Embassy's walls to take shelter. By that time many activists also sought a military intervention of India. As soon as the SLORC (The Military regime then known as the State Law and order Restoration Council) took over power, India only froze its relations with Yangon and opposed the new regime by giving a full and opened support to the pro-democracy movements.

Besides the official diplomatic positions condemning the junta and demanding a return to democracy and humanist values, India did its best to support the pro-democratic activists, students and 'rebels' who fled in 1988-89. India made no effort to conceal its sympathy for the Myanmar exiles and refugee camps were set up in the Northeast, near the Indo- Myanmar border. India defined in the South Block its 'open-door policy' for students and activists. A large campaign condemning the military activities was also launched. As a State controlled institution, the All India Radio broadcast many programmes (especially in Myanmar) denouncing the military. The Myanmar Generals, in turn accused India of collusion with the democratic movements in Yangon (through its Embassy), as well as with ethnic insurgencies all over, especially along the Indo-Myanmar border. India reportedly provided some financial and technical assistance to the Kachins (Kachin Independence Organization) in the Northwest of Myanmar and the Karens, near Thailand (Karen National Union, through its consulate in Chiang Mai, Northern Thailand).

In the summer of 1990, when the so called elections were held and the National League for Democracy (NLD) of Aung San Suu Kayi and U Nu, and ethnic minorities' parties won, the Myanmar Military Government refused to implement the election results and arrested most of the newly elected members. India continued its policy of isolation and opposition to the Myanmar's regime. India held regular meetings at which SLORC was criticized, and the transfer of power to the elected representatives of the people demanded, though this was not officially sponsored, but the presence of members of Parliament from the ruling and other parties in India was noted by SLORC. Indian government spokesmen made regular statements saying the military junta was a major threat to peace in the subcontinent, that India could not remain a silent spectator to the disruption of human rights and dignity in Myanmar. George Fernandes, the then defence minister, gave shelter to Myanmar activists and it is said the All Myanmar Students operated form his residence in New Delhi.

Nonetheless, such activities and statements were toning down. The first stance opted by India a vis-à-vis the new Myanmar junta seemed an idealist one, a policy of opposition and denunciation of the Myanmar military. However, in the early nineties, as the regional order began to be reshaped after the end of the Cold War and the Indo-China Wars, the geopolitics of the region changed, which led to an overhaul of the Indian policy.

By the time the cold war ended Myanmar found itself as an almost isolated country by the international community. Myanmar was desperately looking for an ally. China, having cracked down herself in June 1989 on another student uprising in its country, seized the opportunity and established a very close relationship with its southern neighbour. Taking advantage of the diplomatic and economic vacuum in Myanmar, China built up a "Myanmar strategy", and to a great extent, the Chinese gained a foothold in the country. At the same time, India was also opening a new diplomatic era with the launch of the Look East policy (Kuppuswamy). This new outlook spelt the relations towards Myanmar in three distinct areas. First the instability in the Northeast, second the "China threat", and lastly to capitalize on ASEAN through Myanmar as the bridge between South Asia and the Southeast Asia.

Sec. III. Instability in the Indian North-East: The Myanmar Connection

For decades, the Northeast of India is going through political instability and ethnic insurgencies. The region located at the foothills of the Himalayas, along the Brahmaputra River Basin between Myanmar and the Indian Ocean, is a mosaic of peoples and cultures. Many tribes and ethnic groups live in these landlocked territories, ignoring the delineation of official State borders. Since the independence of India and Myanmar in 1947 and 1948 respectively, many of these ethnic minorities have been struggling with their respective government so as to gain more autonomy (and for some even independence) or at least a specific political and cultural recognition. Most of them are involved in various violent separatist outfits and get sympathy, shelter and finance from across the border.

On the Indian side, the Naga rebellion has been one of the most violent insurgencies in the region for the last fifty years. Claiming the creation of a Greater Nagaland (Nagalim), the National Socialist Council of Nagaland (NSCN), formed in 1980, but inheriting from three decades of struggle, constituted one of the most dangerous insurgent outfit in India, along with the Assamese (United Liberation Front of Asom since 1979) and Mizo (Mizo National Front, having disarmed since the creation of the Indian State of Mizoram in 1987) movements. Since the NSCN split into two rival factions – NSCN (Khaplang) and NSCN (Issac-Muivah) in 1988, the region has been witnessing a rise of violence, through ethnic and criminal clashes, and drugs and weapons trafficking. Myanmar has long served in the 1960s and 1970s as a corridor linking the Indian Northeast's insurgent groups and China (especially through the Communist Party of Myanmar), as one of the then main patrons of the Indian terrorist outfits. Myanmar has long offered a harbour to many of them, seeking shelter beyond the Indo-Myanmar border. As kinships are common across borders, relations between Northeastern insurgents and rebels from Myanmar were quite logical. These ties between Indian insurgents and Myanmar ethnic armed groups have been often reported, particularly with the Kachin Independence Army (mainly Christian, Northern) and the Chin National Front (as the Chin are close to the Mizo ethnicity, further south). Moreover, Khaplang, the Naga leader, is of Myanmar origin and has established bases in Myanmar.

Thus, this imbroglio of ethnic secessionism, religious and political insurgencies, large-scaled smuggling and above all transnational links and cross border supports, have long undermined the relations between New Delhi and Yangon. Myanmar had often turned a blind eye on the home bases, the two NSCNs, the ULFA and Kuki outfits had set up on Myanmar territory and the Indian government has been forever denouncing the indirect (or direct) support the Myanmar junta gave to them. Aware of this bargaining chip that the Myanmar General had in their hands, India began to review its policy towards Myanmar so as to stabilize the region by making Yangon stop aiding the Indian insurgents. The two governments organized new joint military operation to crack down on some insurgents. The two governments organized new joint military operation to crack down on some insurgents' outfits in 2000-2001. Since a couple of years, the Myanmar regime has been keeping on reassuring India that it would not help those outfits nor harbour any of them. Furthermore, courting the junta would also enable India to open up the Northeast and in the long-term crack down on all the smugglings of the region, particularly small and light arms proliferation, since the Indo-Myanmar had become a well-known trafficking corridor.

General Maung Aye during his visit in 2000 had also assured full cooperation in fighting some of the insurgent groups in the Northeastern states. A pragmatic working relationship was re-established in dealing with narcotis trafficking and insurgents along the border. Foreign Minister Win Aung at the end of the week long visit, allayed Indian fears by saying that "Myanmar's soil will not be used as a military base by any power against India".

The Indo- Myanmar bilateral relations received impetus in 2004 from the visit of Than Shwe, the Head of State and Chairman of the State Peace and Development Council (SPDC) of Myanmar. During his visit, Shwe had a very productive meeting with Prime Minister Manmohan Singh on enhancing strategic ties, particularly in areas like security, energy and transportation. Both sides signed a MoU on cooperation on non-traditional security issues. Shwe assured Indian leadership that he would not allow Myanmar to be used for anti-India operations. Myanmar also showed willingness to mount a military operation against northeast and beef up vigil along its border with India.

The MoU would institutionalize security cooperation between India and Myanmar. Apart from operational intelligence, the countries will exchange personnel too. There is also a possibility of joint operations. As part of its security cooperation, India will provide the necessary military hardware to Myanmar and in turn Myanmar's fulfillment of its promise of taking action against the northeast insurgent groups will enhance trade and economic relations and unlock the economic potential of the region and wean away people from these armed groups.

Sec. IV. The China Threat

The second reason, and maybe the most sensitive one, that could justify the realist Myanmar policy of India is the so-called "China Threat". Initially, Myanmar was not been seen as a credible ally that China could use against India's interest in the Northeast. Ne Win's regime had very cold and less than cordial relations with Beijing and Myanmar isolated, itself cutting links with the outside world, India did not perceive any Chinese threat through Myanmar before the early nineties. But during the 1970s, China has been giving support to various Indian insurgents groups, notably those that claimed to follow the Maoist ideology in the 1960s and 1970s. After the Sino-Indian War of 1962, India feared the Chinese militarization of Tibet and Beijing's claim over a large part of Arunachal Pradesh in the Eastern sector.

The advance of the Chinese influence in the Indo-Myanmar region was there for everyone to see. Myanmar rapidly gained favours from China, which took advantage of the situation wherein the rest of the world maintained distance from the Junta regime. After having signed a large trade agreement in August 1988, the Sino-Myanmar cooperation kept on growing through two huge arms deals (in 1989 and 1994), Beijing supplied the Myanmar Army with weapons. The Tatmadaw (Myanmar Army) was thus offered a great opportunity to see its strength increased and its equipment modernized at low cost. It took only a few years for China to get a strong foothold in Myanmar. The Chinese strategy on its southern flank was clear - the main objective of China was to open up the Yunnan and Sichuan provinces to Myanmar, through the Irrawaddy River and road/rail links towards the Myanmar ports on the Indian Ocean. For the southern provinces of China, offered a valuable economic outlet, as the new Myanmar junta opened and liberalized the country's economy in the early nineties. The Myanmar market was seen as a major opportunity for cheap Chinese products. As a consequence, Chinese investors and traders have largely dominated northern Myanmar ever since China's second intention was to ensure a secure and permanent access to the Bay of Bengal, especially in case of a blockade in the South China. The inclusion of Myanmar into China's 'Grade Strategy' was then obvious. Although Beijing tries to give the impression that she has no profound interest in the region, it is obvious that China has now deep strategic links with Myanmar.

This Chinese influence on the Myanmar Junta is seen as a potential threat by India, especially as far as the Chinese presence in the Indian Ocean is concerned. China is reportedly suspected of having significantly up-graded several ports and naval bases. The strengthening of the Myanmar naval infrastructures and the installation of monitoring facilities by the Chinese on the Myanmar territory has long worried India. The construction of several electronic surveillance facilities and listening post along the Myanmar coasts (Hainggyi on the Irrawaddy delta, Zadetkyai and Sakanthit near Mergui in the Tenasserim State) or on Islands (Greater Coco Islands with its 50m-high antenna) are seen as obviously directed against India even though China strongly denies it. George Fernades, in his first days as Minster of Defense in 1998 strongly denounced this alleged Chinese presence in the Bay of Bengal. Nevertheless, pointing out the China Threat and the "Myanmar Pawn", India tried to cope with it. Realizing the likely use of the Myanmar facilities by China India chose to deal carefully with Myanmar instead of opposing head-on the Myanmar military and tried to count the Myanmar Junta so as to avoid it turning into a Chinese military pawn against Indian interests. Myanmar in itself is not at all perceived as a threat by India, even if the Tatmadaw has increased considerably its strength and if the large-scale weaponry present in the country could not be of any risk. Befriending the Myanmar Generals with a 'constructive engagement policy' would in fact, according to Indian strategists, enable India to deal with the Chinese potential threat on its eastern flank. The challenge for India is not to stop Chinese economic presence in the subcontinent but to increase its own commercial integration with Myanmar. The liberalisation of all the South Asian economies under the pressure of globalisation has given India a historic opportunity to integrate the smaller economies of the subcontinent into its own.

Sec. V. Reaching out to South-East Asia

The third reason that can explain the readiness of India to establish close ties with Myanmar is the willingness to reach out to Southeast Asia, especially the ASEAN countries. There is also the objective of maximizing India's economic interests, which is largely a function of domestic policy, both political and economic growth. Foreign policy plays this role in two ways. Firstly, by working to create favourable international economic regimes through multilateral institutions, and second, by getting the best one-to-one deals through bilateral agreements. The Look East policy, aims at getting closer to the booming economies of Southeast Asia. With the turnaround of India's attitude towards Myanmar in the mid-nineties, and with the entry of Myanmar into the ASEAN club in 1997, the integration on Yangon in India's Look East Policy was quite logical. According to Indian officials, Myanmar could be the first step India needs to enter Southeast Asia, and have access to attractive markets and get a strategic foothold there (Kuppuswamy). In the spirit of sub regional economic cooperation, several institutional projects were set up in the region, with Myanmar being the geographical node for them - the BIMST-EC (Bangladesh India Sri Lanka and Thailand Economic Cooperation), the Mekong Ganga Cooperation (MGC) and the Kunming initiative. India chose to engage Myanmar because of its geographical proximity and get closer to it through these regional organizations.

From Myanmar's part, the government suffers economic and a political sanction imposed by the United States and European Union and does not entertain hopes for getting any aid from them. Very recently Myanmar had to give up its turn for the rotating chairmanship of ASEAN, under pressure from United States of America and the European Union to boycott such meetings, if chaired by Myanmar. Despite being admitted to ASEAN, Myanmar's prospects for receiving major economic help are bleak. As mentioned before, only China undertakes some of the significant development projects, mostly in the field of infrastructure. But China alone is not in the position to satisfy Myanmar's needs in foreign aid and investment. Hence, Myanmar looks towards India to receive such support. Accordingly, there has been a drastic change in India's economic relations towards Myanmar in recent years. India decided to engage Myanmar through bilateral as well as multi-lateral means, as its policy of boycott after the 1988 military takeover failed to produce the desired results.

First Border Trade Agreement between India and Myanmar was signed in New Delhi, in January 1994. The Agreement opened the border point between Moreh (Manipur, India) and Tamu (Sagaing Division); this agreement enhanced (and made official) the bilateral border trade between the two countries. Recognizing the centrality of trade in transforming bilateral relations in the subcontinent, India has lobbied to set up an inter-agency task of senior officials to work out a coherent regional trade policy.

India is Myanmar's fourth largest trading partner. Last year bilateral trade between India and Myanmar was worth $428 million. The joint task force of the two countries released which stated that bilateral trade could double to $1 billion by 2006 if the two countries utilize their common border to step up economic cooperation. India wants to develop the industrial potential in its northeastern region and make it a natural base for bilateral trade with Myanmar. It hopes to achieve this by developing roads, airports, railways, telecom, banking and finance. To accelerate border trade, India opened a second transit point at Zowkhathar-Rhi in Mizoram in 2004, in addition to the Moreh-Tamu point in Manipur. The opening of a new trade route also emphasized the need to speedily develop infrastructure facilities at the points of transit, so that trade could take place at the earliest.

India is Myanmar's largest export market, accounting for nearly one-fourth of its exports. In 1999-2000 exports to India were to the tune of $141.14 million, while imports from India were worth $75.36 million. India has emerged as the largest market for Myanmar. Indian imports from Myanmar have touched $400 million while exports are at $100 million. Though India wants to correct this imbalance by increasing exports, it is not in favour of any artificial balancing of trade. It wants a genuine expansion of bilateral cooperation, that could exploit the full economic potential of both countries (Anand Kumar 2004).

During his visit in 2000, General Maung Aye discussed not only about the sensitivity of the India-Myanmar border, but business seemed to be on the agenda. He said that cooperation in hydrocarbon and hydel projects, information technology, tourism and infrastructure development is some of the areas, where the two countries can join hands. The two countries have signed a credit line of $15 million for purchase of Indian goods (Kuppuswamy).

India has been raising Yongon's economic stakes in the region by undertaking various infrastructure projects. The Moreh-Kalemao road, the trilateral highway project from Moreh in Manipur to Kalewa and Kalemyo passing through Myawaddy in Central Myanmar the second largest city and an optical fiber telecommunication network along the highway at a cost of $800 million are some of them. All this in a bid to make the administration take more interest regarding the cross border insurgency problem (Kuppuswamy).

Reflecting good performance of India's "New Age Sector", there has been appreciable increase in the country's exports of drugs and pharmaceuticals products. The growing thaw in Indo-Myanmar relations had augured well for the sector, as pharmaceuticals exports to Myanmar grew by over 36 percent.

India is also helping its neighbour build a $30 million crude oil refinery in Thanlyin – it has invested $4.5 million in the project – and is involved with South Korea's Daewoo in exploration and production in a gas field on the western Rakhine coast. Myanmar is the only Southeast Asian country with which India shares both land and maritime boundaries. India sees Myanmar, not only as a bridge to Southeast Asia, but also as an alternative route for transit of goods. Economic cooperation with Myanmar will definitely speed up economic developments of India's northeastern states, as Myanmar provides the shortest links to Southeast Asian markets by air, land and sea.

It is this magnitude of economic co-ordination and cooperation in the days of globalisation that an India and Myanmar relations are undertaking (Ravni Thakur). Recently there have been talks about the laying of the India-Bangladesh-Myanmar gas pipeline. India is the world's largest energy consumer and its consumption of natural gas is increasing at a rate of 6.1 per cent annually. It jumped from 0.6 trillion cubic feet (tcf) in 2000 and is expected to reach 102 (tcf) by 2006. Though some of this demand is being met domestically, still a large gap remains.

Indian policy makers have initiated numerous policies to address the country's growing energy needs. For example, India is pushing for the creation of 15-45 days of emergency reserves in Rajkot, Mangalore and Visakhapatnam. India is also diversifying beyond oil to access other energy resources, such as nuclear power, coal, natural gas and renewable energy resources, as well as stepping up exploration activities with its borders.

India has also been exploring new options and sources of energy due to its rapidly growing demand. As a result, India is stepping up energy diplomacy with States in the South Asian region, as well as States further allied in Central Asia, Russia and the Middle East and as far away as Latin America and Africa (Anand Kumar).

However, some of the indigenous, cheaper and nearby options closer home are not exploited to their fullest potential due to the unfavourable political climate in the sub-continent, which makes bilateral cooperation very difficult. For the same reason, the issue of 290-kilometre long gas pipeline from Myanmar to India via Bangladesh has been mired in controversy for a long time.

If this proposal materializes, it could change India's ties with Myanmar for the better. This proposal of laying the pipeline it will open the road for further cooperation. If such teamwork happens, then there is sure to be an enduring relationship between SAARC-ASEAN-BIMSTEC. Let it always be borne in mind, what Jacob Viner wrote in the 'The Customs Union Issue' (New York, 1950) "Even the highly technical economic groupings such as Customs Union were primarily the outcome of political and security considerations" (South Asian Politics 2005).

For India, therefore there is once again an opportunity to relate to Myanmar. However, so far our foreign policy has been desultory at best sporadic and episodic. Greater consistency, greater commitment to more open trade and investment relations and a willingness to share in the region's problems and not just in its prosperity will help India move closer.

Sec. VI. Conclusion

While India must Look East with a purpose and commitment, BIMSTEC community must also accept the fact its links with this subcontinent, particularly India run deep into the foundation of our combined history. In Asia, India is both a factor for peace and stability as well as a partner in progress. For India, it is necessary to accept that in Myanmar the liberal democratic paradigm will not come about easily. The changed paradigm will be combined with elements of authoritarianism, as economies will be governed by a varying mix of state control and the market, or cultures that will allow or restrict the entry of foreign influences.

All the same, India's foreign policy must continue to reflect the values of democracy. Being the largest democracy in the world the mantle of safeguarding democracy falls upon India and more so amongst her neighbouring countries. Since India's foreign policy is more political than economic, it must carry on the fight against any kind of domination and uphold the principle of self-determination of the people, their human rights and dignity. To sum up, it is worthwhile to recall the words of Dr.Sein Win, the Prime Minister in exile of the National Coalition Government of the Union of Burma to the Second International Convention for the Restoration of Democracy in Burma in 2004. His appeal was that "India's multifaceted policy should not be restricted to business dealings and short –term military cooperation with the Burmese Generals only and it should include engagement with the Burmese people and their chosen representatives of the democracy movement on moral grounds." India needs to promote her national interest in the world, as it is and not shape them to fit the world. The re-envisioning of the India Myanmar relations linked to each other, culturally and historically is the need of the hour.

References

1. Anand Kumar (2004), "Indo-Myanmar Economic Relations and Northeast Insurgency", *Freelancer*, Article No.1563, November 21.
2. *Ibid.*
3. Dixit J.N (1998), *Across Boarders*, New Delhi: Piscus Books
4. Dutt, V.P (1984), *India's Foreign Policy in a Changing World*, New Delhi: Vikas Publishing House
5. *Ibid.*, p.226
6. *Ibid.*, p.228
7. Kuppuswamy C.S., "Indo-Myanmar Relations – A Volte Face", *South Asia Analysis Group Papers*
8. *Ibid.*
9. *Ibid.*
10. *Ibid.*
11. *Ibid.*
12. Ollapally M. Deepa (2005), "Foreign Policy and Identity Politics: Realist Versus Culturalist Lessons" in Kanti Bajpai and Siddarth Mallavarapu (ed.), *India Theorising the Region and Nation*, New Delhi: Orient Longman Pvt. Ltd.
13. Prakash Chander & Prem Arora (1990), *International Relations*, New Delhi: Bookhive's Publications, p.578.

14. Raja Mohan C (2003), *Crossing the Rubicon*, New Delhi: Penguin Books
15. Ravni Thakur (2004), "Junta Or Not", *Hindustan Times*, November 10.
16. *Ibid.*,
17. *Ibid.*,
18. *South Asian Politics* (2005), Vol.4, No.7, November

14

A Study on India's Political-Economic Relations with Some BIMSTEC Nations

A.Vanajamani

Sec. I. Introduction

The need for a foreign policy of a nation emerges from the desire to establish peaceful external relations, which allows the rulers to concentrate on the aspects of internal development. Foreign policy allows a nation to take economic advantage of the neighbour goodwill in terms trade and business. India has always adopted the policy of non-interference in the internal affairs of the nations and has extended continuous support to establishment of democracy. The tone of Indian foreign policy was set way back in 1855 when the congress denounced the annexation of Burma. Similar stand is being adopted presently in relation to present-day Myanmar and Nepal. Pundit Jawaharlal Nehru in one of his speeches in 1964 said, "We are of Asia and people of Asia are nearer and closer to us". In the past Indian culture has flowed to many of the Asian countries and therefore Nehru desired a closer union. Nehru was creator of the policy for the establishment of Non Aligned Movement (NAM). Nehru always called NAM as non-aligned to any interest bloc, not completely neutral. NAM always denounced aggressionists and colonial tendencies. While NAM represented the political alteration to the cold war environment of that period, formation of South Asian Association for Regional Cooperation (SAARC) ushered in an era of economic cooperation. But SAARC was preceded by formation of as clearing union in 1974. South Asian Free Trade Agreement (SAFTA) was established in 2004, as a separate wing of SAARC.

SAARC agreed to create SAFTA to be implemented over 10 years. Besides regional economic integration, the bilateral free trade agreements between India and Nepal and between India and Sri Lanka have also speeded up the economic integration in the South Asian sub region.

Asian developing countries had made a number of attempts at regional economic cooperation in the 1970s. These include Bangkok agreement of 1975, which covers the exchange of tariff concessions between five member nations –Bangladesh, India, Sri Lanka China, South Korea. Early experiences have not been very successful for which the reasons are various. i) limited coverage of membership, ii) products covered, preference margins not being deep enough, and iii) its scope not extending to the non-tariff barriers. Recent developments in BIMST-EC (renamed as the Bay of Bengal Initiative for Multi-sectoral Technical and Economic Cooperation) could also play a linking role between AFTA and SAFTA, particularly following the adoption of a framework agreement in January 2004 to form an FTA by 2017.

Table - 1

Number of Items Under Bangkok Agreement Concessions

Country	*Current*	*After third round*
Bangladesh	129	129
India	188(33)	577(57)
Srilanka	288 (32)	523(80)

Source: Calculated by the ESCAP secretariat, from *Economic and Political Weekly*, September, 2005.

Note: Special concessions to Least Development Countries (LDCs)

The addition of Bhutan and Nepal as new members and the clear political will that emerged at the first summit for broader economic cooperation, held in July 2004 are indicators for growing desire for regional cooperation. Of particular note is the plan to launch a BIMST-EC business card scheme that could go a long way in promoting cross border trade and investments.

Sec. II. Geography-based Consolidation

Consolidation could take place on a geographical basis. The idea is to build on and rationalize current initiatives on a region-wide basis, while avoiding the creation of a new grouping of countries. The Bangkok Agreement is the only trade agreement that currently links south and east Asia, with three of its members sharing common membership with BIMST-EC and this might eventually coalesce into an initiative that promotes a wider east, south-east and south Asian Free Trade Agreement (FTA). An agreement open to all countries of Asia Pacific, for example the Asia-Pacific agreement as the Bangkok agreement will eventually come to be known, might be a useful vehicle for laying some of the ground work of this framework.

Figure.1

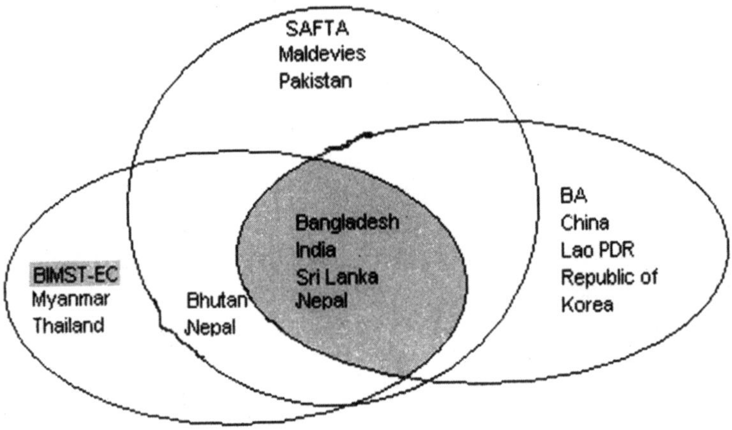

Source:: Economic and Political Weekly, September, 2005

The prospects for consolidation could thus, go further to encompass closely related issues such as trade in services, competition policy and wider forms of economic cooperation like financial and monetary cooperation.

Sec. III. Political and Cultural Relations

3.1. Indo-Sri Lanka Relations

Communal tensions and ethnic rivalry have marked the politics of Sri Lanka since 1950. By 1970, the demand for separate Tamil State was raised and the terrorist activities were attributed to Tamil separatists. The North Communal riots in 1977 and 1983 widened the gulf of mistrust between the communities. Tamil sense of grievances and victimization were increased. Exposed to the largely Simhalese in the South, Tamils sought the support of their ancestral Indian Tamils living in South India. This aspect has been the influencing factor in molding the Indo-Sri Lanka relations.

The mistrust that had started with perceived Indian involvement in the matters of Sri Lankan Tamils, further increased with Sri Lanka, developing its relationship on bilateral level with China and Pakistan. Sri Lanka also got the assistance of pro-western countries to help in improving her economy, which was against Indian policy of Socialism. Though India has assured that it had no intention of invading its neighbors, but criticized the situation in the Jaffna peninsula created by the establishment of the Security Zone, citing the hardship and danger posed to residents of Indian origin. Indian policy on the Sri Lankan ethnic crisis is a shambles, notwithstanding its efforts at mediation and appeals for a negotiated settlement. By virtue of 1987 agreement, India has acquired a definite role in the domestic as well as foreign policies of Sri Lanka. Sri Lanka has been denuded of much of its sovereignty and forfeited its power to seek military or economic assistance from any country without prior clearance from India. The withdrawal of the Indian Peace Keeping Force from Sri Lanka brings to an end a murky phase in Indo- Sri Lankan relations. Hopefully this will remove from the Sri Lankan political agenda – the India attitude that was the hallmark of Sri Lanka's approach to India.

India believes that the essential unity that lies behind diversity needs to be fostered so that aspirations of all sections of the population could be realized. There was also need to strengthen cooperation in the economic field to tap its full potential in the two countries. Indo-Sri Lanka trade had significantly increased in the last two years and efforts were on to identify the various sectors, in which co-operation promised to yield substantial benefits to both countries. The ban on Liberation Tigers of Tamil Elam (LTTE) has also opened up a new, potentially sensitive phase in Indo-Sri Lanka relations The ban coupled with the speed with which India is returning Tamil refugee to Sri lanka, has been welcomed as indication that India was distancing itself form Sri Lankan ethnic conflict

3.2. Indo-Bangladesh Relations

Bangladesh has a special and unique relationship with India since its emergence as a free and independent country. India has played a decisive role in carving Bangladesh out of Pakistan. Initially, India mobilized the world opinion against the atrocities and finally, in the Bangladesh by the Pakistani government; its army fought and brought to knees the Pakistani forces and thus liberated the people of Bangladesh. Refugees from Bangladesh found the conditions propitious to return and settle in their motherland.

A 'Treaty of Friendship, Cooperation and Peace' between India and Bangladesh was signed in March, 1972. After affirming their adherence to the principles of non-alignment, peaceful co-existence, mutual co-operation, non-interference in internal affairs and respect for territorial integrity and sovereignty, the two States agreed to mutual consultations, in order to take appropriate measures in case either was attacked or threatened. It was also decided to improve economic and cultural relations. India and Bangladesh have expressed their determination to stop illegal movement of people into their common borders by all possible means. The two Heads of Governments agreed to arrange speedy repatriation of all Chakma refugees to Bangladesh under fully safety and security. For this purpose, a joint task force headed by home secretaries of the two countries has been set up.

India and Bangladesh have also differed with each other on the issue of Farakka Barrage; fencing the Assam border with barbed wire; sovereignty over New Moore Island and some other economic and political issues. On the non-contentious issues namely, sharing of river waters, there is an evidence of slight forward movement, with both sides agreeing that the Ganga and Teesta river flows fall short during the lead season. They agreed that an equitable long term and comprehensive water sharing arrangement involving these rivers as well as other major ones would serve the best interests of the two countries.

3.2.1 Tin Bigha Corridor: This dispute is outstanding since pre-Bangladesh days. The land boundary agreement of 1974 decided to provide a corridor between Dahagram and Angarpota enclaves. Again in 1982, India agreed to handover the enclave, but till to date there has been no implementation.

3.2.2 Other Disputes: In addition to these irritants border insurgencies are continuing in Chittagong Hill Tract and Tripura. Maritime Boundary disputes and South Talpatty New Moore Isalnd disputes are lingering on adding tension and an unhealthy impact in the region.

In the matter of rivers water, a meeting of Indo-Bangladesh Joint Rivers Commission was held in Dhaka during June 21-22, 1990. It was agreed that an acceptable formula for sharing the waters of the common rivers, including the Ganga and the Teesta, had to be found before, the beginning of the next dry season. It was decided to expedite the work of the secretaries committee in this context.

It also accepted the final report of the Indo-Bangladesh task force, set up in 1988, which recommended as action plan for effective flood management through co-operation. The action plan includes setting up embankments along the common rivers near the border, exchange of expertise for effective river training works in Bangladesh, exchange of flood forecasting data and sharing experience in respect of drainage improvement, flood plain zoning and disaster management.

The fact that Bangladesh now has a democratically elected government that could make it easier for India to build better ties of understanding. The matters discussed were unfavorable balance of trade for Bangladesh, prospects of purchase of more tea for blending requirements, the problems of Chakma refugees, sharing of river waters and the lease of the Tin Bigha to Bangladesh. But there was no progress on the major issues.

3.3. India's Relations with Nepal

Nepal is a land-locked kingdom in the Central Himalayas between the India and Tibetan Autonomous Region of the Chinese People's Republic. The geo-political situation of Nepal has considerably influenced the India attitude toward Nepal, particularly after the occupation of Tibet by China. Another factor, which raised the importance of Nepal, was the deterioration in the Sino-Indian relation in the mid fifties of its strategic location. Nepal being the northern gateway to the Indo-Gangatic plain, the Indian security and stability are in extricable linked with the stability and security of Nepal. Similarly, the same geographical position accounts in a large measure, for her prolonged isolation as well as slow political progress, economic immobility and social backwardness.

Over the decades, India had consistently tried to preserve this special relationship with Nepal. Thus, while there are strict regulations against the employment of foreign nationals in India, millions of Nepalese live and work freely in all parts of it. Nepalese are eligible to join not only the army but also government service in India except IFS, IAS and IPS. Nepalese nationals have extensive property holding in India. They do business here without hindrance.

India has fully financed and implemented co-operation scheme for the development of Nepal's water resources like the Kosi and the

Gandaki projects Around Rupees 20-25 crores is given annually by India for its economic development. About 275 medical and engineering seats are offered to Nepalese students every year under various schemes. In spite of all these, the relations between India and Nepal were not altogether cordial and were not characterized by mutual distrust and acrimony. The Trade and Transit treaties prejudicially signed by the two countries and their differing perceptions in regard to the facilities offered, have been a major source of tension between the countries.

1. The First Trade and Transit Treaty	1950
2. Nepal as a zone of Peace	1975
3. The lapse of Trade and Trasit Treaty	1989
4. Mahakali Treaty	1996
5. New Transit Treaty	1999

3.3.1. Improvements in Relations

A new round of engagement to develop infrastructure, promote trade and improve border management was started in May 2000 during the visit of Nepalese Foreign Minister to India. On July 5, 2000 India and Nepal began discussions on security-related matters including ways to strengthen surveillance along the 1600 km long "highly sensitive' Indo-Nepal border. On August 1, 2000 India and Nepal held a major brain storming session to address threats to their security and ways to orient their relationship to new political and economic demands

3.3.2. International Reactions

In the present-day world of imperialist globalization any internal political event has more international ramifications than ever before. Hence the February 1, royal regression has generated worldwide reactions. None of the major international players have supported Gyanendra's regressive steps so far. The most significant international development has been the suspension of military aid by India and UK. However, the despotic regime is desperately seeking to exploit two issues to gain international support for itself. The first is the 'anti-terrorism' card and the second the 'geopolitical 'card. As far as the "geopolitical' card for the country's strategic positioning between the two nations, China and India is concerned. Gyanendra's attempt to repeat the skilful diplomatic maneuvering of playing one neighbor against the other can not be expected to bear much fruit in the changed situation of international balance of forces.

Sec. IV. Economic Relations

Economic historians of the coming centuries might describe the shift in policy paradigm of the developing countries from import substitution to outward orientation during the closing decades of the 20th century as a major landmark in the history of the developing world. The South Asian economies were not mere passive spectators to this whirlpool, but joined the process earnestly (Kumar 2005). Inter country differences in the extent and timing notwithstanding; there have been comprehensive policy reforms in the 1990s, covering different sectors of these economies, especially liberalization of trade and investment regimes with deliberate initiatives to integrate their economies with the rest of the world (Kumar).

4.1. Policy Reforms

The 1990's witnessed comprehensive reform programs in almost all the countries in South Asia. With possible exception of Sri Lanka, which began opening up of trade and capital flows little later, all the other countries in the region have initiated major policy reforms with respect to the external sector which interalia, included reduction in the level and dispersion of tariffs and quantitative restrictions and removing regulations on foreign investments. The period also witnessed the launching of new plans in Bhutan (9th Plan) India (10th Plan) and Nepal (10th Plan). Since there was inter-country variation in the focus as well as the pace of reforms a country level approach is called for.

Given below is the country-wise economic indicators like GDP Growth, inflation rate, merchandise export and import growth, Fiscal Balance etc in per cent ages.

4.1.1. Economy of Bangladesh

- Prior to 1986 there were 24 tariff slabs, which have been rationalized to 12 by 93-94; 6 by 96-97; and 4 by 99-00.
- Preferential rates of duties applicable to public sector enterprise were eliminated in 1989.
- The maximum tariff rate was reduced from a level of 350 percent in 91-92 to 37.5percent in 99-00
- Bangladesh shifted from a fixed exchange rate regime to a managed system of floating exchange rate.
- The foreign investment policy was revised in 1991 and it removed the limit on foreign equity participation.

Table - 2

Major Economic Indicators, Bangladesh, 2000-2004 (%)

ITEM	*2000*	*2001*	*2002*	*2003*	*2004*
GDP growth	5.9	5.3	4.4	5.2	5.8
Gross domestic investment/GDP	23.0	23.1	23.2	24.0	25.5
Gross domestic saving/GDP	22.1	20.8	23.6	22.7	23.0
Inflation rate (consumer price index)	3.4	1.6	2.4	3.8	4.5
Money supply (M2e) b growth	18.6	16.6	13.1	12.8	14.2
Fiscal balance/ GDP	-6.2	-6.1	-4.4	-3.9	-5.2
Merchandise export growth	8.2	11.4	-7.6	9.5	10.5
Merchandise import growth	4.8	11.3	-8.7	3.5	7.5
Current account balance/GDP	-0.9	-2.3	0.4	-1.3	-2.5
Debt service ratio	8.0	8.2	8.7	8.6	8.4

Source: Asian Development Bank (2003), *Asian Development outlook*, New York: Oxford University Press

Note: Policy Reforms which had its beginning in the 1980s, accelerated in the 1990s.

4.1.2. Trade Policy of Bangladesh

- Liberalized imports and import procedures with no need of licensing
- Reduction in Quantitative Restrictions (QRs), the coverage of which has been reduced from 42 per cent in 1985 to only 2 percent of imports in 1996
- Local currency Taka is freely convertible for current account transactions.
- IMF consistent counter trade/special Trading Arrangements are allowed.
- Export promotion measures are specific and transparent.

These policy measures encourages Free Trade and able to gain fruits of LPG

4.1.2. Economy of India

Table - 3

Major Economic Indicators, India, 2000-2004 (%)

Item	*2000*	*2001*	*2002*	*2003*	*2004*
GDP growth	4.4	5.6	4.4	6.0	6.3
Gross domestic investment/GDP	24.0	23.7	23.9	24.0	25.0
Gross domestic saving/GDP	23.4	24.0	24.5	24.1	25.2
Inflation rate (consumer price index)	7.2	3.6	2.8	5.0	5.0
Money supply (M2e) b growth	16.8	14.2	15.7	16.0	16.0
Fiscal balance/ GDP	-9.5	-10.0	-9.3	-9.5	-9.0
Merchandise export growth	19.6	0.1	11.4	15.1	16.6
Merchandise import growth	7.0	-2.8	6.3	11.8	12.2
Current account balance/GDP	-0.6	0.3	0.6	0.3	0.2
External debt/GDP	22.4	20.9	19.5	18.0	16.0

Sources: Asian Development Bank (2003), *Asian Development Outlook*, New York: Oxford University Press, p.118

The move towards a more open and market-oriented economy could be traced back to the mid 1980s.

Policy Reforms of India

- Dismantling of the import licensing system
- Phasing out of almost all of the non-tariff barriers
- The QRs on imports of around 2300 items had been removed unilaterally in 1998
- Tariff rates have been brought down to a maximum of 50 per cent from 355 percent
- Average weighted tariff rates have come down from 87 percent to just 20 per cent by 1999.
- A reduction in peak customs duty from 35 percent to 30 per cent
- Further reductions in these duties into only two slabs of 10 percent (for raw material, intermediate and components) and 20 percent (for final products) by 2004-05.
- Foreign ownership upto 100 percent is permitted in most manufacturing sectors
- Automatic approval of outward FDI proposals by India companies to the extent of US$ 10 million.
- A competition Act was passed in 2002

Government of India took lead role in the sub-region to implement LPG through these trade policies.

4.1.3. Economy of Nepal

Nepal also opened up it economy in the early 1990s, with the adoption of liberalization policy. The main goal of Tenth Plan of Nepal (2003-2007) is to bring about a substantial, positive and sustainable change in the living standards of Nepalese people.

- High, sustainable and broad based economic growth with the aim of resurgence of broad-based economic activities
- Agriculture development, sustainable management of natural resources and biodiversity
- Development of tourism, water resources, information Technology, industry and commerce sector with an important role for private sector.
- Social sector and infrastructure development

Sec.V. Composition of Merchandise Trade

All nations agreed to accelerate cooperation in the core areas of trade, finance and investment to realize the goal of an integrated South

Asian economy in a step-by step manner. The nations aspire to make full use of regional synergy to maximize the benefits of globalization and liberalization and to minimize their negative impacts on the region. Recognizing the close relationship between trade and economic expansion, an attempt is made to analyze the structure of service sector exports and imports.

The South Asian countries exports of services have also grown in recent times. Especially commercial service exports of India showed significant growth, largely owing to exports of IT software and related services that have grown at a compound rate of over 50 percent over the past five to six years. In case of Sri Lanka, commercial services have become vibrant in growth and more than half of the services exports are emanating from this sector. In case of Bangladesh, transport sector recorded remarkable increase in its share.

Table - 4
Major Economic Indicators, Nepal 2000-2004 (%)

Item	*2000*	*2001*	*2002*	*2003*	*2004*
GDP growth[a]	6.0	4.6	-0.6	1.5	3.5
Gross domestic Investment/GDP	24.2	23.8	24.4	22.0	22.0
Gross domestic Savings/GDP	18.8	19.0	17.4	17.0	17.0
Inflation rate (consumer price index)	3.5	2.4	2.9	5.0	5.0
Money supply (M2) growth	21.8	15.2	6.3	12.0	12.0
Fiscal balance[b] /GDP	-3.3	-4.5	-3.3	-4.0	-4.0
Merchandise export growth	37.5	4.6	-18.0	5.0	10.0
Merchandise import growth	22.0	-0.2	-11.4	5.0	10.0
Current account balance/GDP	-5.3	-5.4	-7.0	-5.0	-5.0
Debt service ratio[c]	6.0	6.8	9.7	7.0	7.0

Source: RIS (2004), *South Asia Development and Cooperation Report*, New Delhi.

Transport services are the leading item in their import basket. In Bangladesh, India, and Sri Lanka transport services account for around 60-70 percent of total imports of commercial services during the 1990s. However, in 2001, it appears that imports of transport services in the case of India and Sri Lanka have slowed down. For Nepal, import of travel services have been quite prominent.

Table - 5

Structure of Service Exports

	Commercial service exports ($mn.)		*Transport (%of total service)*		*Travel (% of total service)*		*Other (% of total service)*	
	1990	*2001*	*1990*	*2001*	*1990*	*2001*	*1990*	*2001*
Bangladesh	296	242	12.9	29.5	6.4	19.6	80.6	50.8
India	4610	20390	20.8	10.6	33.8	17.9	45.4	71.4
Nepal	166	303	3.6	15.6	65.6	47.5	30.8	36.9
Sri Lanka	425	1344	39.7	29.7	30.2	15.8	30.1	54.5

Source: RIS (2004), *South Asia Development and Cooperation Report*, New Delhi

Table - 6

Structure of Service Imports

Countries	*Commercial Service imports ($mn)*		*Transport (%of total services)*		*Travel (%of total services)*		*Other (%of total services)*	
	1990	2001	1990	2001	1990	2001	1990	2001
Bangladesh	554	1375	71.1	75.0	14.1	12.0	14.9	12.9
India	5943	23419	57.5	41.1	6.6	13.1	35.9	45.8
Nepal	159	205	40.8	34.9	28.5	38.8	30.7	26.3
Sri Lanka	620	1729	64.2	48.9	11.9	14.2	23.9	36.9

Source: As in Table.5

Table - 7

Trade performance Index in Basis Manufactures in South Asian Countries

Indicators	*Bangladesh*	*Bhutan*	*India*	*Nepal*	*Sri Lanka*
Relative Ranking among184countries	122	124	129	----	129
Trend of exports	18	123	53	70	105
Average annual change in per capital exports	105	121	80	25	99
Share in world market	83	119	34	121	93
Product Diversification	81	123	24	90	94
Product spread (concentration)	71	124	19	103	81
Market diversification	53	122	32	44	71
Market spread (concentration)	62	122	14	88	74

Source: As in Table.5

Note: Data year for Bangladesh is 1997-2001, data year for Bhutan is 1995-1999, data year for India is 1997-2001, data year for Nepal is 1995-1999, and data year for Sri Lanka is 1997-2001.

Sec. VI. Trade Performance of BIMSTEC Countries

To get a more comprehensive picture of their trade performance an attempt has been made to analyze the trade performance of these countries by referring to the trade performance index, as developed by the International Trade Center (ITC)

It is evident from the table that the trade performance of these countries at the global level has been dismal in relative sense. This is clear from the fact that in the area of basic manufacture, out of 184 countries in the world. The Rank of these nations ranged between 122 and 129. During the some of the recent years (in most cases the period is 1997-2001) some countries such as Bangladesh, India have shown dynamism as compared to other countries in terms of exports of basic manufactures. However in terms of rate of per capital exports, only Nepal appeared to have fared better than others. This indicator is important because, it may be argued that the level of exports is determined by the demand for a country's products in world markets and a country's ability to satisfy that demand, which can be related to its size. Hence, the value of per capita exports shows how outward looking is a country, and the extent to which the population produces for the world market. In terms of share in global market in basic manufactures, except India, other countries have not performed very well. While India's rank has been 34, other countries have ranked in the range of 83 to 121. There are two more aspects that need to be taken into account while assessing the trade performance, viz., product diversification as well as market diversification. The South Asian countries have performed relatively better in terms of market diversification, as compared to product diversification.

6.1. BIMSTEC Countries' Outlook

Economic performance will depend heavily on the domestic security and political scenario, and developments in the global economy. Domestic factors played a more important role, such as the security situation in Nepal, tensions between India and Pakistan and progress on peace talks in Sri Lanka.

The figure 2 is indicating the BIMSTEC countries' outlook by considering GDP Growth percent in the years from 2001 to 2004.

Growth in GDP for the sub region declined to 4.2 percent from 5.0 percent in 2001, instead of increasing as forecasting in ADO 2002, primarily as a result of adverse weather conditions in Bangladesh, India and Nepal. In addition, the economies of Bangladesh and Nepal suffered from extremely weak external demand. In contrast Sri Lanka experienced stronger growth in 2002 compared with the previous year.

Figure 2

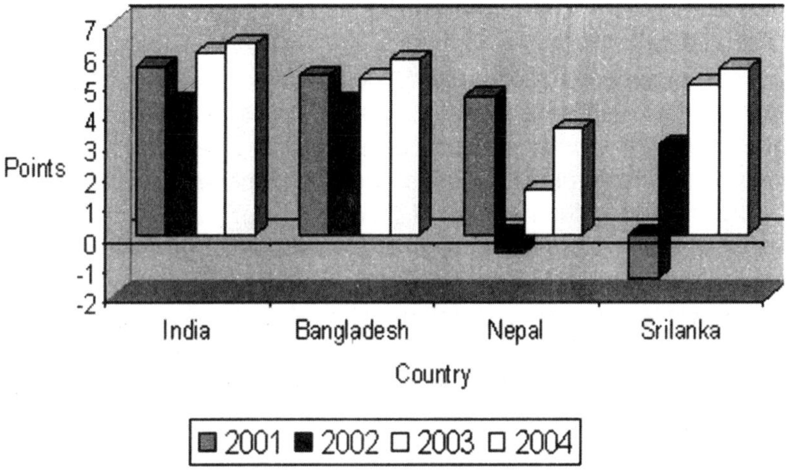

Source: Asian Development Bank (2003), *Asian Development Outlook*, New York: Oxford University Press

Inflation remained generally mild at 4.0 percent as most economies adopted macro economic policies that kept prices stable, while Sri Lanka still had double digit inflation in 2002 Export Growth in the region picked up to 7.0 percent in 2002, as India's exports recovered, in spite of weak external demand. Import growth also recovered to 2.5 on account of India's strong demand. The outlook for South Asia is based on an assumed acceleration in global economic growth improved political stability and security in the countries and normal weather conditions. In this context, growth is expected to increase to 5.7 percent in 2003 and to 6.1 percent in 2004 led by strong expansion in India which accounts for roughly three-fourths of the sub region's economy. With continued economic liberalization and private sector-led growth, gross domestic investment as a share of GDP is expected to increase in most countries.

Sec. VII. Conclusion

For South Asia where regional cooperation is influenced by bilateral issues, as seen in the case of SAARC. The formation of BIMSTEC has been indeed a welcome sign that some efforts have been undertaken. So far whatever has been done, no doubt, constitutes small beginning, but perhaps an irreversible movement has begun which in due course may develop into substantially mutual beneficial activity. It is a fact that BIMSTEC has many things in common, culturally, geographically, socially and economically to certain extent, but unfortunately not politically.

In no other region of the world, do we have such a big country as India, surrounded by a number of small ones. It has the major concentration of mineral resources of the region and far more advanced technological base and structure of production, covering entire range of modern industry than the rest of the countries of the region, who are almost in early stages of industrial development. In view of such peculiar feature of India, relative to the rest of the region, there can be no worthwhile regional cooperation without full Indian participation in such an endeavor. Thus, it would not be an exaggeration to say that, as Indian role is crucial for meaningful cooperation in the area of Bay of Bengal. Their sizes, economic dynamism, political stability, military power contrives to assure that the major regional influences, which originate within are going to emanate from this nation. In other words, India is to be central to the future of co-operation in South Asia in general and BIMSTEC in particular.

References

1. Asher G mukul, Rahul Sen (2005), "East Asia Integration: A Win - Win Situation for Asia", *Economic and Political Weekly,* September 3- 9, pp.3932 – 3938.
2. Asian Development Bank (2003), *Asian Development Outlook*, New York: Oxford University Press, p.11
3. *Ibid.*, p.118
4. Bonapack Tiziana (2005), "Regional Trade and Investment Architecture in Asia-Pacific", *Economic and Political Weekly*, September 3, pp.3941–3947.
5. Asian Development Bank (2003), *Op.cit.*, p.118
6. Kumar Nagesh (2005), "A Broader Asian Community and a possible Roadmap", *Economic and Political Weekly*, September 3, pp.3928 – 3930.
7. RIS (2004), *South Asia Development & Cooperation Report*, New Delhi.
8. Subrahmaniam Narendra (2005), "Political Formation of Cultures, The South Asian Experience", *Economic and Political Weekly*, September 3, pp.3821 – 3827.

15

Oceanic Resources of Bay of Bengal : Scope for Scientific and Technical Collaboration

P. Rajendra Prasad

The Bay of Bengal and the associated coastal zone encompasses enormous quantities of natural resources, both living and non-living. With an exponential depletion of land natural resources, the focus of the humankind is drifted on to the near shore and ocean fronts. The major discoveries of hydrocarbon resources in the off shore regions and the increasing dependence on marine food have given additional importance to the oceans. Neighbouring countries of Bay of Bengal i.e., India, Bangladesh, Thailand, Myanmar, Sri Lanka etc. by virtue of similar socio-economic status have very high potential and ample scope for scientific and technical collaboration. India, with its vast potential in intellectual human resource and technological skills, can perhaps take a leading role in conceptualizing and evolving strategic R & D and capacity building activities in exploration, exploitation and management of the coastal zone and natural resources of the Bay of Bengal region.

Sec. I. Introduction

The huge quantities of sediment piles, reaching a thickness of more than 25 km at places, make the off shore regions of Bengal basin, a potential hydrocarbon sink. The thick mangrove vegetation belts bounding the bay supplement the conventional local energy source and also forms one of the major raw materials for 'medicines from

Fig. 1 Bay of Bengal Community

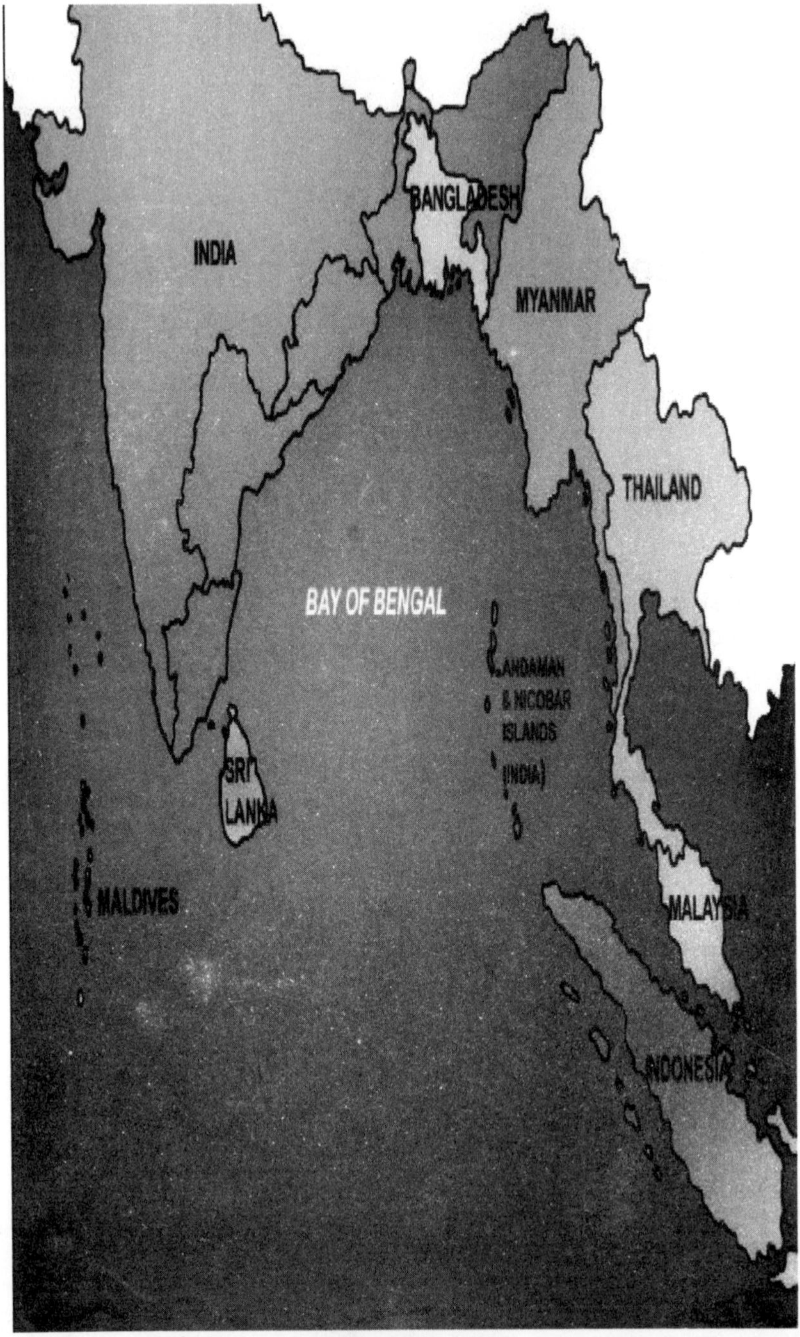

natural sources'. The algae and the benthos in the Bay of Bengal and its costal regions are the exclusive raw materials for the 'medicines from oceans'. The coastal and the ocean waters, ones known for a regular maritime activity, if revitalized, can not only provide an excellent means of 'waterways' for transportation but also significantly reduce the pressure on the highway traffic. The coastal population mostly involved in the fishing activity needs a philip to improve their life standards by adopting new and state of the art technology. Tourism on the coast is the least focused activity in the Indian scenario. Natural resources like ilmenite, monazite, rutile, garnet etc., need to be explored in an effective way.

India, with its relatively better position among the Bay of Bengal Community and other SAARC countries from socio-economic and science and technology points of view complimented by competent human resource, can take a leading role in the development and execution and transfer of state of the art technology and capacity building among the neighbouring countries.

Sec. II. Natural Resources

The natural resources of the country along the coast, the near shore and the deep environments include valuable living and non-living resources that can significantly contribute to the economic growth of any country with ocean boundaries. While most of the living resources are replenishable, a proper management and exploitation strategies of some of the non-living resources can also be treated as replenishable. Various living and non-living resources, their nature and abundance of occurrence and the scientific strategies that can be adopted in their exploration and exploitation are briefly discussed. This will provide a deep insight into the possible collaboration that can be initiated and organized in the direction of BIMSTEC.

2.1 Non Living Resources

Non-living resources mainly comprise of mineral resources, including hydrocarbons. The coastal and the near shore regions constitutes high grade silica sands, coral reefs, radioactive minerals like ilmenite and monazite and other economic minerals like rutile, garnet etc.. The manganese nodules available on the deep water sea bed contain heavy metals like nickel, cadmium, gold, etc., Though, apparently, these resources do not seem to be renewable resources, they can, in fact be treated as renewable resources from a scientific dimension. The inland geological formations disintegrate and decomposes due to geological processes like weathering, fracturing etc. and carried into the oceans through fluvial regime. The enrichment of these minerals take place wherever favourable hydrographic, sedimentological and oceanographic processes prevail in the nearshore regions. However, occasionally these heavy minerals are generated in the oceanic region and are transported towards the coast. The manganese nodules, rich in their heavy mineral constituents, are generated in the deep ocean either with a biological or geological nuclei. With time, the nodules grow in size of abundance. Thus, the coastal and near shore mineral resources, the coral reefs and the nodules to some extent can be treated as partially renewable resources.

The huge sediment piles carried by fluvial system from hinterland towards the coast contain significant quantities of organic matter that gets deposited in the ocean sediments. The thick piles of sediments over a period of time get enriched in their organic content leading to the generation of hydrocarbons. The hydrocarbons thus, generated migrate to get entrapped in favourable structures. The off shore structures off Krishna – Godavari basins and Cauvery basin are proved to be highly potential sources for hydrocarbons with a number of production wells in operation. Gas hydrates is one more significant natural energy, which is gaining high importance in the recent years. Gashydrates essentially contains methane in frozen state under water depths of 1500-2000 m.

2.1.1. Mineral Resources: The hinterland geological formations constitute a number of minerals. Many of these economic minerals may not have commercial viability from production point of view. One of the best examples is the khondolite suit of rocks, metamorphic in nature, do contain heavy minerals like ilmenite, monazite and highly economic minerals like rutile, garnet etc., but they cannot be produced through an economically viable process. But the same rock formation, while being exposed to a number of geological processes like weathering, fracturing etc., disintegrates into loose sediments and gets transported through aeoline and fluvial processes. In this processes due to their natural physical characteristics like varying densities, grain size characteristics and other distinct physical and chemical properties, segregates, while they are transported, leading to a partial state of enrichment. These minerals in due course of time reach the nearshore regions of the coastal waters and get enriched under favourable hydrographic, sedimentological and oceanographic process response phenomenon. Figure 2 depicts one such example on the east coast.

Figure 2: Heavy Mineral Concentrations along the East Coast

Thus, these valuable minerals which in their original form of occurrence are not viable for economic processing become highly economic for their exploitation and extraction. However, though the processes appears to be so simple to understand the scientific strategies that are required to fix their provinance, process-response characteristics, assessment of occurrence and their abundance in various geological formations and physical states will play a critical role. One specific example of such mineral occurrences is the placer mineral deposits of the coastal and the nearshore regions of East and West coasts of India. The entire coastal belt of West Bengal, Orissa, Andhra Pradesh, Tamil Nadu, Kerala Ratnagiri etc. contains huge quantities of placer minerals. The Sri Lankan coast is also known for abundance of ilmenite and leucoxene palcers. The Indian Rare Earths and the Department of Atomic Energy have developed excellent scientific skills to map, assess and evaluate these placer minerals. The existing technology can further be enhanced to process the heavy minerals to be used as raw materials for our nuclear energy requirements. This is an area, which deserves the attention of not only the Government of India but also all the Bay of Bengal community nations who can derive an unassumingly high benefit in this field, if a concerted effort is put in. Though no gold placers are reported as such, they are obtained through panning in the sands of Subernarekha river in the Bengal delta region which hints at the possibility of their presence in the relict beaches and buried river channels. The Orissa and the Andhra coast are potential areas for the occurrence of gold. Similarly chromite and antimony are expected from the ultra maphic rocks near Andaman Sea.

2.1.2. Polymetalic Nodules: Manganese, iron, nickel, copper, cobalt, led, melodium, cadnium, titanium etc., constituent's a polymetalic nodule. However, cobalt, copper and manganese are

Figure 3: Various Modes of Manganese Nodules

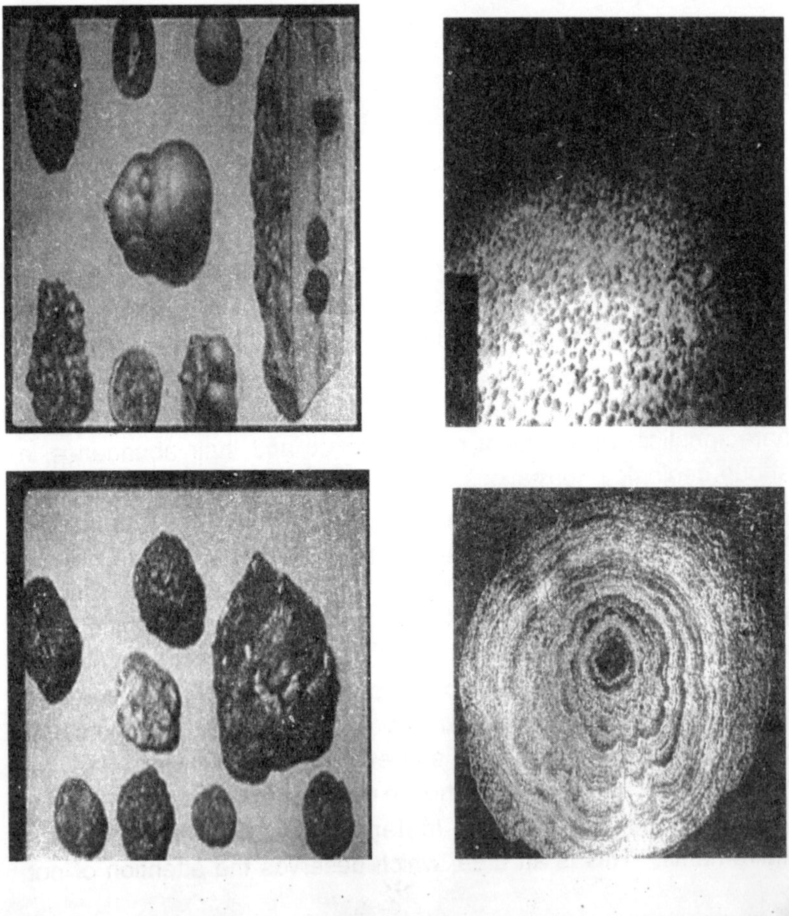

considered to be of great strategy importance. Normally the involved geological phenomena itself is very slow when compared to the time spans of non-living regime. The growth and development of the polymetalic nodules is one of the slowest of all the known geological phenomena. They are almost of the order of a few cms over several million years. This makes these resources more precious and attributes a more non-renewable character to them. The origin of the polymetalic nodules could be both hydrogeonic, diagenic, hydrothermal and halmyrolitic. Deep-sea manganese nodules are found in abundance, mostly in intraplate regions. The depth and the sedimentation rates control the abundance of these nodules. Figure 3 shows various modes of Polymetalic nodules present in Indian Ocean region.

2.1.3. Hydrocarbon Resources: The oil and natural gas forms the major chunk of the hydrocarbons resources in the entire world. Degeneration of organic matter is proved to be one of the major sources for these valuable resources. In the recent years, it is proved that this resource is no more confined to continental region but is also abundant in the offshore region. However, the structural controls which are observed to follow the landmasses are observed to provide the primary signatures for their locations in the offshore regions. These hydrocarbon resources are located at depths following from 1.5 to 3.5 km from seabed, making the task of both exploration and exploitation very tough. The geophysical exploration techniques, which are the only tools to identify the oil bearing structures below the sea bed are not only expensive but also involve a very high degree of technical skills in the processes of data acquisition and interpretation. These require an integrated knowledge of geology, geophysics, mathematics and certain engineering aspects. India, with its very rich human resources, over the last five decades has developed world-class technology in the field of hydrocarbon exploration and exploitation. Organizations like Oil and Natural Gas Commission has an established track record in this field, which prompted countries like Russia, Iran etc to hire their services. This is an area, where India can play a very significant role in helping BIMSTEC in the field of natural oil and gas

2.1.4. Gas-hydrates: Apart from the well-known oil and natural gas, which are of organic origin, gas- hydrates are crystalline compounds of water and methane molecules formed at high pressure and low temperature. They occur naturally in the outer continental margins and the permafrost regions of the world. The energy contained in the gas-hydrates is estimated to be double the amount of total fossil fuel reserves in the world. Further, one volume of hydrate produces around 150 times volume of gas at STP. This makes the gas-hydrate as the future energy source (Figure 4).

When they were discovered way back in 1810, they could not be realized as an economically viable resource. These gas hydrates are associated with a conspicuous seismic property known as Bottom Simulation Reflector (BSR). The BSR has a characteristic of reversing the seismic phase. The known gas hydrates are estimated to be at least two times more than the fossil fuels on the global scale. Again, India is one of the most competent countries that can handle the gas hydrates regime both in off shore and nearshore regions. The geophysical strengths of India are highly comparable with any developed nation to explore, exploit these non-living resources of the world's oceans. A concerted and cooperative effort by the Bay of Bengal community could elevate their economic strengths.

Figure 4 : Gas Hydrates

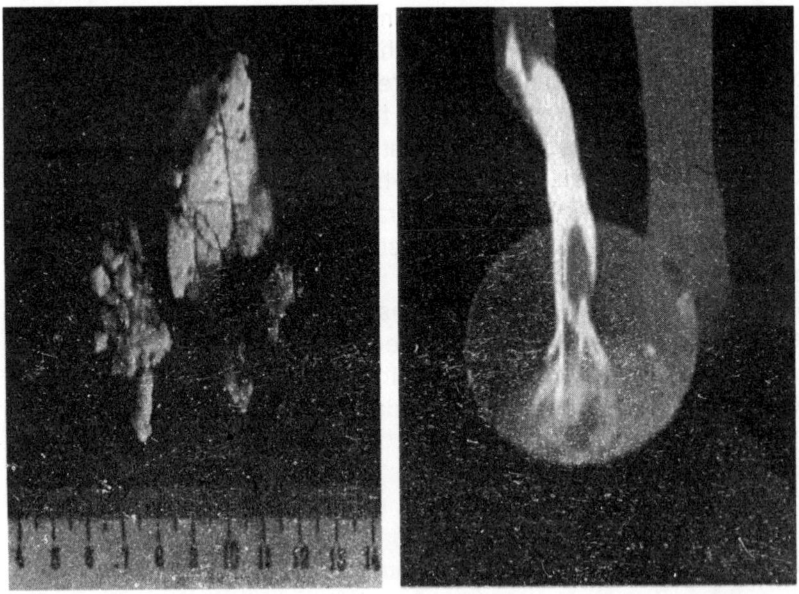

2.2. Living Resources

The living resources of the Bay of Bengal and its coastal regions includes the mangrove ecosystems and fisheries. The mangrove ecosystems are normally distributed along the coast and the estuaries of major rivers near their confluence. The mangroves of Krishna-Godavari and the Cauvery are spread out in large areas representing more than sixty species. Most of the species, being oil rich, are usually used as firewood by the coastal population mostly by the low-income community. However, many species are observed to be of medicinal value. Apart from their economic and medicinal importance, many natural events like tidal waves, tsunamis, and storm surges have proved that the mangroves can act as natural barriers to absorb the impact of such natural events saving mankind from their fury.

2.2.1. Fisheries: The participation of the India, Bangladesh, Sri Lanka and Myanmar in the Bay of Bengal project is observed to be a very successful collaborative programme not only in the improvement of marine food production, but also in the field of technology transfer. A huge quantum of literature has been generated on the fishing species available in various kinds of waters on improvement of fishing gears, operational procedures, food processing and production. This is a living example in the field of marine biology for the BIMSTEC to follow. Inspite of such great developments taking in this field, India has advanced far beyond these latest developments in the field of identification of potential fishing zones using remote sensing technologies. India could make an indelible mark in this field, which was very well recognized by the entire western world. The fundamental concept of this technology is based on Ocean Color Monitoring (OCM) data from the satellites and interpreting them for the presence of high chlorophyll content, which is supposed to be the best nutrient for the marine organisms. Under suitable temperature salinity DO, light chlorophyll and other nutrient conditions the marine organisms folk together for breeding as well as fooding designating them as a potential fishing zones.

There are more than six million fishermen in the country, out of which 2.5 million are full time while the rest 1.5 million work on part time basis. More than two lakh traditional crafts and about a lack of mechanized boats operating in !ndian waters of focus their activity at both pelagic and demersal fishes. Due to the increasing population of the fishing community and intensifying fishing operations the fish catches have been on a degenerative phase. However, the tradition and the heritage doesn't provide an alternative for this activity. As a result, the Department of Space in collaboration with the Ocean Development and several institutions under Ministry of Agriculture have put up a concentrated endeavor for more than a decade to provide potential fishing zone advisories for the sea going community. These sights can be identified from the sea surface temperatures and the chlorophyll concentrations.

Fig. 5. Schematic Diagram of PFZ

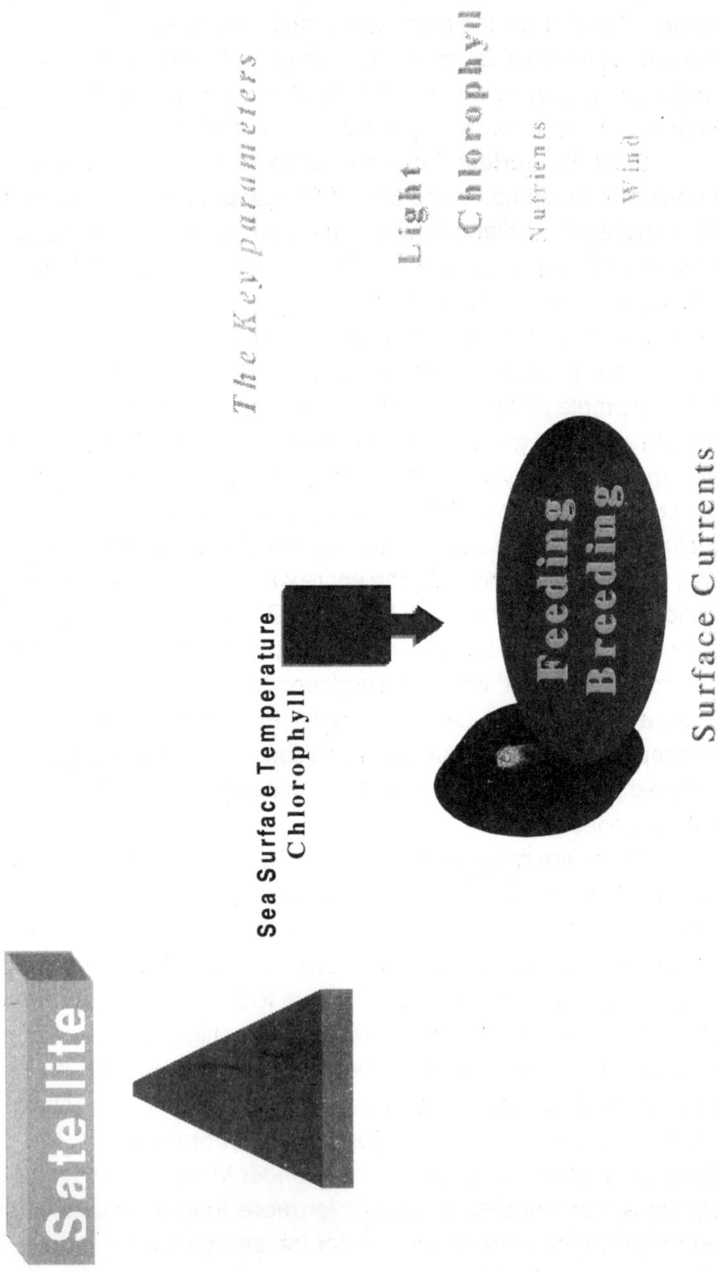

A number of algorithms developed and tested in this field proved to enhance the fish production at least by 50 per cent. The concept of the location of Potential Fishing Zones is shown in figure 5. This is a field where India can provide a leading technology to the neighbors.

2.2.2. Mangrove Ecosystems: Mangroves are plants, which live in muddy and wet soil in tropical and subtropical tidal waters. The biological and plant community, their relationship and inter dependence can be treated under Mangrove ecosystem. Mangroves can be trees, shrubs, palms or ground ferns growing in the zone between high and low tides. Mangroves are often found in regions such as estuaries, embayment and muddy tidal flats. The benthic community represented mollusks, crustaceans, echinoderms, hydroids, actinarians, planarians, etc., and the pelagic community forms the part of the interrelated ecosystems. Mangroves are very fragile and dynamic ecosystems and depend on climatic factors like temperature, rainfall, wind, radiation etc., Sedimentation and tidal amplitude plays a significant role. The Indian mangroves comprise of approximately 60 species belonging to different families and they are abundant both along the east and west coasts of India, including the Andaman Islands. However, almost 80 percent of the mangrove system is located along the east coast. Almost 60 percent of the Indian coastal marine living species is dependent on the mangrove estuarine complex.

A typical mangrove complex of the Indian coast is shown in figure 6.

Figure 6: Typical Mangrove Complex

Uses of Mangroves: Traditionally, in India, the mangrove forests have been used for a variety of purposes like boat building, tannin extraction, firewood, stake for fishing, fodder, natural fertilizer etc.,. Except in Sunderban region, the human habitation is not within the mangrove forest. As a result, the Sunderban mangroves have been extincting due to agricultural and other activities intensified by the habitants. Most of the times the mangrove forests are exploited for timber on a commercial scale. However, the coastal community depends heavily on the mangrove system as the only source of firewood since ancient times. Apart from the traditional uses of Mangrove plant products in India, some of the mangroves and their associates listed in table 1 are found to be of great medicinal importance.

Table - 1

Mangroves and their Associates, with Medicinal Importance

Acanthus ebracteatus	Acanthus ilicifolius	Acrostichum aureum
Aegiceras corniculatum	Avicennia alba	Avicennia marina
Avicennia officinalis	Bruguiera gymnorrhiza	Bruguiera sexangula
Bruguiera parviflora	Ceriops tagal	Cynometra ramiflora
Derris trifoliata	Excoecaria agallocha	Heritiera fomes
Heritiera littoralis	Kandelia candel	Lumnitzera racemosa
Rhizophora mucronata	Rhizophora apiculata	Scyphiphora hydrophyllacea
Sonneratia caseolaris	Xylocarpus mollusis	Xylocarpus grantum

Of late, it is realized that mangroves are playing very significant role in protecting the coastal regions and coastal habitants from natural calamities like storm surges, cyclones, tsunamis, tidal waves etc., In the light of the above findings the geographical location of the Bay of Bengal community along the ocean banks makes it necessary to undertake a concerted R & D and management strategies of the mangrove ecosystems unitedly.

Sec.III. Drugs from the Oceans:

The large biodiversity of the oceans still remained unexplored. Isolation of drugs from the marine flora and fauna for human treatment is a very recent action initiated by many pharmacy companies and Indian and foreign R & D and academic organizations. The need for new drug development and the associated coast are ever increasing and also making it difficult to identify the bioresources. Unlike the terrestrial bioresources, the marine bioresources have been relatively less explored. The first isolation of prostaglandsins from soft corals

Table - 2

Natural Products - Examples of Some Drugs from Oceans

Compound	*Source*	*Application*
Asocalipyrrolidinone	Ascochyta salicorniae	Antimalarial
galactans Sulfated	Botrocladia occidentalis alga and from invertebrates	Anticoagulant
17-Dimethylamino lobohedleolide	Soft coral Lobophytum	Anti-HIV
Eicosapentaenoic acid	Theonella swinboei-sponge	Cardiovascular
Hydroxyakalone	Agobacterium aurantiacum	Hyperuricademigout
Pyrizinostatin	Marine sediments	PGP discs
B-90063	Sea Water	Hypertension

from fauna and flora in late sixties has given great impetus to the probability of discovering new drugs from marine sources in a very large scale compared to those from the terrestrial sources. In the recent years many bioactive molecules exhibiting strong activities against a variety of infections like HIV, malaria, fungal infections, cancers, asthma, inflammation etc. have been isolated and a few of them are under in an advanced state of clinical trails in India and abroad. The CSIR institutions and a few private sector pharmacy companies in India have been working seriously on this topic since 1990. Some of the marine materials being used to extract drugs and chemicals are presented in table 2. Though it appears to be quite promising to extract drugs from the oceans, the risks involved are at least comparable to similar efforts from terrestrial resources.

Sec.IV. Ocean Thermal Energy

The oceans are great repositories of thermal energy. The coastal regions are gifted with high wind and tidal energies. These energies, when coupled with the advanced technologies can provide a number of alternative energy to other resources.The Indian scientific community has been working on the production of alternative energy resources from the tidal and the coastal winds. In the recent years, the National Institute of Ocean Technology, a technical arm of the Department of the Ocean Development of India has built up a 1 MW OTEC plant to produce electricity. Further, they have developed expertise in typing the ocean thermal energy conversion to produce fresh water from seawater with minimum cost.

Sec.V. The Scope

Keeping in view the similarities in coastal, near shore and ocean environment of the countries of the Bay of Bengal Community, there is enormous scope to initiate and strengthen mutual cooperation between these counties in the following fields.

Hydrocarbon exploitation including Gas-hydrates
Mangrove ecosystems
Placer mineral deposits
Marine fisheries
Water ways
Non-conventional energy resources
Drugs from oceans
Pollution and health of seas
Coastal Zone Management
Development of base line data
Monitoring and mitigation of natural hazards
Sustainable development of Living and Non-living Resources
Natural hazards- monitoring and mitigation
Capacity building including human resources
Conventional and Non-Conventional energy Sources
Marine Minerals Resources
Marine Fisheries and Aquaculture
Re-defining EEZ

These are only a few to mention and to start with. There is vast scope for further cooperation in many areas.

Selected Bibliography/References for Further Study

1. Cronam ,D S (1980), *Underwater Minerals*, London: Academic Press, p.362.
2. Cronam, D S (1992), *Marine Minerals in Exclusive Economic Zone*, London: Chapman and Hall, p.209.
3. Ginsburg G D & Soloviev V A (1998), *Submarine Gas-hydrates*, St. Petersburg: VNII Okeangeologia
4. Gupta, H K et al. (1998), *Analysis of single channel seismic data from the continental margins of India for exploration of gas-hydrates: Effective medium modeling*, Geophysics Res. Lett., 26: 2021-2024.
5. Harsh K. Gupta (2005), *Oceanology*: University Press, p.215.
6. Makogon Yu F (1981), *Hydrates of natural gas*, Tulsa: Pennwell, p.237.
7. Murty, T S (1984), *Storm surges-Meteorological Ocean Tides*, Ottawa, (Canada): Department of Fisheries and Oceans, , p.897
8. Nebojsa et al. (1998), *Global Energy Perspectives*, p.50.
9. O'Connor L (2002), *3D International*, p.9.
10. Sharma R. Sudhakar M & Iyer, S D (1994), "Distribution of manganese nodules, rocks and sediments in the Central Indian Basin: Factors influencing performance of mining system" in Sushil Kumar et.al (ed.), *Ocean Technology Perspective*, New Delhi: CSIR-PID.
11. Uhera H & Ikegami Y (1990), "Optimization of a Closed Cycle OTEC System", in *ASME Journal of Solar Engineering*, 112 No.4.

16

Some Views on Possible Collaboration in Science and Technology among Bay of Bengal Economic Community with Emphasis on Space, Earth and Atmospheric Sciences

A. Narayana Swamy

A. Siva Parvathi

Sec. I. Introduction

Science and Technology are shared heritage of all mankind. All the countries of our globe have equally participated in their creation during the past. Subsequently, wide gaps in the knowledge and application of science and technology among these countries were developed resulting in the socio-economic abnormalities and categorization of developed/industrialized and developing countries However, in recent years, there is a wide spread feeling in the developing countries that acquiring science and science based high technology through collaboration is hard. The most revolutionary aspect of technology is anybody can learn it. It jumps easily over barriers of race and language. It took three generations of misery for the older industrial countries to master the technology of coal and iron. The new industrial countries of Southeast Asia like Singapore, South Korea etc., mastered new technology and made the jump from poverty to wealth in a single generation (Salam 1989). One should realize that technology is a part of the planetary environment and to be shared like air and water with the rest of the mankind through proper cooperation. The science and technology used for civilian purposes as well as for possible collaboration among various countries may be classified into four categories viz., basic sciences, applied sciences, conventional low technology and science based high technology.

Sec. II. Basic and Applied Sciences

The basic sciences can be classified as Physics (including Geophysics, Space and Astrophysics) Chemistry, Mathematics, Biology and basic Medical sciences. The developing countries (including countries of Bay of Bengal community) have tended to neglect this area of basic science assuming for some reason that one could live off the scientific results obtained by other developed countries. Research and training in basic sciences is conducted in the universities and research centers of the developed world. Hence, it is perfectly possible to change over from basic to applied research in developed world. However, in our countries this is not the case due to lack of proper development and opportunity.

There are several areas of applied science like agriculture (including livestock, fisheries and forests, medicine, health and population, energy resources, environment and pollution, earth sciences, including irrigation and soils, exploration for renewable and non-renewable resources, meteorology-cyclones, hydrology-floods and droughts and oceanography-tsunami, seismology-earth quakes, remote sensing in earth and atmospheric sciences etc., in which collaboration among countries of Bay of Bengal community can be worked out. It is necessary to emphasize the importance of harnessing applied scientists for economic growth and for the betterment of human conditions.

2.1. Technology

The technology can be divided into classical low technology and science-based high technology. Some of the areas of classical low technology include bulk chemicals, iron and steel, petroleum technology including exploration and exploitation, power generation and transmission by establishing industries like nuclear/hydropower plants. These are the areas of negotiated technology transfer, on which some of the developing countries like India placed emphasis. Any other country, wishing to industrialize will have to develop one or more of the technologies listed above. Low technology played major role in building up of the technological base of several countries like Japan, South Korea and Russia. It is interesting to note that Switzerland with a population of 6.4 million is a world leader in pharmaceuticals, specialized engineering and high technology.

The areas of science-based high technology comprise communications and information technology (hardware and software), space technologies (design, launch and operate various types of satellites and acquire and utilize the relevant data), pharmaceuticals and fine chemicals, biotechnology and superconductors. Electronics has been the main engine of innovation since the inventory of the transistor around 1950. The electron has been identified about a century ago and the microchip on which today's information technology industry depends has been around for 35 years. However, electronics gave way to a superior technology based not on electricity but on light (photons). Science has made startling progress in manipulating photons. The photons travel faster than electrons. Unlike electrons, which interfere with each other, photons can be made to pass through each other unperturbed. The customary way to make computer cheaper and faster is to squeeze electronic components close together. The number that can be fitted on a single chip has grown from a dozen, 35 years ago, to several millions today. Sending several electric currents through one chip at the same time risks cross-talk and disaster. However, this is not so with light. A chip could process several light photons at once without interfering with each other. In communication, the companies have replaced the copper cables with hair thin optical fibers made of glass, proving that light is a better messenger than electricity.

Biotechnology thrives on new knowledge generated by molecular biology, genetics and microbiology, but these disciplines are weak, often nonexistent in the underdeveloped world (Lai, 1987). During the recent years, the bio-revolution has begun to spin off significant new developments in areas of agriculture. These include gene-splicing that has revolutionized the economics of dairy farming with increases in milk yields of 15 to 20 percent without raising feed costs. Similarly, calves can now be harvested from cows at a greatly increased rhythm thanks to embryo duplication technologies that enable a single cow to produce twin calves five times a year. Industrial tissue culture technologies may soon eliminate the need to grow whole plants.

High technology differs from classical low technologies in that high expertise in the relevant basic sciences (physics, chemistry, biology and mathematics) is crucial. Very few of the countries under Bay of Bengal community (except India and Thailand) are conscious of the need for or have made progress in high technologies.

2.2. Priorities for Development

It has been established that standards of a nation depends on its strength in Science and Technology. An index of the strength in the science and technology is the numbers of those engaged actively in this activity. According to UNESCO in the industrialized countries an order of several thousand inhabitants per million are engaged in research, development and implementation and the number keep rising year after year (UNESCO, 1989), while those similarly engaged in developing countries are seldom exceed at best more than a few hundred. One of the revealing indices of the size of the science and technology in our countries is the funding. The industrialized and developing countries spend almost equal percent of their GNP's on defense and education. For health expenditure, there is three fold variation. The ratio of expenditure on science and technology range between a factor of seven or more. Even the available funds are not distributed properly, due to lack of talented and committed manpower to execute the task.

Of the several aspects of science and technology which have been mentioned above, the first to be developed in our countries is classical low technology. The next may be application science (assuming expertise in basic sciences is already available). The last cooperation can be science-based high technology. Of course, for a moderate sized developing country there is no option to develop all the four areas of science and technology enumerated above.

The widening gap in economics and influence between nations of the Bay of Bengal economic community is essentially the science and technology gap. The reasons for the existence and widening of gap as well as under utilization of science and technology in our region are to be studied under joint collaboration. The joint endeavor in science will be one of the unifying forces among the diverse people living in the countries of Bay of Bengal community. It is time to recognize the fundamental importance of science in socio-economic and cultural development as well as technological progress and resolve to work towards giving science and technology a position of highest priority within the countries of Bay of Bengal economic community.

2.3. Reasons for Lagging Behind

Some of the reasons for poor development and under utilization of science and technology in South and Southeast Asia are: (i) Lack of meaningful commitment towards basic or applied science. The consequences are weak universities in sciences and research centers of applied sciences, isolated communities of scientists/academicians with scant provision for infrastructure, scientific literature, international contacts, weakness in scientific and technological education and little expenditure on sciences; (ii) no commitment to self-reliance in technology. The situation may be some what better for low technologies but is dismal in the case of high technologies; (iii) inadequate institutional and legal framework and in respect of political actions, there is a necessity to have institutional and legal enactments; (iv) the manner in which the enterprise of science has been run is another concern and an active enterprise of science must be run by committed scientists themselves and not by professional administrators or business managers or scientists who were active some time ago but not at present; (v) lack of political stability, which may be either external or internal and the internal dangers may stem from unsettled borders, tribalism, religious intolerance, sectarianism, corruption etc.; and (vi) attitude of the suppliers of technology towards technology transfer and one of the failures of our countries has been the concentration on imported technology, neglecting at the same time the development of their own scientific and technological base.

2.4. Steps to Strengthen

There are five classes of communities in our society which could be involved in the building up and utilization of the enterprise of science and technology. First there are our rulers who determine the priorities. Second, there are planners, the economists and the international bankers who advise them. Third may be the entrepreneurs with their management skills. Fourth are the educators and media people-plus the religious leaders in some of the countries who interact directly with the public. Fifth and last come the scientists and technologists.

Different countries have different experiences in regard to one or more of these classes. For India, Nehru's influence has conditioned by his background as a science student at Cambridge was paramount in laying down the traditions for scientific and technological research in the country. The religious leaders of some countries like Bhavawan Sri Satya Sai Baba can play a leading role in popularizing science and technology for the masses.

Sec. III. Environmental Conservation for Economic Growth

As discussed earlier, collaboration among Bay of Bengal community is essential for the development of scientific and technological education, higher training, application sciences and building up of technology. This is because of similarity of the problems and the experiences among these countries. The collaboration among the scientists/academicians of the above countries may take place at some of the centers like for example, full pledged SAARC centers in respective countries where infrastructure facilities may be developed to host scientists from Bay of Bengal community, so that they can visit periodically, discuss and develop the possible joint programs for the Higher Technological Education and Research.

The environment-development linkage is important to Bay of Bengal community. This is most obviously the case where environmental resources require regional management as with the global 'commons' like the oceans, the atmosphere and space. There are shared environmental resources which are already approaching the point of diminishing returns, for example, ocean fishing. Remote Sensing satellite derived phytoplankton concentration in conjunction with Sea Surface Temperature (SST) values may be utilized for identifying potential fishing areas in the marine environment and thus may help the fishermen community. It may also help the countries to strengthen its economy due to improving marine exports. The data derived from Oceansat – 1 Indian Remote Sensing Satellite, which carries an optical sensor known as Ocean Color Monitor (OCM) is being used for mapping Chlorophyll/Phytoplankton distribution in Indian offshore region. This data is being utilized in association with Sea Surface Temperature values derived from Advanced Very High Resolution Radiometer (AVHRR) Sensor on board NOAA Satellite to forecast potential fishing zones and forecasts are being regularly dissipated to user community in India. Figure 1 shows the distribution of Oceansat – I, derived Chlorophyll in Bay of Bengal (Siva Parvathi, 2004). Figure 2 presents an example of the distribution of Sea Surface Temperature in Arabian Sea (Nagalakshmi, 2004). The countries of Bay of Bengal community may develop collaboration with India in utilization of Oceansat – I data as well as future Oceansat-II data, which is expected to be launched in 2007 so as to develop fisheries forecast models.

In some other cases, there are signs of serious abnormalities like ozone layer depletion and the accumulation of greenhouse gases, deforestation and fires associated with tropical forests and extinction of several species, depletion of renewable and non-renewable resources, dumping of toxic wastes etc. Figure 3 shows the distribution

Figure 1 Chlorophyll distribution over Bay of Bengal derived from Oceansat – I

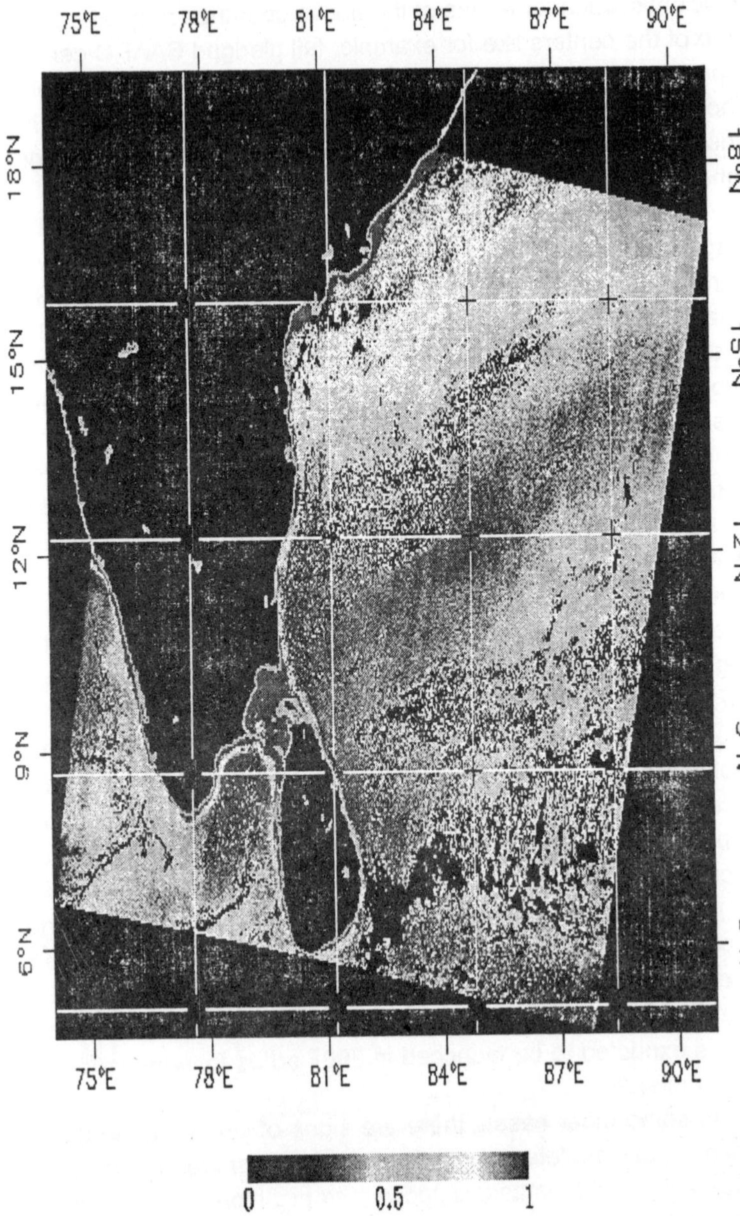

(Courtesy: SAC/ISRO)

Figure 2 Sea Surface Temperature of Arabian Sea from NOAA-AVHRR

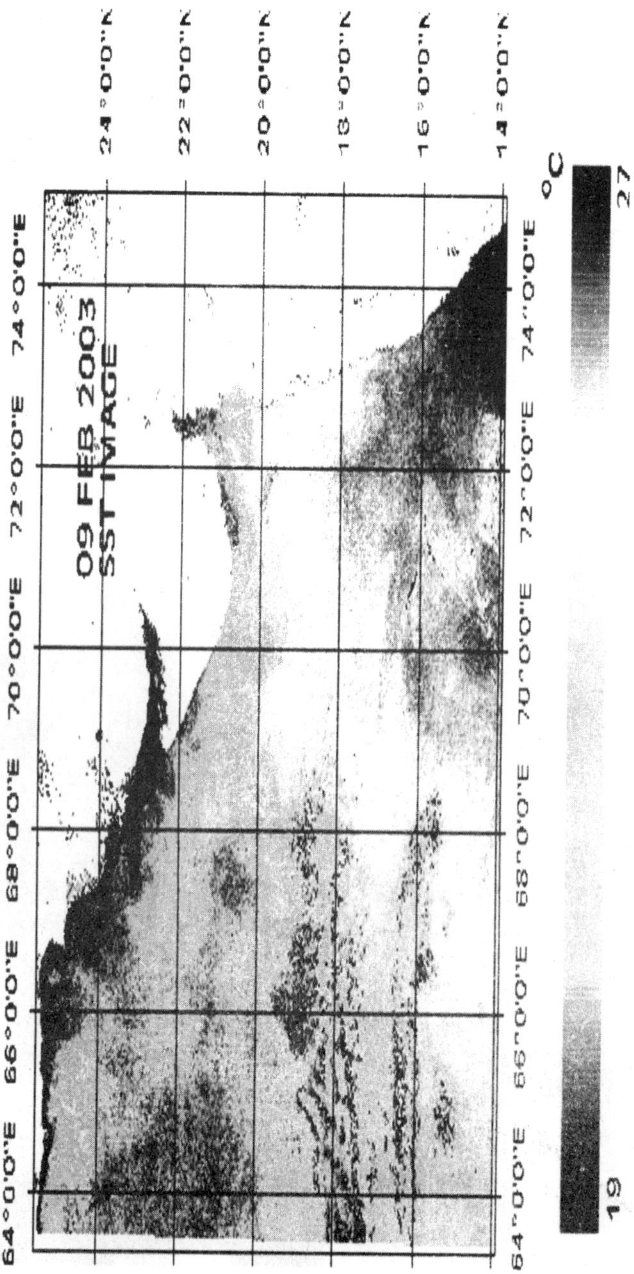

(Courtesy: NOAA/SAC/ISRO)

of NOAA AVHRR derived forest cover in South and Southeast Asia region. Indian Remote Sensing Satellites IRS –1C and 1D provides relatively high spatial and reasonably goodtemporal resolution forest cover derived from Advanced Wide Field Sensor (AwiFS). The resolution has been further increased in the IRS RESOURCESAT. The Indian Remote Sensing Satellite data would be quite useful to monitor forest cover depletion and forest fires over South and South East Asian region for every two days.

There is also hardening consensus that the average global temperature is rising and continue to rise. To assess the above phenomena accurately, it is necessary to determine local and regional level spatial and temporal variations in temperature so as to integrate the same to derive global variations. There exist several other problems in South and Southeast Asia related to joint management of shared river basins, forests, seas and land.

Figure 3 Forest cover over South and South East Asia derived from NOAA-AVHRR

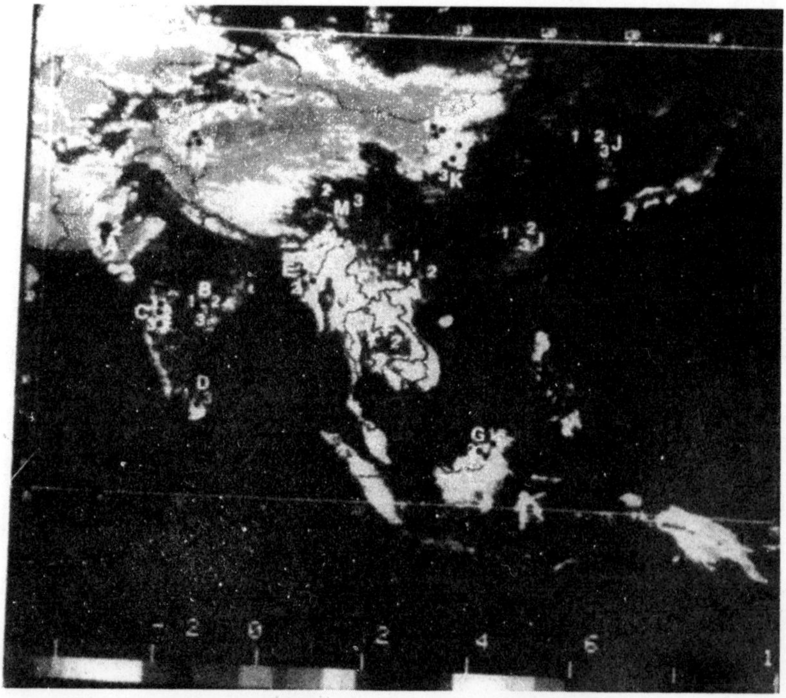

(Courtesy: Curtis Woodcock)

For example, one of the fruitful area of mutual cooperation can be on the studies related to Transport and Deposition of Atmospheric Pollutants by the monsoon winds on the terrestrial environment of the region. The Bay of Bengal community region is strongly influenced by monsoonal flow of moisture and marine/terrestrial/anthropogenic pollutant laden air masses. The transport and deposition of atmospheric pollutants over various countries of the region is being controlled by south west monsoon winds (June-September) and the north east monsoon winds (October-December) which travel over Bay of Bengal in opposite direction to South West mansoon winds (Swamy 1991). Figure 4 presents the flow direction of monsoonal winds during

Figure 4: Distribution of South West Monsoon Winds over Indian Off-shore

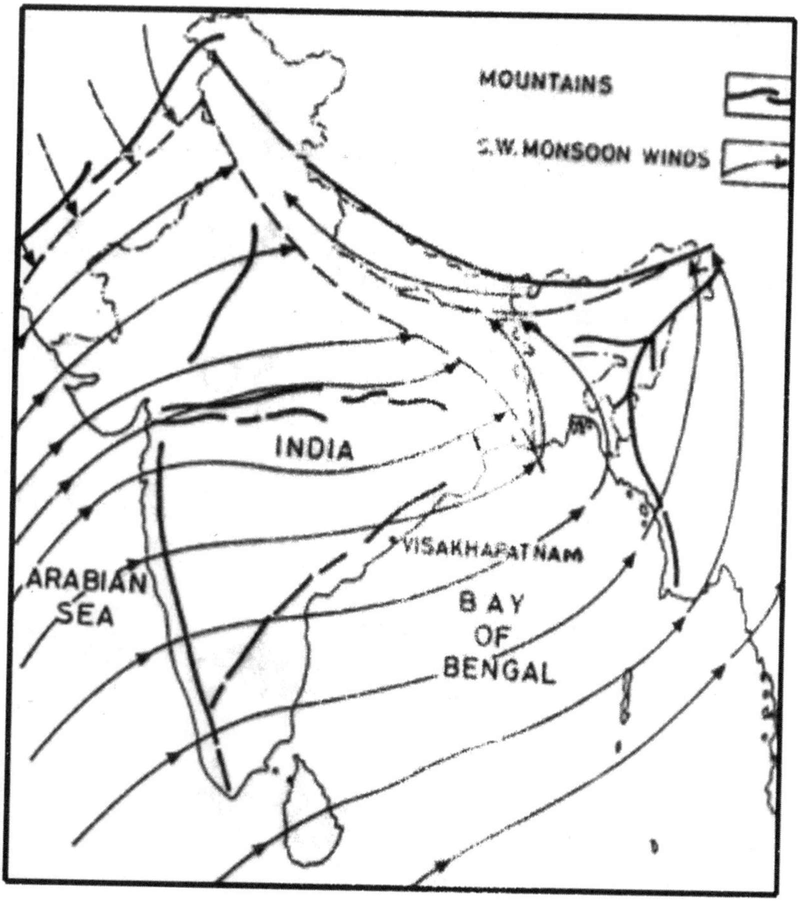

south west monsoon period. Figure 5 presents the atmospheric deposition of various pollutants during summer, south west monsoon and north east monsoon periods monitored at the coastal city of Visakhapatnam adjoining Bay of Bengal. To understand the anomalous distribution of various ionic concentrations, it is necessary to establish a network of observation sites and carry out further analyses using appropriate transport and depositional model.resulting from the possible global climate change. Such study has already been initiated by some of the South and Southeast Asian countries under Asia Pacific Network (APN).

Figure 5: Atmospheric Deposition of Major Ionic Concentrations during Different Seasons at Visakhapatnam City

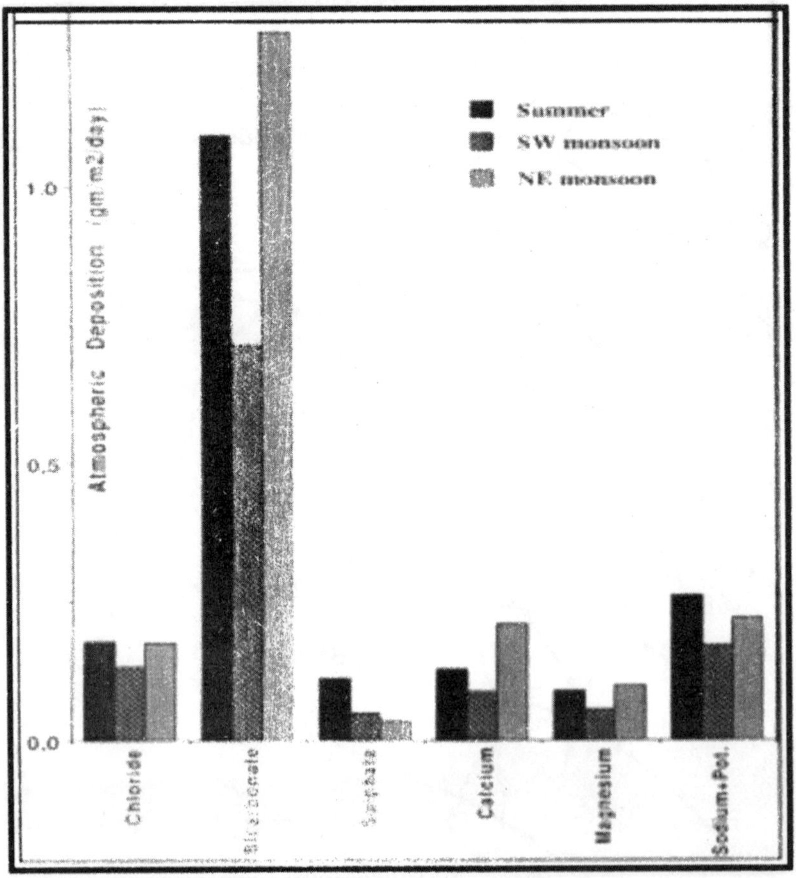

3.1. Capable Project 2004-CB01NSY: The first author (A. Narayana Swamy) is the investigator from India along with scientists from Japan, Thailand, Sri Lanka, Bangladesh, Vietnam and Pakistan. University of Tokyo Institute of Industrial Science Hydrological Model and Japan Public Works Research Institute Hydrological Model have been used under technology cooperation program and tested for their suitability on various selected coastal regions to determine the future possible spatial-temporal flood inundation for different climatic change scenarios and sea level rise and analyses of socio-economic impacts have been carried out (Swamy et. A.l 2005). Similarly the authors are willing to collaborate in research areas of their expertise related to Satellite derived geophysical data analyses for identification of favorable reservoir sites in marine environment for exploration of Oil and Natural Gas, forecasting of river discharges for water resources management as well as disaster management etc.

The Bay of Bengal community must play an appropriate role in the area of Global Science, for example Global Change Research Program of International Council of Scientific Unions (ICSU) and UNESCO Program relating to the Biosphere. All the countries in the world are currently responsible for the damage to the earth and atmospheric environment. It is necessary to understand several facets of our environment like short and long term weather forecasts, hurricane tracking, detecting changes on the earth's surface, shifting of the climate and its impact on people whose livelihoods depend on the climate such as farmers, water managers, fishermen, urban planners etc. It is also necessary to understand how do the earth's land, water, air and life interact to produce the environment, in which we live and is going to be affected due to climatic shifts/changes, as it will have enormous impact on the economy of the countries of our region.

References

1. Lai, C. H. (ed.) (1987), *Ideals and Realities*, World Scientific Publishing Co., p. 379.
2. Nagalakshmi V. (2004), "Studies on Physical and Biological Coupling of Ocean waters based on Chlorophyll and Sea Surface Temperature derived from Satellite Remote Sensing", M.Sc.(Tech), Dissertation of Andhra University, Visakhapatnam, p.57.
3. Salam, M. A. (1989), *Notes on Science and Technology and Science Education in the Development of the South*, Publication of TWAS, p.295.

4. Siva Parvathi, A. (2004), "Application of Neural Networks, Band Ratio and Bio-Optical Algorithms to retrieve Chlorophyll from Remote Sensing data over Marine Environment", M.Sc.(Tech) Dissertation of Andhra University, Visakhapatnam, p.90.

5. Swamy, A. N. (1991), "Atmospheric deposition from bulk precipitation at Visakhapatnam, India", paper presented at NATO Advanced Study Institute on *Energy and Water Cycles in the Climate System*, Glucksburg, Germany, September 30 – October 11, & Ehrhard Raschke and Daniela Jacob (eds.), *Global Environmental Change*, NATO ASI Series I:Vol.5, Springer-Verlag Berlin, Heidelberg 1993, pp.454-455.

6. Swamy, A. N., D. Dutta and S. M. Asokan (2005), "Flood inundation modeling during severe cyclonic storms and socio-economic impact analyses of various climate change scenarios over Mahanadi Delta, India", proceedings of the International Symposium on *Floods in Coastal Cities under Climate Change conditions*, Bangkok, (Thailand): Asian Institute of Technology, June, ISBN: 974-93889-3-3, pp. 11 – 18.

7. UNESCO (1989), *UNESCO Statistical Year* Book, Paris: UNESCO Publication.

17

International Cooperation in BIMSTEC for Marine Archaeology

E.V. Gangadharam

Sec. I. Introduction

Marine archaeology seeks to unravel men's past activities on, at or near the Sea. The terms marine archaeology and maritime archaeology are often used synonymously. The term underwater archaeology covers the discipline without restricting its scope. The term nautical archaeology is somewhat more specific in that it refers to archaeology of boats, boat-building ethnology and navigational knowledge.

Projects of marine archaeology are generally expensive. The object of this paper is to indicate the tremendous potential to develop this important subject at reasonable cost in South Asia in general and BIMSTEC countries in particular. It also suggests that there is potential for cost-effective training in marine archaeology in these countries.

Marine Archaeology is often misunderstood to be a subject of humanities. In fact, it has more to do with sciences and technology than with history and archaeology. However, it is acknowledged that marine archaeological research begins with historians or archaeologists identifying potential sites for investigation. Scientists and technologists then take over, since the methodologies to be followed are entirely scientific and technical in nature. From locating the underwater site, documenting it, recovering and bringing artefacts to surface, conservation and restoration procedures, are complex procedures combining sciences and ocean engineering. For example,

* *Satellite remote sensing* helps to locate underwater sites with precision.
* *Marine geophysical instrumentation* is used to study geology of the seabed and underwater site
* *Manned or unmanned submersibles* are used where depth of the site is greater than about 20 metres.
* *Divers* and *diving equipment* are employed to document *in-situ* the submerged remnants using underwater surveying, photography and videography.
* *Ocean technology* canvas balloons, barges and specially designed pontoons are required for lifting heavy artefacts such as cannon and sometimes the entire ship hull from the seabed.
* *Chemical treatment and analysis* are critically important for proper conservation, restoration and ultimate museum display.

United States, Australia, United Kingdom and many European countries have been pursuing marine archaeological studies routinely for the last fifty years. In India, it made its debut in 1970s and the details are dealt with in detail in a later section. Developing countries are just beginning to establish marine archaeology. Advanced countries with expertise and experience in this subject are assisting other nations in providing equipment, assistance and training to develop this field.

Sect. II. The Importance of Marine Archaeology

2.1. Study of Prehistoric Dwellings

As civilization advanced, it spread from fertile inland areas such as riverbanks or secure mountainous areas to the edges of the continents, namely shores of the seas. People who settled along the shore first constructed simple shelters and homesteads with stone-boulders and wooden logs. These may have increased in number and sophistication, to become townships. There are examples in the Scandinavian and other regions, of such dwellings in the midst of lakes or at seashore, which became submerged over the course of time.

2.2. Study of Prehistoric Settlements, Townships and Ports

Clusters of such dwellings progressively increased in number and sophistication and became settlements and townships. As the commerce and business at the coastal townships diversified, into coastal maritime trade, they evolved into prehistoric ports.

Marine archaeological research focuses on a range of topics from the architecture of individual structures to the spatial arrangement and planning of settlements. This valuable information is fundamental to the historical and anthropological investigations of that locality, the age, and those times.

2.3. Boat-building Ethnology

Ancient man developed the skills to cross-lakes and rivers using hollowed out tree trunks and makeshift wooden rafts to keep him self-afloat. His skills, however, were hampered at the edge of the sea. Standing on the shores on a starry night, man must have wondered what is on the other side of the forbidding water body that is the sea. His adventurous spirit led to the fashioning of simple log-boats or two-piece catamarans, identifying ancient port sites long since forgotten, which he used to venture out on to the tumultuous seas. Further innovation led to the development of boats in the ancient times. Study of these archaeological artefacts now found buried at coastal sites is the foundation for boat-building ethnology, and marine archaeology contributes to this fascinating area of human history.

Sec. III. Examples of Well Known Marine Archaeological Case Histories in the World

Marine archaeology is an exciting field of study, which helps to build up forgotten aspects of human history with concrete evidence for all to see. Examples of marine archaeology include identifying and studying ancient port sites and ports long since forgotten, locating, bringing to surface and restoring famous old boats and sunken ships ranging in age from the ancient to the modern. In other words, this is the stuff of which the excellent documentaries on the *National Geographic*, *Discovery and History Channel* are made of. Some well-known examples are given below as case histories.

3.1. Port Alexandria (Egypt)

It is the historically most famous port of the Egyptian Civilization which served the Mediterranean region from the times of Cleopatra, and regarded as one of the Seven Wonders of the World. The huge structures of the port, now dilapidated, are half submerged in the sea. Historians have chronicled the usage of the port from historic accounts of Greek, Chinese and other travellers. From early 1900s, divers investigated the offshore region of the Mediterranean and discovered huge fragments of sculptured stone statues and other decorative sculptures such as gate-guarding lions. Archaeologists joined the activity and a wealth of information was gathered. The latest efforts were made in 2002, when a highly technological survey confirmed the stone remnants of sculptures on seabed. A well-known woman archaeologist dived and confirmed that it was part of the ancient Egyptian heritage. The huge pieces are now recovered and set up in an archaeological museum in Cairo, and draws thousands of tourists every day.

In BIMSTEC countries, there must be sites of submerged ports either historically chronicled in old literature or recently documented by archaeological studies. These provide an excellent opportunity to develop and establish knowledge and expertise in all sub-disciplines of marine archaeology in these countries.

3.2. The Warship *Vasa* Stockholm Harbour

This Swedish sailing vessel sank in 1628 during the launching, much to the embarrassment of the King of Sweden who was present. Various reasons were attributed to the sinking: poor design of the ship, imbalance of the hull created by the emplacement of cannon on the gun-deck. In a major well-coordinated effort, the ship was recovered intact in 1961, with more than 3,500 artefacts, which provide valuable information on life aboard ship in the 17th century. The restored vessel is moored in the Stockholm harbour and draws a steady stream of marine archaeologists and tourists alike.

3.3. HMS Mary Rose (1545)

This was a sailing vessel – a prestigious battleship built for King Henry VIII of England in 1509, which sank in 1545 near Portsmouth. The wreck was discovered in 1965 by diving marine archaeologists. A mammoth project was taken up by Mary Rose Trust with Prince Charles as Patron. Ms. Margaret Rule, a distinguished woman archaeologist learnt diving at the age of about 50, and was in charge of the Project. The ship's fragile wooden hull was lifted to surface using a specially designed cradle and brought ashore pulled by specially designed pontoon. The entire ship hull is presently undergoing preservation while on display at the Historic Dockyard at Portsmouth, near London. A wealth of artefacts of the ship, its crew and workers were recovered and preserved along with bows and arrows, bronze cannon and exquisite navigational devices. The author was given the privilege to handle and view a special collection normally not shown to visitors.

On the shores of every maritime nation in the BIMSTEC grouping, there are bound to be wrecks of boats and ships. These, if excavated would provide material evidence of maritime history and heritage of these countries, to be admired by the posterity.

3.4. Geldermalssen (1752) South China Sea

This wreck represents a dream-come-true story of an English adventurer who discovered it and became rich overnight. *Geldermalssen* built in Holland, was loaded with cargo in China and set sail for Batavia (now Jakarta), Indonesia. It sank somewhere in South China Sea in 1752. Michael Hatcher, an English diver discovered it in 1985. The cargo list preserved in the Dutch archives in Holland was secured. It showed that tea was the major commodity in the inventory, when the ship sailed to South China Sea. The Chinese porcelain was less important.

When the wreck was discovered the tea decayed in the seawater and was worthless, while the Ming dynasty Chinese porcelain stayed fresh as new and was the most valuable cargo recovered. Further, 46 kg of gold in the form of ingots was also found. The blue-and-white Ming dynasty porcelain consisted of tea and dinner sets, exquisite vases, jugs and statuettes. An exhibition of the recovered artefacts was held in Malaysia in 1986. The author was Honorary Curator of *Muzium Negara* at the time and had the privilege to help organize the excellent exhibition of the recovered cargo, which included the gold ingots.

Sec.IV. Examples from India

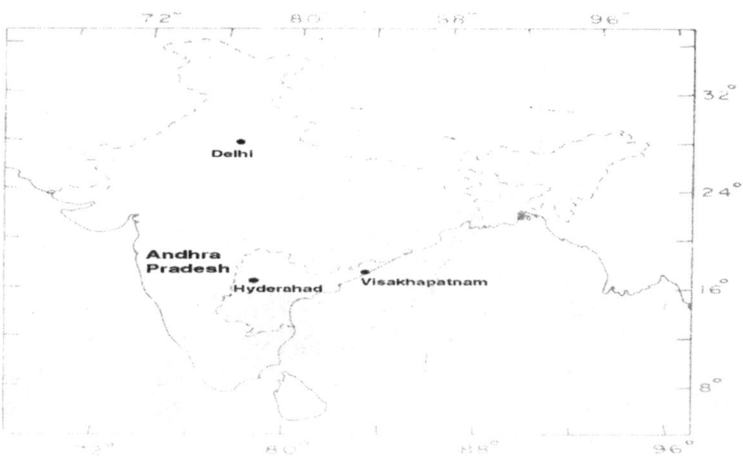

4.1. Dwarka

Underwater exploration at Dwarka on the west coast of Gujarat by Dr. S. R. Rao of NIO, is the first and best known example for Marine Archaeology in India. As Superintending Archaeologist of Archaeological Survey of India, he discovered five layers of foundations of temples at ancient habitation levels close to the present Dwarakadheesh temple in Dwarka, on the west coast of Gujarat. Under the visionary patronage of National Institute of Oceanography, Goa, he investigated the offshore area near Dwarka with token funds from Indian National Science Academy (INSA).

Using divers, he found remnants of a settlement (township), bastions, jetties etc. and some artefacts indicating that these are indicative of Dwaraka mentioned as having been submerged, in the epic *Mahabharata*. Subsequently using an archaeologist trained in diving (Mr. Gudigara) and the technical support of the NIO Regional Centre at Visakhapatnam, he established that the site is indeed that of ancient Dwarka, dated to 3rd Century B.C. This has placed India firmly on the marine archaeology map of the world.

Anchor stones recovered at Dwaraka

4.2.Cambay

In the early 2000, scientists of the National Institute of Ocean Technology (NIOT) Chennai discovered unexpectedly, a submerged site in Gulf of Khambat (Cambay) which turns out to be about 7,500 BC (NIOT, 2002). When this discovery was announced in India that this site would be the oldest human habitation site not only in India but in the world, considerable debate was generated in the Press and Internet media (INIDIA TODAY 2002, FRONTLINE 2002a, FRONTLINE 2002b and anonymous author on Internet, 2002). Since this would be the world's oldest habitation site, some details are given here.

The site, about 20 km off Hazarika, Surat District, Gujarat in the Gulf of Khambat, the Arabian Sea (NIOT 2002). Marine geophysical survey of sea bottom using Side scan Sonar indicated the presence of a palaeo-channel (ancient river bed) over a length of about 9 km. Regular geometric grid patterns recognizable on either side of the palaeo channel suggested that this could be an urban habitation site. During further visits to the area marine geophysical sub-bottom profiling was carried out and brought to light large wall-like structures and rectangular basements at a depth of 20 to 40 m. Since the depth of site precludes sending divers, a dredge sampler was used as the next best thing, though strictly unacceptable according to marine archaeological standards. A large number of archaeological and geological samples were collected.

Underneath the marine sediments obviously the youngest in the sequence, river sediments, alluvium and sand with fresh water shells, river conglomerates and root casts, suggesting that the area was a sub aerial terrain at one time. Items of archaeological significance were pre-historic scrapers of chert, potsherds, bead fragments, perforated pieces of stone, bones and human teeth. The recovery of a large piece of carbonized wood was the most significant find, since it can be dated. Carbon-14 dating of the wood yielded a preliminary date of 8450 to 8350. This date, though it belongs to the dated wood, can be attributed to the habitation site, *making it the oldest known habitation site any where in the world.* Because of the significance of the find from the point of view of ancient history of India and the world, the then Minister for Ocean Development (Dr. Murli Manohar Joshi) made a public announcement at Delhi on May 19, 2001. Subsequently the NIOT organized an expert's meeting at Chennai on July 1-2, 2002, at which the author was an invited speaker.

BIMSTEC countries with a sea-coast would also most definitely have several sites which must have served as "ports", with ships anchoring about half a mile from shore and smaller "masula" boats ferrying cargo and passengers.

Enthusiastic historians, archaeologists and scientists in these countries have a potential field for pioneering research, which can lead to immediate publication. This will promote the cause of creating awareness and national pride in those countries for their maritime heritage. For example, Rangoon (Yangon) was the active port for indentured labour brought by the British from northern Andhra to Burma (Myanmar). Our Centre has already collected specific and detailed information, which is under publication (Gangadharam, 2006). Similar information on ancient port sites in other BIMSTEC countries is lacking.

Under a properly drafted Memorandum of Understanding (MoU), the concerned countries share the artefacts recovered, and share the historical information. It is very well known that in many cases, the shipwrecks yield treasures such as gold, silver ingots, jewellery, ancient porcelain and sculptures.

Sec.V. International Cooperation

5.1. Malaysia

Malaysian archaeologists undertook their first marine archaeology project in 1984. A Dutch shipwreck *RISDAM* (1727) off Mersing, Johor was documented and artefacts recovered, helped by specialists from Australian, the Netherlands and Singapore. The author had the opportunity to participate in the work for four years, in the recovery and field preservation of cargo, which included tin ingots, elephant tusks and guns.

Research was carried out by the author at University of Malaya on the chemistry and metallurgy of the tin ingots, mineralogy and provenance of the ballast bricks, identification of the timber used for the ship, and X-ray examination of the hand guns in concretions. The results are currently on display in the Maritime Archaeology gallery.

5.2. Australia

Australia offers excellent courses in marine archaeology, one of which was taken by the author. Advice, cooperation and technical support are being extended by Australia to Thailand and Sri Lanka.

5.3. UNESCO, SEAMEO-SPAFFA

International organizations like UNESCO and SEAMEO (SPAFFA), professional associations for marine archaeology such as Nautical Archaeology Society (UK) and Professional Association of Diving Instructors (PADI, USA) have programmes to cooperate with Universities and government Departments. The programmes are cost-effective and time-bound and enable the recipient countries to or expand marine archaeology programmes.

Sec. VI. Less well-known Examples from India

6.1. Poompuhar (TamilNadu)

Located about 300 km south of Chennai, Poomppuhar is known as the capital of the Chola kingdom, *circa* 1100 AD. The classic *Silappathikaram* by Illango Adigal is taken to be a realistic account of the romantic tale of Kannagi and Kovalan, which contains references to a legendary township of Poompuhar, or *Kaveripoompaṭṭinam* which according to the legend, is submerged under the sea on account of curse of *Indra*.

NIO Goa undertook a marine archaeological expedition at Poompuhar with the technical support of NIO Regional Centre, Visakhapatnam. It located some archaeological features such as ring wells. However, a British steamer with lead ingots was also accidentally discovered.

6.2.Vaisakheswara Temple (*circa* 1127 AD) of Visakhapatnam

There is well-known legend that an ancient temple lies submerged just off shore in Visakhapatnam. Our Centre has collected specific information in the form of a 11th century Tamil inscription on a stone tablet, evidence of a bronze statue dredged up in the channel of Visakhapatnam Port, references in old gazetteers and architectural indicators from an existing temple opposite to the suspected site of the submerged temple. We applied Remote Sensing studies and found distinct "anomaly" which could be the remnants of the submerged temple in the area of the suspected site. The Eastern Naval Command has been helping with divers for this Project. The work is necessarily slow and takes considerable time like similar investigations elsewhere in the world.

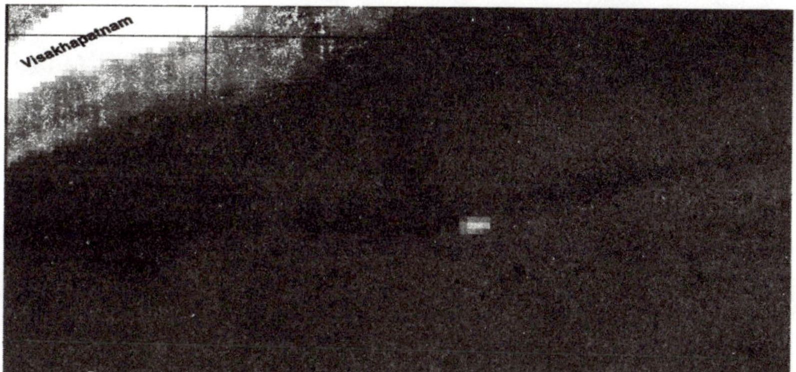

Suspected submerged Temple near Coastal Battery as seen in Satellite imagery

If the anomaly turns out to be a positive indicator on the seabed for the submerged temple, the remnants would be photographed and surveyed underwater, recovered using techniques developed for marine archaeology, restored and displayed for posterity. The Project is continuing, and is necessarily slow because of lack of funds and other factors. If successful, it would be a great attraction, first of its kind in the country, for Indian and foreign tourists.

Ancient port sites and ports played a vital role in establishing maritime contacts between nations and regions whether for trade, spreading of religion or for colonizing. ancient townships or temples may have been submerged because of sea-level changes or local tectonic disturbances or changes in coast line. These result in potential sites for investigation by marine archaeological methods. The foregoing examples in India show that there is potential for academic and professional archaeologists, historians, scientists and engineers of BIMSTEC countries to join hands with experts from other countries and help to develop and establish marine archaeology in their own land.

6.3. Dutch Cannon from Seabed at Visakhapatnam

A seabed concretion about 2.3m long and estimated to weigh about 2 tons was dredged up accidentally in the entrance channel of Visakhapatnam port in 1997.

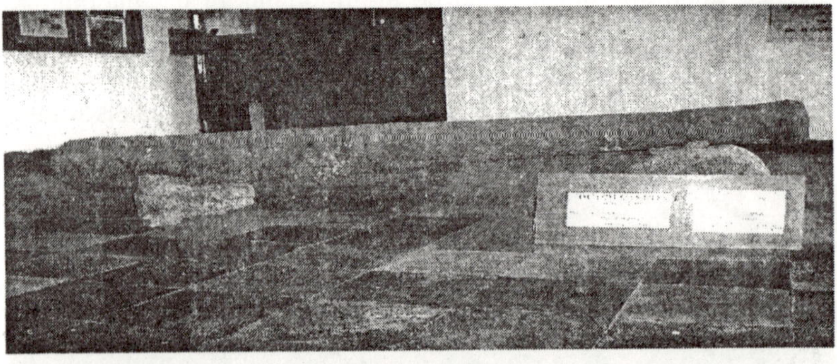

At the request of Port authorities, the Centre for Marine Archaeology investigated the unique find and determined that the concretion contains cannon. Careful chiselling of the outer layer of sand, mud, calcium carbonate and shells revealed that the object is indeed cannon, made of cast iron. Further studies of old maritime publications on the region indicated the possibility that the cannon might have rolled off the northern slope of the Dolphin's nose Hill into the port channel. It was determined that the cannon could be of Dutch origin, *circa* 1700 AD.

The cannon was presented to the Centre by the Visakhapatnam Port Trust in 1998 and was a major exhibit of the Centre's mini-museum ever since. The restoration and conservation of the cannon was made one of four items proposed in the UGC Project on Maritime History of Andhra.

The inscription, insignia or number usually present on cannon was missing because of intense corrosion. The cannon was kept in a large tank and soaked in sodium hydroxide solution for eight weeks for removal of chloride, and the cast iron was stabilized. Work is continuing to determine the composition of the cast iron for comparison with data available in the literature on Dutch metallurgy of 18th century, and attempts will be made to reduce the rust back to metallic iron by reverse electrolysis.

The above details are given to indicate the scope and range of multi-disciplinary studies that can be carried out on marine archaeological finds. These include X-raying concretions to reveal contents, chemical analysis for metallic objects, identification of wood for boat timbers, geological studies on bricks and stone objects, zoological studies on animal remains and anthropological examination of human bones etc. Restoration of the cannon to meet standards of display requires the construction of the gun carriage with Dutch design from contemporary illustrations available in literature.

6.4. Baruva, Srikakulam Dt., (Andhra Pradesh)

Baruva was an important historic port of northern Andhra. It was embarkation port for indentured labour to be taken to Burma (Rangoon) and Malaya (Kelang, Peninsula Malaysia). The ships would anchor just off the coast and small "Masula" boats were used to load and unload passengers and cargo. The Centre had investigated the British East India Company ship, which was very active during that period, when "Vizagapatam" was less important than "Bimilipatam".

Regarding migrant labour, Telugu population of northern Andhra migrated by the hundreds to Burma and Malaya during the period. The author's 17-year stay in Malaysia helped to collect corresponding information from the 3rd generation Malaysian Telugus. This is being integrated with research data from Baruva and a comprehensive account of Malaysian Telugu Diaspora will be attempted.

Port pillars (*circa* 1850 A.D.), Baruva, Srikakulam Dt.

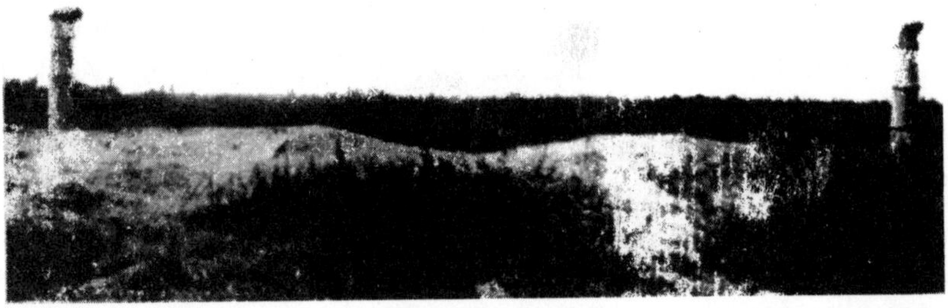

6.5. Bimilipatnam (Visakhapatnam Dt.)

The Centre collected records of the largest private shipping company during the British period, which used to operate from Bhimilipatnam with offices at Vizagapatam. The 1929 records of Ripley & Co. give names of ships (Clan Buchanan, S.S. Hesperides, SS Macfarlane), cargo (manganese ore, jute, coconut fibre, myrabolams), dates of sailing, ports of destination (Rotterdam, Hamburg, Antwerp, Glasgow, New York) freight rates and dates of arrival at destination. Study and analysis of such records is in progress, which would help to derive valuable economic data concerning the prevailing trade between India and Europe in the 1850's. This is an important by-product of Marine Archaeological studies.

Sec. VII. Marine Archaeology in BIMSTEC Countries

BIMSTEC countries are part of the Indian subcontinent and share a common maritime heritage. Historians and archaeologists have established that these countries had regional and foreign maritime contacts for centuries. Further, India, Bangladesh, Myanmar and Sri Lanka were part of the British Empire, and were involved in maritime trade, shipbuilding for over 150 years. Several sites of ancient ports and shipwrecks with valuable cargo are known to be present. Two examples relevant to BIMSTEC countries will illustrate.

7.1. Myanmar

Gold coins "weighing 65 to 66 grains of paddy" believed to be of the period of Raja-raja Narendra were found in a shipwreck located on the shores of Ramri island, near Chedoba port, Kioh Kohi Pia district of Aarakon region of Burma (Myenmar). Southern Burma was referred to as "Suvarna Boomi" in ancient Indian literature. Similarly, Burmese traders are known to have visited Tamralipti (present Tamluk West Bengal, India), which was an active international maritime trading centre, as per Chinese travelogues, and studies by Indian historians.

7.2. Sri Lanka

A sailing vessel of the British period carrying cargo of valuable marble statues of historic importance from India to England wrecked in Sri Lankan waters. Its location is known, and can be recovered under bi-lateral cooperation between India and Sri Lanka.

Sec.VIII. Training in Marine Archaeology for BIMSTEC Countries

The objective of this presentation is to propose that universities and institutions in these countries may consult mutually and evolve a practical way of initiating marine archaeology projects. International organizations and professional societies are interested in providing technical expertise.

Possibilities for assembling a team of international experts to assist South Asian countries have been discussed earlier at the international conference in Singapore. A preliminary proposal to organize an international Consortium for Marine Archaeology in South Asia is likely to be discussed in Singapore in 2006. BIMSTEC countries could join this effort. A consortium approach by maritime nations in the BIMSTEC results in promoting marine archaeology projects.

References

1. Anonymous (2002), *Submerged city in the Gulf of Khambat: Neolithic precursor of the Sarasvati Sindhu Valley Civilization,* (Internet article), p.13.
2. Anonymous (1985), Mary Rose (1545), *Guide to Ship Hall Museum, Historic Docks*, Portsmouth: The Mary Rose Trust, p.37.
3. Anonymous (1972). *National Maritime Museum* (1972), *VASSA* (1533), Brochure: Stockholm Heritage Press, p.86.
4. Anonymous (1990), *Port Alexandira Antiquities, 330 B.C.: Guidebook*, National Archaeological Commissioner, Egypt: Port Alexandria, p.22.

5. *Frontline* (2002a), "Questionable Claims", March 01-15, pp. 67 – 71.
6. *Frontline* (2002b), "The Gulf of Khambat debat", April 12, pp. 94 – 98.
7. Gangadharam, E. V. (1986), "The sunken Dutch trading vessel off Mersing Coast, Johor – preliminary study of the geological environment of the shipwreck, its artifacts and their initial field preservation" in *Kapal dan Harta Karam* (Ships and sunken Treasure). Kuala Lumpur: United Selangor Press Sdn. Bhd., p.181.
8. Gangadharam E. V. (1991), "The legend of Vaisakheswara Temple of Visakhapatnam *in:* Workshop on Potential for Marine Archaeology research in Andhra", Centre for Marine Archaeology, Andhra University, Waltair, p.32.
9. Gangadharam E. V. (1991), "The Lost Temple for Vaisakheswara off Visakhapatnam, Andhra Pradesh, India (Abstract) in *Recent Advances in Marine Archaeology*, proceedings of *Second Indian Conference on Marine Archaeology of Indian Ocean Countries* (Bangalore), Goa: National Institute of Oceanography.
10. Gangadharam E. V. (1994), "The submerged Vaisakheswara Temple off Visakhapatnam – A Major Project of the Centre", in *Saga of Marine Archaeology in India*, Centre for Marine Archaeology, Andhra University, Waltair, p.82.
11. Gangadharam E. V. (1994), "Searching for the Lost Temple for Vaisakheswara – the first major Project of the Centre", in *Saga of Marine Archaeology in India*, Centre for Marine Archaeology, Andhra University, Waltair, p.82.
12. Gangadharam E. V. (2002), "*Comprehensive geological and geochemical studies on samples recovered from Cambay site*, paper presented at the Experts' Meeting on *Marine Archaeology in the Gulf of Cambay*, April 1 – 2, Chennai, p.4.
13. Gangadharam, E. V. (2006), "The historic port of Baruva, Srikakulam District : The gateway for indentured labor to Burma and Malaya", Centre for Marine Archaeology, Andhra University, Waltair (unpublished report),p.8.
14. Green, Jeremy and E. V. Gangadharam (1985), *The Dutch Fluit RISDAM (1727)Excavation Report*, Western Australian maritime Museum,Western Australia: Fremantle (Perth), p.88.
15. Green, Jeremy and Somasiri Devendra (eds.,1993), *Marine Archaeology in Sri Lanka The Galle Barbour Project – 1992*, Colombo: PGIAR (University of Kelaniya) Publication.
16. India Today (2002), *Found! World's oldest city (Cover story).* February 11, pp. 42 - 50.

17. Jorg, C.J.A. (1986), *The Geldermalssen: History and Porcelain*, Groningen: Kemper Publishers, p.123.

18. National Institute of Ocean Technology (2002), "A study on the Archaeological, Geological and Engineering Significance of the Gulf of Cambay, Background paper for the experts meeting at NIOT, Chennai, July 1.

19. Rao S.R. (1988), "Excavation of Submerged Ports – Dwarka a Case Study ***in:*** Marine Archaeology of Indian Ocean Countries", Proceedings of *First Indian Conference on Marine Archaeology* (Jamnagar,1987), Goa: National Institute of Oceanography.

20. Rao, S.R. (Ed.) (1994), "An Integrated Approach to Marine Archaeology", Proceedings of the *Fourth Indian Conference on Marine Archaeology of Indian Ocean Countries* (Visakhapatnam), Goa (Dona Paula): National Institute of Oceanography, p.141.

18

The Asian Drama of BIMSTEC, SAARC, and ASEAN Countries (An Analysis of Human Poverty of the Nations)

G. Ramachandrudu

Ch. Appa Rao

A. Rajani

Sec.I. Introduction

BIMSTEC (Bangladesh, India, Myanmar, Sri Lanka, and Thailand Economic Cooperation) is the latest sub- regional grouping of Asian Countries. Bhutan and Nepal are the new entrants into BIMSTEC. The viability and sustainability of this new combination of nations having the common legacy of the sea, the Bay of Bengal, on which millions of fishermen depend for their livelihoods. The people in this region have many other common socio-economic problems of human poverty, illiteracy, unemployment, natural disasters like the recent Tsunami, and the last but not the least the terrorism, which is largely due to the neglect of the respective governments to address the problems mentioned above. The formation of the new grouping without Pakistan and China has to be analyzed in the new global and Asian regimes.

The objectives of this paper are a) to examine the extent of human poverty in BIMSTEC, SAARC, and ASEAN countries; b) to analyze the regional and international political economies; and c) to reflect on the future of the sub-regions without China.

Sec. II. BIMSTEC

There is also an alternative abbreviation for BIMSTEC (Bay of Bengal Initiative for Multi-Sectoral Technical and Economic Cooperation). Formerly the Bangladesh – India – Myanmar – Sri Lanka – Thailand – Economic Cooperation is a sub- regional grouping, combining the geographically contiguous countries of Bangladesh, Bhutan, India, Nepal and Sri Lanka from the SAARC and Myanmar and Thailand from ASEAN regions. The BIMSTEC region has identified six sectors for cooperation, viz., trade and investment, technology, transport and communication, energy, tourism and fisheries. The formation of BIMSTEC in 1997, with the objective of promoting harmonious development of economic relations among the members through fair conditions of competition for trade is welcoming.

2.1. Human Poverty of BIMSTEC Countries

Table.1 presents key Socio-economic indicators of BIMSTEC Countries. The total population of BIMSTEC countries in 1,378 million, out of which 1,080 (78 percent) of the people are from India. Thailand with just 62 million people has got the highest per capita income (US $ 2540), when compared to India's (US $ 620). Thailand has got all the characteristics of More Developed Countries with a population growth rate of 0.7 percent per annum, density of population being 122 persons per sq. k.m., fairly high life expectancy (72), adult literacy (90 percent) and less poverty (6 percent). Sri Lanka stands second in socio-economic indicators. Myanmar is the country for which, not much data are available seems to have been doing better than may other countries in the region. The table also presents Coefficient of Variation of all indicators. The C.V is highest in population density (0.88), maternal mortality ratio (0.82) and Adult Literacy (0.76)

Table.2 presents certain key human development indicators of BIMSTEC countries. More or less socio-economic indicators confirm the status of these countries. Thailand and Sri Lanka are leading in human development status and having the least human poverty index. India is leading with the skilled human resources like doctors and technicians. However, it is yet to achieve results in population control, access to sanitation and drinking water. Myanmar seems to be doing better than India in almost all the human development aspects. The table also presents Coefficient of Variation of all indicators. It can be observed that there are greater variations with regard to the number of doctors (0.62), access to sanitation (0.45), human poverty index (0.43), Family planning, (0.40), and T.F.R (0.35)

Table - 1

Key Socio-Economic Indicators of BIMSTEC Countries

S.No.	*Country*	*Population (2004)*			*Percapita income(US$)*	*Life expectancy (2003)*		*Adult literacy (%)*	*Income Poverty (%)*	*MMR*
		Size (Mill)	*Growth rate of popn.*	*Population Density*		*Male*	*Female*			
1.	Bangladesh	141	1.7	1079	440	62	63	41	36	380
2.	India	1080	1.5	363	620	63	64	61	35	540
3.	Myanmar (Burma)	49	1.2	76	- -	55	60	- -	- -	- -
4.	Sri Lanka	19	1.3	301	1010	72	76	90	6	92
5.	Thailand	62	0.7	122	2540	67	72	93	2	44
6.	Bhutan	0.89	2.7	19	760	62	65	- -	- -	- -
7.	Nepal	25	2.2	176	260	60	60	49	39	740
	C.V	1.99	0.40	1.18	0.88	0.08	0.09	0.35	0.76	0.82

Source: (1) World Bank (2006), *World Development Report*, New York: Oxford University Press.
(2) UNDP (2005), *Human Development Report*, New York: Oxford University Press.

Table – 2

Key Human Development Indicators of BIMSTEC Countries

S.No.	*Country*	*HDI (2003)*	*HPI (%) (2003)*	*TFR (2005)*	*Family planning (2003)*	*Doctors per lakh population*	*Access to Sanitation (%)*	*Access to Drinking water (%) (2002)*
1.	Bangladesh	0.52	44	2.0	72	30	48	75
2.	India	0.60	31	3.1	48	51	30	86
3.	Myanmar (Burma)	0.58	22	2.5	37	30	73	80
4.	Sri Lanka	0.75	18	2.0	70	43	91	78
5.	Thailand	0.78	13	1.9	72	30	99	85
6.	Bhutan	0.54	- -	4.4	19	5	70	62
7.	Nepal	0.53	39	3.7	39	5	27	84
	C.V	0.18	0.43	0.35	0.40	0.62	0.45	0.10

Source: UNDP (2005), *Human Development Report*, New York: Oxford University Press.

Sec. III. SAARC

The SAARC consisting of India, Pakistan, Bangladesh, Sri Lanka, Nepal, Bhutan and Maldives was started in 1985. Internal political inconsistencies and external pressures have virtually weakened the spirits of SAARC. This regional grouping has not even strengthened at least the academic infrastructure like statistical database for further explanation of co-operative possibilities. It is rightly proposed by our Prime Minister to start SAARC University in the Dhaka summit on November 12, 2005. They have to learn lessons from comparative cost and advantage thesis. With vast natural and human resources, one should wonder why this region should be suffering with author human poverty. Nations fail because of the failure of politicians who lack statesmanship, thinkness and visionaries like Nehru, Indira Gandhi, Bhutto, Muzibur Rahman, and others.

The Association provides a platform for the peoples of South Asia to work together in a spirit of friendship, trust and understanding. It aims to promote the welfare of the peoples of South Asia and to improve their quality of life through accelerated economic growth, social progress and cultural development in the region. Cooperation in the SAARC is based on respect for the principles of sovereignty, equality, territorial integrity, political independence, non-interference in internal affairs of the member States and mutual benefit. Regional cooperation is seen as a complement to the bilateral and multilateral relations of SAARC member States. Decisions are taken on the basis of unanimity. Bilateral and contentious issues are excluded from the deliberations of SAARC.

Working Groups have been established in the areas of: Information and Communications Technology (ICT); Biotechnology; Intellectual Property Rights (IPR); Tourism; and Energy Summits, which are the highest authority in SAARC are to be held annually. The country hosting the Summit holds the Chair of the Association. Pakistan, which hosted the Twelfth Summit in January 2004, was the Chairperson of the Association and now it is handed over to Bangladesh in the Thirteenth summit in Dhaka in November 2005.The Council of Ministers comprising Foreign Ministers, meets at least twice a year. Its functions include formulating policy, reviewing progress of regional cooperation, identifying new areas of cooperation and establishing additional mechanisms that may be necessary. The Standing Committee comprising Foreign Secretaries, monitors and coordinates SAARC programmes of cooperation, approves projects including their financing and mobilizes regional and external resources. It meets as often as necessary and reports to the Council of Ministers. The Association also convenes meetings at Ministerial Level on specialized themes. The Committee on Economic Cooperation, consisting of Secretaries of Commerce oversees regional cooperation in the economic field.

The Agreement on SAARC Preferential Trading Arrangement (SAPTA) was signed in 1993 and four rounds of trade negotiations have been concluded. With the objective of moving towards a South Asian Economic Union (SAEU), the Agreement on South Asian Free Trade Area (SAFTA) was signed during the Twelfth Summit in Islamabad in January 2004. SAFTA has enter into force from January 2006.The Association has carried out regional studies on trade, manufactures and services, environment and poverty alleviation, SAFTA and customs matters. During the Twelfth Summit in Islamabad, the SAARC Social Charter was signed in order to address social issues, such as population stabilization, empowerment of women, youth mobilization, human resource development, promotion of health and nutrition, and protection of children, which are keys to the welfare and well-being of all South Asians. The Governors of the Central Banks of member States under the auspices of SAARC finance meet regularly to consider cooperation in financial matters.

The Twelfth Summit renewed the urgency to deal with poverty in the region. For this purpose, the Summit directed the Independent South Asian Commission on Poverty Alleviation (ISACPA) to submit to the next Summit a comprehensive and realistic blue-print setting out SAARC Development Goals for the next five years in the areas of poverty alleviation, education, health and environment. Memoranda of Understanding have been signed to promote collaboration with UNCTAD (United Nations Conference on Trade and Development), UNICEF (United Nations Children's Fund), UNDP (United Nations Development Programme), UNESCAP (United Nations Economic and Social Commission for Asia and Pacific), UNDCP (United Nations Drug Control Programme), ITU (International Telecommunications Union), APT (Asia Pacific Telecommunity), WHO (World Health Organization), UNIFEM (Untied Nations Fund for Women), CIDA (Canadian International Development Agency), EC (European Commission), PTB (German Meteorology Institute), WB (World Bank), ADB (Asian Development Bank), UNAIDS (Joint United Nations Programme on HIV/AIDS) and SACEP (South Asia Cooperative Environment Programme).

Table - 3

Human Poverty Indices in SAARC Countries

Country	*2003 HDI*	*2003 HPI*	*2005 TFR*	*1990-2004 Doctors per lakh population*	*2002 Access to sanitation*	*2002 Access to drinking water*
India	0.602(127)	31.3(58)	3.1	51	30	86
Pakistan	0.527(135)	37.1(68)	4.3	66	54	90
Bangladesh	0.520(139)	44.1(86)	3.2	23	48	75
Sri Lanka	0.751(93)	18.0(42)	2.0	43	92	78
Nepal	0.526(136)	38.7(74)	3.7	5	27	84
Bhutan	0.536(134)	–	4.4	5	70	62
Maldives	0.745(96)	16.6(37)	4.3	78	58	84
C.V		0.366	0.24	0.74	0.41	0.116

Source: As in Table.2

Regular dialogues with other regional organisations such as ASEAN (Association of South-East Asian Nations), ECO (Economic Cooperation Organisation) and PIFS (Pacific Islands Forum Secretariat) are held with a view to promoting cooperation among sub-regional automatically. The Association promotes interaction on multilateral issues of common concern to its members and has identified areas in which collective positions could be projected at international forums. These include trade, finance, environment, agriculture, women and children, and information and telecommunications. Beyond official linkages, SAARC also encourages and facilitates cooperation in privatesector through the SAARC Chamber of Commerce and Industry (SCCI), which is a SAARC Apex Body. Other such bodies are SAARC LAW and the South Asian Federation of Accountants (SAFA). In addition, status as SAARC Recognized Body has been accorded to professional groups in South Asia including Architects, Management Development Institutions, University Women, Town Planners, Cardiologists, Dermatologists, Teachers, Writers, Insurance Organizations, Diploma Engineers, Radiological and Surgical Care Societies.

Table. 3 presents the selected human poverty indices for SAARC countries. This region is perhaps one of the most backward regions of the world, with acute income poverty as well as human poverty. Sri Lanka is relatively better-performed country both in economic as well as human development. Bangladesh is on the lowest ladder of the socio-economic scale with 44 percent human poverty, followed by Nepal (39 percent) and Pakistan (37 percent). India is not far away from these least performing States, with 31 percent of the suffering under acute human poverty. The most important single reason is that these governments are framing policies for rapid growth with the assumption that the economic growth shall "trickle down" automatically to the lower strata of the society and their investments in social sectors are decreasing year after year. The table also presents Coefficient of Variation of all indicators. It can be observed from the table that the larger variations in the variables of the number of doctors 0.74, access to sanitation 0.41, and H.P.I 0.37.

Sec. IV. ASEAN

The Association of Southeast Asian Nations or ASEAN was established on August 8, 1967 at Bangkok by the five original member countries, namely, Indonesia, Malaysia, Philippines, Singapore, and

Thailand. Brunei Darussalam joined on January 8, 1984, Vietnam on July 28, 1995, Laos and Myanmar on July 23, 1997, and Cambodia on April 30, 1999. The ASEAN region has a population of about 500 million, a total area of 4.5 million square kilometers, a combined gross domestic product of US$737 billion, and a total trade of US$ 720 billion.

The ASEAN Declaration states that the aims and purposes of the Association are: (i) to accelerate the economic growth, social progress and cultural development in the region through joint endeavors in the spirit of equality and partnership in order to strengthen the foundation for a prosperous and peaceful community of Southeast Asian nations; and (ii) to promote regional peace and stability through abiding respect for justice and the rule of law in the relationship among countries in the region and adherence to the principles of the United Nations Charter. In 1995, the ASEAN Heads of States and Government re-affirmed, "Cooperative peace and shared prosperity shall be the fundamental goals of ASEAN."

The Treaty of Amity and Cooperation (TAC) in Southeast Asia, signed at the First ASEAN Summit on February 24, 1976, declared that in their relations with one another, the High Contracting Parties should be guided by the following fundamental principles:

- Mutual respect for the independence, sovereignty, equality, territorial integrity, and national identity of all nations;
- The right of every State to lead its national existence free from external interference, subversion or coercion;
- Non-interference in the internal affairs of one another;
- Settlement of differences or disputes by peaceful manner;
- Renunciation of the threat or use of force; and
- Effective cooperation among themselves.

4.1. Political Cooperation

The TAC stated that ASEAN political and security dialogue and cooperation should aim to promote regional peace and stability by enhancing regional resilience. Regional resilience shall be achieved by cooperating in all fields based on the principles of self-confidence, self-reliance, mutual respect, cooperation, and solidarity, which shall constitute the foundation for a strong and viable community of nations in Southeast Asia.

Some of the major political accords of ASEAN are as follows:

- ASEAN Declaration, Bangkok, August 8, 1967;
- Zone of Peace, Freedom and Neutrality Declaration, Kuala Lumpur, November 27, 1971;

- Declaration of ASEAN Concord, Bali, February 24, 1976;
- Treaty of Amity and Cooperation in Southeast Asia, Bali, February 24, 1976;
- ASEAN Declaration on the South China Sea, Manila, July 22,1992;
- Treaty on the Southeast Asia Nuclear Weapon-Free Zone, Bangkok, December 15, 1997; and
- ASEAN Vision 2020, Kuala Lumpur, December 15, 1997.
- Declaration of ASEAN Concord II, Bali, October 7, 2003

The ASEAN Security Community is envisaged to bring ASEAN's political and security cooperation to a higher plane to ensure that countries in the region live at peace with one another and with the world at large in a just, democratic and harmonious environment.

In 1992, the ASEAN Heads of State and Government declared that ASEAN should intensify its external dialogues in political and security matters, as a means of building cooperative ties with States in the Asia-Pacific region. Two years later, the ASEAN Regional Forum or ARF was established. The ARF aims to promote confidence-building, preventive diplomacy and conflict resolution in the region. The present participants in the ARF include: Australia, Brunei Darussalam, Cambodia, Canada, China, European Union, India, Indonesia, Japan, Democratic Peoples' Republic of Korea, Republic of Korea, Laos, Malaysia, Myanmar, Mongolia, New Zealand, Pakistan, Papua New Guinea, Philippines, Russian Federation, Singapore, Thailand, United States and Vietnam. Through political dialogue and confidence building, no tension has escalated into armed confrontation among ASEAN members, since its establishment more than three decades ago.

4.2. Economic and Functional Cooperation

When ASEAN was established, trade among the member Countries was insignificant. Estimates between 1967 and the early 1970s showed that the share of intra-ASEAN trade from the total trade of the Member Countries was between 12 and 15 per cent. Thus, some of the earliest economic cooperation schemes of ASEAN were aimed at addressing this situation. One of these was the Preferential Trading Arrangement of 1977, which accorded tariff preferences for trade among ASEAN economies. Ten years later, an enhanced PTA Programme was adopted at the Third ASEAN Summit at Manila further increasing intra-ASEAN trade.

The Framework Agreement on Enhancing Economic Cooperation was adopted at the Fourth ASEAN Summit in Singapore in 1992, which included the launching of a scheme toward an ASEAN Free Trade Area or AFTA. The strategic objective of AFTA is to increase the ASEAN region's competitive advantage as a single production unit. The elimination of tariff and non-tariff barriers among the member countries is expected to promote greater economic efficiency, productivity, and competitiveness. The Fifth ASEAN Summit held at Bangkok in 1995 adopted the Agenda for Greater Economic Integration, which included the acceleration of the timetable for the realization of AFTA from the original 15-year timeframe to 10 years.

In 1997, the ASEAN leaders adopted the ASEAN Vision 2020, which called for ASEAN Partnership in Dynamic Development aimed at forging closer economic integration within the region. The vision statement also resolved to create a stable, prosperous and highly competitive ASEAN Economic Region, in which there is a free flow of goods, services, investments, capital, and equitable economic development and reduced poverty and socio-economic disparities. The Hanoi Plan of Action, adopted in 1998, serves as the first in a series of plans of action leading up to the realization of the ASEAN vision.

In addition to trade and investment liberalization, regional economic integration is being pursued through the development of Trans-ASEAN transportation network consisting of major inter-state highway and railway networks, principal ports and sea lanes for maritime traffic, inland waterway transport, and major civil aviation links. ASEAN is promoting the interoperability and interconnectivity of the national telecommunications equipment and services. Building of Trans-ASEAN energy networks, which consist of the ASEAN Power Grid and the Trans-ASEAN Gas Pipeline Projects, are also being developed.

ASEAN cooperation has resulted in greater regional integration. Within three years from the launching of AFTA, exports among ASEAN countries grew from US$43.26 billion in 1993 to almost US$80 billion in 1996, an average yearly growth rate of 28.3 per cent. In the process, the share of intra-regional trade from ASEAN's total trade rose from 20 per cent to almost 25 per cent. Tourists from ASEAN countries themselves have been representing an increasingly important share of tourism in the region. In 1996, of the 28.6 million tourist arrivals in ASEAN, 11.2 million or almost 40 per cent, came from within ASEAN itself. Today, ASEAN economic cooperation covers the following areas: trade, investment, industry, services, finance, agriculture, forestry, energy, transportation and communication, intellectual property, small and medium enterprises, and tourism.

Functional cooperation is guided by the following plans:

- ASEAN Plan of Action on Social Development;
- ASEAN Plan of Action on Culture and Information;
- ASEAN Plan of Action on Science and Technology;
- ASEAN Strategic Plan of Action on the Environment;
- ASEAN Plan of Action on Drug Abuse Control; and
- ASEAN Plan of Action in Combating Transnational Crime

4.3. External Relations

The ASEAN Vision 2020 affirmed an outward-looking ASEAN playing a pivotal role in the international community and advancing ASEAN's common interests. ASEAN has made major strides in building cooperative ties with States in the Asia-Pacific region and shall continue to accord them a high priority. Cooperation with other East Asian countries has accelerated with the holding of an annual dialogue among the leaders of ASEAN, China, Japan, and the Republic of Korea. In 1997, a joint statement between ASEAN and each of them was signed providing for framework for cooperation towards the 21st century. In November 1999, the leaders of ASEAN, China, Japan and the Republic of Korea issued a Joint Statement on East Asia Cooperation outlining the areas of cooperation among them.

The ASEAN Summit of 1992 mandated that "ASEAN, as part of an increasingly interdependent world, should intensify cooperative relationships with its Dialogue Partners." Consultations between ASEAN and its Dialogue Partners are held at the Foreign Ministers' level on an annual basis. ASEAN's Dialogue Partners include Australia, Canada, China, the European Union, India, Japan, the Republic of Korea, New Zealand, the Russian Federation, the United States of America, and the United Nations Development Programme. ASEAN also promotes cooperation with Pakistan on certain sectors. Consistent with its resolve to enhance cooperation with other developing regions, ASEAN maintains contact with other inter-governmental organizations, namely, the Economic Cooperation Organization, the Gulf Cooperation Council, the Rio Group, the South Asian Association for Regional Cooperation, and the South Pacific Forum. Most ASEAN Member Countries also participate actively in the activities of the Asia-Pacific Economic Cooperation (APEC), the Asia-Europe Meeting (ASEM), the East Asia-Latin America Forum (EALAF).

4.4. Structures and Mechanisms

The highest decision-making organ of ASEAN is the Meeting of the ASEAN Heads of State and Government. The ASEAN Summit is convened every year. The ASEAN Ministerial Meeting (Foreign Ministers) is held on an annual basis. Ministerial meetings on several other sectors are also held: agriculture and forestry, economics, energy, environment, finance, information, investment, labour, law, regional haze, rural development and poverty alleviation, science and technology, social welfare, transnational crime, transportation, tourism, youth, the AIA Council and, the AFTA Council. Supporting these ministerial bodies are 29 committees of senior officials and 122 technical working groups. To support the conduct of ASEAN's external relations, ASEAN has established committees composed of heads of diplomatic missions in the following capitals: Brussels, London, Paris, Washington D.C., Tokyo, Canberra, Ottawa, Wellington, Geneva, Seoul, New Delhi, New York, Beijing, Moscow, and Islamabad.

The Secretary-General of ASEAN is appointed on merit and accorded ministerial status. The Secretary-General of ASEAN, who has a five-year term, is mandated to initiate, advise, coordinate, and implement ASEAN activities. The members of the professional staff of the ASEAN Secretariat are appointed on the principle of open recruitment and region-wide competition. ASEAN has several specialized bodies and arrangements promoting inter-governmental cooperation in various fields: ASEAN University Network, ASEAN-EC Management Centre, ASEAN Centre for Energy, ASEAN Agricultural Development Planning Centre, ASEAN Earthquake Information Centre, ASEAN Poultry Research and Training Centre, ASEAN Regional Centre for Biodiversity Conservation, ASEAN Rural Youth Development Centre, ASEAN Specialized Meteorological Center, ASEAN Tourism Information Centre, and ASEAN Timber Technology Centre. In addition, ASEAN promotes cooperative activities with organizations with related aims and purposes: ASEAN-Chambers of Commerce and Industry, ASEAN Business Forum, ASEAN Tourism Association, ASEAN Council on Petroleum, ASEAN Ports Association, ASEAN Vegetable Oils Club, and the ASEAN-Institutes for Strategic and International Studies. Furthermore, there are 53 Non-Governmental Organizations (NGOs), which have formal affiliations with ASEAN.

Table. 4 presents the human development and poverty indices of the ASEAN countries. Singapore is leading the countries in almost all the indicators of development. Its HDI rank is 25 with an index of 0.907, followed by Brunei (0.866), Malaysia (0.796) and Thailand (0.778). There are fewer inequalities in this region. Cambodia, Myanmar and Vietnam are the less developed countries in the region. These

Table - 4

Human Poverty Indicators of ASEAN Countries

S.No.	*Country*	**HDI*	*HPI (%) (2003)*	*TFR (2005)*	*Doctors per lakh population 2004*	*Access to Sanitation*	*Access to Drinking Water (%)*
1.	Brunie	0.866 (33)	- -	2.5	101	- -	- -
2.	Cambodia	0.571 (130)	41.3 (81)	4.1	16	16 (2002)	34 (2002)
3.	Indonesia	0.697 (110)	17.8 (110)	2.4	16	52 (2002)	78(2002)
4.	Laos	- -	- -	- -	- -	- -	- -
5.	Malaysia	0.796 (61)	8.9 (16)	2.9	70	96(1996)	95(2002)
6.	Myanmar	0.578 (129)	21.9 (50)	2.5	30	73(2002)	80(2002)
7.	Philippians	0.654 (84)	16.3 (35)	3.2	116	73(2002)	85(2002)
8.	Singapore	0.907 (25)	6.3 (6)	1.4	140	- -	- -
9.	Thailand	0.778 (73)	12.8 (28)	1.9	30	99(2002)	85(2002)
10.	Vietnam	0.704 (108)	21.2 (47)	2.3	53	41(2002)	73(2002)
C.V		0.16	0.58	0.29	0.72	0.466	0.25

indices reflect in human poverty index as well. Singapore is having the least HPI with 6.3 percent and the highest is in Cambodia with 41.3 percent. The same status is maintained in TFR, doctors per a lakh population, accesses to sanitation and drinking water. The table also presents Coefficient of Variation of all indicators. There are larger variations in the variables, the number of doctors (0.72), H.P.I (0.58) and access to sanitation.

Sec.V. The Asian Drama

J.K. Galbraith (1964) in his popular book on *Economic Development* said that the principles of good government, the inducements to individual performance, the role of popular enlightenment, the foundations of thrift, the effect of competition and of monopoly, the relation between social classes the reasons why some people worked hard and others were idle were all grist for their highly diversified mill. In fact, he opined that it has given little attention to what made for economic progress or on the other hand, what led to stagnation.

Gunnar Myrdal (1982) in his famous book on *Asian Drama* mentioned that a major source of bias in much economic research on poor countries is the endeavor to treat the internal problems of the Asian Countries from the point of view of the western political and military interest in saving them from communities. The Asian Drama, the conception of the problems of South Asia is not a mere artifice, but an image that comes naturally to an observer of the present life of these nations.

Amartya Sen (2005) in his recent book on *The Argumentative Indian* argued that in India, social progress and equity remains as a serious concern even though economic growth rate of 5 to 8 per cent is satisfactory during 1990s. However, it is lower than that of ASEAN countries like South Korea, Taiwan, and Singapore. The overall performance of the economy may not have matched to China's growth rate of 8 to 10 per cent. Sen opined that India can learn a lot from the experience of China and South Korea. Making good use of global trade opportunities is among the lessons that China and South Korea offer to India.

Sen argued in his book that it is important to avoid the much–aired simplification that all India needs to do is to achieve fast economic growth and speedy reduction of poverty and greater relation on the global market. This reflects, in fact, a serious misreading of the variety of factors that have contributed to the kind of economic success achieved in China, South Korea, Thailand and other East and South East Asia. These countries did emphasize international trade and made fine use of the global market mechanism. But they also made it possible to have broad-based public participation in economic expansion, through such policies as extensive schooling and high literacy, good health care, widespread land reforms, and some considerable fostering of gender equity (not least through female education and employment). Sen explains that the products China exports to the outside world include a great many that are made by not particularly highly skilled labour, but schooled and literate labour nevertheless. Their production generates much employment with a great deal of income going to poorer sections of the Community.

To counter the growing imperialist policies of the USA, a new imperial formation is emerging and globalization today has much in common with globalization a century ago. Then there was the British Empire, now there is US Empire. In a global development discourse, each national State governs its economy, and each developing economy is developing itself, in a global context, but in South Asia and elsewhere, national development regimes can also be understood realistically as officially, but not operationally independent territories in a global development regime. Who is leading development, which is benefiting, and where today's trends are moving remain debatable. It is more accurate to say that development has entered a confusing phase of flux and uncertainty. China not figuring in any of these Asian regional groupings is perhaps the biggest lapse on the part of the three organizations of BIMSTEC, SAARC, and ASEAN. Russia, China and India could lead the whole region, with the new grouping called the United States of Asia (USA), that can counter act the imperialist tendencies of the United States of America (USA).

Sec. VII. Conclusion

The Asian Drama of forming and sustaining the regional groupings of BIMSTEC, SAARC, and ASEAN is well in tune with the fast changing global scenario. Many thinkers feel that these regional groups lost their relevance with the signing of several agreements under WTO. As East Asian economies begin to emerge from the shadows of the 1997 crisis, there appears to be an increasing coordination and cooperation among the major Asian countries, which is essential to manage global challenges and to enhance Asia's role in world affairs.

In fact, India's deliberate look east policies have resulted in greater integration with the rest of Asia. If Asia is to increase its economic and political weight in world affairs, India's involvement would have to be integral part of the Asian Drama of cooperative politics. It is in this context that closer cooperation among Japan, Russia, and China along with BIMSTEC, SAARC and ASEAN countries would provide considerable win-win opportunities and will have far reaching implications for the peace and progress of world.

References

1. Amartya Sen (2005), *The Argumentative Indian*, Penguin
2. Asher M.G. and Rahul Sen (2005), "India-East Asia Integration: A Win-Win for Asia," *Economic and Political Weekly*, Vol.40 (36), pp.3932-3940
3. Gunnar Myrdal (1982), "*The Asian Drama*," New Delhi: Kalyani Publishers
4. Galbraith,J.K. (1964), "*Economic Development*," Cambridge: Harvard University Press
5. Horst Rolly (2005), *Concerning India and China: Huntington Sees no Way of Removing the Existing Fault Line between the Two Nations*, p.354
6. Kokichi ITO, LI Zhidong, Ryoichi Komiyama (2005), "Asian Energy Outlook up to 2020," *Economic and Political Weekly*, Vol.40 (36), pp.3953-3959.
7. Nagesh Kumar (2005): "A Broader Asian Community and a Possible Roadmap", *Economic and Political Weekly*, Vol.40 (36), pp.3926-3931.
8. RIS (2002), *South Asian Development and Cooperation Report*, New Delhi.
9. Tiziana Bonapace (2005): "Regional Trade And Investment Architecture in Asia – Pacific Emerging Trends and Imperatives," *Economic and Political Weekly*, Vol. 40(36), pp.3941-3948.
10. Yao Chao Cheng (2005): "China's Role in the Asian Economic Unification Process," *Economic and Political Weekly*, Vol. 40(36), pp.3949-3952.

19

Strategies for the Achievement of Regional Cooperation in BIMSTEC With Special Focus on Road Transport

D. Panduranga Rao

K.V. Mohan Kumar

Sec. I. Introduction

The regional cooperation bodies of developed countries such as European Union, ESCAP, NATO, etc. have attained regional cooperation in optimum manner and turned out optimum benefits in various sectors such as, international trade, resource development, transport and communications even though several traditional hurdles exist among member countries in the above mentioned bodies. All these differences are eliminated through healthy bi-lateral and regional cooperative policies. Moreover, these bodies become strong trade blocs and establish monopolistic trends especially in international trade at global level. As a result, the Asian countries face adverse effects and not able to withstand competition of the above mentioned regional bodies, even though they have good potential for the development trade.

The Asian countries have also recognized the importance of regional cooperation, especially the South Asian countries and formed as SAARC. The achievements of the SAARC in respect of regional cooperation is not up to the mark and lagging behind, when compared to the achievements of developed countries' regional cooperative bodies. The experience of the successful regional cooperative bodies envisages that the regional cooperation in the field of transport and communication plays vital role to achieve optimum development in regional cooperation especially, in the field of trade (Technical Committee on Transport 1994).

Keeping the above aspects under consideration, an attempt is made in this paper to identify the potential areas for the achievement of regional cooperation in the field of transport as well as to suggest strategies for the attainment of regional cooperation in an optimum manner. There is a paramount need for attaining regional cooperation in transport sector in BIMSTEC countries (Waquif Arif A 1995). This regional cooperation has not only improved the economic status especially economy and international trade of these countries, but also established healthy bilateral relations. Moreover, this cooperation paved the path for optimum utilization of the resources of water, forest and agriculture. All these are member countries of SAARC. Moreover, India and Bangladesh are the member countries of BIMSTEC region. This study is confined to road transport only which is a more crucial and needy area for attaining the optimum level regional cooperation. The coverage is also limited to India, Nepal, Bhutan and Bangladesh only.

Sec. II. Benefits to be derived from Regional Cooperation in the field of Transport

The benefits to be derived from the regional cooperation in the field of transport are:

(i) develop more cost effective and reliable and speedier intra regional movements of goods and people;
(ii) contribute to increased people-people contacts;
(iii) to increase prospects for mutually beneficial regional cooperation in many other areas;
(iv) expanded intra regional markets especially in international trade;
(v) facilitate to develop multi model transport through integration of road, rail, ship and inland water transport;
(vi) reduce travel time;
(vii) reduce transport cost;
(viii) reduce transit handling at cross boarder areas;
ix) strengthen the transport linkages in between trade centres and their hinter lands;
(x) facilitate faster movement of goods and material through integrated system of handling and clearance;

(xi) facilitate intra regional travel to avoid additional demands to foreign exchange resources;

(xii) reduce tariffs in more rationalized manner; and

(xiii) strengthen and also extend the regional cooperation in other areas. (Institute for Sustainable Development 1994)

It is evident that the regional cooperation in the field of transport creates immense development in the other areas and also improve the status of bi-lateral relations among countries.

2.1. Identification of the Potential Areas

The major routes required for regional cooperation are:

India:

Boarder Roads – highways connecting to Bangladesh, Nepal and Bhutan.

Bangladesh:

1. With India NH34 (Bangaion, Petrayole – connecting Dhaka)
2. NH31 – (Silguri to Dhaka – Via Dinajpur Bogon)
3. NH44 (Shillang – Agartala – Dhaka)
4. NH51 (Dalu – Dhaka – via – Silhet)

Nepal – India:

1. With India – NH28 (Raxaul – Kathmandu)
2. NH31 (Siliguri – Pithargarh connected to East West highway in Nepal)
3. with Bangladesh through India.

Bhutan – India:

1. With India Rengiya road/Daranga road to Tashigung road in Bhutan
2. Gombasha road (Bhutan)
3. Bongaigaon – Hasimara road connects to Phunt sholing (Bhutan)
4. with Bangladesh (through India via Gapaigori (India) – to Kochbehar (Bangladesh).

Sec.III. Asian Highways

India:

A1 stretch:

Passes through Ludhiana, Delhi, Agra, Kanlpur Calcutta, Bangaon enters Bangladesh at Jessore

A2 stretch:

From Ferozpur passes through Delhi, Muradabad and enter Nepal at Banbasa, reenters India at Siligari and then enters Bangladesh at Dinajpur

A5 stretch:

Connects Jhumritaliya, passes through Bihar, Muzaffarpur, Raxaul connects Nepal at Birgunj

AHR 45; AH 47; AHR4; AHR45

AHR 45 + 47:

Connects at Chennai, goes upto Paramagudi where it becomes AHR 4 & goes at Dhanushkodi.

Bangladesh:

A1 stretch:

From Jessore goes by ferry service to Dhaka, Chitagong & enters Burma through Technaf from Bangladesh enter into Burma & enters in Hochimin city in Vietnam.

A2 stretch:

From Dinajpur passes through Rangplur, Bogra, Dhaka & connects route A1 or Commilla & then goes to Chittagong.

Nepal:

A1 stretch enters from India at Babasa

A5 stretch:

From Birgunj goes to Kathmandu

A43 stretch:

From Muzaffarpur (India) passes through Sitamari (India)I and re-enters Nepal at Janakpudham

Bhutan:

No highway net work available

All these route are permitted to move International traffic through regional cooperation among these countries (Raghavan S.N 1995).

3.1 Problems and Deficiencies in the Inter-Country Routes

The major problems and deficiencies that exist in inter country routes are:

1. inadequate inter model transfer facilities between rail, road, and shipping;
2. inadequate number of cross border surface transfer points for goods and people;
3. absence of fast track routes, by passes and adequate repairs and maintenance facilities;
4. higher rates of road accidents;
5. high congestion and delays at transport centres and transfer points;
6. non-uniform technical standards and administrative formalities across countries;
7. national restrictions on cross-border for movements of goods and people;
8. under utilization of inland water and coastal routes within and across borders;
9. low handling capacities; and
10. absence of regional and sub regional conventions agreements or protocols on road and rail transport, shipping and inland water transport.

The above mentioned problems and deficiencies are significantly affect the benefits derived from the inter-country routes as well as to restrict the regional cooperation among countries.

Sec. IV. Strategies for attaining Regional Cooperation

After the critical examination of the situation, the study suggested strategies for attaining regional cooperation in the field of transport in between India, Nepal, Bhutanm and Bangladesh are:

1. simplification, rationalization, standardization and harmonization of cross-borders formalities, procedures, administrative and managerial systems;
2. harmonization of cross-border transit charges, frameworks for insurance claims and compensation and promotion of inter-country payments for these in local currencies;
3. reduction in the differences between intra-regional transport tariffs and charges on the one hand and intra-country and international tariffs and charges on the other;

4. continual increase in the availability and transparency of information flows related to capacities, cost prices, intra-regional flows of goods people and information through the development of regional electronic information and transfer systems;
5. promotion of common standards and certification of quality through the evolution of a regional standards organization;
6. mobilization of support for cooperative and collaborative development from various sectors of industry, labour, trade and financial institutions, concerned government agencies, international and multi-lateral organizations by increasing interactions among above mentioned organizations;
7. t work out forecasts to predict demand and supply of movements of goods, people and information flows in medium and long term scenarios;
8. delineation of areas for regional cooperation;
9. design of the plans for bi-lateral and multi-lateral joint ventures, projects, programmes and other collaborative activities for the development of road infrastructure; and
10. should elicit the cost of non-cooperation in the transport sector to consumers, producers, and governments in the region.

These suggested strategies are helpful not only to achieve regional cooperation in the field of transport but also strengthen the bilateral relations and also strengthen and extend regional cooperation in other areas among the BIMSTEC countries.

References

1. Institute for Sustainable Development (1994), "Report on Transport Infrastructure and Transit Facilities in the SAARC Region", Lalithpur: Nepal, pp.33-36.
2. Raghavan S.N (1995), *Regional Economic Cooperation among SAARC Countries*, New Delhi: Allied Publishers, pp.79-85.
3. Technical Committee on Transport (1994), Report of the 30th Meeting (December, New Delhi, SAARC Secretariat, Kathmandu), pp.12-18.
4. Waqif Arif A (1995), Prospects for Regional Cooperation in Transport and Communication Sectors in South Asia", New Delhi: MacMillan India, pp.28-32.

20

Disaster Management in BIMSTEC with a Special Focus on Indian Scenario

C. Praseeda

Sec.I. Introduction:

Disaster is defined as a serious disruption of the functioning of the society causing widespread human, material or environment loses which exceed the ability of the affected society to cope using its own resources. Disaster is the product of vulnerability and hazard. An area may be hazard prone yet may be able to withstand the risk due to lower vulnerability. For instance, Japan with its advanced research in the area of construction of buildings, is able to avoid human and material losses despite being prone to continuous earthquakes. The suffering and distress of people facing disasters in many countries are further compounded by disaster overlap – a situation where another over takes one disaster in quick succession by other. The recent cyclones in BIMSTEC countries, particularly Thailand, Sri Lanka and South India and the consequent flooding in some of the major cities are an example of this situation. This paper attempts to explain the disaster management programmes in the BIMSTEC region in the wake of the recent Tsunami occurred in Thailand, Sri Lanka and India with a special focus on the latter.

Sec. II. Classification of Disasters

Classification of disasters, as appended in Charts 1 and 2, are self-explanatory.

Chart-1

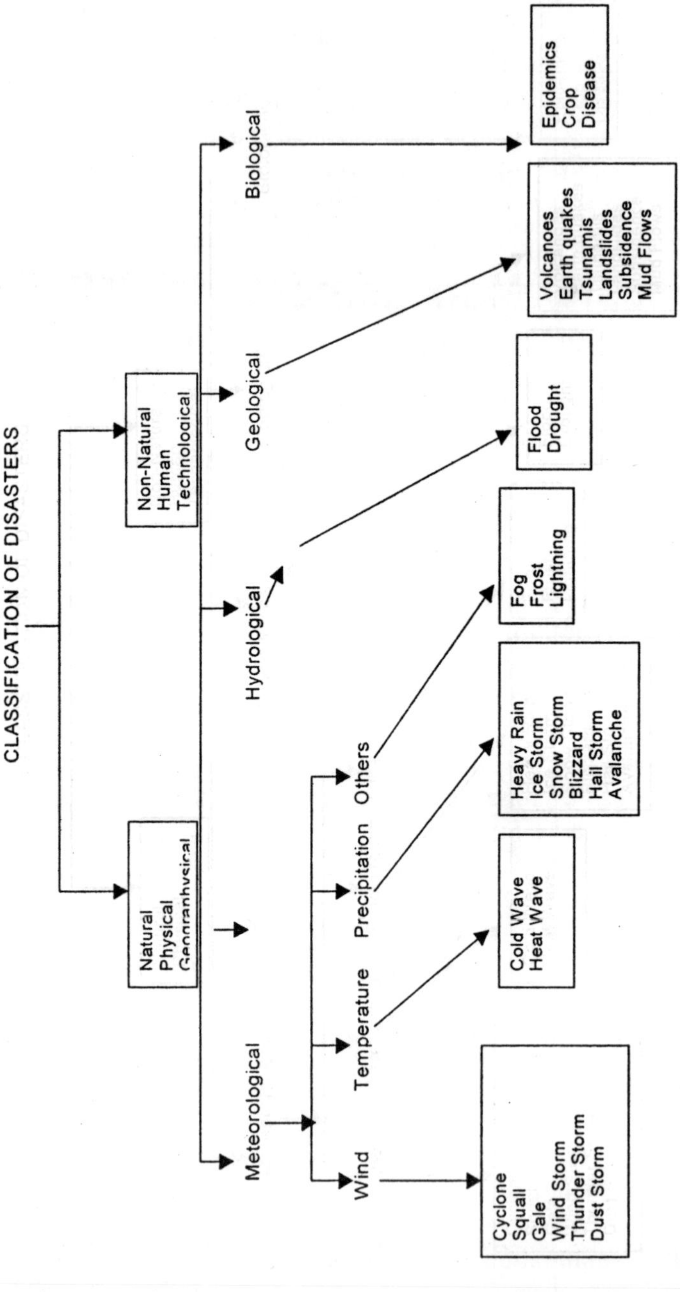

Source: Economic and Political Weekly, October 15, 2005,p.455

Chart-2

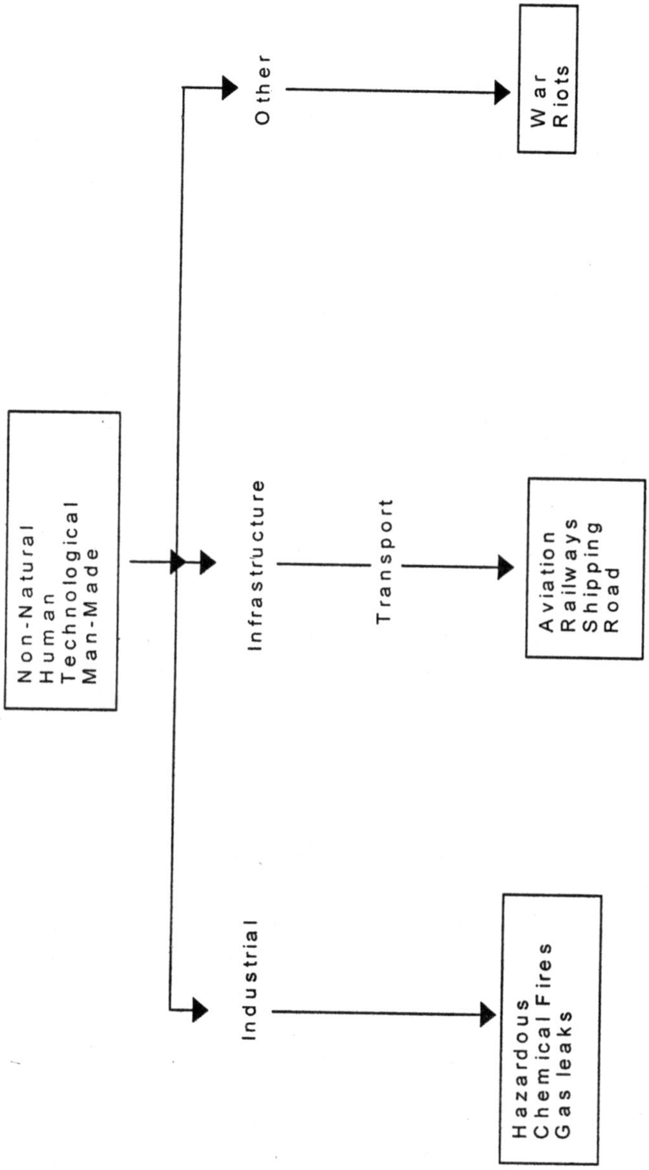

Source: *Economic and Political Weekly*, October 15, p.455

Table - 1

Human Development Profile of some of the BIMSTEC Members

	India	*Bangladesh*	*Nepal*	*Sri Lanka*	*Bhutan*	*Weighted Average*	*Developing Countries*
Population below income poverty line (%) -$ 1 a day (1993 PPP US$) 1983-2000* national poverty line 1987-2000	44.2 26.1	29.1 35.6	37.7 42	6.6 25	-- --	41 --	-- --
Population without access to health service 1995 number (millions) as a % of total population	143 15	68 55	-- --	1.3a 7c	0.6 35	276T 22	910T 20
Population without access to safe water 2000 – number (millions) as a %of total population	122 12	4 3	5 19	3 17	0.8 38	151T 11	-- 22
Population without access to sanitation 2000 – number (millions) as a % of total population	700 69	61 47	18 73	3.2 17	0.7 31	835T 63	2349T 48
Illiterate adults 2000 – number (millions) as a % total adult population	434 42.8	76 58.7	14 58.2	1.6 8.4	-- --	604T 45.5	-- 26.3

(Contd.)

(Contd. Table-1)

	India	*Bangladesh*	*Nepal*	*Sri Lanka*	*Bhutan*	*Weighted Average*	*Developing Countries*
Illiterate female adults 2000 – number (millions) as a % of total adult female population.	270 55	44 70	9 76	1 11	-- --	372T 58	-- 31
Children malnutrition(weight for age) 2000 - % of children under 5	47	61	47	33	--	47	--
Under 5 mortality rate (Per 1000 live Births) 2000	96	82	100	19	100	95	59
People living with HIV/AIDS Adult (% age 1-49) 2001**	0.79	<0.1	0.49	<0.1	<0.1	--	1.32

Source: Mahbub ul Haq Human Development Center (2002), *Human development in South Asia*, New York: Oxford University Press, Government of India (Ministry of Finance, 2001-02), *Economic Survey.*

Sec.III. Socio-Economic Status of the BIMSTEC Region:

The BIMSTEC grouping was established to encourage economic and technical co-operation and necessarily focus has also given on the safety aspects of the region. The natural disasters jeopardize the safety of not just one nation but other neighboring nations in the same area. The situation is further aggravated by the low human development profile. It may be stated that while liberalization and economic reforms have had a positive impact on the growth rate of the economies of the BIMSTEC nations, the present state of human development still remains a challenge. Though the public expenditure in the health and education sector in India has increased, the increase has not been proportionate during the 1990s. In fact, as a proportion of GNP, public expenditure on education declined from 3.9 to 3.2 percent in the post-structural reforms period in India . (South Asia Development and Cooperation Report 2004).

As per the table- 1, except in the area of sanitation India's performance in the area of human development is comparatively better. Similarly, India's spending in public health is also relatively higher than its neighbors, as indicated in the table below.

Table - 2

Public Expenditure on Education and Health of some of the BIMSTEC Members

Countries	*Public Expenditure on Education (as % of GNP)*		*Public Expenditure on Health (as % of GDP)*	
	1990	1995-97	1990	1996 – 98
Bangladesh	1.5b	2.2b	0.8	1.6
Bhutan	--	4.1	2.1	3.2
India	3.9	3.2	0.2	0.6
Nepal	2.0	3.2	0.8	1.3
Sri Lanka	2.7	3.4	1.7	1.4

Source: RIS based on UNDP (2000).

Thus, the role of India in BIMSTEC as an integrating agent cannot be gainsaid. India's ability to launch satellites and its elaborate research establishment can be of use immense to the Bay of Bengal region as a whole. The comparative political stability of India is also an advantage, which gives India a lead role in the disaster management programme.

Sec.IV. Tsunami and BIMSTEC:

The Tsunami, which hit the India, Thailand and Sri Lanka on December 26, 2004 was instrumental in creating immediate awareness on a larger scale. Tsunami is a Japanese word, which means a train of waves at the harbor, as the deep sea is comparatively calm. Usually an earthquake and the chain of waves created move away from the source at great speed cause a Tsunami. The Tsunami occurred in the South Asian countries in the past are given in table-3.

Table – 3
Tsunamis in South Asia

Date	Location
1524	Near Dabhol, Maharastra
02 April, 1762	Arakan Coast, Myanmar
16 June, 1819	Rann of Kutch, Gujarat
31 October, 1847	Great Nicobar Island
31 December, 1881	Car Nicobar Island
26 August, 1883	Karkatoa volcanic eruption
28 November, 1845	Merkan Coast, Baluchistan.

Source: Amateur Seismic Centre.

The recent post-Tsunami field surveys in 2005 have identified that the eaweed and sea grass between Parmeshwaran and Kanyakumari has been uprooted. Many marine organisms have been dislocated. Breeding grounds have been destroyed. For instance, olive ridley turtles and mangrooves have been either damaged or adversely affected (Ramesh 2005). Tsunami studies have also cast a shadow over the Sethusamudram project. The clearance given by the government to SSLP is being berated by various experts, as this will lead to dredging in the Palk strait to create depth needed for navigation and at the same time, it can lead to heavy destruction from Dhanuskodi to Erunakulam in the event of a Tsunami in future, as Tsunami waves travel faster in depth. Palk strait being a shallow area hampered the speed of the last wave on December 24, 2004.

Sri Lankan authorities reported 30,196 confirmed deaths, after the island was hit by the Tsunami. One and half million people were displaced from their homes. The agriculture and tourism sectors were severely damaged. The Naval Base at Tricomalee has been submerged. The Sri Lankan economy has suffered a serious set back due to the sudden disaster. In Thailand, 5,246 people (official estimates) were killed by the Tsunami. Thai tourism has incurred enormous losses with a number of holiday resorts either damaged beyond recognition or submerged in the waters. The most popular resort of Phuket was totally destroyed. Similarly, fishing activity, which next to tourism contributes considerably to the national income has been crippled with the fishing equipment severely damaged.

Sec.V. Geographical Division of Disasters in India

The BIMSTEC countries are geographically located in the hazardous belts of the earth's surface. The climatic and seismic factors are responsible for the regular disasters faced by them in terms of floods, draughts, cyclones earthquakes, windstorms, tidal waves, and landslides (Sekhar 2005). In this relation India has experienced high number of disasters and ranks 10th in the world's list of countries facing worst disasters. It has the dubious distinction of occupying second rank, with China and Bangladesh occupying, first and third ranks respectively in total number of deaths due to natural disasters.

Traditionally the major disasters in India can be classified, basing on certain geographical divisions. The northern part of India is prone to earthquakes and landslides. Floods best eastern India and Southern India, which is the lower part of the Peninsula with 8000km long coastline, is usually prone to cyclones, and floods.

5.1. Earthquakes

As per the latest seismic map, India is divided into five seismic zones. Earthquakes in India occur in the Himalayan areas whenever the Indian plate collides with the Eurasian plates. This leads to a series of under ground shock waves and culminates in the movement of earth surface.

5.2. Floods

The record 944 mm rainfall in Mumbai, 540 mm rainfall in Chennai, and around 400mm rainfall in Bangalore is the highest in 100 years to have been experienced by any of these cites. This deluge resulted in flooding of the cities leading to paralysis of regular life, transport and business of the Cities. It has also exposed the vulnerability

Table – 4

List of Some Significant Earthquakes in India and Its Neighbourhood

Date	*Epicentre*		*Location*	*Magnitude*
	Lat (Deg N)	*Long (Deg E)*		
1819 Jun 16	23.6	68.6	Kutch, Gujarat	8.0
1869 Jan 10	25	93	Near Cachar, Assam	7.5
1885 May 30	34.1	74.6	Sopore, J&K	7.0
1897 Jun 12	26	91	Shillong Plateau	8.7
1905 Apr 04	32.3	76.3	Kangra, H.P	8.0
1918 Jul 08	24.5	91.0	Srimangal, Assam	7.6
1930 Jul 02	25.8	90.2	Dhubri, Assam	7.1
1934 Jan 15	26.6	86.8	Bihar-Nepal Border	8.3
1941 Jun 26	12.4	92.5	Andaman Islands	8.1
1943 Oct 23	26.8	94.0	Assam	7.2
1950 Aug 15	28.5	96.7	Arunachal Pradesh - China Border	8.5
1956 Jul 21	23.3	70.0	Anjar, Gujarat	7.0
1967 Dec 10	17.37	73.75	Koyna, Maharashtra	6.5
1975 Jan 19	32.38	78.49	Kinnaur, H.P	6.2
1988 Aug 06	25.13	95.15	Manipur-Myanmar Border	6.6
1988 Aug 21	26.72	86.63	Bihar – Nepal Border	6.4
1991 Oct 20	30.75	78.86	Uttarkashi, U.P Hills	6.6
1993 Sep 30	18.07	76.62	Latur-Osmanabad, Maharastra	6.3
1997 May 22	23.08	80.06	Jabalpur, M.P	6.0
1999 Mar 29	30.41	79.42	Chamoli Dist, U.P	6.8
2001 Jan 26	23.40	70.28	Bhuj, Gujarat	6.9

Source: Government of India (Ministry of Home Affairs), *Hazards Disasters and your* Community.

Table-5
Death Toll in Major Floods of India

Year	*Number of People killed*	*Location*
1968	4,892	(1) Rajasthan, Gujarat (2) North – East, West Bengal, Assam
1978	3,800	North, Northeast
1964	2,001	Assam, Arunachal Pradesh, Jammu & Kashmir, Himachal Pradesh, Punjab, Uttar Pradesh, Goa, Kerala, Gujarat states
1961	2,000	North
1968	1,811	Assam, Arunachal, Bihar, Kerala, Meghalaya, Punjab, Sikkim, Uttar Pradesh, West Bengal states
1980	1,600	Uttar Pradesh, Bihar, Gujarat, Kerala, Haryana
1989	1,591	Maharashtra, Andhra Pradesh, Gujarat
1995	1,479	Bihar, Haryana, Jammu & Kashmir, Punjab, Uttar Pradesh, West Bengal & Maharashtra.
1997	1,442	Andhra Pradesh, Arunachal Pradesh, Assam, Bihar, Gujarat, Himachal Pradesh, Jammu & Kishmar, Karnataka, Kerala, Maharashtra, Madhya Pradesh, Orissa, Punjab, Rajasthan, Sikkim, Uttar Pradesh and West Bengal.
S2000	1,290	Gujarat, Andhra Pradesh, Assam, Arunachal Pradesh, Bihar, Himachal Pradesh, Kerala, Madhya Pradesh, Punjab, Uttar Pradesh and West Bengal
1971	1,023	North India

Source: As in table-4.

of the so-called IT hubs of the country. These cities are a part of some of the fast developing urban areas of Asia. Some of the problems being faced by them are skewed development, lack of proper planning, unauthorized occupations, and mismanagement by vested interest. This scenario is not unique to India alone, it has been noticed in UK, USA and Europe, which experienced very fast rate of development. South Asia presently has a share of 9 of the 17 cities of the world experiencing high urbanization rate (Mohan, Dasgupta 2005). They are Dhaka, Mumbai, Delhi, Jakarta, Kolkata, Karachi, Shanghai, Metro Manilla, and Beijing. Rapid urbanization draws heavily on the natural resources of an area resulting in creation of unplanned building activity, slums, and squatter establishments. Such fast pace of development needs highly alert administration and use of strategies like action planning supported by evaluation checks and feedback. It requires committed participation from all the stakeholders.

The disasters being faced by these cities is aggravated by their geographical make up. Mumbai for instance basically an island city, is formed with a linear central bowl of depression with lowest level at Mahalakshmi race course (Srivastava, Mukharjee). Chennai and Bangalore though devoid of similar geographical construction face similar problems due to improper urban planning.

A close look at the table- 5 reveals that so far metropolitan cities have never been flooded, as it happened in the case of Mumbai, Chennai, and Bangalore. The inundation of Mumbai was unprecedented in its scale and devastation. The single important factor responsible for the disaster is human intervention in its greediest form. In 2002, Hyderabad too was flooded though not as severely as Mumbai. In the light of both these experiences the State Government of Andhra Pradesh immediately called for a meeting of officials to discuss the possible effect on Hyderabad in case of a similar situation. The discussion yielded some disturbing conclusions. It was unanimously felt that given the topography of the city and the numerous encroachments on the Musi River, the plight of Hyderabad could be worse than Mumbai. This move of the State government is a good beginning in the sense that there is an effort being made to realize and learn from other's experiences.

Sec. VI. Challenges to Disaster Management in India

Reactive Measures: The disaster management network which has been designed with due care has not been totally successfully as

Chart - 3

Disaster Management Systems in India

National Level	*Structure / Function*
National Disaster Management Authority (Proposed)	With Representation from relevant departments from centre and state.
National Emergency Management Authority (Proposed)	To be headed by secretary of Home affairs and representatives from various departments.
NIDM	Office at IIPA, conducts disaster research and training.
Departments Involved in preparedness.	Indian Metrology Science and Technology and Telecommunication.
Departments involved in Prevention.	Environments Forecasts
Departments involved in relief and rehabilitation.	Poverty elevation and Rural development.
STATE LEVEL	Health Railways
Department of Disaster Management	Water resources Agriculture and urban employments.
DISTRICT LEVEL	
Disaster Management Committees,	Hazard Mitigation, Preparedness, Capacity Building, Relief and Response, Administration, Finance,
BLOCK / TALUK LEVEL	To co-ordinate relief work through relief committees
Disaster Management Teems	To make youth to participate in Disaster Training. Training provided in areas like Evacuation, Search, Rescue, First aid, Trauma, Counseling.

Source: *Disaster Management in India – A Status Report* 2004

the concentration of the system is of fire fighting nature. The measures adopted in terms of preparedness mitigation and relief is more reactive in nature. As it is seen both in the cases of tsunami and rain induced floods, despite the extent of training and preparation the administration machinery was rendered helpless. Some of the factors that challenge effective disaster management in India are as given below.

Political Dynamics: The initial reaction of most of the political parties is to announce liberal help and compensation followed by a whirlwind tour of the area, and appointment of committees. The real estate developers backed by political patronage are continuous obstacles to meaningful development (Souza 2005). Thus the steps taken by them are only quick fix solutions, not long term plans. The Tsunami relief material was either dropped in unaffected areas (Tamilnadu) or left rotting instead of immediate distribution (Car Nicobar Islands). This suggests lack of co-ordination between organizers and implementers (Banerjee 2005) It is also noticed that states like Assam which are in high earthquake prone area and experience consistent floods have no basic database on key personnel, infrastructure, life line backlogs or a development plan (Saikia 2005).

Disinterested Academia: The situation is compounded by the fact that very low research has been under taken in the area of disasters.

Table - 6

Research on Disasters in Social Science Projects: 1969-2003

Year	*Projects*	*On Disasters*
1969-1974	451	2
1975-1981	769	4
1982-1991	650	4
1991-1996	299	1
1996 – 2001	253	4
2001 – 2003	71	0
Total	2,493	15

Source: Based on *Annual reports* of Indian Council of Social Science Research, 1969-2003,

Note: Data for 1987-88 unavailable.

Table – 6 reveals that scientific and incisive studies on disaster management are very less in number. It is time that the researchers focus on Disaster management related areas.

Ecological Fallout: The millennium ecosystems synthesis report compiled by 1300 natural and social scientists from 94 countries discovered a range of factors responsible for disasters. It identifies emergence of dead zones of coasters waters, collapse of fisheries and shift in regional climates. Most of the cities of South Asia are also slowly turning into concrete jungles. The natural green cover is reducing at a fast rate leading to degradation of land. Reclamations have also influenced the delicate ecological balance (Srivastav and Mukharjee 2005); Reduced flow of rivers into the ocean due to accumulation of debris has resulted in the ocean incursion into the land. The Mahim river of Bombay has been reduced to the level of a drainage with sewage and filth (Arunachalam 2005). Hills in the area of Mumbai face extensive quarrying, resulted in loosening of surface material, and landslides (Srivastav Mukharjee 2005). Heavy discharge of industrial and domestic effluents into sea has increased the levels of magnesium and cadmium in seawaters, rendering them dangerous for Sea Organisms and may also affect general populace. (Chopra 2005).

Skewed Development: The major cities of India lack proper planning and development. Cities like Shangai, Chennai, and Mumbai rose to prominence during the late 19th century due to their ports and infrastructure. Soon they emerged as industrial destinations of the nation attracting manpower in search of employment from all over their countries. Thus, these cities experienced skewed development in the absence of proper urban planning right from the pre-independence period. The development plans of Maharastra which are to be prepared once in 10 years have been prepared only twice from 1966. Besides this almost 6.5 millions population in the city of Mumbai alone live in slums chawls and squatter settlements (Review 2005).

Proactive Alternatives: The National Institute of Disaster Management of India has rendered yeoman service to the establishment of a holistic system of disaster management. Its multi-pronged approach towards disasters preparedness mitigation, and relief and rehabilitation are highly comprehensive and scientific. The Status Report on Disaster Management in India published by the National Disaster Management division; Ministry of Home Affairs provides ample information about the plans and proposals of the Government of India. Though the report has touched on almost all the dimensions of managing a disaster, certain areas may be further explored. The following are some proactive alternatives that may add value to the already existing system.

Preparedness: Disaster Management is not the responsibility of government alone. There is a need for stakeholder participation. Most of the well laid plans go awry because the general public is not aware of them and often resist their implementation. Therefore there is a need to spread information until it becomes common knowledge. The disaster administration may conduct awareness seminar and open houses where popular participation should be encouraged. Presentation can be made in cities, town, and villages alike, and discussion and question answer sessions can be initiated. These open houses help in promoting general understanding.

Understanding of the extent of planning being undertaken by the government and empathic response can be elicited. Information campaigns provide only piecemeal information but not the complete picture. Open houses can provide not only complete information of the disaster management structure and its functions, but also provide information in an interrelated way. A flow chart model representation of the total disaster management tree can be shown and each segment of population should be made to identify their place in the structure and their role either as planner, participant or as a victim of disaster.

Disaster Awareness: Media can be used to the fullest extent to create disaster related awareness. Innovative and informative advertisement should be designed to be telecast by all channels. Famous film personalities can be used to spread disaster preparedness messages as in the case of Polio Abhiyan. District administration can conduct competitions in educational institutions and disaster relief runs can be organized. In the rural areas located in disaster zones, disaster response emergency contact numbers and list of related authorities should be conspicuously available in town halls and panchayat offices etc. The services of theater groups, alternative media, and other cultural organisations can be roped in to spread the message in rural areas.

Capacity Building and Training: The segment that is usually and invariably affected by disaster is the poor and under privileged. Therefore besides training other agencies like Government and Technical Personnel, training should also be given to slum dwellers and fishing community. The slum dwellers can be trained in matters of hygiene and health especially during disasters. The fishing community, living near the shore need training in evacuation and understanding the signals of nature. Though, their ability to do so is a part of their traditional knowledge, their need to understand the scientific and technical aspects of the same can enhance their chances of

Chart - 4

Disaster Management

Preparedness	*Mitigation*	*Relief/Rehabilitation*
Social Participation in community Training. Mock exercises Role of media. Training to public transport agents. Sea safety signals. Training to Youth of fishing community. Encouraging disaster research. Including disaster awareness in school syllabus. Designing a disaster response regimen on an inter-related basis.	Planting trees. Fisher folk housing. Enforcing population control. Strengthening city management. Corporatisation of some services. Linking ecologically sensitive projects to disaster mapping. Research of disaster resilient construction especially in earthquake areas and costal areas. Maintenance of drainage sanitation or environment representation	Disaster management fund. Temporary employment in post disaster period. Construction of multipurpose shelters.

survival. Their understanding of the meteorological science and uncertainties in weather forecasting can elicit empathetic response and true involvement with authorities wanting to help them.

Role of NGOs: Training people in disaster prone areas should be continuous. Refresher training should be provided at regular intervals to ensure preparedness in all eventualities. This task may be entrusted to the Non-government Organizations. The NGO's are more successful in implementing the various programmes undertaken and can also afford to be innovative in the process, as they are not guided by bureaucratic procedures and rules. Yet there is a need to exercise caution in the selection of NGO's to ensure qualitative training. The NGO's can recruit volunteers from the area where they are to train and thereby gain access to the inner circle of community. Mock emergency exercises can be taken up to provide practical training especially in schools and densely populated areas where panic due to fear causes more damage than the actual disaster.

Corporate Contribution: Corporate and multinational giants of India need to make significant contribution to disaster management as a part of Corporate Social responsibility. Their role can be in terms of providing infrastructure and financial support. They can also contribute to funding disaster related research. Due to their multinational character they can bring about geographical integration in the activity of disaster management.

Mitigation and Rehabilitation: Prevention of a disaster is an uncertain task especially in the case of a natural disaster. Therefore efforts should be channeled towards mitigating their impact. The measures would go a long way in mitigating the impact of disasters are: the shore areas can be liberally planted with casuarinas trees and coconut trees as trees impede the speed of an oncoming wave; ecologically sensitive projects like Sethusamudram need to be linked to disaster mapping and disaster research; civic system like sanitation and drainage should be well maintained; and open spaces should be protected and maintained to enhance natural percolation of water.

Likewise, the relief measures are: creation of youth rescue teams; creation of Disaster Management info systems; and creating clear channel of communication.

Sec.VII. Role of India in achieving Integrated Disasters Management System

Environment was identified as an area, which required immediate action, by SAARC way back in 1987. A commission was constituted to study the causes and consequences of natural disasters. A proposal was made to monitor the climate by creating a network of member countries and through SAARC meteorological research center. A SAARC environmental Ministers conference was held in New Delhi in April 1992. Recurrence of disasters in the area of Bay of Bengal and the increasing awareness has motivated many nations to establish separate departments and structures to address the issue.

7.1. Integrated Disaster Management

The principal reasons for the continuing increase in the loss levels caused by natural disasters include (i) the continuing growth of the population, (ii) the rapid increase in building activity caused by the growing concentration of people and the economic assets in urban areas, and (iii) a constant migration of people to coastal areas that are generally more exposed to natural disasters. For example, in Bangladesh over a million people are living on islands formed by silt deposits and along the vulnerable flood plains and coastal areas. Over 85 per cent of the population of China lives on alluvial plains or along river basins concentrated in one third of the total area of the country. The situation is quite similar in Viet Nam, where the dykes along rivers providing protection are sometimes breached by floodwaters causing extensive inundation. The development of industry in regions that are subject to natural hazards, without appropriate protective measures being taken, is another reason for the growing losses due to disasters.

Sec.VIII. Conclusion

Some of the measures that may be adopted for integrated disaster management system are:

- Establishment of Disaster Hotline, or a warning system, which can convey disaster related information immediately.

- The meteorological department of member countries should establish an elaborate network to ensure coordination in the prediction of disasters. A common website of disaster awareness can be developed in which information on disasters can be shared and measures being taken up by each nation can be posted. This can also act as a learning device.

- Integrated and inter-related disasters research can enhance in building a holistic profile of disasters in the area.

- A Bay of Bengal disaster management fund can be created to help a member country facing a major disaster.

- Disaster management experts exchange programmes can be taken up to develop understanding of similarities and differences in the disaster being faced by these countries.

- A Disaster Management Training and education institute can be established to conduct, introduce integrated training and ensure free flow of information.

Except Nepal and Bhutan, which are landlocked the other member countries of the BIMSTEC are exposed to the rough and tumble of the Bay of Bengal. The tsunami had caused extensive damage to India Sri Lanka and Thailand that lie in the seismic zone and are susceptible to massive landslides. In this backdrop, it is suggested that the BIMSTEC has to incorporate common disaster management programme into its agenda.

References

1. Arunachalam B (2005), "Drainage Problems of Birhan Mumbai", *Economic and Political Weekly,* September 3-9, pp.3909-3911.
2. Banerjee Sumanta (2005), "Reflections On Tsunami", *Economic and Political Weekly*, January 8-14, pp.97 – 98.
3. Barthwal Brijesh, Sadhana (2005), "The Seismic World", *Yojana,* February,
4. Chopra. Kanchan (2005), "A Land Report on Eco Systems of the World", *Economic and Political Weekly*, May 7-13, pp.1942 – 1943.
5. Dash. Biswanath (2005), "Tsunami Warning System, Beyond Technological Fixes", *Economic and Political Weekly*, January 22 – 28, pp.269 - 271.
6. Government of India (Ministry of Home Affairs, NDM Division), *Disaster Management in India: A Status Report.*
7. *Ibid.*, (2005)
8. D'Suuza J B (2005), "Disastrous Management", *Economic and Political Weekly*, September 3 – 9, pp.3900 – 3901.
9. Kapur Anu (2005", "Insensitive India, Attitude towards Disaster Prevention and Management", *Economic and Political Weekly,* October 15 – 21, pp. 4551 - 4560.

10. Goyari Phanindra (2005), "Flood Damages and Sustainability of agriculture in Assam", *Economic and Political Weekly*, June 25- July 1, pp.2723 – 2729.

11. Kurien Jhon (2005), "Securing the Future Against Tsunami", *Economic and Political Weekly,* January 8 – 14, pp.98 – 99.

12. Mehta. Lyla (2005), "The Tsunami and Globalized Uncertainty", *Economic and Political Weekly*, January 15 – 21, pp.194 - 195.

13. Mohan. Rakesh (2005), "The 21st Century: Asia Becomes Urban", *Economic and Political Weekly* January 15 – 21, pp.213 – 223.

14. Pathak K Vidyadharan, Sirish B Patil (2005), "Would Decentralization have made a difference", *Economic and Political Weekly*, September 3 – 9, pp.3902 – 3904.

15. Ramesh R (2005), "Will To Disaster", *Economic and Political Weekly,* June 1 – July 1, pp.2648 – 2653.

16. Saikia Anup (2005), "Disaster Unprepared ness in Assam", *Economic and Political Weekly*, June 11-17, pp.2389 – 2391.

17. Sekhar. R. Madhu (2005), "Tsunami Waves", *Yojana*, February

18. Standing Guy (2005), "Tsunami Recovery Grants: Looking at Long Term Sustainable Plans", *Economic and Political Weekly*, Feb 5 – 11, pp.510 – 514.

19. Government of India (Ministry of Home Affairs), *Hazards, Disasters and your community*.

21

Social and Economic Aspects of Development in BIMSTEC with Special Focus on Women

P. Tara Kumari

Sec. I. Introduction

The overall trend in development thinking in recent years has been towards emphasising the indicators of development, other than just economic growth of the per capita income. The social and economic aspects of development, especially those relating to basic needs, have received greater attention by the world community. The ILO conference (1976), South Commission (1990), Tenth Non-Aligned Summit (1992) and UNDP (1990, 1993 and 2004) recognised that the basic amenities of life have to be ensured through the priority area of development planning. In view of these shifts in development thinking, it is felt that an account of socio-economic development experience of the BIMISTEC countries has been undertaken with special focus on women.

Development is not only the transformation of the economy and its real meaning is the transformation of society as a whole and the living conditions of its people. There is a special focus on those critical areas (demographic situation, employment, social exclusion), which were perhaps bypassed by the concentration on economic growth alone. Among all these social areas of relative neglect, the focus must especially fall on women, who together constitute about 50 per cent of the world population. This is essential because i) they are of considerable share of the world population, ii) women are especially disadvantaged and under-privileged in many areas like health, education, employment, income, social status, participation in decision-making and so on, particularly in Third World counties, iii) women themselves have a tremendous potential, so far un-harnessed to contribute to both economic and social development. In light of this, there is a need for focus on women in BIMSTEC regional grouping, comprising of Bangladesh, Bhutan, India, Myanmar, Nepal, Sri Lanka and Thailand.

In tune with the global thinking, the economic status of women in India too is now accepted, as an indicator of society's development. Maintenance of proper qualitative balance among various economic activities is one of the principal functions of the economic systems, which would operate to give equal freedom of choice to men and women. The orientation of the society as a whole is now that women should play an equal part in the development of the countries, which is an important pre-condition for the advancement not only of women but also of the country as a whole. Women are lagging behind socially, politically and economically in the society in BIMSTEC countries also. The position of women in employment, earning, education, health status and decision-making opportunities is not upto the mark in these countries, and they indicate the low status of women in the economy. In this direction, the present paper assesses the economic and social aspects of women's development in BIMSTEC countries.

Sec. II. Comparison of Women in BIMSTEC Countries

Before examining the status of women, an attempt is made to examine the socio-economic indicators of the BIMSTEC nations. The data in table-1 indicates the size of the economy of the BIMSTEC countries. India with more than one billion population is the largest in these countries, followed by Bangladesh. Among the BIMSTEC countries, Bhutan is having the lowest size of population. The population per sq. km. is the highest in Bangladesh followed by India while it is the lowest in Bhutan. Among the BIMSTEC countries, Sri Lanka stands at the third position in the population density. It is interesting to note that Bangadesh with lower population than India is having higher population density.

All the BIMSTEC countries belong to the middle-income group. The gross national income of these countries, shown in table-1,

Table - 1

Size of the Economy-2004

Country	*Population Millions 2004*	*Surface area in thousand sq. kms.*	*Population density per sq. km.*	*Gross national income $ Billions*	*GNI per capita ($)*	*PPP GNI $ million*
Bangladesh	140.5	14,750	1079	61.2	440	1,980
Bhutan	2.7	46,500	19	0.554	630	-
India	1,079.7	32,87,263	363	674.6	620	3,100
Myanmar	49,910	6,56,678	76	-	-	-
Nepal	25.2	1,47,181	176	6.5	260	1,470
Sri Lanka	19.4	65,610	301	19.6	1,010	4,000
Thailand	62.4	5,13,120	122	158.7	2,540	8,020

Source: World Bank (2003-05), *World Development Indicators*, Washington D.C

World Bank (2006), *World Development Report*, New York: Oxford University Press

Table - 2

Population Dynamics

Country	*Average annual growth rate of population (%)*		*Population composition (in per cent)*			*Dependency Ratio dependants as (proportion of working age population)*	*Crude death rate (housand per people)*	*Crude birth rate (thousand per people)*
	1980-2001	*2015*	*0-14*	*15-64*	*>64*		*2001*	*2001*
Bangladesh	2.2	1.7	36.3	52	2.8	0.7	9	28
Bhutan	2.7	2.2	39.5	47	3.6	-	-	-
India	1.9	1.4	32.9	52	4.1	0.6	9	26
Myanmar	1.8	0.9	30.8	54	4.0	0.5	10	26
Nepal	2.3	1.9	39.9	48	2.9	0.8	10	34
Sri Lanka	1.3	0.7	24.8	56	5.8	0.5	6	17
Thailand	1.5	0.7	24.5	57	5.4	0.5	7	17

Source: World Bank (2003), *World Development Indicators,* Washington D.C

UNSCAP (2003), *Statistical Year Book for Asia and the Pacific*, Bangkok

indicates that Thailand has the highest gross national income per capita followed by Sri Lanka in absolute terms. Among the remaining countries, Butan and India are having middle level of per capita income. Even in the PPP terms, GNI per capita of Thailand is the highest followed by Sri Lanka. Thus, it is found that though India ranks first in terms of population, Thailand stands at the top in per capita income in both terms, followed by Sri Lanka.

Table - 2 shows the population dynamics of BIMSTEC countries. The average annual growth rate of population during the period 1980-2001 is highest in Bhutan, despite the fact that this country has the lowest population among the BIMSTEC countries. Nepal and Bangaldesh had 2.3 and 2.2. average annual population growth rates respectively. Among the remaining countries, India's average annual population growth rate is higher.

The population age composition shows that, above 64 age group accounts for highest percentage in Sri Lanka followed by Thailand. India and Myanmar rank next to the above in aged population. Interestingly, Thailand and Sri Lanka have high share of working group population also. On the other hand, Nepal, Bhutan and Bangladesh have high percentage of children age group of population. The dependency ratio analysis indicates that Nepal has more dependents followed by Bangladesh and India, on the working age population. The remaining countries have less dependents of working age population. The crude death rate shows the highest rate in in Myanmar and Nepal, followed by Bengladesh and India, while crude birth rate is the highest in Nepal and Bangladesh. Sri Lanka and Thailand registered lowest crude birth rate as well as crude death rate.

It is thus evident from table-2 that Sri Lanka has the lowest average annual population growth rate followed by Thailand, while Bhutan has the lowest population with highest growth rate. Aged population is found to be highest in Sri Lanka followed by Thailand. Health is one of the crucial factors of the human development and the health status of the people determines the well-being and the pace of economic and social development. Life expectancy, crude birth and death rates are the key indicators of health. Thus BIMSTEC countries are still far away from the reasonably good health status, as is evident from high crude death rates and crude birth rates, however, the data indicate better health status in Sri Lanka and Thailand, compared to the remaining BIMSTEC countries.

Table - 3 indicates the structure of output of BIMSTEC countries. It is clear that there has been a shift from agriculture to service sector

Table - 3

Sectoral Distribution of Output – 2004

Country	*Agricultural value added % of GDP*	*Industrial value added % of GDP*	*Service value added % of GDP*
Bangladesh	21	27	53
Bhutan	-	-	-
India	22	26	52
Myanmar	-	-	-
Nepal	40	23	37
Sri Lanka	17	25	58
Thailand	10	44	46

Source: World Bank (2006), *World Development Report*, New York: Oxford University Press.

in Sri Lanka, India, Bangladesh and Thailand, while in Nepal, the agriculture still dominates. Among the BIMSTEC countries, the agricultural value added as per cent of GDP in Nepal ranks the highest followed by India and Bangladesh. In the case of industry value added as per cent of GDP, Thailand stands at the highest, followed by Bangladesh and India. There has been more than 50 per cent of contribution of service value added to the GDP in Sri Lanka, Bangladesh and India.

Sec. III. Women in Development in BIMSTEC

Table - 4 shows that the women in development in BIMSTEC countries. The female life expectancy is the highest in Sri Lanka followed by Thailand, in which the male life expectrancy is also high. India stands at fourth position of female life expectancy, after Sri Lanka, Thailand land Bhutan. The gap between male and female life expectancy is narrow in Nepal, Bangaldesh and also in India, indicating the inadequate health status of women.

The adult litracy rate of females is significant in Thailand, Sri Lanka and Myanmar, while it is unimpressive in Nepal, India and Bangladesh. The gap between female and male literacy rates is also

Table-4

Women in Development-2004

Country	*Life expectancy (in years)*		*Adult literacy rate per cent age 15 and older*		*Labour force participation rate female to male rate*	*Women in decision making per cent of total at ministerial level*	*Female population per cent of total*
	Male	*Female*	*Male*	*Female*			
Bangladesh	62.0	63.0	58	41	0.7	3	49.5
Bhutan	62.0	65.0	-	-	-	-	-
India	63.0	64.0	80	65	0.7	3	48.4
Myanmar	55.0	60.0	96	93	0.8	0	50.2
Nepal	61.2	62.0	81	60	0.7	3	49.4
Sri Lanka	71.5	76.8	97	97	0.6	13	49.2
Thailand	66.3	73.8	98	98	0.9	4	50.1

Source: World Bank (2003-05), *World Development Indicators*, Washington D.C

high in Nepal and Bangladesh including India. In the labour force participation, female to male rate is also not appreciable in most of the BIMSTEC countries. As seen from the table, the women in decision making at ministerial level is also poor in this region, with the exception of Sri Lanka. The role of gender in the socio-economic profile of BIMSTEC countries thus, appears to be secondary owing to the strong roots of patriarchy.

Table - 5 indicates employment by economic activity of males and females in BIMSTEC countries. The data shows that the higher number of people, irrespective of gender is involved in agriculture in Nepal, followed by India and Bangladesh. There are about 50 per cent of females engaged in agriculture in Thailand and Sri Lanka. When it comes to industry, a marginal gender difference is seen in Sri Lanka.

Table – 5

Employment by Economic Activity - 2003

Country	*Agriculture*		*Industry*		*Service*	
	male labour (%)	*Female labour (%)*	*Male labour (%)*	*female labour (%)*	*male labour (%)*	*female labour (%)*
Bangladesh	54	78	11	8	34	11
Bhutan	-	-	-	-	-	-
India	63	42	21	16	39	42
Myanmar	-	-	-	-	-	-
Nepal	91	98	1	0	8	2
Sri Lanka	38	49	23	22	37	27
Thailand	52	50	19	16	29	34

Source: World Bank (2003-05), *World Development Indicators*, Washington D.C

UNDP (2005), *Human Development Report*, New York: Oxford University Press

A considerable percentage of population with marginal gender difference is engaged in service sector in India, as against the significant variation of 10 per cent in Sri Lanka. In Thailand, the per cent of male labour in total is also low in service sector, when compared to the per cent of female labour. While in Bangladesh, the per cent of male labour is high than the female labour. In India, the per cent of female labour in total is higher when compared the per cent of male labour, as the service sector has absorbed more females due to industrialization, growth of banking, finance, trade & commerce sectors. Employment by economic activity indicates that female workers are found to be highest in Nepal followed by Bangladesh in agriculture; in Sri Lanka and to some extent in India and Thailand in industry; and in India followed by Thailand in services.

Sec. IV. Conclusion

In terms of social and economic indicators, development of women is found to be better in Sri Lanka and Thailand when compared to Bangladesh, Bhutan and Nepal. India and Myanmar are placed in between these two categories of countries. The position of women in employment, earning, education health status and decision making opportunity is not impressive in these countries and the government should support the enhancement of empowerment of women.

Selected Bibliography

1. Bhabani Sen Gupta (ed., 1988), *SAARC-ASEAN Prospects and Problems of Inter-regional Cooperation*, New Delhi: South-Asian Publisher.
2. Krishna Ahooja Patel, S. Uma Devi, G.A. Tades, (eds.,1999), *Women and development*, New Delhi: Har-Anad Publication Pvt Ltd.
3. Panchamukhi, V.R & Rehman Sabhan (1995), *Towards An Asian Economic Area South Centre*, Geneva.

22

Gender Mainstreaming in Trade Policies in BIMSTEC

B. Ratna Kumari

Sec. I. Introduction

The BIMSTEC is a sub-regional grouping, combining some geographically contiguous countries of South and South-east Asia, viz. Bangladesh, Bhutan, India, Myanmar, Nepal, Srilanka and Thailand. The objective of this paper is to assess the progress towards gender equality and poverty reduction through women's access and control over economic activities, in terms of trade liberalization policies of Asian countries at micro and macro level. After briefly setting out a frame work for understanding of the participation of women in trade activities, changes in the labour market, their access and control over the resources in the current context of structural reforms are discussed in this paper. The paper also identifies a few key policy options in terms of mainstreaming gender in trade development programmes to achieve the Millennium Devolpment Goals (MDGs).

Sec. II. Gender Mainstreaming in the BIMSTEC Development

Gender mainstreaming is a process to achieve greater gender equality and overcome the costs of women's marginalisation. The costs of gender inequality are particularly noted in hindering development in terms of more poverty, increased deprivation and chronic failure in satisfaction of social needs (nutrition, health, education, dignity, social prestige and self-esteem). Thus, the term of "gender mainstreaming" has been referred to as a comprehensive strategy that involves the integration of women-oriented programmes and gender issues into development institutions by allotting a special budget. As the BIMSTEC community is totally dominated by the patriarchal and hierarchal values, mainstreaming requires (a) incorporation of gender concerns in planning, policy and implementation to provide effective rights and dignity to the disadvantaged; (b) women inclusive in social, political and economic institutions, (c) transformation of cultural structures of power with themselves, with in home and outside, (d) ending domestic and public violence, (e) recognition of women's work (productive and reproductive) and contribution to economy as well as their economic agency (Govind Kelkar, 2005).

Unequal gender relations affect the way in which the burden of poverty is distributed and unequal gender relations can also be the cause of the poverty among women and girls in otherwise non-poor families under globalization processes. Thus, unequal gender relations need to be addressed both as a cause and as a factor in the intensification of poverty under trade policies at micro and macro level.

A large number of reviews from UN Convention on Elimination of All Forms of Discrimination against Women (CEDAW), in 1979 to World Bank development report (2004) noted that all BIMSTEC countries have improved their development policies in relation to gender and efficiency of resource mobilization for poverty reduction. However, the South Asian countries have an HDI value of 0.1584 and GDI value of 0.535, which is 99 points lower than the average for developing countries (UN/HDR 2002) is exacerbated in most cases by unequal allocation of food, lower wage rates, lack of inheritance rights of women (Ramakrishna and Rangacharyulu, 1999). Despite numerous cases of success in managing the village level governance and microfinance or self help groups (SHGs), rural women of this BIMSTEC have significantly less access than men to livelihood resources, assets, health care, education, technology and community management. In addition to that, the liberalization of trade policies in this region has a negative impact on women empowerment.

Sec.III. Gender Gap Index

The World Economic Forum (WEF) released in May 2005 is the first ever study that attempts to the size of the "gender-gap" in 58 countries. The study results show that Sweden, Norway, Iceland, Denmark, and Finland at the top of the list, as the countries have the smallest "gender-gap". Whereas the large populous Asian nations such as India (53), China (33), Thailand (44), Bangladesh (39), Pakistan (56) and Turkey (57) hold lowest positions in the rankings (see table.1). It is evident from table-1 that their rankings reflect large disparities between men and women on all five areas of index: economic participation, economic opportunity, educational attainment, political empowerment and health and well-being. On the whole, India ranks good score in the area of political empowerment (24), a development that may be taken as a good omen for the future. However, Bangladesh is even ahead of European countries like Italy(45) and Greece(50) in terms of overall ranking in the above. It scores over its neighbours India and Pakistan as far as economic participation and educational attainment is concerned (www.weforum.org).

Women's movements, feminist researchers and numerous civil society organizations in the region have expressed deep dissatisfaction over the current poverty assessments for failing to incorporate women's concerns or overlooking gender relations of inequality. However, the measures like Gender Development Index (GDI) and Gender Empowerment measure (GEM) adopted to indicate the level of women's development have not been able to capture the position gained by women in accessing livelihoods under globalization process. Hence there is a need to study the components of gender mainstreaming in trade policies of BIMSTEC region.

Sec. IV. Women's Economic Participation in BIMSTEC

4.1. Emerging issues in Women Labour Market

It is observed that there are certain issues / changes that have occurred in the position of women in the labour market in last three decades. In many Asian developing countries, women in rural areas are farmers (Uma Devi 1996). In countries like Malaysia and Sri Lanka, a larger percentage of female labour is engaged in tea, rubber, coconut plantation as casual and permanent workers. Many women are enrolled themselves in home-based production activities, such as rolling beedis and lace making where wages (piece rate payments) are very low. Recently, this system has changed into the manufacturing of modern products such as electronic assembly units (OECD, 1994).

Export-led growth strategies have been adopted in Asian countries such as Malaysia, Philippines and Singapore. The countries

Table -1

Women's Empowerment: Measuring the Global Gender Gap Index

Country	*Overall rank*	*Overall Score**	*Economic Participation*	*Economic Opportunity*	*Political Empowerment*	*Educational Attainment*	*Health & well-being*
China	33	4.01	9	23	40	46	36
Bangladesh	39	3.74	18	53	42	37	37
Thailand	44	3.61	1	39	49	54	32
India	53	3.27	54	35	24	57	34
Pakistan	56	2.90	53	54	37	58	33
Turkey	57	2.47	22	58	53	55	50

Source: (1) UNIFEM(2005), "Women's Empowerment :Measuring the global gender gap" in *World Economic Forum Report*.

(2) DFID(2005), *Mainstreaming ICTs* ,Vol. II, No.3 p.17, New Delhi.

Note: * All scores are reported on a scale of 1 to 7, with 7 representing maximum gender equality.

are interested in employing young unmarried female labour force in export goods making industries, relaying on a cheaper intensive labour process. However this technology is out of reach for the poor women.

But workingwomen are not benefited much as the industrial employees prefer only young women for their speed, discipline, docile and many women are ready to accept low wages. Moreover, the employers are likely to employ women in industries such as textile, ready-made clothing, electronics, foods and beverages where wages are comparatively less (Asian Development Bank 1995). And also mostly young girls are given preference to work in the call-centres due to the Business Outsourcing (BOS) trade policies. Women could find more jobs such as hostesses and receptionists but these jobs are outside the purview of labour regulations. In service sector, jobs are such as teachers and secretaries are still feminised. But in social and health services women are engaged in low status occupation. In trade also, women are engaged in retail trade; while men are in wholesale trade.

Important changes caused by the globalization and liberalization of trade policies are: (i) young girls are given preference to work in the call-centres and higher technology oriented industries; (ii) women managers are increasing upto middle level management; (iii) generational changes in the family structures; (iv) feminisation of poverty enhances for long working hours with low-wages; and (v) the sudden shift in the work culture due to changes in the trade policies brought vast changes in the life style of women, in terms of flexible working hours, disturbances in their familial relationships and causes mental pressure in their marital life.

Sec. V. Liberalisation of Trade Policies in a Comparative Perspective

Therefore, the present study has made an attempt to correlate the world market economy with globalisation in terms of the creation of specialisesd sires for capital investment and labour control. In Nepal, tourist sites and hydroelectric projects attract foreign and domestic partnerships. Srilanka is a free trade zone. India is now a collection of regional development histories (Drez and Sen 1998). Bangalore and Hyderabad are growth nodes for global high technology business collaboration. In Bangladesh, an under garment industry has been the fastest growing employer, primarily of women, relying on imports of material inputs and exporting all its output and specific rural sites for shrimp cultivation, natural gas extraction, and coal mining preoccupy development news. The Sylhet region of Bangladesh specializes in the restaurant business in Britain, and natural gas production, compete with recurring disasters caused by foreign investors who buy rights to national resources at bargain rates dictated by national needs for FDI and secured by shady deals with government officials (David Ludden, 2005). Hence in a global development discourse, each national State governs its economy. Each 'developing economy' is developing by itself, in a global context, but in Asian countries and elsewhere, national development regimes can also be understood realistically as officially but not operationally independent territories in a global development regime under world trade policies. Who is leading development, which is benefiting and where today's trade policies trends are moving remain debatable. It is more accurate to say that the development caused by the due trade liberalization policies for women in these countries has entered confusing phase of flux and uncertainty.

5.1. Challenges

The challenges that call for gender analysis and mainstreaming also reverberates on the trade front within WTO and other trade fora. Official efforts to engender trade rules and reforms in general, whether at the global or regional levels, have so far resulted in two near universal outcomes. Either gender analysis and mainstreaming end up softening the impact of de-stebilising trade liberalization policies through targeted social safety nets, or they lead to intervention that make poor women more efficient contributors to and women in politics more effective policy makers for the systematic expansion and deepening of trade liberalization reforms (Gigi Fransisco, DAWN informs, 2003). Very often, these are inter-linked objectives.

Such interpretations and outcomes emerge out of a narrow, instrumentalist managerialist understanding of gender by governments and multi-lateral bodies. For them, it is a single matter of women getting their share of benefits from, while uncritically participating in, policies and programmes just like the men.

5.2. Some Policy Implications

"Structural reforms and policies linked to trade intensifications and financial liberalization are peddled as engines of women's increased access to incomes and employment. However, studies shows that these policies and reforms have generated a host of concerns over poor women's rights and welfare. ....At the same time, it has increased vulnerability of women's health, bodily integrity, and well being as they are forced to manoeure both the productive economy and the socially reproductive care economy"(Mariamma.W 2003).

Hence, there is a need to interconnect women's organizations and networks through gender analysis, in order to challenge and resist unfair and undemocratic WTO rules and processes, and to enforce alternative trade, development and governance arrangements.

Sec.VI. Conclusion

A set of rules for trade, development and governance in this region must insists on the centrality of the market forces above persons, communities and governments promotes the rights of the business sector overthrows the people, communities and States; and countries to overlook the structural, institutional and cultural barriers to women's self autonomy, is immediately and fundamentally in discord with the visions and politics of gender transformation.

References

1. Drez and Sen (1996) *Indian Economic Development and Social Opportunity*, New Delhi: Oxford university Press.
2. David Ludden (2005) (2005) "Development Regims in South Asia History and the Governance conundrums" *Economic and Political Weekly* Vol.37, Sept10-16
3. Govind Kelkar (2005), "Development effectiveness through gender mainstreaming: Gender equality and poverty reduction in South Asia". *Economic and Political Weekly*, Vol.XL, Nos. 44 and 45, pp. 46-90.
4. Murthy .S and Gaur. K.D (2002), *Women Work Participation and Empowerment*, Jaipur (India): RBSA publishers
5. Uma Devi (1996), *Role of Women in Economic Development*, Kanpur (India): Bodh Publications
6. UNDP (2002), *Human Development Report*, New York: Oxford University press.

23

Gender Inequity in BIMSTEC Countries: An Overview

G. Lakshmi

S. Vanaja Rani

Sec. I. Introduction

A decade after the Beijing Conference, it is apropos to take stock of the modest advances made by the seven countries in the South and Southeast Asian region viz., Bangladesh, Bhutan, India, Myanmar, Nepal, Sri Lanka and Thailand towards the goal of gender equity and promoting women's political participation, probe the obstacles and examine the opportunities. These geographically contiguous countries have entered into a sub-regional grouping — The Bay of Bengal Initiative for Multi-Sectoral Technical and Economic Cooperation, BIMSTEC for short, addressing only economic and technical issues, grossly overlooking the more important political and gender issues in this forum.

This paper gives an overview of gender inequity in BIMSTEC countries in one basic dimension of human development – i.e. political participation of women and unequal position of women in governance and stresses on the need to address gender disparity questions in regional forums. Gender inequity effects the overall development and progress of a nation. Gender equity in terms of political participation is an area of critical importance for development, which is woefully lacking in these countries. Given the gender disparities in the South and Southeast Asian countries, gender may be a fit area for sub-regional approaches. The BIMSTEC countries should also address gender relations through this forum. There is much to be gained from regional cooperation in terms of political participation of women.

To start with, South and South East Asia is primarily a gender inequity region, where the picture of women is most ignoble and inequitable. Of course, gender-gap is worldwide but the problem of gender inequity is even more serious in the so-called BIMSTEC countries. A serious "development gap" exists in these countries. Despite making gains following the Fourth World Conference on Women, women in the region continue to be excluded, marginalized, and prevented from enjoying seats of power in the decision-making bodies and public policy-making processes.

Women's political participation, in the region as elsewhere, is a fundamental challenge for the coming millennium. It will engage half of the world's population—the women, their organizations and movements. But it will also demand a commitment from government and other social institutions: media, schools, the business sector, trade unions, cooperatives—to help, not hinder, the cause of equality. Governments in this region generally affirm equality principles, which are enshrined in all, if not most, of their laws. But legal rights are often not reflected in reality: Women in the region have yet to achieve equality, particularly in their right to self-representation and self-determination.

One way of exploring, at least in a shorthand way, the status of women in these countries, in terms of political participation and governance, is through comparative statistics. This paper has primarily drawn from the data/figures taken from the Human Development Report (HDR 2005), latest statistics from the Inter-Parliamentary Union as well as studies undertaken by the network of the Center in Asia-Pacific for Women in Politics (CAPWIP). These statistics provide evidence to show gender inequity in terms of political participation in the said region.

As part of the millennium development goals, the UNDP compiled the Human Development Report [HDR] 2005, entitled 'International Cooperation at a Crossroads: Aid, Trade and Security in an unequal world'. The report was prepared by the Pakistan-based Mahbub ul Haq Human Development Center, which was set up in 1995 by late Dr Mahbub ul Haq, founder and chief architect of the United Nations Development Program (UNDP) Human Development Reports. Analysis of the figures and tables in the HDR suggests that women in developing countries seem to be worse off than those in developed countries. For instance, women in the BIMSTEC region participate less in governance than the women in European countries.

Sec. II. Political Participation: A Measure of Equity

Despite many advances in every aspect of life including representation in the public realm, gender inequity still persists globally and especially in the South and Southeast Asian region. The HDR 2005 rankings of countries are according to the Human Development Index (HDI) which is based on a combined measure of longevity, educational attainment and ability to buy basic goods and services and the Gender Empowerment Measure (GEM) that identifies gender inequality in three key areas, the primary area being political participation and decision-making power, as measured by women's and men's percentage of shares of parliamentary seats. The HDI and the GEM indicators in BIMSTEC countries as given in the HDR [2005] show consistent disparities between women and men in the basic dimensions of human development such as economic and political participation.

Table 1 shows that as far as the HDI ranking in the BIMSTEC countries are concerned, India is placed at 127th position (UNDP 2005a) embarrassingly behind, Thailand (at 73) and Sri Lanka (at 93), which is a matter of great concern. However, India is ahead of Myanmar (at 129), Bhutan (at 134), Nepal (at 136) and Bangladesh (at 139) (UNDP 2005b). The figures in Table 1 are self-explanatory. The figures show that only a handful of European nations – mostly the Nordic state – Norway, Iceland, Sweden, Luxembourg have 'succeeded best' in narrowing the gender gap. Other 'gender fair' countries include Canada and Australia (UNDP 2005c).

Yet another statistical data compiled by the Inter-Parliamentary Union provides illustration of women's 'development gap' in the BIMSTEC countries. As Table 3 shows despite the fact that India is the largest democracy in the Asia-Pacific region it only has 8.3 percent women Members of Parliament (MPs) in its Lower House and in terms of world classification of women in national parliaments it stands at 109 rank, which is again embarrassingly below Bangladesh (at 71), Thailand (at 71) and Bhutan (at 102). While in Bangladesh 14.8 percent of the national MPs are women, including the Prime Minister, in Thailand and Bhutan there are 10.8 percent and 9.3 percent respectively, women parliamentarians. Lagging behind India are Sri Lanka (at 124) with 4.9 percent women's representation and Nepal (at 124) with 0 percent women's representation in the lower house.

Table-1
Women's Political Participation

HDI Rank	*Countries*	*Year women Received right: To vote*	*To stand For election*	*Year first women Elected (E) or Appointed (A) to Parliament*	*Women in govt. at ministerial level (as % of total) 2005*	*Seats in Parliament held by women as % of total: Lower/ Single [1990-2005*	*Upper/ Senate 2005]*
1.	Norway	1907	1907,1913	1911 - A	44.4	36 - 38.2	---
2.	Iceland	1915,1920	1915, 1920	1922 - E	27.3	21 - 30.2	---
3.	Australia	1902,1962	1902, 1962	1943 - E	20.0	6 - 24.7	35.5
4.	Luxembourg	1919	1919	1919 - E	14.3	13 - 23.3	--
5.	Canada	1917, 1960	1920,1960	1921 - E	23.1	13 - 21.1	37.1
6	Sweden	1862,1921	1907 1921	1921 - E	52.4	38 - 45.3	--
BIMSTEC Countries (Medium Human Development)							
73	Thailand	1932	1932	1948 - A	7.7	3 - 10.6	10.5
93	Sri Lanka	1931	1931	1947 - E	10.3	5 - 4.9	---
127	India	1950	1950	! 952 - E	3.4	5 - 8.3	11.6
129	Myanmar	1935	1946	1947 - E	---	--- --	---
134	Bhutan	1953	1953	1975 - E	0	2 - 8.7	---
136	Nepal	1951	1951	1952 - A	7.4	6 - 5.9	8.3
139	Bangladesh	1972	1972	1973 - E	8.3	10 - 2.0	---

Source: UNDP (2005), *Human Development Report*, New York: Oxford University Press

Table-2

Women in National Parliaments
World Average

Both Houses Combined	
Total MPs	43'961
Gender breakdown known for	43'961
Men	36'766
Women	7'195
Percentage of women	16.4%

Single House or Lower House	
Total MPs	37'054
Gender breakdown known for	37'054
Men	30'912
Women	6'142
Percentage of women	16.6%
Upper House or Senate	
Total MPs	6'907
Gender breakdown known for	6'907
Men	5'854
Women	1'053
Percentage of women	15.2%

Source: The data in the table below has been compiled by the *Inter-Parliamentary Union* on the basis of information provided by National Parliaments as on February 2006.

As given in Table 1 and Table 3, one can find a relationship between increased political participation of women and improved development outcomes. One can infer from the given data that the continued absence of women's voices in governance is largely due to inequitable representation and participation in institutional structures, such as government and their political participation.

Table-3
Classification in BIMSTEC and Some Select Countries

Rank	Country	Lower or single House				Upper House or Senate			
		Elections	Seats*	Women	% W	Elections	Seats*	Women	% W
1	Rwanda	09 2003	80	39	48.8	09 2003	26	9	34.6
2	Sweden	09 2002	349	158	45.3	---	---	---	---
3	Norway	09 2005	169	64	37.9	---	---	---	---
4	Finland	03 2003	200	75	37.5	---	---	---	---
5	Denmark	02 2005	179	66	36.9	---	---	---	---
6	Netherlands	01 2003	150	55	36.7	06 2003	75	22	29.3
13	Iceland	05 2003	63	21	33.3	---	---	---	---
28	Switzerland	10 2003	200	50	25.0	10 2003	46	11	23.9
44	Canada	01 2006	308	64	20.8	N.A.	100	35	35.0
71	Bangladesh *	10 2001	345	51	14.8	---	---	---	---
"	Thailand	02 2005	500	54	10.8	03 2000	200	21	10.5
102	Bhutan	N.A.	150	14	9.3	---	---	---	---
109	India	04 2004	543	45	8.3	06 2004	242	28	11.6
124	Sri Lanka	04 2004	225	11	4.9	---	---	---	---
"	Nepal	05 1999	2	0	0.0	06 2001	19	3	15.8

(Contd.)

(Contd. Table 3)

Source: The data in the table below has been compiled by the *Inter-Parliamentary Union* on the basis of information provided by National Parliaments as on February 2006. 187 countries are classified by descending order of the percentage of women in the lower or single House; a select few are given in the table. Accessed from Internet - www.ipu.org

Note: 1. Figures correspond to the number of seats currently filled in Parliament,

2. Data regarding the political situation of women in Myanmar is not readily available.

3. * Bangladesh: In 2004, the number of seats in parliament was raised from 300 to 345, with the addition of 45 reserved seats for women. These reserved seats were filled in September and October 2005, being allocated to political parties in proportion to their share of the national vote received in the 2001 election.

Women's political participation needs to go beyond raw numbers to encompass the complex relationship between power, participation and poverty. In the HDR 2003, Mahbub-ul-Haq warns that "Human development, if not engendered, is fatally endangered" (UNDP 2003), what he means is that unless providing gender equity is considered an urgent priority, South and South East Asia will continue to be one of the most impoverished, malnourished, illiterate and gender – insensitive regions of the world and the subordinate status of the women may derail whatever little advancement made in this nations.

Countries that do not fully take account of one half of their population are undermining their competitive potential. Gender exclusion is widely prevalent in political governance, in a region which has boasted women heads of government in India, Bangladesh, and Sri Lanka and yet in which women are a minority in the parliament and hold only a few seats in government cabinets. Women continue to be in the minority in the area of power and decision-making although progress in improving the proportion of women serving in politics and administration has been steady. One can say marginalization of women in the political process and governance in general has been both the cause and effect of the slow progress made in the advancement of women in these countries.

Sec. III. Obstacles to Women's Political Participation

Women around the world at every socio-political level find themselves underrepresented in parliament and far removed from decision-making levels. While the political playing field in each country has its own particular characteristics, one feature remains common to all: it is uneven and not conducive to women's participation. Women who want to enter politics find that the political, public, cultural and social environments are often unfriendly or even hostile to them. Even a quick glance at the current composition of political decision-makers in any region provides evidence that women still face numerous obstacles in articulating and shaping their own interests. What are the obstacles women faces in entering parliament? How can women better cope with these hindrances? Not only does this inequity threatens the very survival of women and girls in these countries, but also deprives the talents of more than half its population.

Many factors hinder women's equal access to power and decision-making. Gender inequity and its cultural acceptance are endemic in the region. Pervasive influence of traditional gender roles constricts women's participation in leadership and decision-making roles. Historically, socially prescribed roles have limited women's access to political participation, and other forms of decision-making. Besides this, persistent institutional barriers to women's access to power that cut across various socio-political institutions.

Sec. IV. General Strategies

General strategies include mechanisms that enhance women's political participation such as:

(i) Work for gender quotas that allot 30 to 50 percent of decision-making positions for women at every level— "half the world, half the power" concept —. A policy of positive discrimination such as the Women Reservation Bill in India (which is yet to see the light of the day), and allotting Cabinet ranks for women ministers;

(ii) Lobby for electoral reform. Efforts should be made to bring about legal and institutional changes to promote women's political participation, including constitutional amendments;

(iii) Work for quotas in political bodies - appointive and elected positions, structures of political parties as a short-term measure to increase the number of women in such bodies;

(iv) Gender mainstreaming strategies that promote a culture of gender sensitivity in government; national machineries for women, which have the primary role of leading and monitoring;

(v) Gender mainstreaming strategies of governments; gender or women's budgets that allot a percentage of national budget for gender mainstreaming and affirmative action for women's advancement; and

(vi) In legislatures of some democratic countries, women's sectoral representatives have been appointed on terms and capacities at par with elected representatives. A more recent mechanism that provides a leeway for women's political participation is the party list system where women's groups can bid for seats in the legislature.

In light of the above, in the area of gender equity the focus on development by governments should thus be on devising polices to increase women's access to political institutions and increased participation. From the point of view of human development and gender equity, gender equality in governance is further imperative.

On the eve of the millennium and almost half a decade after Beijing, the question of what still needs to be done to achieve women's equal access to power and decision-making remains of little or no priority. Notwithstanding their reported accomplishments, countries in the region have not recorded a dramatic increase in women's political participation.

The absence of women's voices is shaping the most fundamental political instrument – the most critical of which is the national budget - has ensured the preservation of gender inequity in all spheres. Until gender parity is reached in governance, women cannot reach full equality with men in any sphere. Equality emphasizes treating people same. However, treating people the same does not accommodate significant differences which may affect the outcomes of 'equal treatment' where conditions, do not take into account the differences in people, 'equal treatment' tends to default to unequal status quo. Equity then would recognize differences and accommodate it in order to prevent the inequitable status quo. Equity emphasizes fairness in process and outcomes. There is a growing recognition that economic participation and political participation cannot be separated. Politics and participation range from the home through the locality to the national level. Women need to participate at the micro-level of the home, the meso-level of the community organizations, and local Government, and at the macro-level of national party, parliamentary and governmental politics.

The problem today is what should the policy makers otherwise do to enhance women's achievement of equity. Measuring the magnitude of the problem is a first step and it is hoped that the governments in the BIMSTEC nations can use the HDR ranking as shown in the Table 1, to identify issue areas and to learn from the experience of nations that have even more successful in narrowing the gender gap. The HDR rankings in the table can be seen as a benchmark for improvement.

Improving political participation of women, particularly in the decision-making positions should be the main priority for the South and South East Asian nations. Gender equity and gender parity with regard to political participation is the most important catalyst for change in society. Progress and empowerment in other areas would automatically follow political empowerment of women, since gender equity is an essential condition towards achieving gender equality and empowerment.

Sec.V. Conclusion

Promoting gender equality and empowering women is one of the millennium goals of the UNDP and gender equity should precede the latter. Women's full participation in politics is a fundamental and non-negotiable right. The United Nations Secretary General's report on Equality in Political Participation and Decision Making posed this question: "To what extent is the general advancement of women needed before it is possible to have full participation in politics? Or rather, is it the case that full participation in politics is necessary to achieve the general advancement of women?" (UN 1996). Each question presupposes a different strategy in addressing the problem of broadening women's political participation.

The first question makes as a precondition to women's full participation in politics the satisfaction of their practical needs such as access to education, health care, livelihood and legal status. But if it has been women's absence from positions of power that occasioned their marginalization, the question is: How can they push for their practical needs to be prioritized in a situation where men still dominate in decision-making in government?

The second question underscores the need to promote women's full and equal participation in decision-making positions to ensure that their needs are prioritized and addressed. This strategy further implies that women can and should take control of their future instead of being dependent on the action of others. Women can set and pursue their own agenda. Increased political participation of women is, after all, not only an end in itself but also a means to address issues that are of importance to them.

Hence again, regional cooperation can help, the challenge will be to identify and define the opportunities and modalities. Ultimately, unless and until gender equity is provided, women equality and empowerment remains a distant dream.

References

1. UNDP (2005), *Human Development Report*, New York: Oxford University Press, p.319
2. *Ibid.*, p. 317
3. *Ibid.*, p. 316
4. *Ibid.*, (2003), p.319.
5. United Nations (1996), *Platform for Action and the Beijing Declaration*, New York: United Nations Department of Public Information.

Appendix - I

Declaration on the Establishment of the Bangladesh-India-Sri Lanka-Thailand Economic Cooperation (BIST-EC)
Bangkok 6 june 1997

The Minister of State for Foreign Affairs of Bangladesh, the Minister of State of India, the Deputy Minister of Foreign Affairs of Sri Lanka and the Deputy Minister of Foreign Affairs of Thailand, acting on behalf of their respective Governments;

MINDFUL of the existence of mutual interests and common concerns among their countries and complementarities of their economies and convinced of the potential for strengthening further the existing bonds of friendship and cooperation;

DESIRING to establish a firm foundation for common action to promote sub-regional cooperation in the areas of trade, investment, technological exchange and other interrelated areas in a spirit of equality and partnership and thereby contribute towards peace, progress and prosperity in their common region;

CONSCIOUS that in an increasingly interdependent world, the cherished ideals of peace, freedom, and economic well-being are best attained by fostering greater understanding, good neighbourliness and meaningful cooperation among countries of the same sub-region already bound together by ties of history and culture;

CONSIDERING that countries share a primary responsibility for strengthening the economic and social stability of their sub-region and ensuring peaceful and progressive national development;

DO HEREBY DECLARE:

FIRST, the establishment of Bangladesh-India-Sri Lanka-Thailand Economic Cooperation to be known as the BIST-EC.
SECOND, that the aims and purposes of the BIST-EC shall be:

1. To create an enabling environment for rapid economic development through identification and implementation of specific cooperation projects in the sectors of trade, investment and industry, technology, human resource development, tourism, agriculture, energy, and infrastructure and transportation.
2. To accelerate the economic growth and social progress in the sub-region through joint endeavours in a spirit of equality and partnership.
3. To promote active collaboration and mutual assistance on matters of common interest in the economic, social, technical and scientific fields.
4. To provide assistance to each other in the form of training and research facilities in the educational, professional and technical spheres.
5. To cooperate more effectively in joint efforts that are supportive of and complementary to national development plans of Member States, which result in tangible benefits to the people in raising their living standards, including through generating employment and improving transportation and communication infrastructure.
6. To maintain close and beneficial cooperation with existing international and regional organizations with similar aims and purposes.

7. To cooperate in projects that can be dealt with most productively on a sub-regional basis among the BIST-EC countries and that make best use of available synergies.

THIRD, the BIST-EC will observe the following principles in all its activities:

(a) Cooperation within the BIST-EC will be based on respect for the principle of sovereign equality, territorial integrity, political independence, and non-interference in internal affairs, peaceful co-existence and mutual benefit.
(b) Cooperation within the BIST-EC will constitute an additionality to and not be a substitute for bilateral, regional or multilateral cooperation involving the Member States.

FOURTH, that to carry out the aims and purposes of the BIST-EC, the following institutional mechanisms shall be established:

(a) Annual Ministerial Meetings, which shall be hosted by the Member States on the basis of alphabetical rotation.
(b) Senior Officials Committee, which shall meet on a regular basis as and when required.
(c) A Working Group, under the chairmanship of Thailand and having as its members the accredited Ambassadors to Thailand, or their representatives, of the other Member States, to carry on the work in between Annual Ministerial Meetings.
(d) Specialized task forces and other mechanisms as may be deemed necessary by the senior Officials to be coordinated by Member States as appropriate.

DONE in Bangkok on the Sixth Day of June in the Year One Thousand Nine Hundred and Ninety Seven.

(*Source:*http://mofa.gov.bd/bimstec/dec_establis.html)

Appendix - II

Joint Statement of the BIMST-EC Ministerial Meeting – December 1997

A special Ministerial Meeting was convened in Bangkok on 22 December 1997 attended by H.E. Mr. Abul Hasan Chowdhury, Minister of State for Foreign Affairs, the People's Republic of Bangladesh; H.E. Mr. A. N. Ram, Secretary, Ministry of External Affairs, Republic of India; H.E. U. Nyunt Swe, Deputy Minister of Foreign Affairs, Union of Myanmar; the Hon. Mr. Lakshman Kiriella, Deputy Minister of Foreign Affairs, the Democratic Socialist Republic of Sri Lanka; and H.E. M.R. Sukhumbhand Paribatra, Deputy Minister of Foreign Affairs, Kingdom of Thailand, and their respective delegations.

At the conclusion of their Meeting, the Leaders of Delegation issued the following Joint Statement:

We reaffirmed the aims, purposes and principles contained in the Bangkok Declaration of 6 June 1997 on the Establishment of the Bangladesh – India – Sri Lanka – Thailand Economic Cooperation (BIST-EC).

We welcomed the Union of Myanmar into the grouping and decided to rename our organization "BIMST-EC" (Bangladesh – India – Myanmar – Sri Lanka – Thailand Economic Cooperation).

We were highly satisfied with the substantive progress that has been made in forging greater understanding and trust among Member States over the past six months. We were confident that BIMST-EC has the potential to be a key building block in the architecture of peace, stability and economic well being in Asia.

We strongly reaffirmed our intention to work closely together to strengthen various infrastructural linkages between Member States, especially in the transport and communication sectors that would reinforce complementarities arising out of the Bay of Bengal rim identity of BIMST-EC. We expressed our resolve and determination to move the organization expeditiously into an operational phase through the immediate implementation of a range of cooperative projects.

In this connection, we expressed our appreciation to the ESCAP for drawing up a development programme of sectoral cooperation for consideration of BIMST-EC.

On the basis of the ESCAP study, we have agreed to implement immediately an integrated Cooperative Work Programme composed of the following elements:

(i) The establishment of an Economic Forum with the participation of public and private sector representatives to promote economic cooperation among Member States, identify and assist in the implementation of cooperative projects in the fields of trade and investment and infrastructure, and provide a forum for high-level exchange of views between policy makers and the business community;

(ii) The promotion of trade and investment cooperation through the holding of private sector forums in five key sectors, namely textiles and clothing, drugs and pharmaceuticals, gems and jewellery, horticultural and floricultural products, and information technology products and services with technical support from ESCAP;

(iii) The holding of a senior economic officials meeting to promote intra-regional cooperation on elimination of non-tariff barriers, market access issues, services, and preferential trading arrangements among Member States;

(iv) The cooperation on technology transfer and endogenous capability building;

(v) The reinforcement of transport and communication linkages among Member States through:
   - Identification and promotion of new inter-modal linkages within Member States
   - Improving efficiency of international land transport in Member States
   - Promotion of multi-modal transport practices among Member States
   - Study of transport demand and capacity requirements for intra-regional commodity flows with a view to drawing up an action plan to remove any constraints to a potential transport network among Member States.

- Streamlining and reducing costs of transport system through site studies to identify and propose measures for removing present institutional, operational and infrastructure bottlenecks.
- Promotion of international transport along inland waterways;

(vi) The enhancement of intra-regional energy cooperation through an action plan for the
Development and utilization of natural gas, wind, solar and water/ tidal wave energy resources. A roundtable would be held in conjunction with ESCAP to evolve this plan.

(vii) The establishment of a Working Group on Tourism and the holding of a BIMST-EC
Meet on Tourism in 1998 in India to develop an action plan for cooperation in the tourism sector.

(viii) The promotion of cooperation in fisheries through the conduct of a comprehensive
Study on marine resources, processing and marketing, to be conducted in coordination with the FAO.

In the implementation of the above Cooperative Work Programme, we agreed to continue our close cooperation with the ESCAP and to seek to engage interested States who can contribute to the progress of the work programme, and the UNDP, ADB, IBRD/Word Bank and other relevant international organizations in similar collaborative efforts.

In addition to the Cooperative Work Programme, we agreed to pursue the following:

(i) Establish intra-regional linkages among central banks, financial institutions and credit agencies and exchange views on macro-economic policies;

(ii) Cooperation to address and remove obstacles to intra-regional cooperation on transport and communications such as providing transit agreements, relaxation of documentation requirements, support for multi-modal transport operations, and establishment of transportation links;

(iii) Conclusion of bilateral investment promotion and guarantee agreements and avoidance of double taxation agreements among Member States;

(iv) Cooperation among civil aviation authorities and representatives of national airlines of Member States to discuss modalities for expansion of air services through, inter alia, inter-line arrangements, synchronization of schedules, code-sharing, cargo and charter arrangements.

We reiterated the commitment of BIMST-EC to the principle of open regionalism and reaffirm that this would be emphasized through dialogue with non-Member States, other regional groupings and international organizations that share similar aims and principles.

In order to allow for a requisite period of consolidation to permit the expeditious implementation of the Cooperative Work Programme, we have agreed on a five-year moratorium on the consideration of application for new membership. We also agreed that a geographical definition focused on the Bay of Bengal rim would be one of the key criteria for full membership. Observers and guests would be invited to attend appropriate meetings and participate in various BIMST-EC activities. The criteria for such participation will be drawn up.

On behalf of the Member States of BIMST-EC, we underlined the importance of Asian solidarity, enhanced South-South cooperation, and coordination among developing countries in the face of challenges that are being posed by the globalization of international trading and financial systems. We reiterated the call for the major economies of the G-7 to assume a proportionate role in restoring stability to the financial situation in Asia, which could potentially have wider adverse consequences for the international economic system.

(*Source*: website: www.bimstec.org)

Appendix - III

BIMST-EC Summit Declaration
Bangkok, 31 July 2004

We, the Prime Minister of the People's Republic of Bangladesh, the Prime Minster of the Kingdom of Bhutan, the Prime Minister of the Republic of India, The Prime Minister of the Union of Myanmar, the Prime Minister of the Kingdom of Nepal, the President of the Democratic Socialist Republic of Sri Lanka and the Prime Minister of The Kingdom of Thailand gathered in Bangkok, Thailand, on 31 July 2004 for the first BIMST-EC Summit Meeting;

Convinced that the geographical location if our countries and our rich natural and human resources provide a sound basis for mutually beneficial cooperation,

Recognizing that the pluralistic nature of our societies, our shared cultural heritage and the rich diversity of languages, arts, crafts and traditions provide ample opportunity for multi-dimensional cooperation within our region;

Convinced that regional and sub-regional economic cooperation such as ours contribute to efforts towards global free and fair trade being pursued under the multilateral trading regime,

Affirming that the above realities provide a firm foundation on which to build our partnership and overall cooperation;

Resolving to foster a sense of community that will lead to the economic and social development of the entire region;

Do hereby:

Agree that our grouping shall henceforth be known as BIMST-EC of the Bay of Bengal Initiative for Multi-Sectoral Technical and Economic Cooperation.

Commit us to the founding objectives and'principles of BIMST-EC; to assess the challenges and opportunities for economic cooperation in our region; and to strengthen BIMST-EC's ability to find ways and means to realize those challenges and opportunities effectively and efficiency.

Note with satisfaction BIMST-EC's achievements so far, including the signing of the Framework Agreement for a BIMST-EC Free Trade Area, the launch of Visit BIMST-EC Year 2004-2005 and the year-long Plan of Action on tourism, the establishment of the BIMST-EC Chamber of Commerce, the first BIMST-EC Youth Football Tournament held in Phuket, the establishment of the BIMST-EC Center in Bangkok, and a biomass gasifier plant Myanmar, and pledge to move forward with renewed vigor.

Agree to focus on specific areas of cooperation, including but not limited to trade and investment, transport and communications, tourism, energy, human resources development, agriculture, fisheries, science and technology and people-to-people contact.

Agree to explore the expansion of BIMST-EC Cooperation into the areas of culture, education, and public health, protection of biodiversity and traditional knowledge, rural community development, small and medium-scale enterprise, construction, environment, information and cOommunciations technology, biotechnology, weather and climate research, natural disaster mitigation and management.

Agree to take all possible steps including timely completion of the Free Trade Area negotiations for realization of the full potential of BIMST-EC trade and investment, taking into account the special needs of individual member countries.

Recognize that future cooperation under BIMST-EC requires the development of key infrastructure, in particular transportation & communication linkages, to facilitate tourism, trade and investment and accordingly agree to strengthen and accelerate cooperation for developing concrete regional project proposals such as the ongoing negotiations on road linkages between the member countries.

Agree to promote sustainable and optimal energy utilization through development of new hydrocarbon and hydropower projects, interconnection of electricity and natural gas grids, energy technologies.

Agree to coordinate our diverse strengths in the tourism sector to derive maximum benefit from our natural, cultural and historical attractions, and recognize the need to enhance inter-regional tourism through such strategies as joint marketing of intra-BIMSTEC tourism packages, exchange of visits and information as well as sub regional tourism co-operation.

Agree to facilitate travel within the region for business travel, exchange programmes and tourism, including through the introduction of a BIMSTEC Business Travel Card/Visa.

Encourage the private sector to explore ways to tap the economic partnership potential of the member economies and make full use of BIMSTEC opportunities.

Agree to intensify cooperation to promote the sustainable use of the marine resources in the Bay of Bengal through effective management and conservation in close coordination with the already existing frameworks, including the Bay of Bengal Programme-Inter-Governmental Organisation (BOBP-IGO).

Agree to enhance technical cooperation aimed at capacity building, and recognize the potential for public and private organizations to expand existing cooperation in this area.

Express grave concern at the continuing threat of international terrorism and transnational crime that has adversely affected the economic and social progress of the peoples of the BIMSTEC region; recognize that the solidarity and friendship existing among member states could be utilized as a basis to counter this threat; agree, as an urgent priority, to co-ordinate our efforts to combat this menace; including through the exchange of information among concerned agencies, and other concrete programmes of co-operation, and resolve to continue active co-operation in ongoing efforts of the international community in combating terrorism in all its forms and manifestations, by whosoever it is perpetrated irrespective of its cause or stated rationale.

Agree to coordinate our efforts to address, as a matter of priority, transactional issues that threaten the economic and social progress of peoples of the BIMSTEC region, including HIV/Aids and other threats to public health such as malaria, tuberculosis, and polio; and encourage active cooperation among concerned agencies, including through the exchange of information, sharing of experiences and other concrete programmes.

Decide to proactively promote increased interaction among our peoples through programmes, such as exchanges of parliamentarians, media persons, students and faculty, sports persons, as well as exchanges in the fields of performing arts and entertainment, such as motion pictures, television programmes and music.

Decide to accord priority to projects that could be clearly conceptualized, adequately funded and effectively implemented, with well-defined goals and tangible results relevant to the needs of our peoples, based, as far as possible, on internal financing from within the BIMSTEC countries.

Agree to streamline procedures and protocols to make BIMSTEC more efficient and output-based.

Agree that once a clear and focused programme of cooperation is in place, appropriate formal institutional mechanisms would be established, jointly and within each member country, for effective coordination and implementation.

Agree to task their Foreign Ministers with the responsibility of coordinating overall BIMSTEC cooperation.

We express our gratitude to the Government of Thailand for the warm hospitality and excellent arrangements made for the Summit.

(*Source*: website: www.bimstec.org)

Index

C